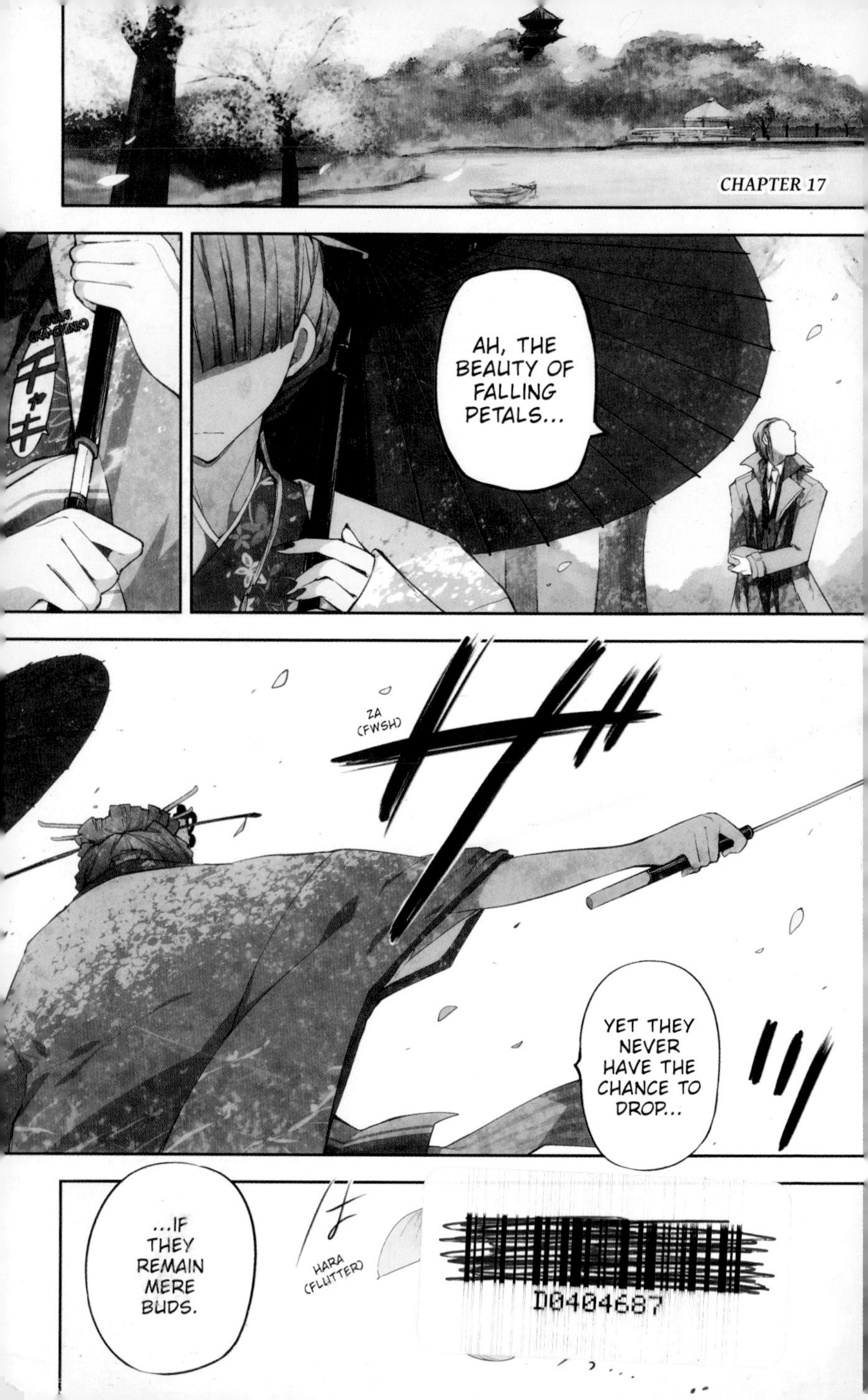
CHAPTER 17
AH, THE BEAUTY OF FALLING PETALS...
CHAKI (KA-CHINK)
チャキ
ZA (FWSH)
YET THEY NEVER HAVE THE CHANCE TO DROP...
HARA (FLUTTER)
...IF THEY REMAIN MERE BUDS.

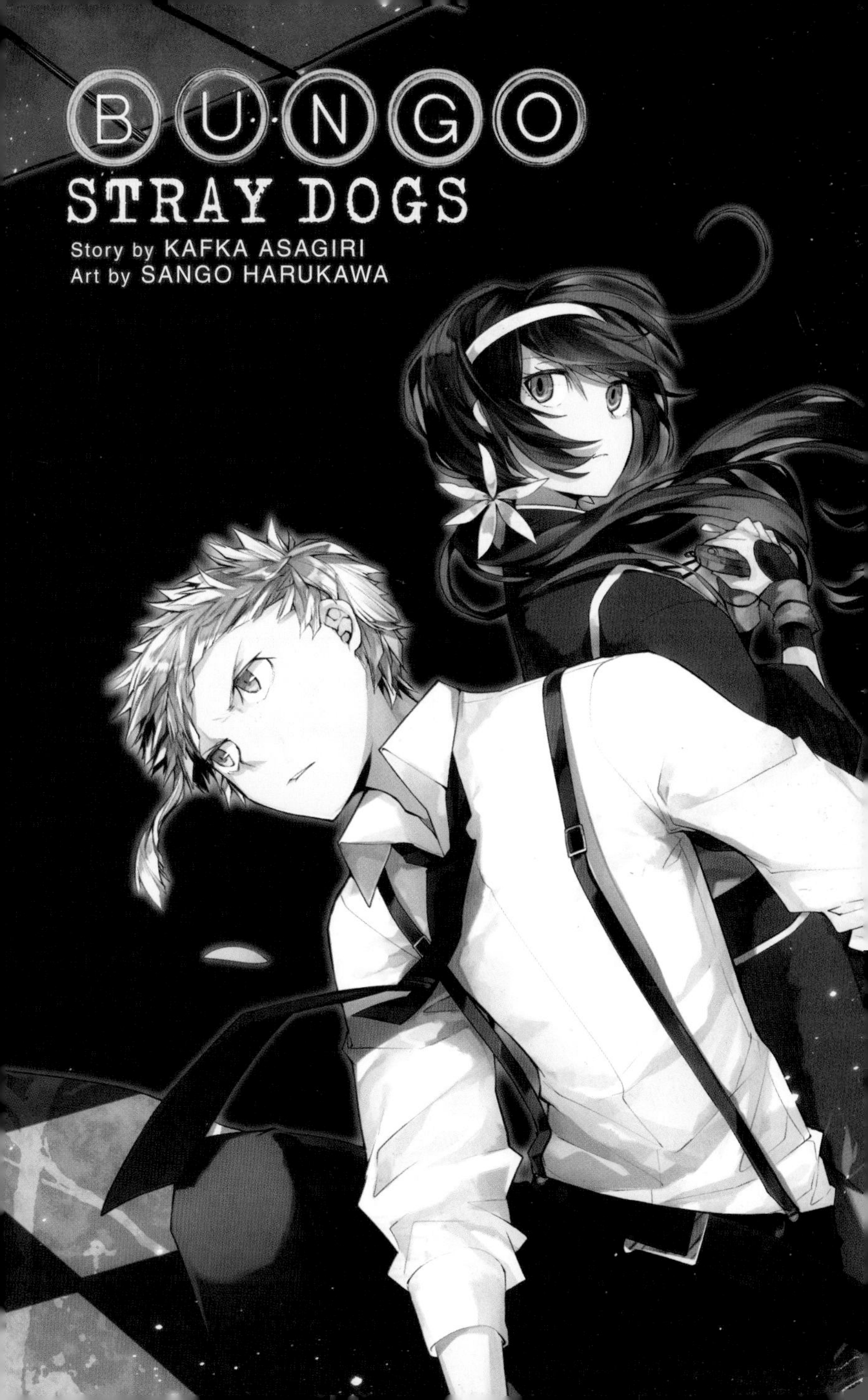
BUNGO
STRAY DOGS
Story by KAFKA ASAGIRI
Art by SANGO HARUKAWA

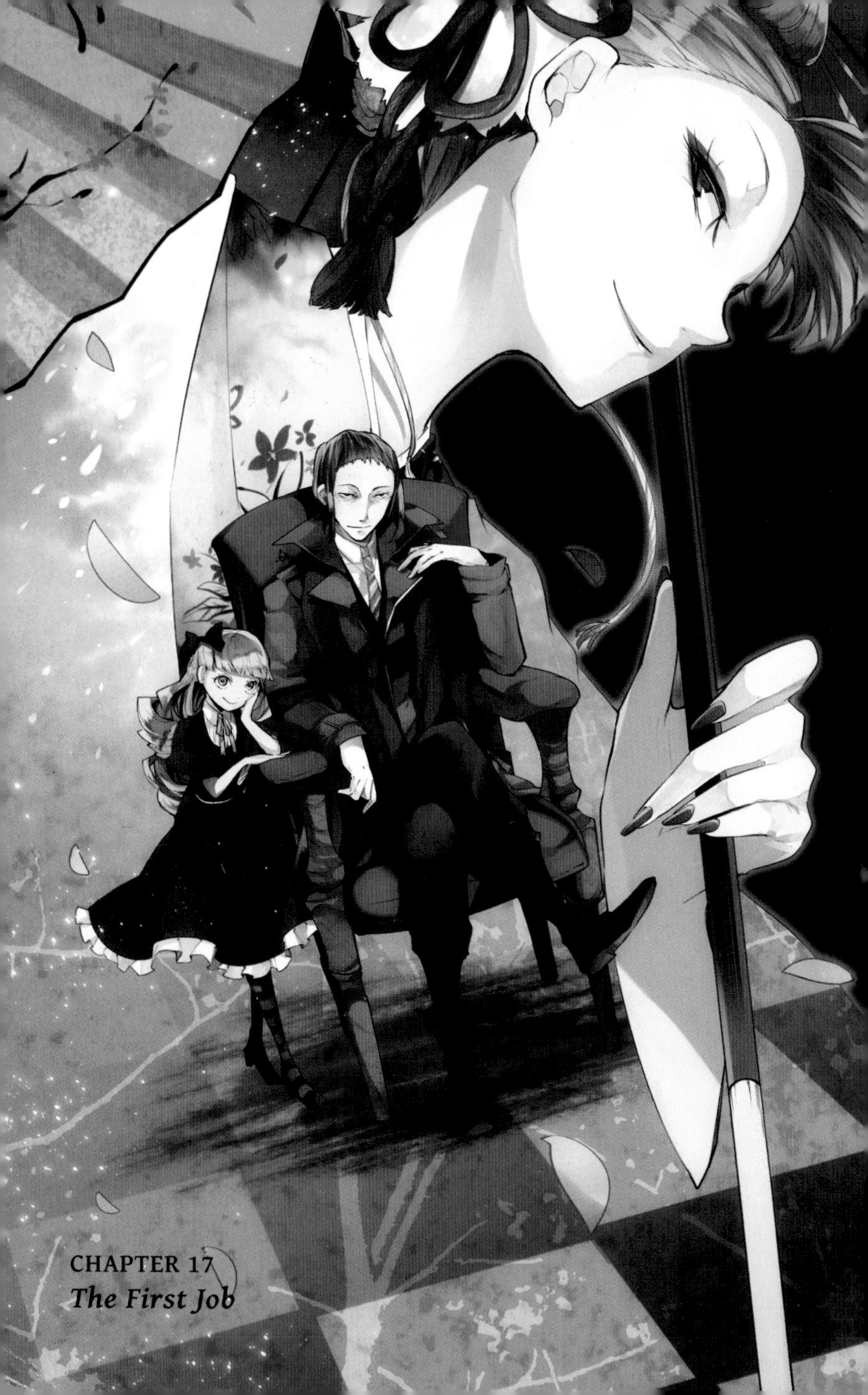
CHAPTER 17
The First Job

TABLE of CONTENTS

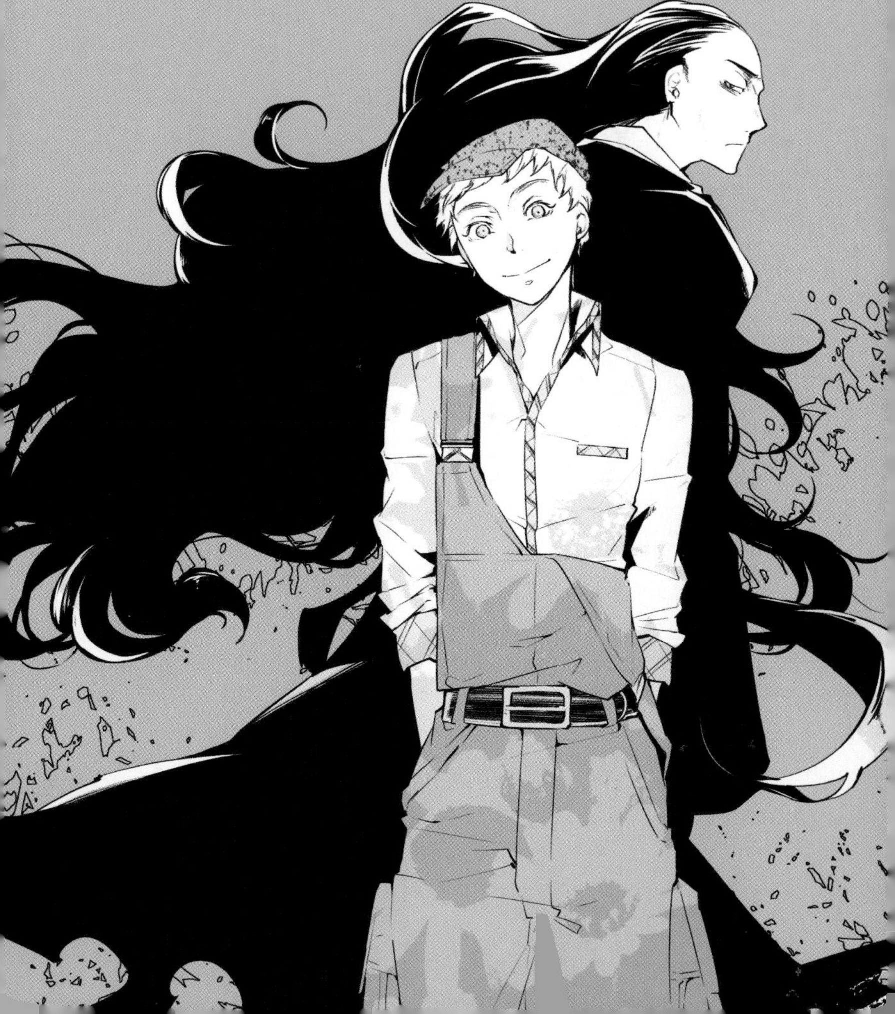

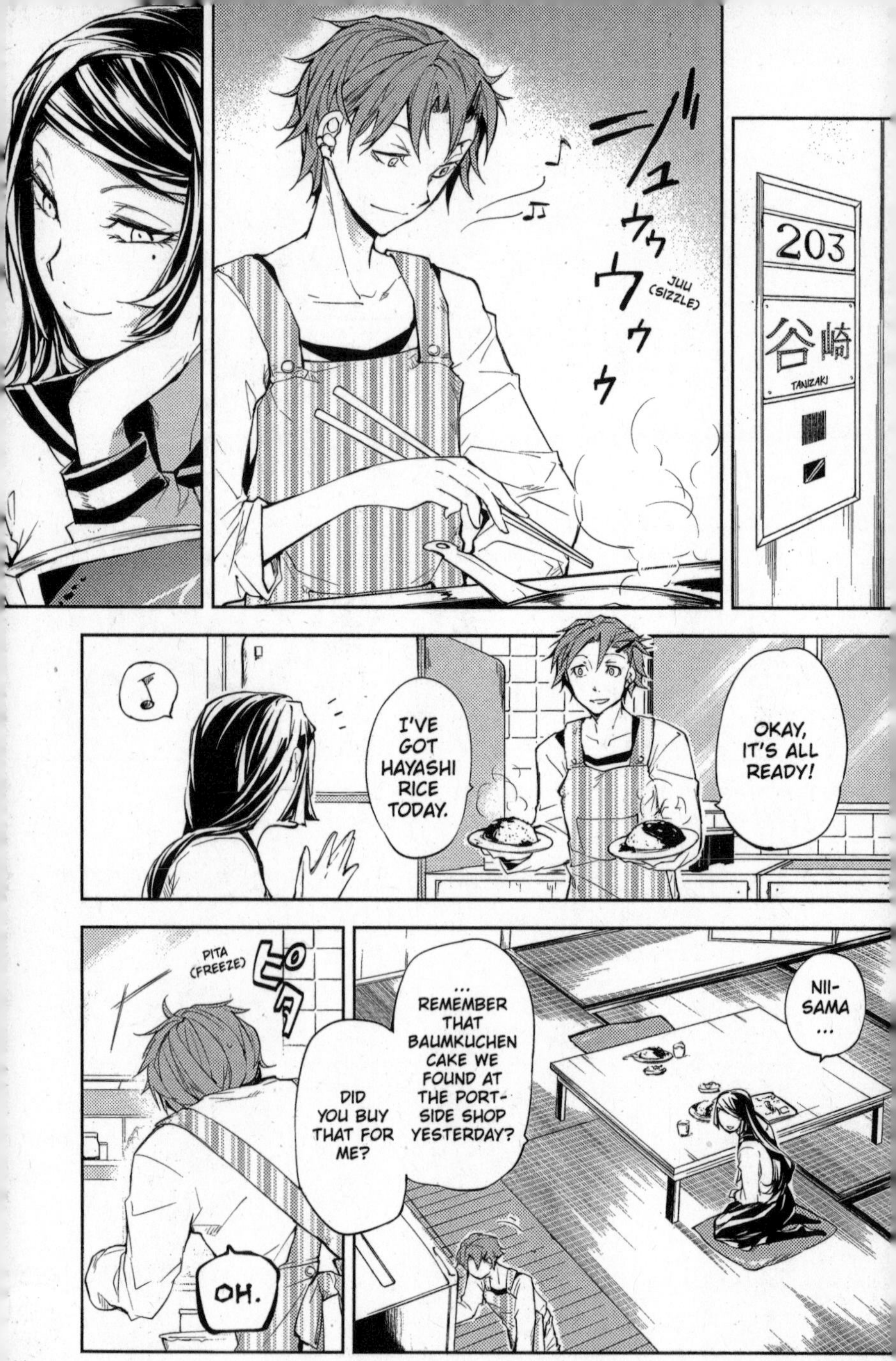
203
谷崎
TANIZAKI
JUU (SIZZLE)
OKAY, IT'S ALL READY!
I'VE GOT HAYASHI RICE TODAY.
NII-SAMA...
...REMEMBER THAT BAUMKUCHEN CAKE WE FOUND AT THE PORT-SIDE SHOP YESTERDAY?
DID YOU BUY THAT FOR ME?
PITA (FREEZE)
OH.

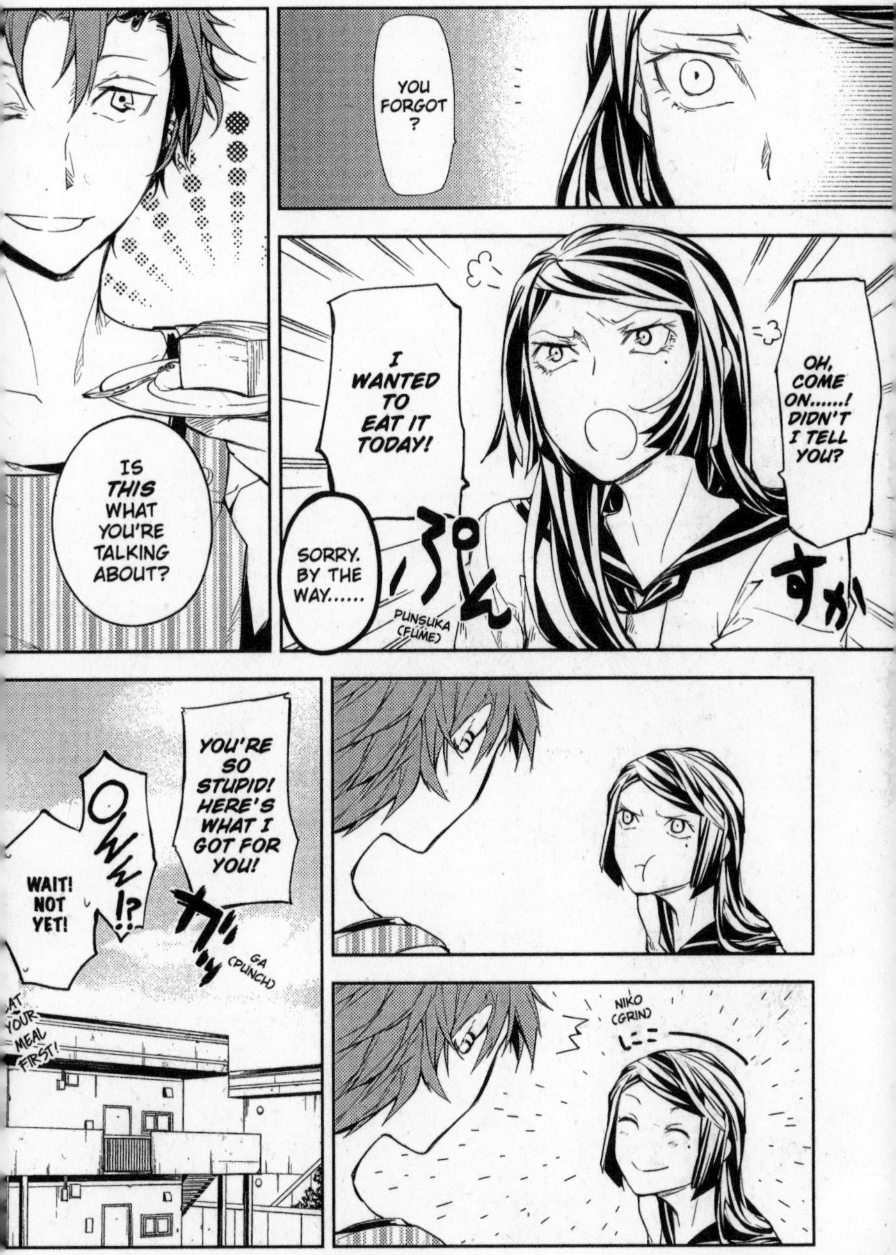
YOU FORGOT ?
OH, COME ON......! DIDN'T I TELL YOU?
すか
I WANTED TO EAT IT TODAY!
ぷん
PUNSUKA (FUME)
SORRY. BY THE WAY......
IS THIS WHAT YOU'RE TALKING ABOUT?
NIKO (GRIN)
にこ
YOU'RE SO STUPID! HERE'S WHAT I GOT FOR YOU!
OWW!?
WAIT! NOT YET!
ガッ
GA (PUNCH)
EAT YOUR MEAL FIRST!

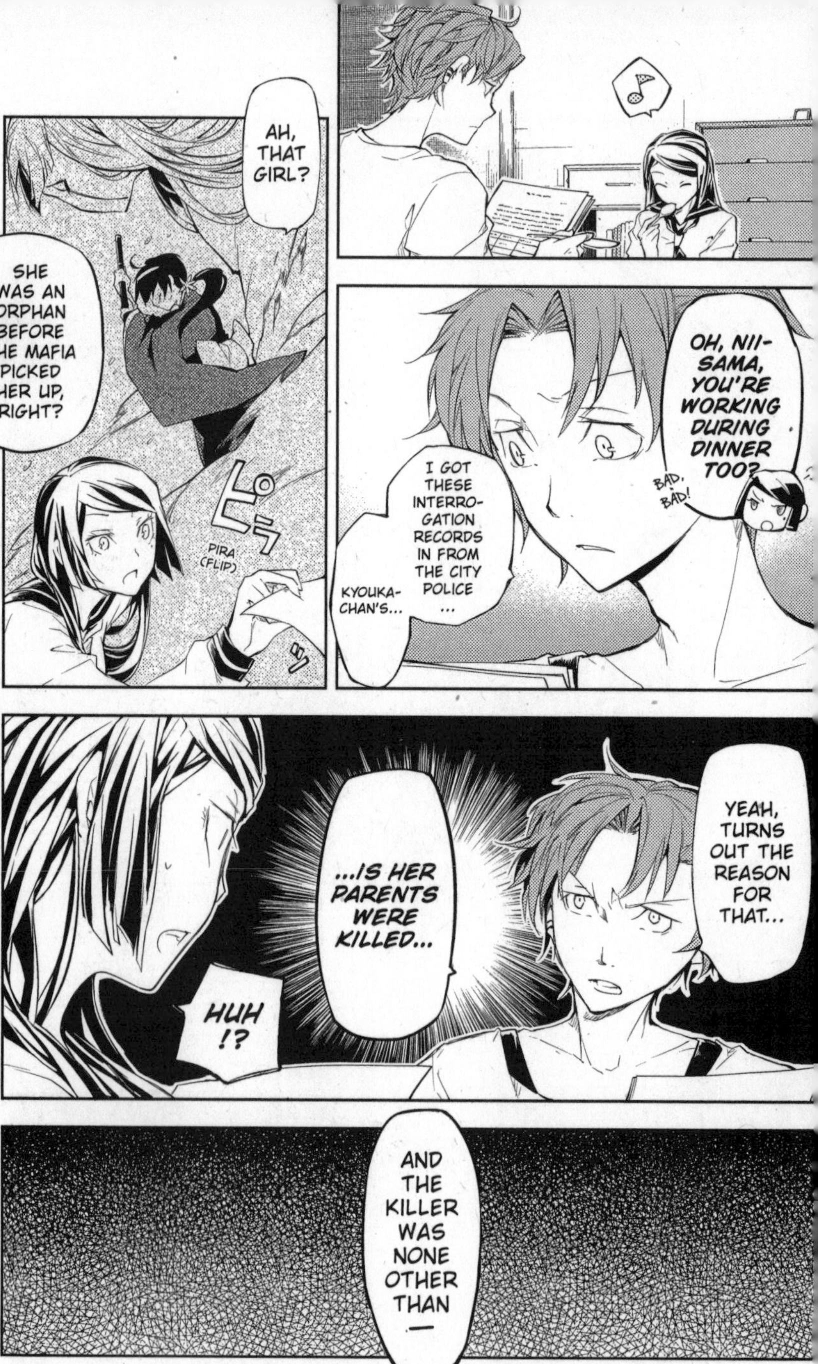
OH, NII-SAMA, YOU'RE WORKING DURING DINNER TOO?
BAD, BAD!
I GOT THESE INTERROGATION RECORDS IN FROM THE CITY POLICE...
KYOUKA-CHAN'S...
AH, THAT GIRL?
SHE WAS AN ORPHAN BEFORE THE MAFIA PICKED HER UP, RIGHT?
PIRA (FLIP)
YEAH, TURNS OUT THE REASON FOR THAT...
...IS HER PARENTS WERE KILLED...
HUH!?
AND THE KILLER WAS NONE OTHER THAN —

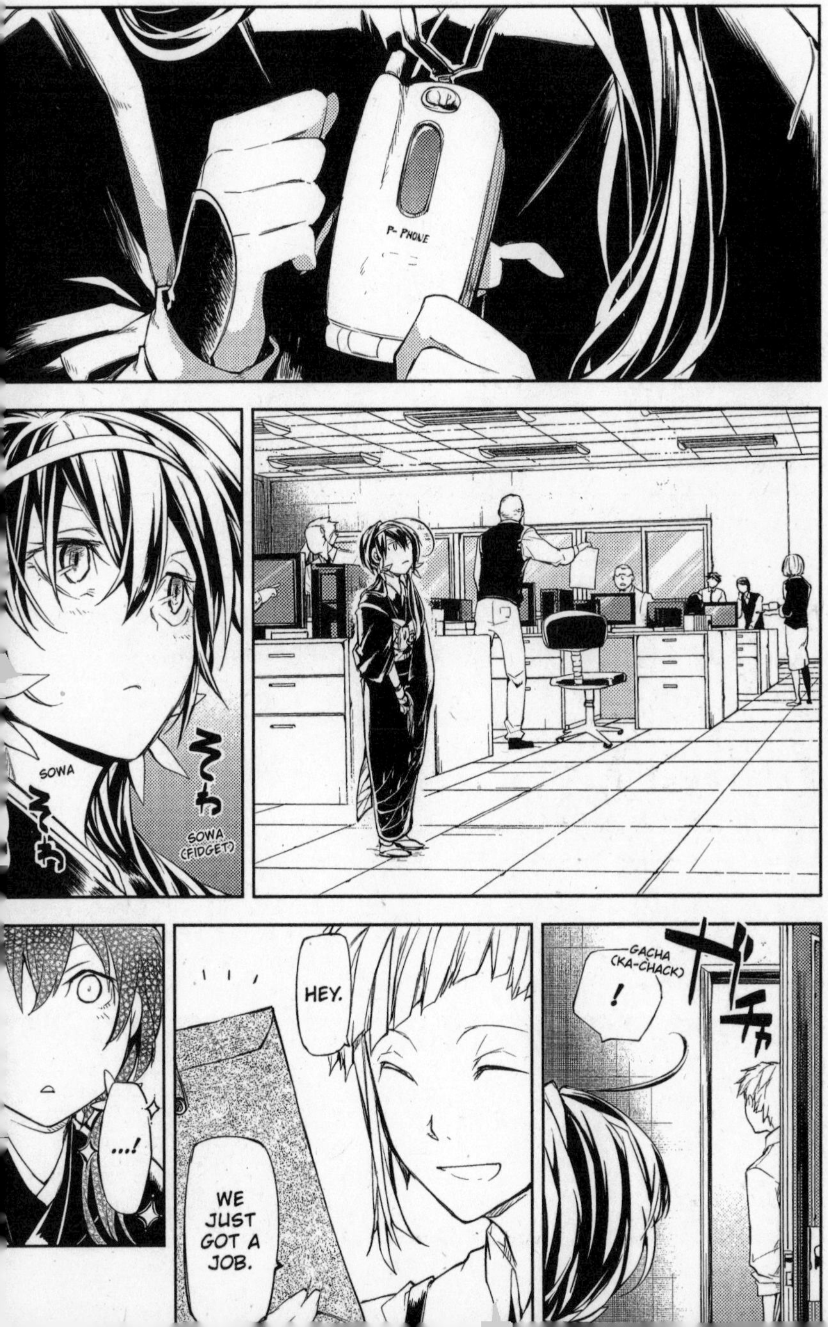
P-PHONE
そわ
SOWA
そわ
SOWA (FIDGET)
ガチャ
GACHA (KA-CHACK)
!
HEY.
WE JUST GOT A JOB.
...!

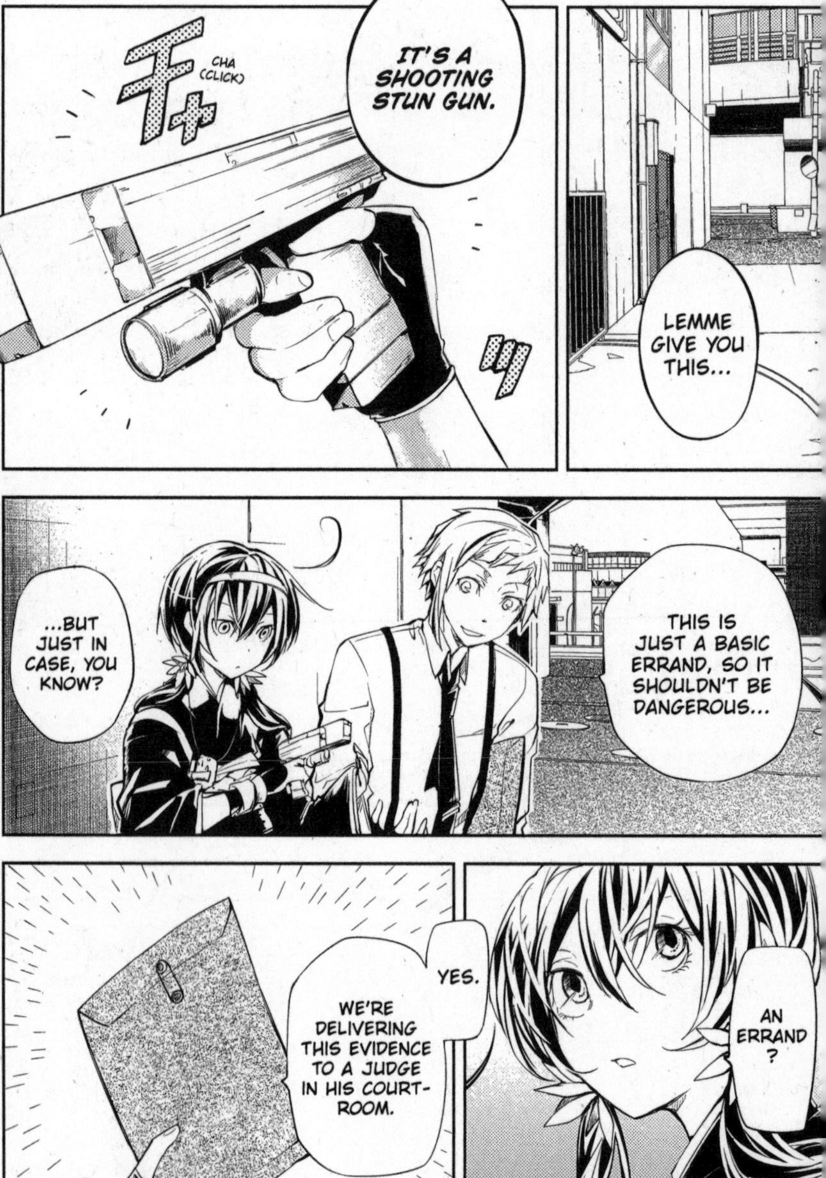
LEMME GIVE YOU THIS...
CHA (CLICK)
IT'S A SHOOTING STUN GUN.
THIS IS JUST A BASIC ERRAND, SO IT SHOULDN'T BE DANGEROUS...
...BUT JUST IN CASE, YOU KNOW?
AN ERRAND?
YES.
WE'RE DELIVERING THIS EVIDENCE TO A JUDGE IN HIS COURT-ROOM.

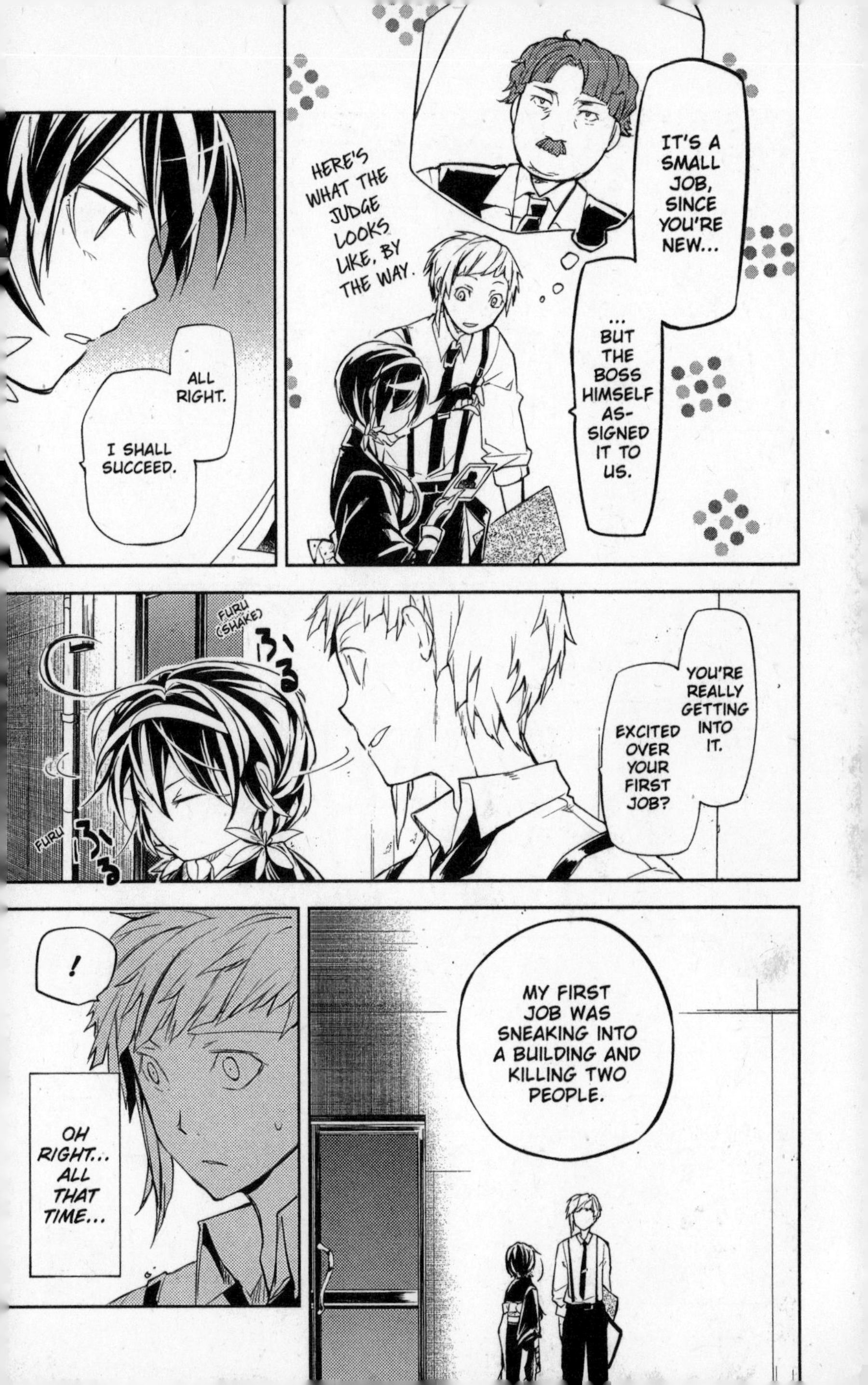
IT'S A SMALL JOB, SINCE YOU'RE NEW...
...BUT THE BOSS HIMSELF AS-SIGNED IT TO US.
HERE'S WHAT THE JUDGE LOOKS LIKE, BY THE WAY.
ALL RIGHT.
I SHALL SUCCEED.
YOU'RE REALLY GETTING INTO IT.
EXCITED OVER YOUR FIRST JOB?
FURU (SHAKE)
ふる
FURU
ふる
MY FIRST JOB WAS SNEAKING INTO A BUILDING AND KILLING TWO PEOPLE.
!
OH RIGHT... ALL THAT TIME...

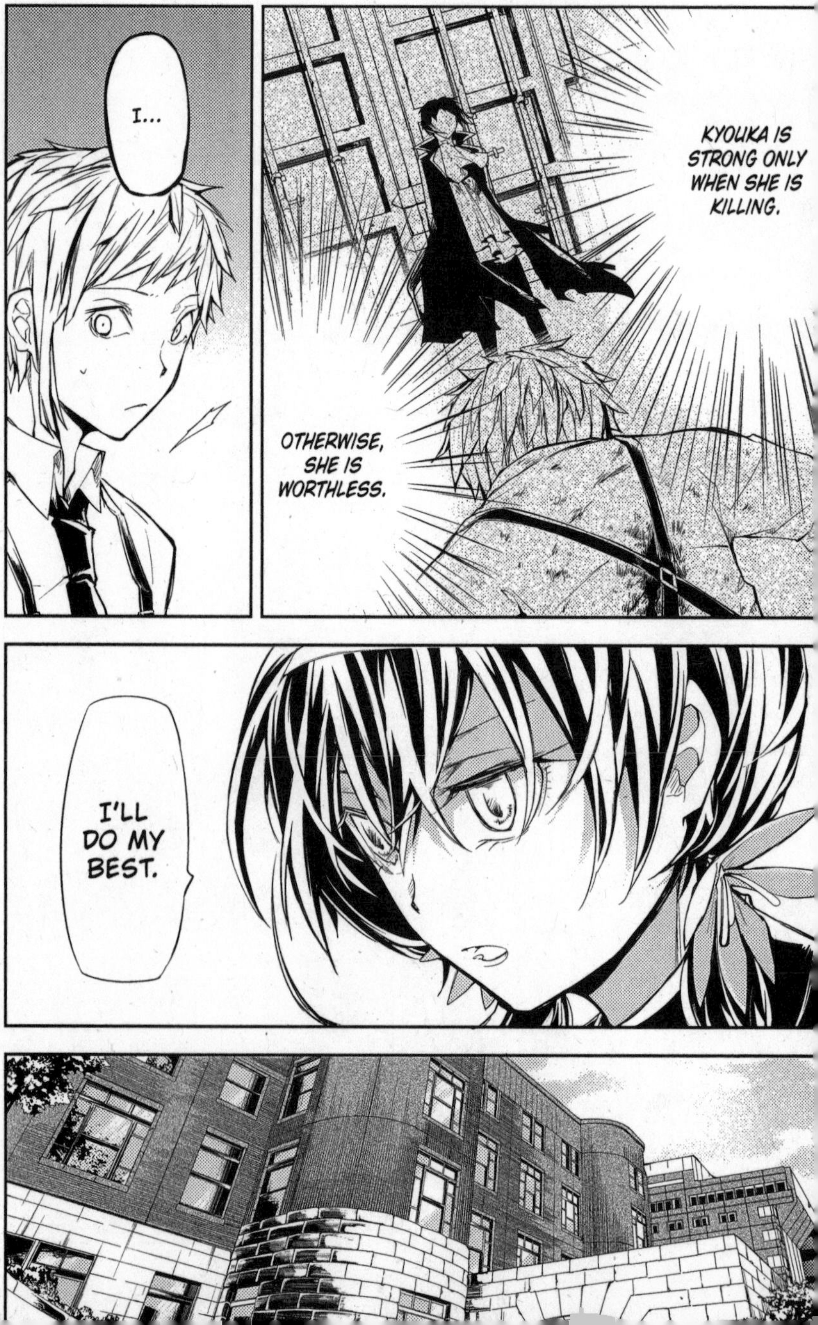
KYOUKA IS STRONG ONLY WHEN SHE IS KILLING.
OTHERWISE, SHE IS WORTHLESS.
I...
I'LL DO MY BEST.

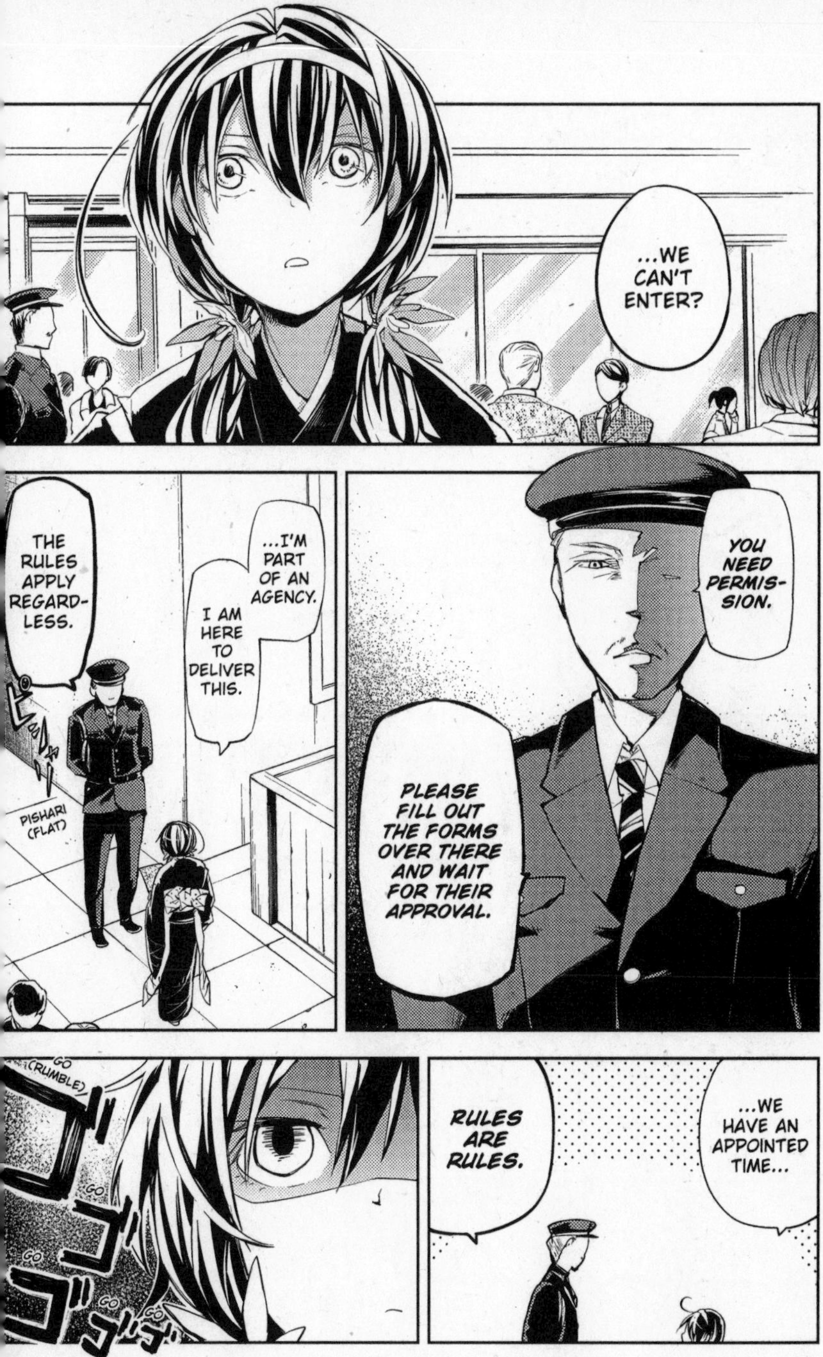
...WE CAN'T ENTER?
YOU NEED PERMIS-SION.
PLEASE FILL OUT THE FORMS OVER THERE AND WAIT FOR THEIR APPROVAL.
...I'M PART OF AN AGENCY.
I AM HERE TO DELIVER THIS.
THE RULES APPLY REGARD-LESS.
PISHARI (FLAT)
...WE HAVE AN APPOINTED TIME...
RULES ARE RULES.
GO (RUMBLE)
GO
GO
GO
GO

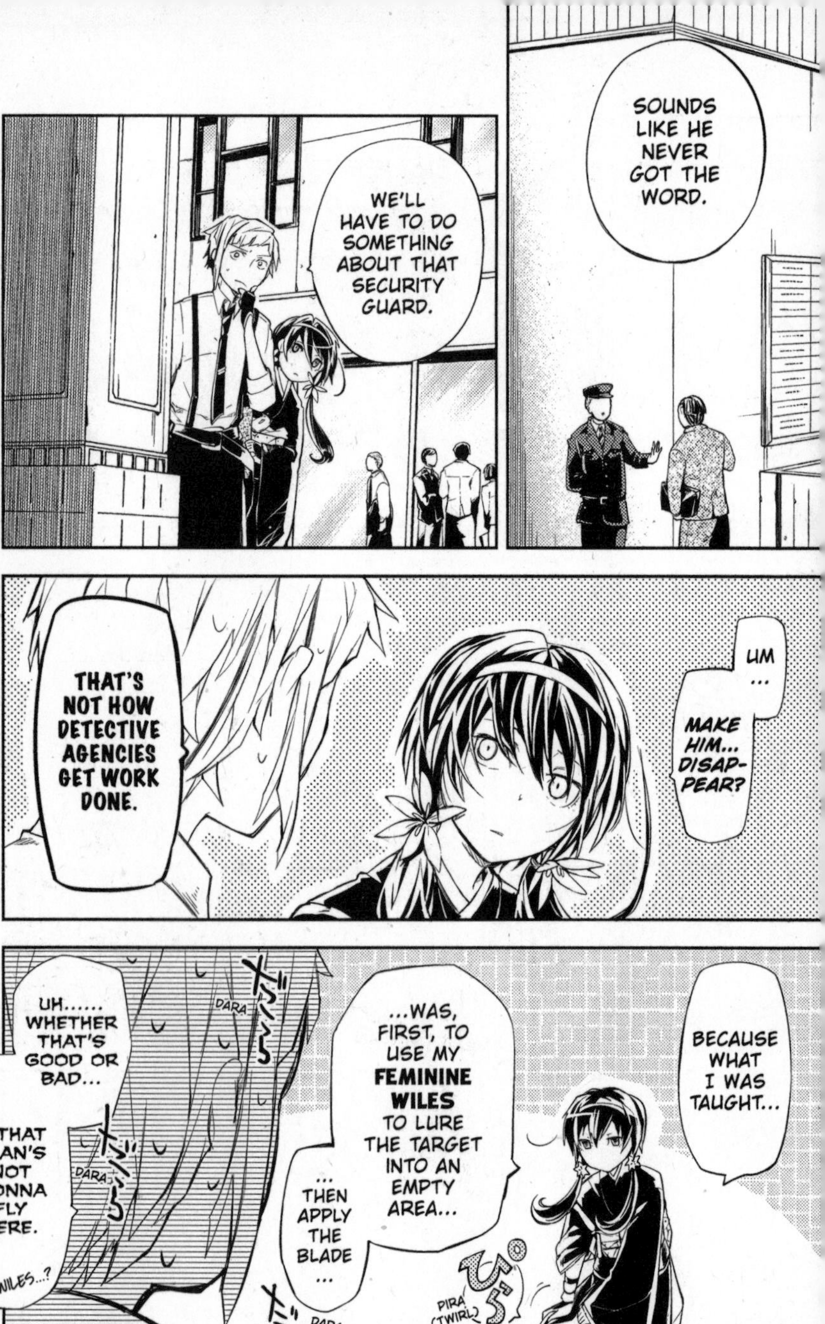
SOUNDS LIKE HE NEVER GOT THE WORD.
WE'LL HAVE TO DO SOMETHING ABOUT THAT SECURITY GUARD.
UM ...
MAKE HIM... DISAPPEAR?
THAT'S NOT HOW DETECTIVE AGENCIES GET WORK DONE.
BECAUSE WHAT I WAS TAUGHT...
PIRA (TWIRL)
...WAS, FIRST, TO USE MY FEMININE WILES TO LURE THE TARGET INTO AN EMPTY AREA...
... THEN APPLY THE BLADE ...
DARA (SWEAT)
DARA
DARA
UH...... WHETHER THAT'S GOOD OR BAD...
...THAT PLAN'S NOT GONNA FLY HERE.
WILES...?

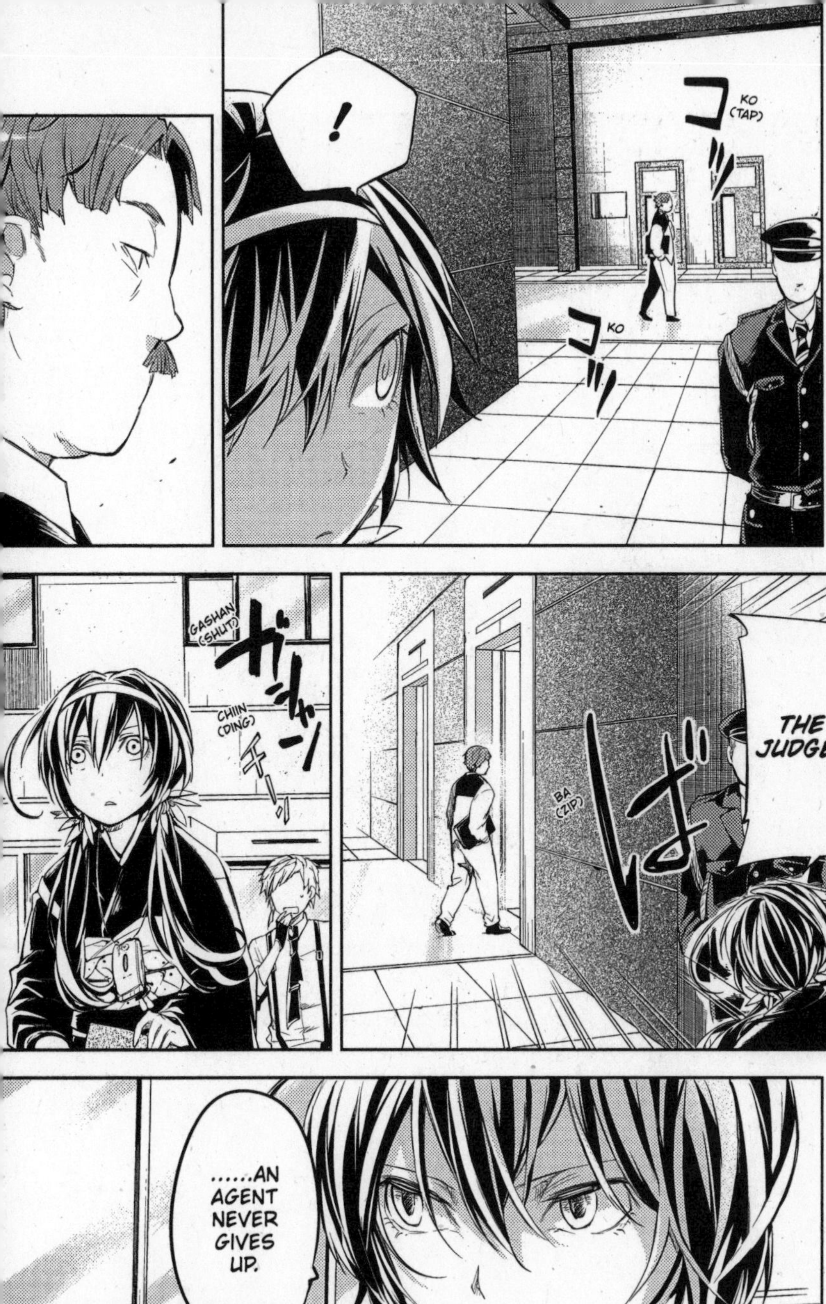
KO (TAP)
KO
!
BA (ZIP)
THE JUDGE!
GASHAN (SHUT)
CHIIN (DING)
......AN AGENT NEVER GIVES UP.

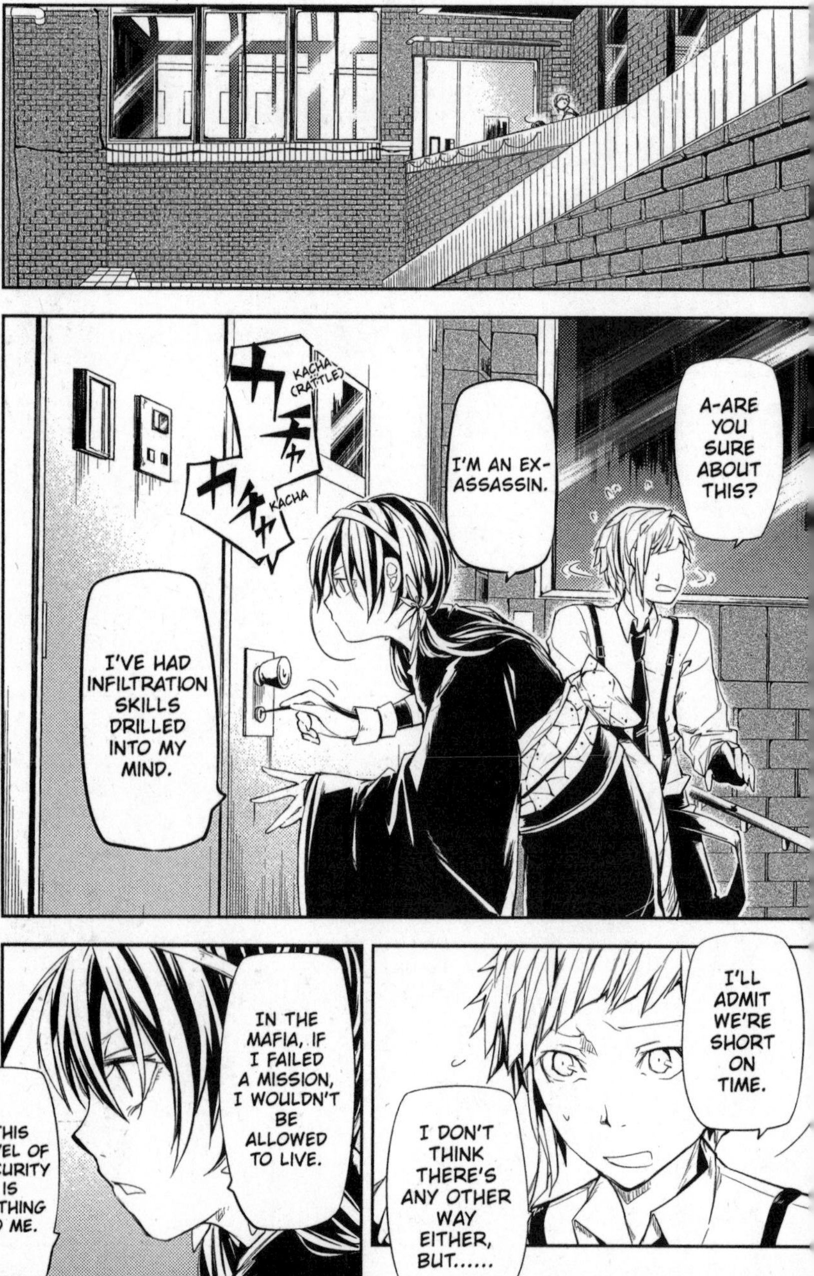

A-ARE YOU SURE ABOUT THIS?
カチャ
KACHA (RATTLE)
カチャ
KACHA
I'M AN EX-ASSASSIN.
I'VE HAD INFILTRATION SKILLS DRILLED INTO MY MIND.
I'LL ADMIT WE'RE SHORT ON TIME.
I DON'T THINK THERE'S ANY OTHER WAY EITHER, BUT......
IN THE MAFIA, IF I FAILED A MISSION, I WOULDN'T BE ALLOWED TO LIVE.
THIS LEVEL OF SECURITY IS NOTHING TO ME.

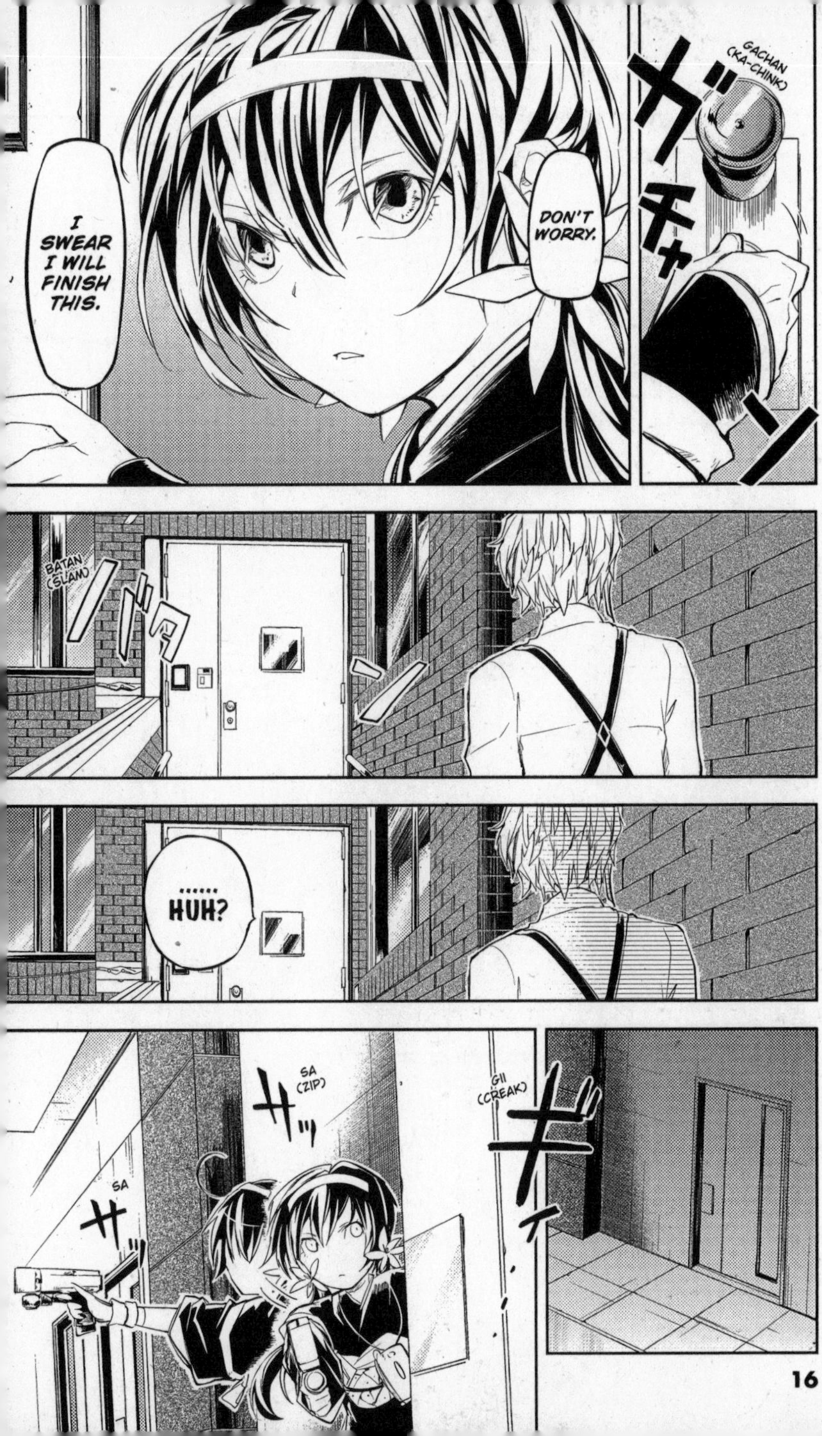
GACHAN (KA-CHINK)
DON'T WORRY.
I SWEAR I WILL FINISH THIS.
BATAN (SLAM)
......HUH?
GII (CREAK)
SA (ZIP)
SA

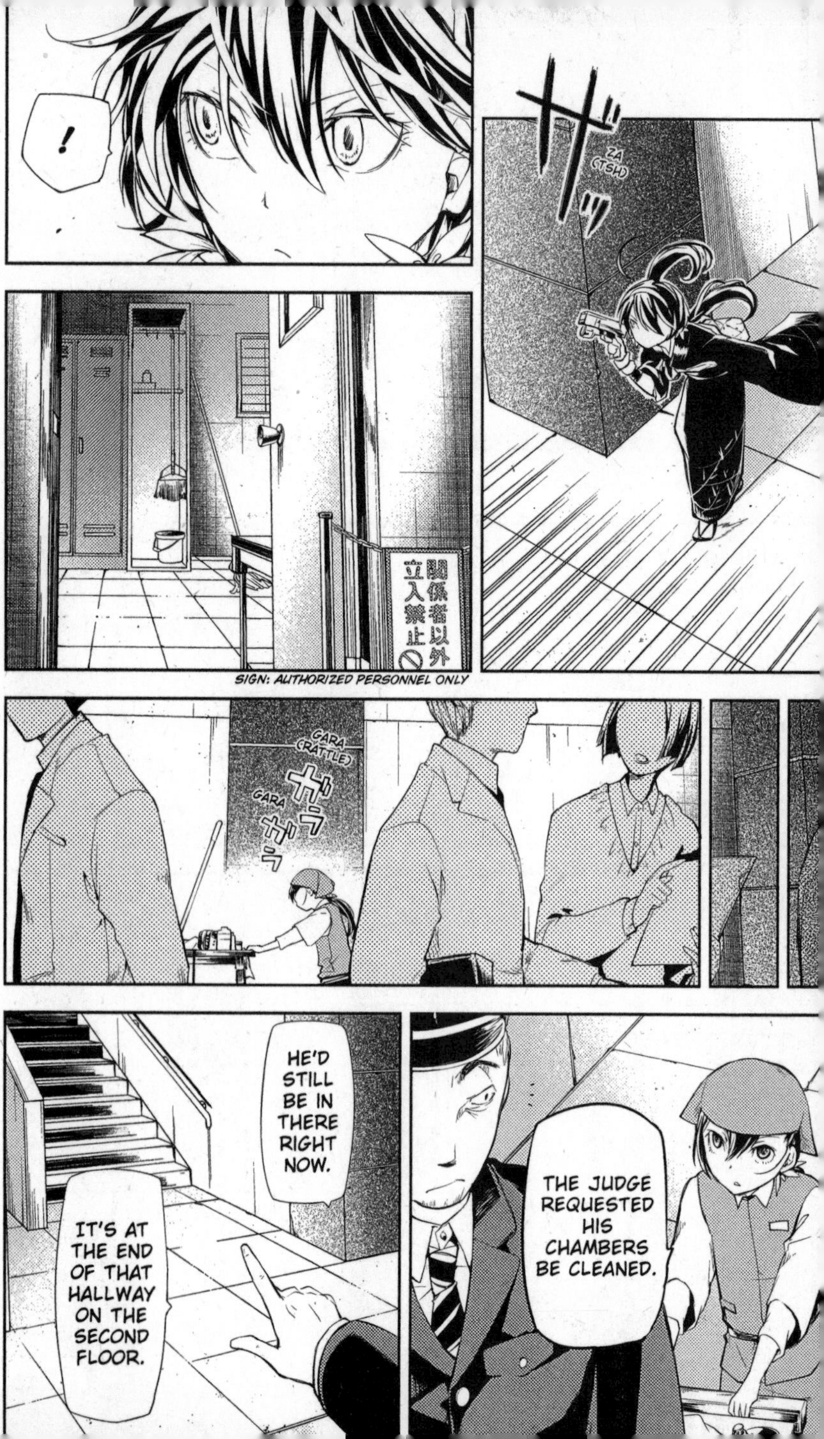
ザッ
ZA (TSH)
!
関係者以外立入禁止
SIGN: AUTHORIZED PERSONNEL ONLY
ガラ
GARA (RATTLE)
ガラ
GARA
THE JUDGE REQUESTED HIS CHAMBERS BE CLEANED.
HE'D STILL BE IN THERE RIGHT NOW.
IT'S AT THE END OF THAT HALLWAY ON THE SECOND FLOOR.

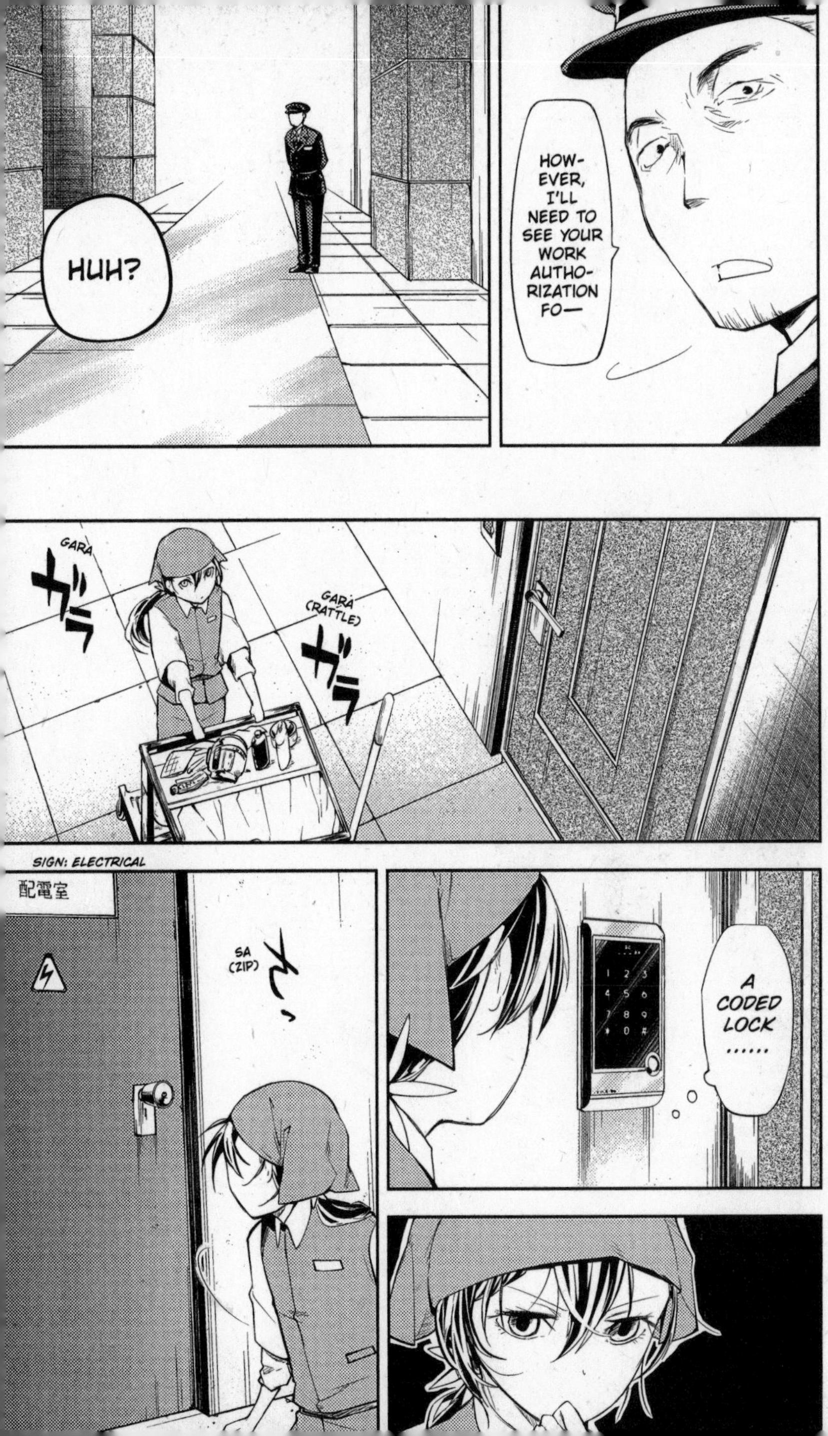
HOW-EVER, I'LL NEED TO SEE YOUR WORK AUTHORIZATION FO—
HUH?
GARA (RATTLE)
GARA
A CODED LOCK......
SIGN: ELECTRICAL
配電室
SA (ZIP)

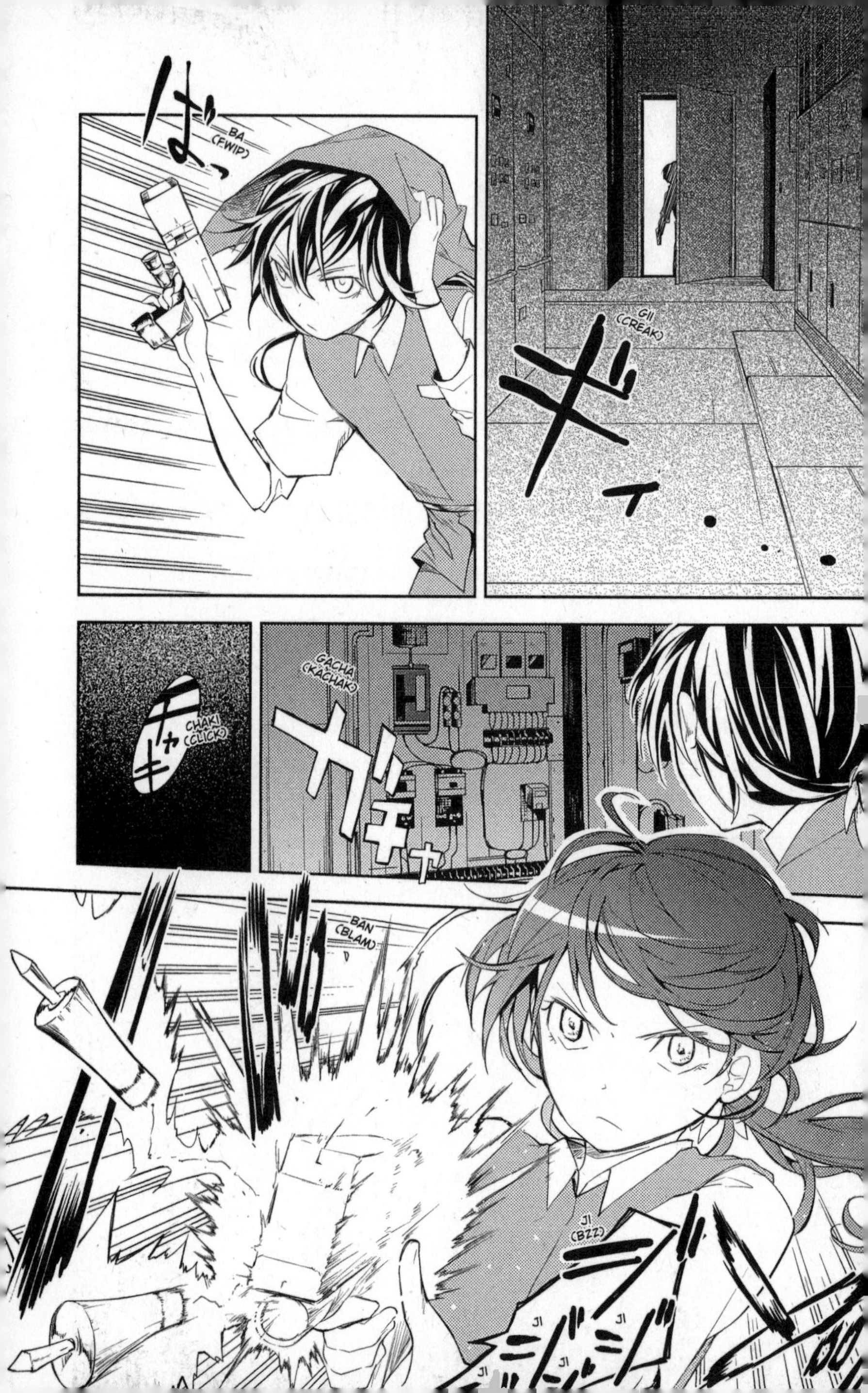
GII (CREAK)
BA (FWIP)
GACHA (KACHAK)
CHAKI (CLICK)
BAN (BLAM)
JI (BZZ)
JI
JI
JI
JI

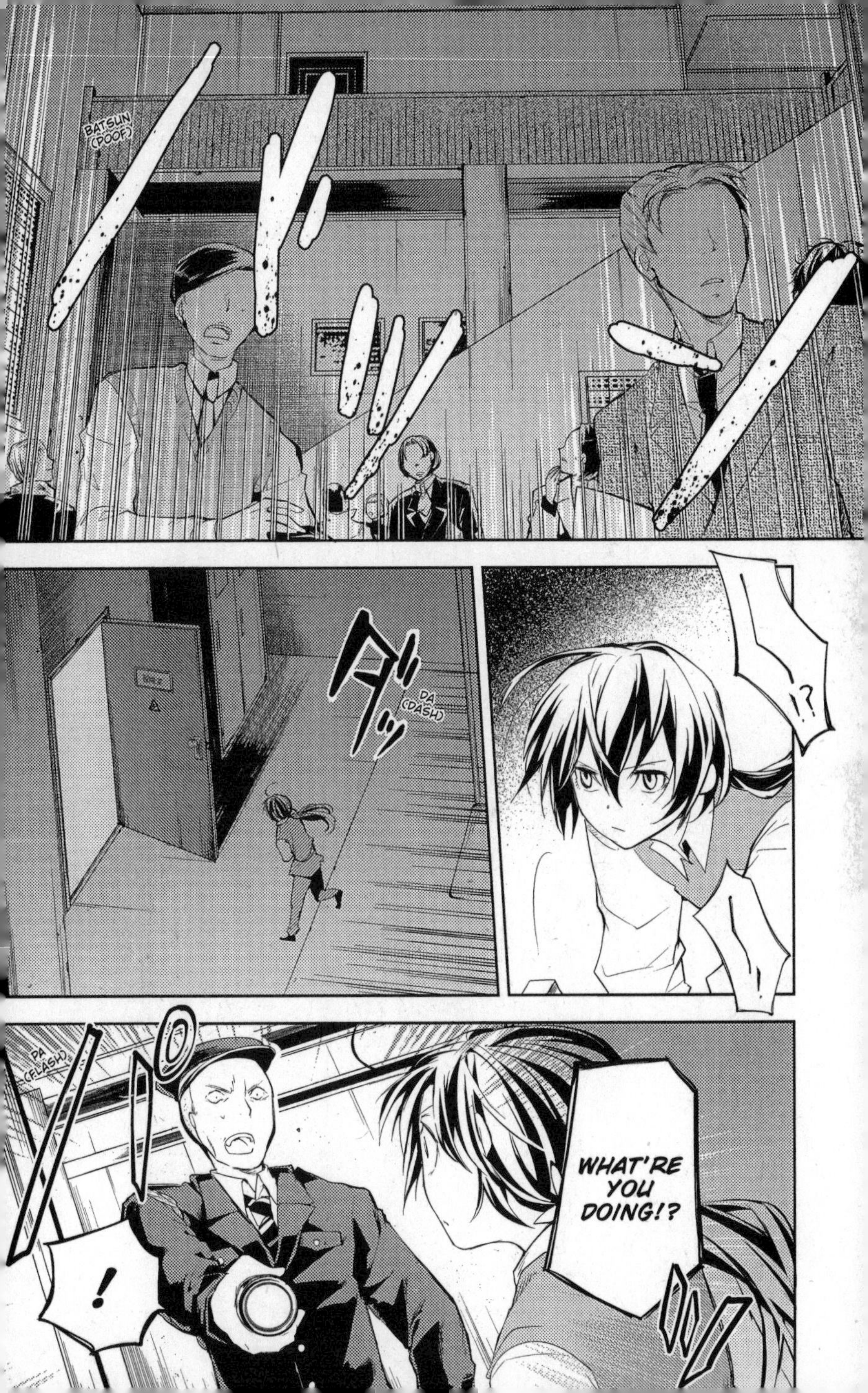
BATSUN (POOF)
!?
DA (DASH)
WHAT'RE YOU DOING!?
PA (FLASH)
!

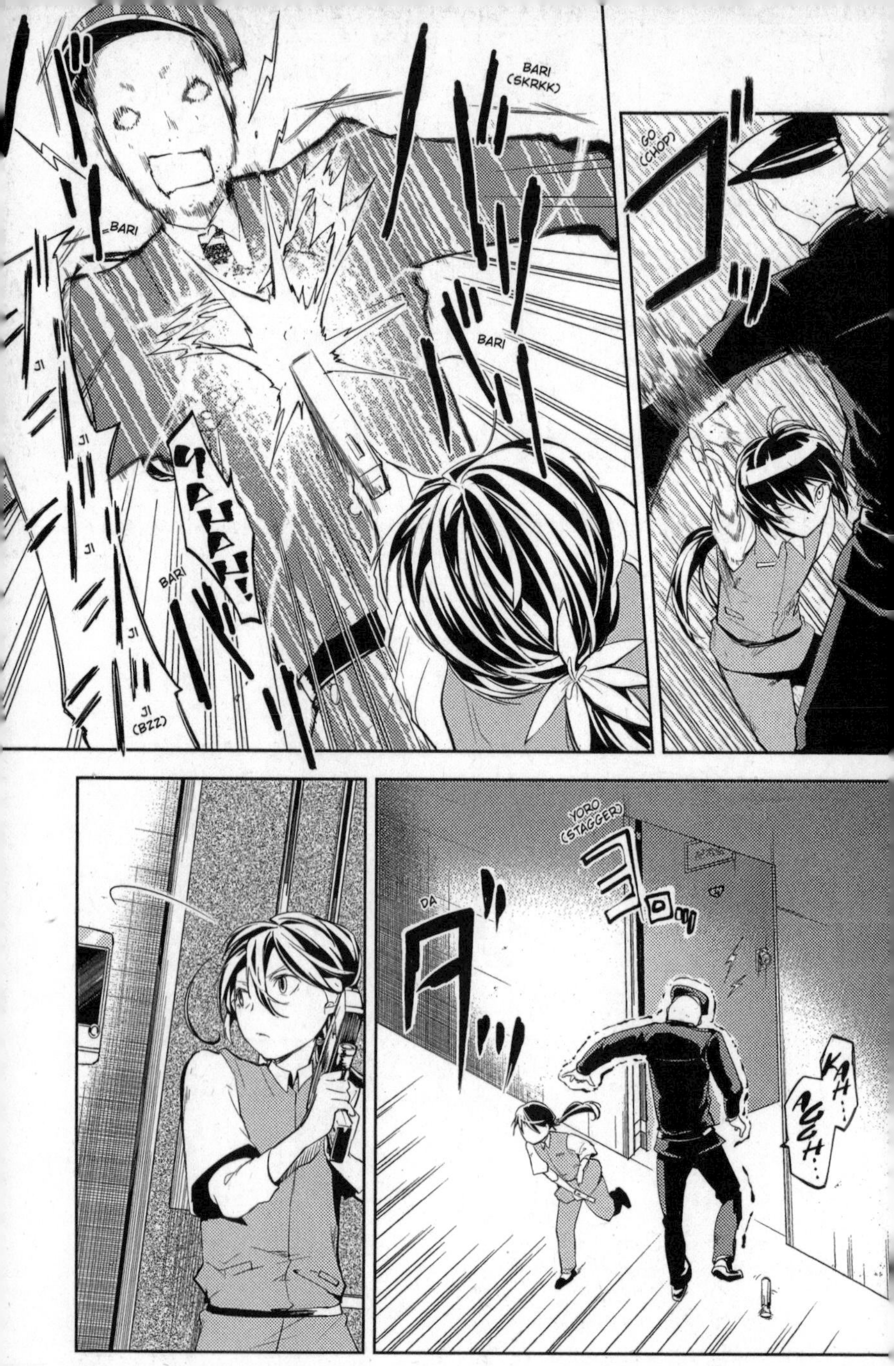
GO (CHOP)
BARI (SKRKK)
BARI
=BARI
JI
JI
JI
GAHAH!!
BARI
JI
JI (BZZ)
YORO (STAGGER)
DA
KAH... AUGH...

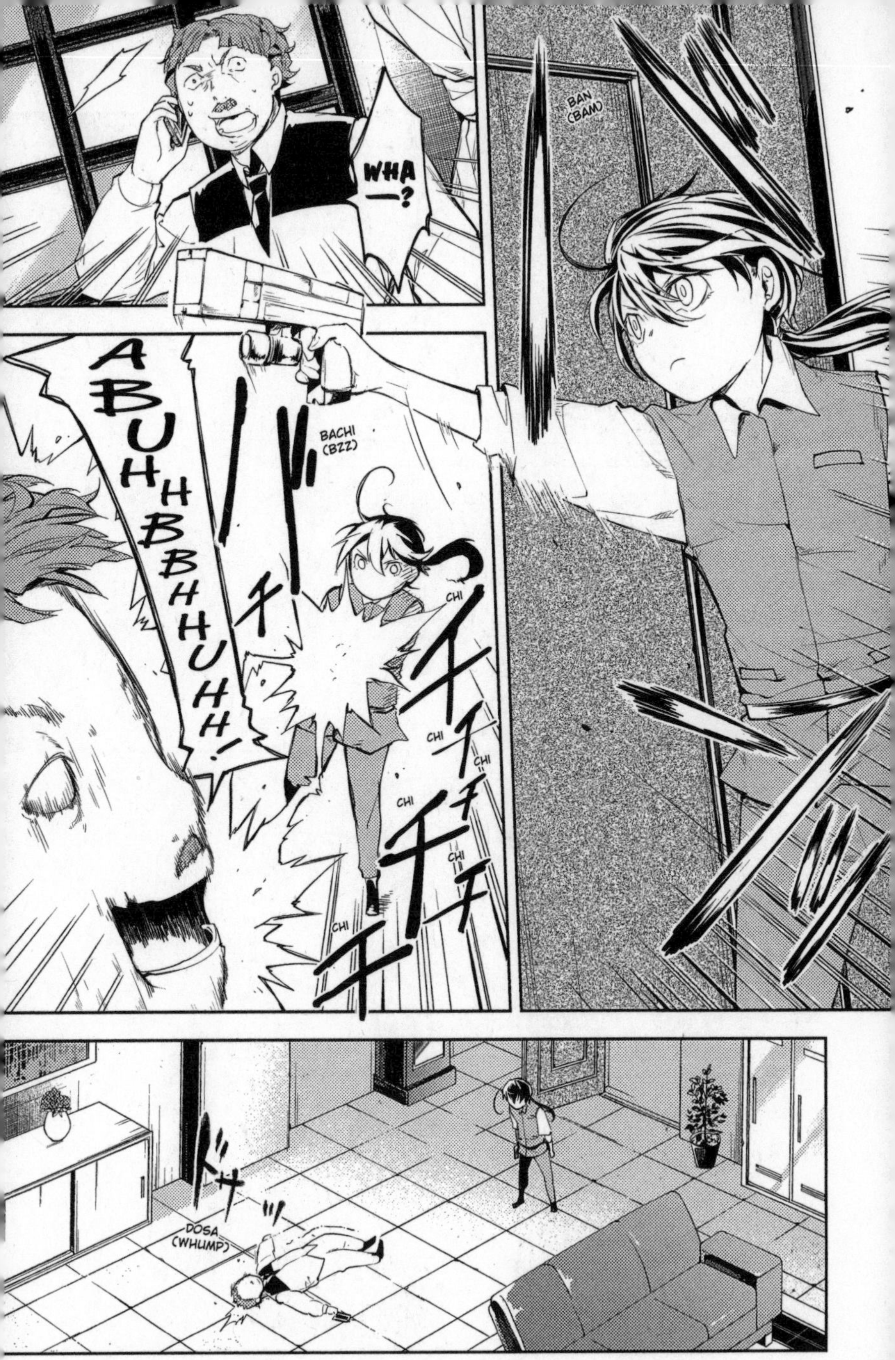
BAN (BAM)
WHA—?
ABUHHBBHHUHH!
BACHI (BZZ)
CHI
CHI
CHI
CHI
CHI
CHI
DOSA (WHUMP)

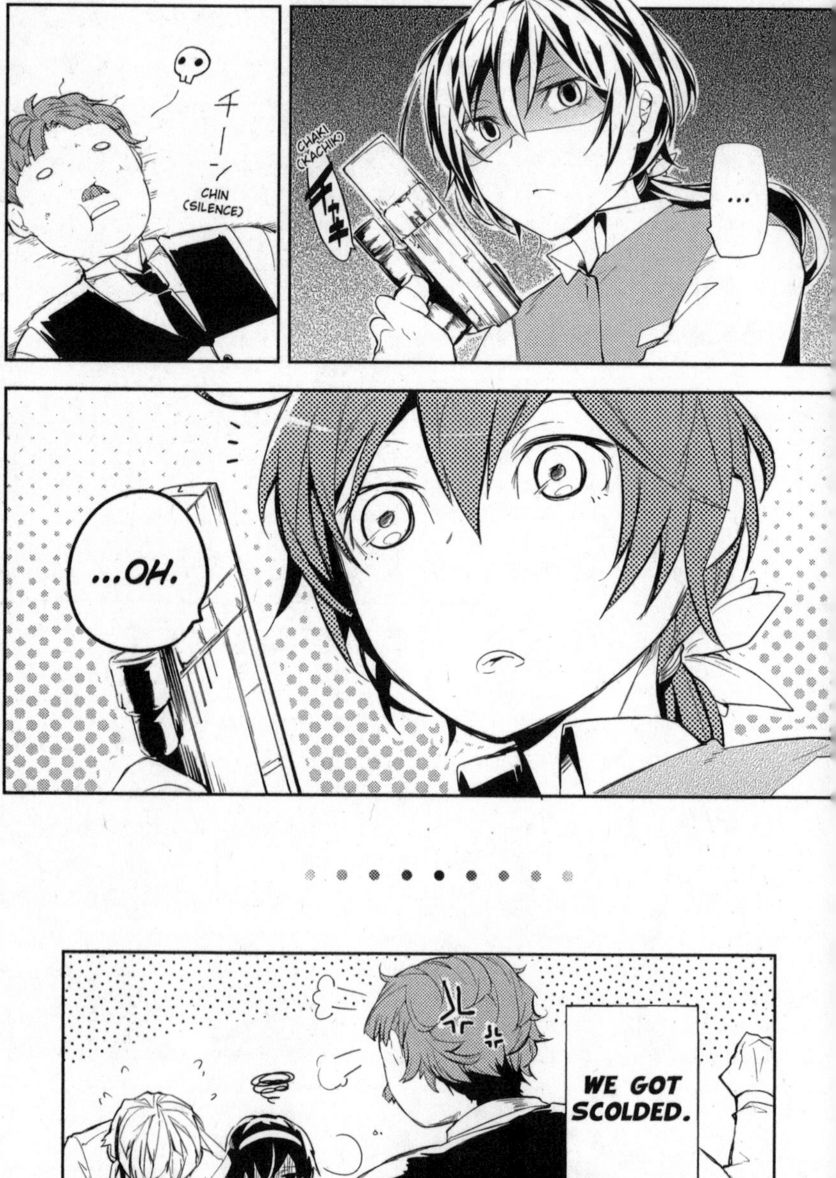
...
CHAKI (KACHIK)
チャキ
チーン
CHIN (SILENCE)
...OH.
WE GOT SCOLDED.

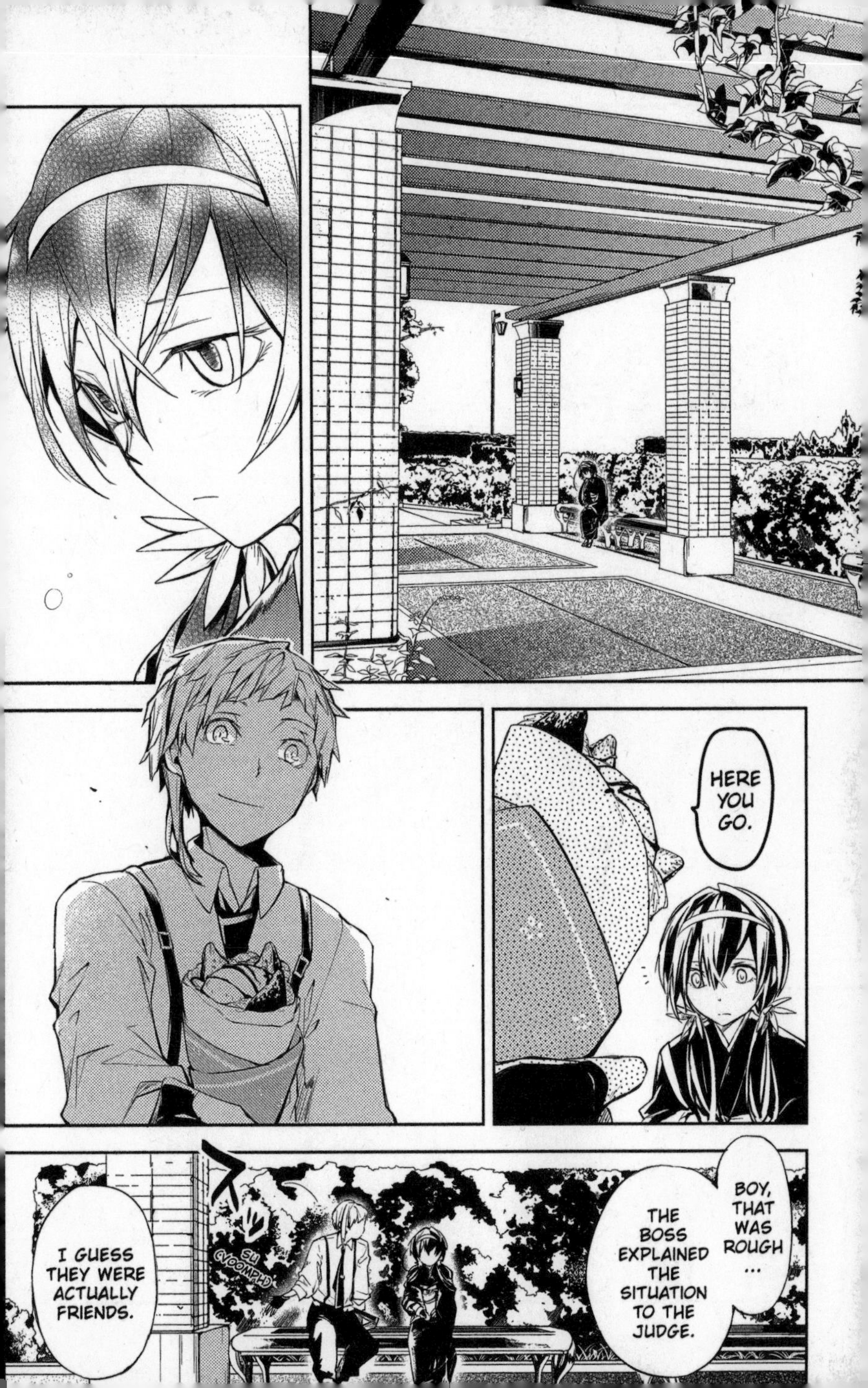
HERE YOU GO.
BOY, THAT WAS ROUGH ...
THE BOSS EXPLAINED THE SITUATION TO THE JUDGE.
SU (VOOMPH)
I GUESS THEY WERE ACTUALLY FRIENDS.

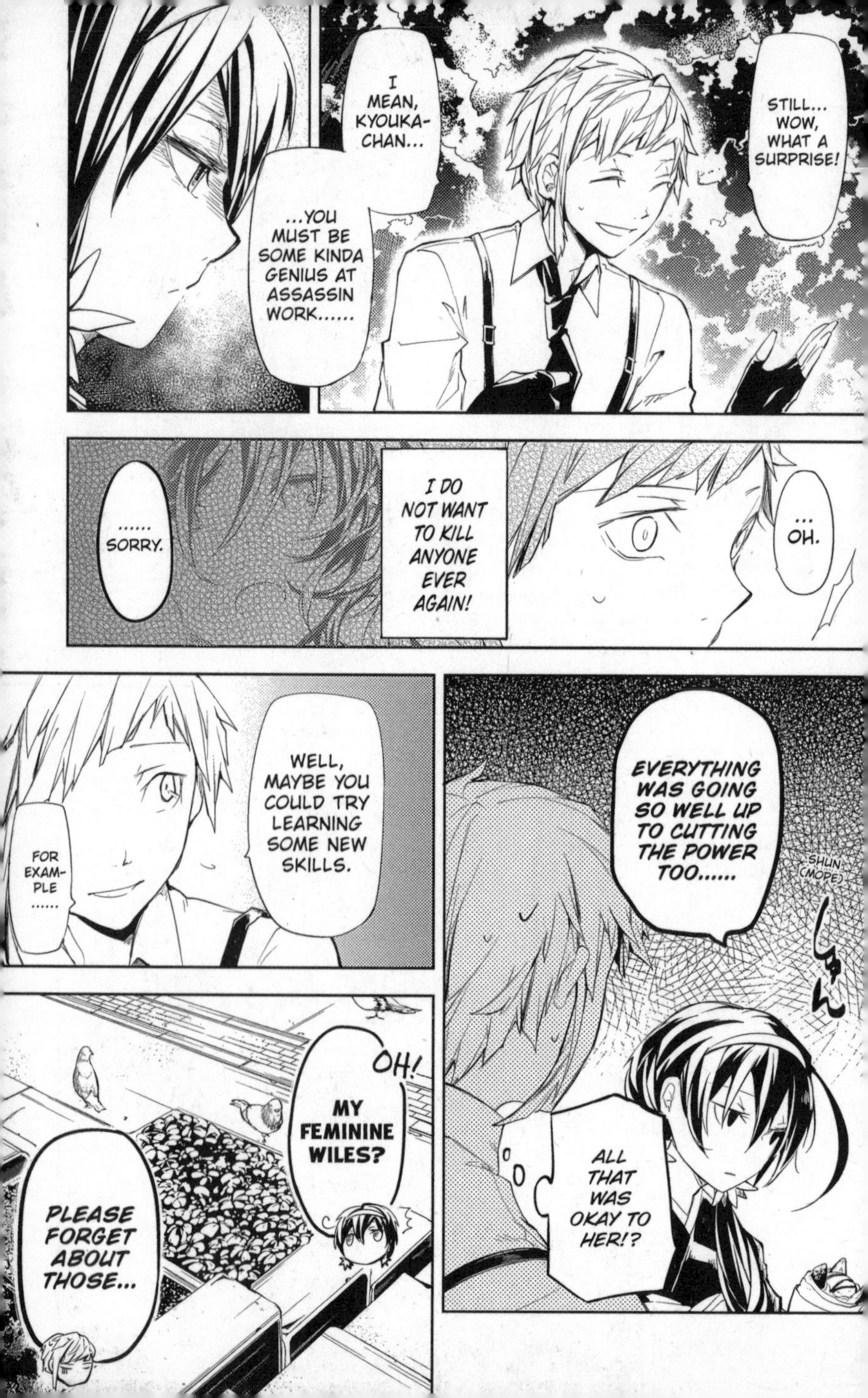
STILL... WOW, WHAT A SURPRISE!
I MEAN, KYOUKA-CHAN...
...YOU MUST BE SOME KINDA GENIUS AT ASSASSIN WORK......
...OH.
I DO NOT WANT TO KILL ANYONE EVER AGAIN!
......SORRY.
EVERYTHING WAS GOING SO WELL UP TO CUTTING THE POWER TOO......
SHUN (MOPE)
ALL THAT WAS OKAY TO HER!?
WELL, MAYBE YOU COULD TRY LEARNING SOME NEW SKILLS.
FOR EXAMPLE......
OH!
MY FEMININE WILES?
PLEASE FORGET ABOUT THOSE...

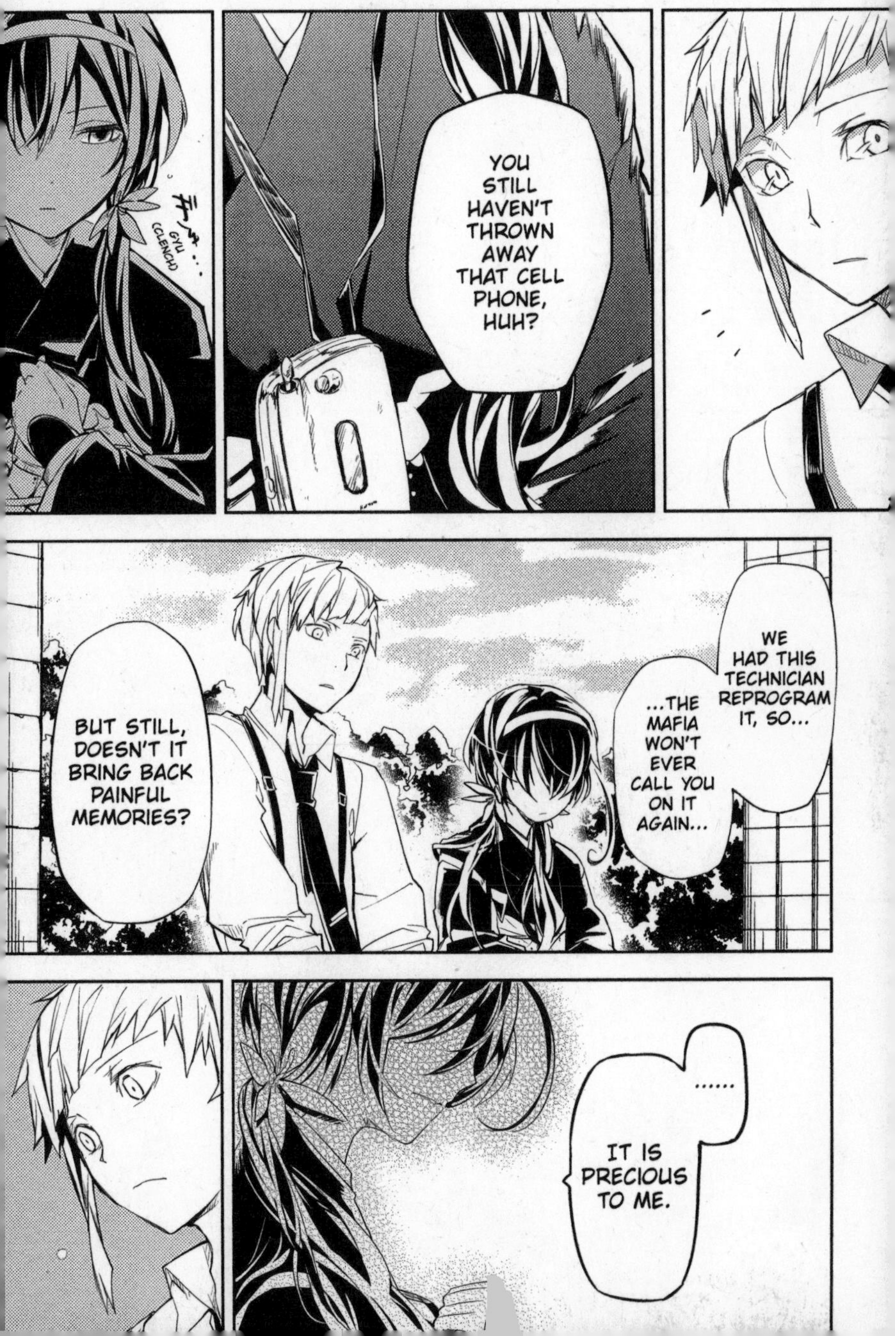
YOU STILL HAVEN'T THROWN AWAY THAT CELL PHONE, HUH?
GYU (CLENCH)
WE HAD THIS TECHNICIAN REPROGRAM IT, SO...
...THE MAFIA WON'T EVER CALL YOU ON IT AGAIN...
BUT STILL, DOESN'T IT BRING BACK PAINFUL MEMORIES?
......
IT IS PRECIOUS TO ME.

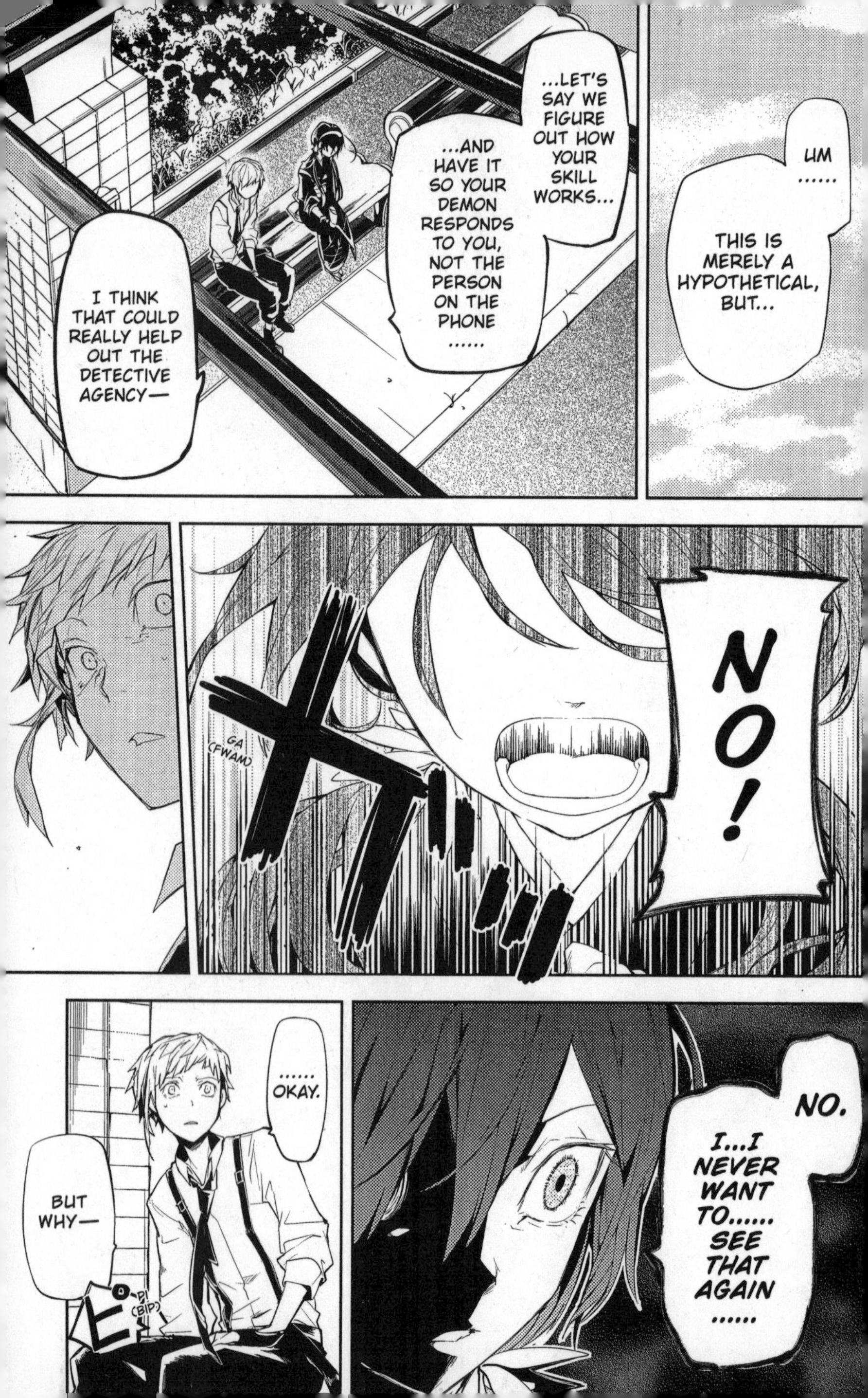
UM ......
THIS IS MERELY A HYPOTHETICAL, BUT...
...LET'S SAY WE FIGURE OUT HOW YOUR SKILL WORKS...
...AND HAVE IT SO YOUR DEMON RESPONDS TO YOU, NOT THE PERSON ON THE PHONE ......
I THINK THAT COULD REALLY HELP OUT THE DETECTIVE AGENCY—
NO!
GA (FWAM)
NO.
I...I NEVER WANT TO...... SEE THAT AGAIN ......
...... OKAY.
BUT WHY—
PI (BIP)

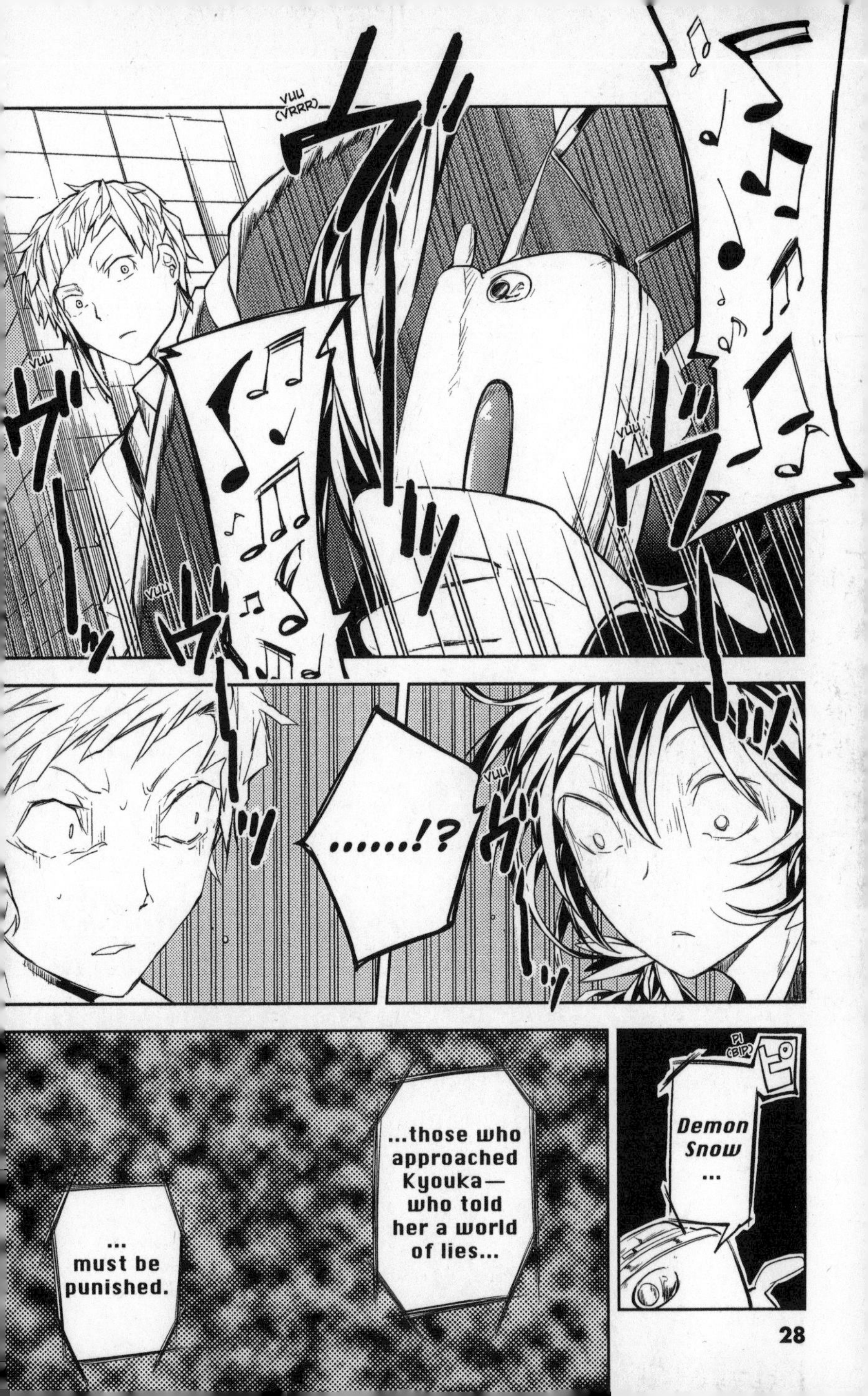
VUU (VRRR)
VUU
VUU
VUU
VUU
......!?
PI (BIP)
Demon Snow ...
...those who approached Kyouka—who told her a world of lies...
... must be punished.

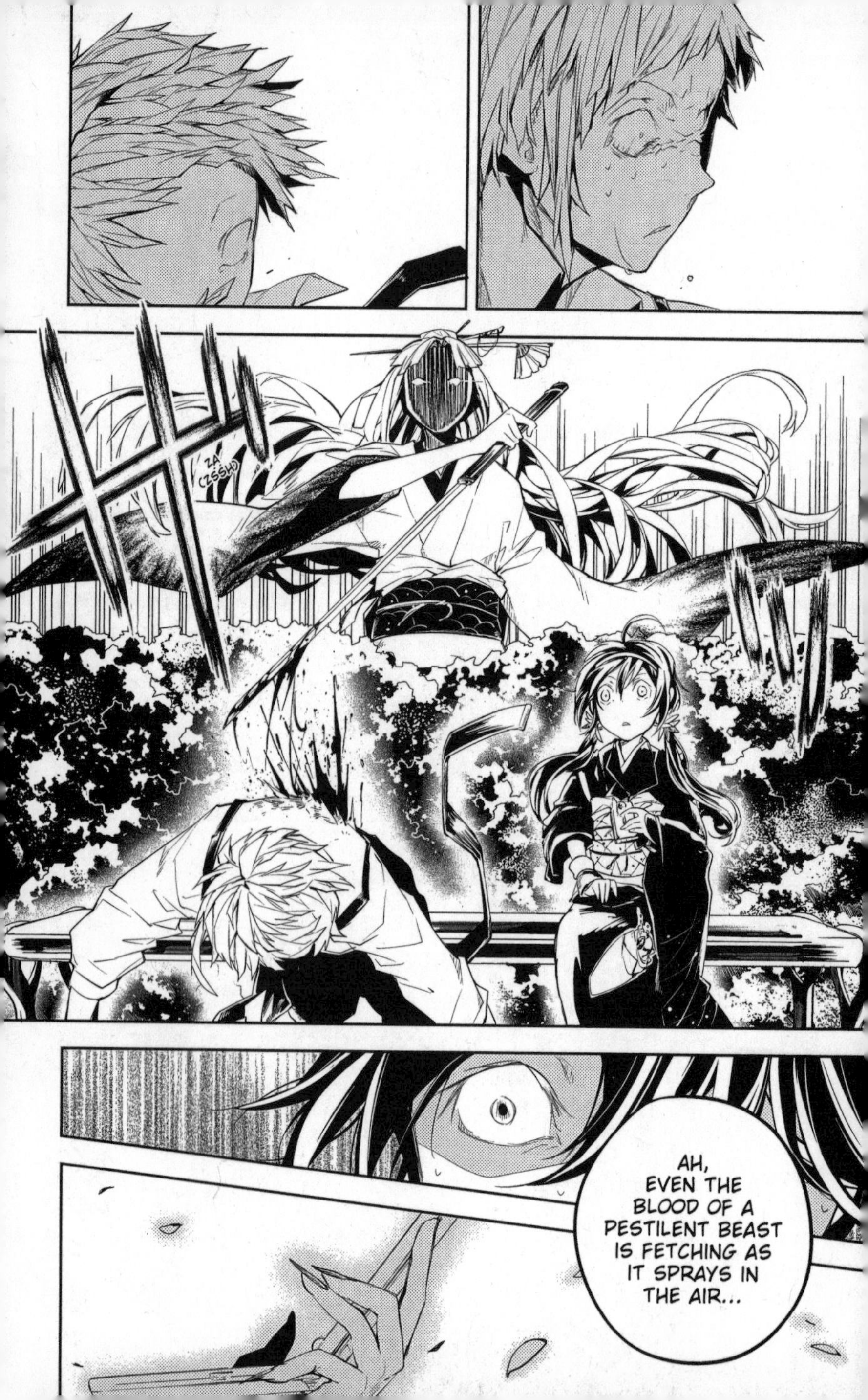
ZA ZSSH
AH, EVEN THE BLOOD OF A PESTILENT BEAST IS FETCHING AS IT SPRAYS IN THE AIR...

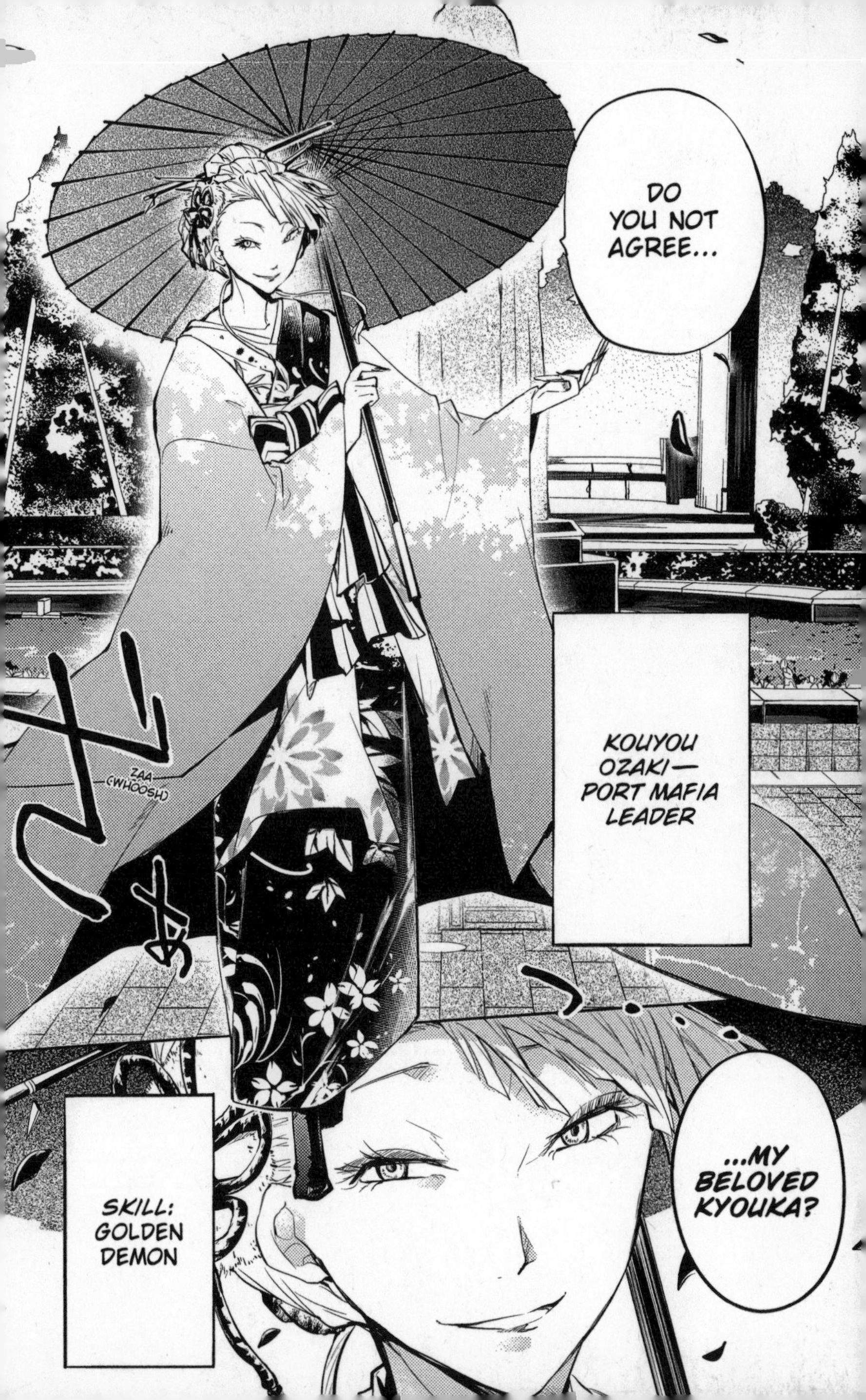
DO YOU NOT AGREE...
KOUYOU OZAKI—PORT MAFIA LEADER
ZAA (WHOOSH)
...MY BELOVED KYOUKA?
SKILL: GOLDEN DEMON

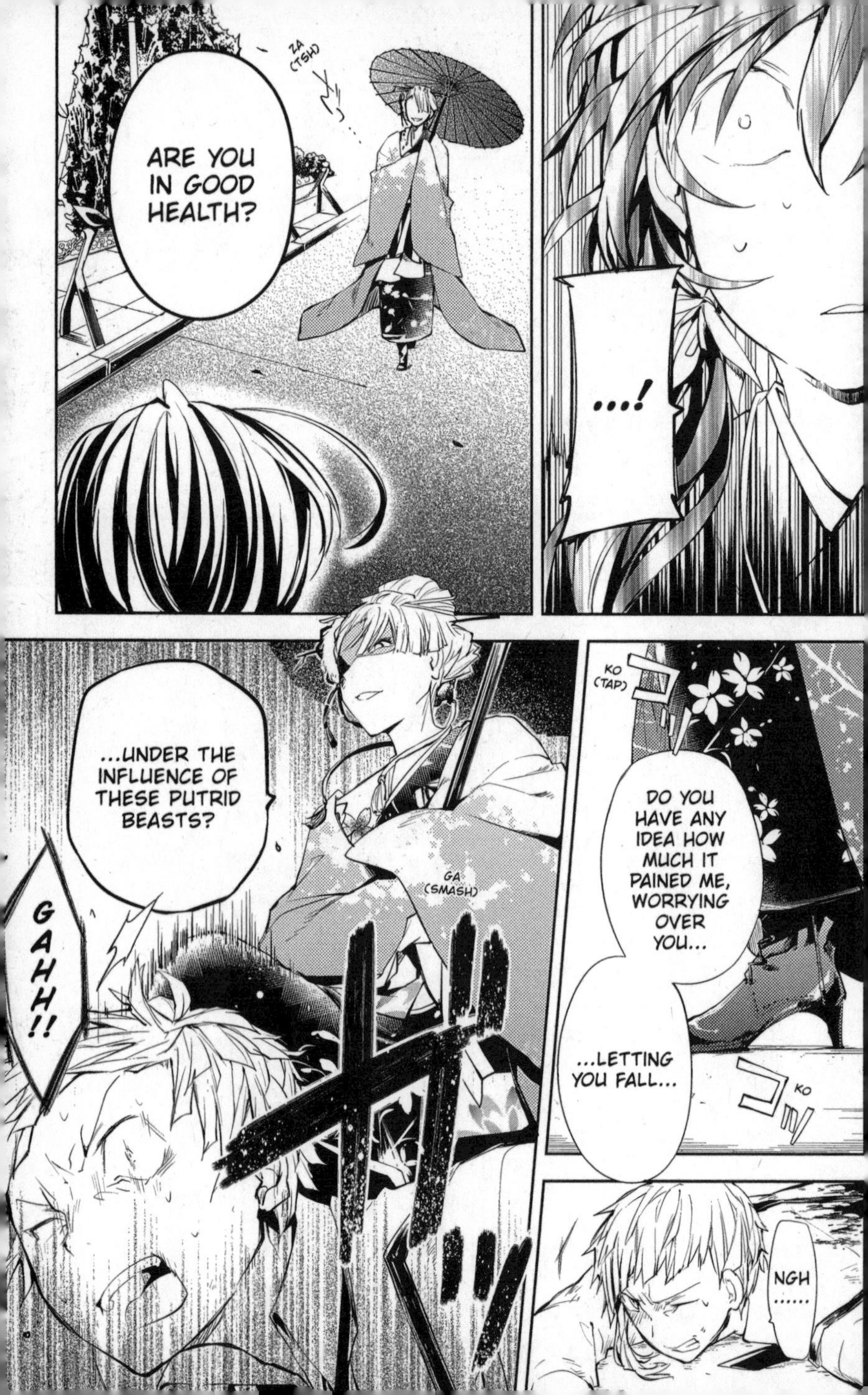
...!
ZA (TSH)
ARE YOU IN GOOD HEALTH?
KO (TAP)
DO YOU HAVE ANY IDEA HOW MUCH IT PAINED ME, WORRYING OVER YOU...
...LETTING YOU FALL...
KO
NGH ......
...UNDER THE INFLUENCE OF THESE PUTRID BEASTS?
GA (SMASH)
GAHH!!

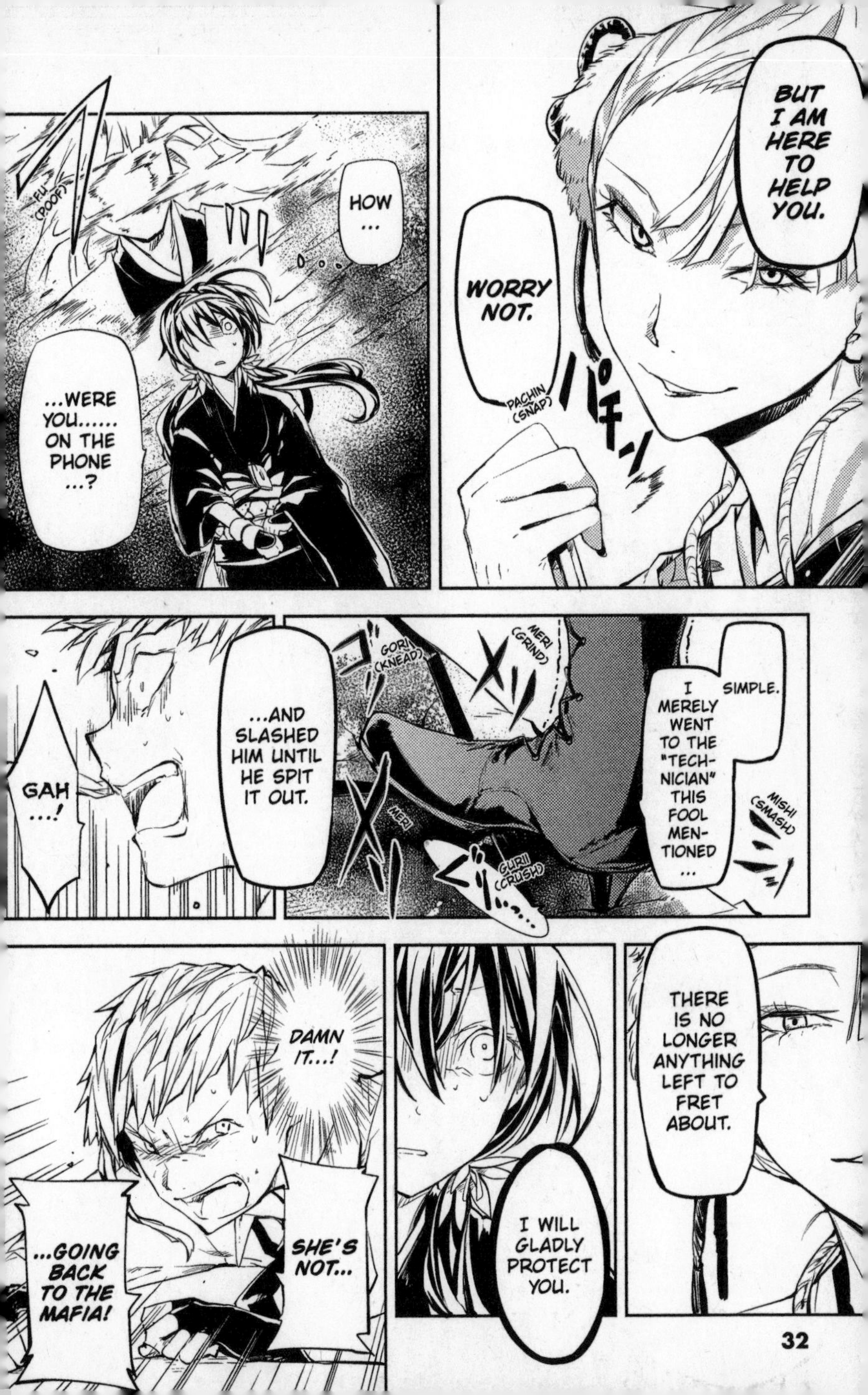
BUT I AM HERE TO HELP YOU.
WORRY NOT.
PACHIN (SNAP)
HOW ...
...WERE YOU...... ON THE PHONE ...?
FU- (POOF)
SIMPLE.
I MERELY WENT TO THE "TECH-NICIAN" THIS FOOL MEN-TIONED ...
MISHI (SMASH)
MERI (GRIND)
GORI (KNEAD)
MERI
GURI (CRUSH)
...AND SLASHED HIM UNTIL HE SPIT IT OUT.
GAH ...!
THERE IS NO LONGER ANYTHING LEFT TO FRET ABOUT.
I WILL GLADLY PROTECT YOU.
DAMN IT...!
SHE'S NOT...
...GOING BACK TO THE MAFIA!

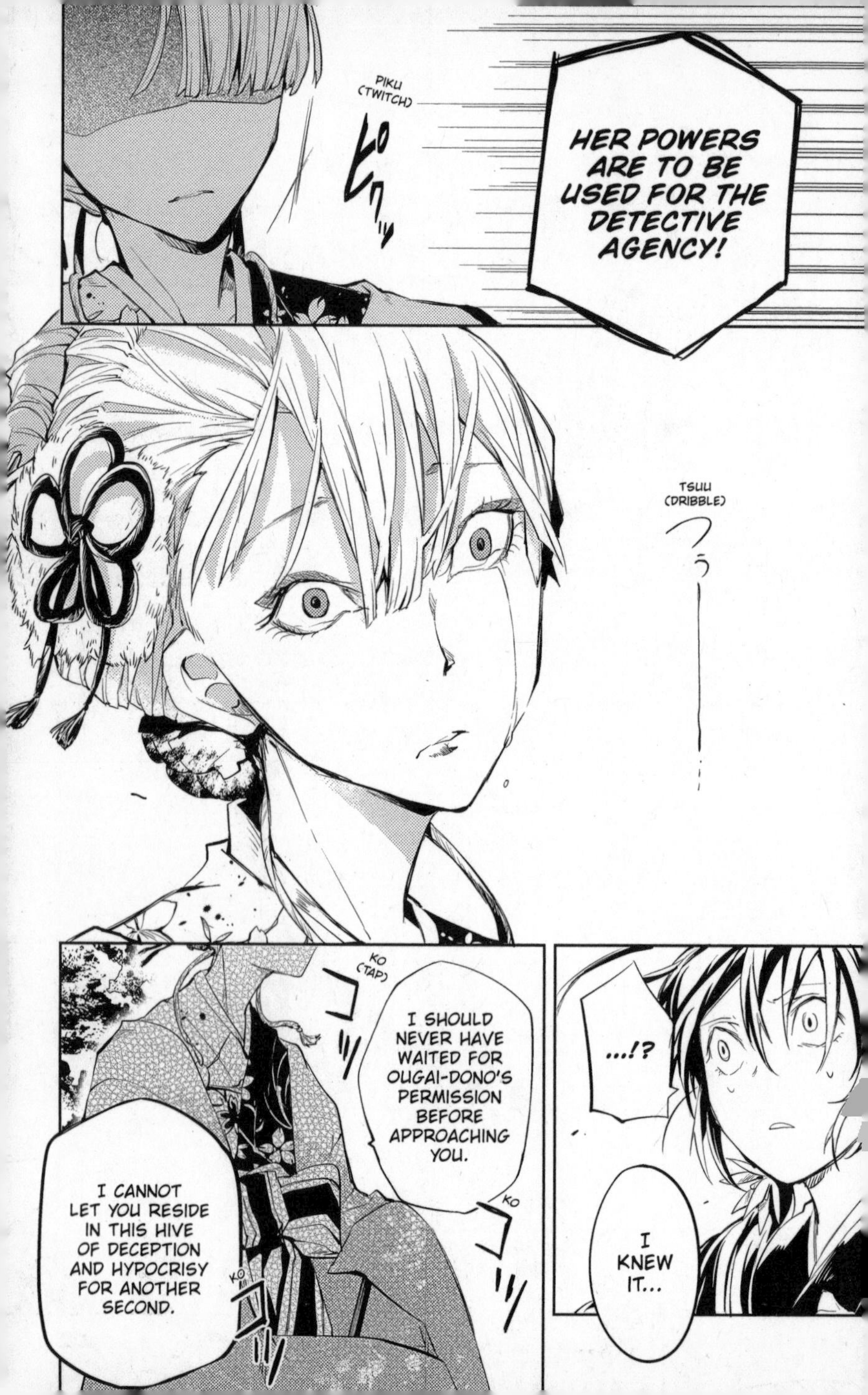
HER POWERS ARE TO BE USED FOR THE DETECTIVE AGENCY!
PIKU (TWITCH)
TSUU (DRIBBLE)
...!?
I KNEW IT...
KO (TAP)
I SHOULD NEVER HAVE WAITED FOR OUGAI-DONO'S PERMISSION BEFORE APPROACHING YOU.
KO
I CANNOT LET YOU RESIDE IN THIS HIVE OF DECEPTION AND HYPOCRISY FOR ANOTHER SECOND.
KO

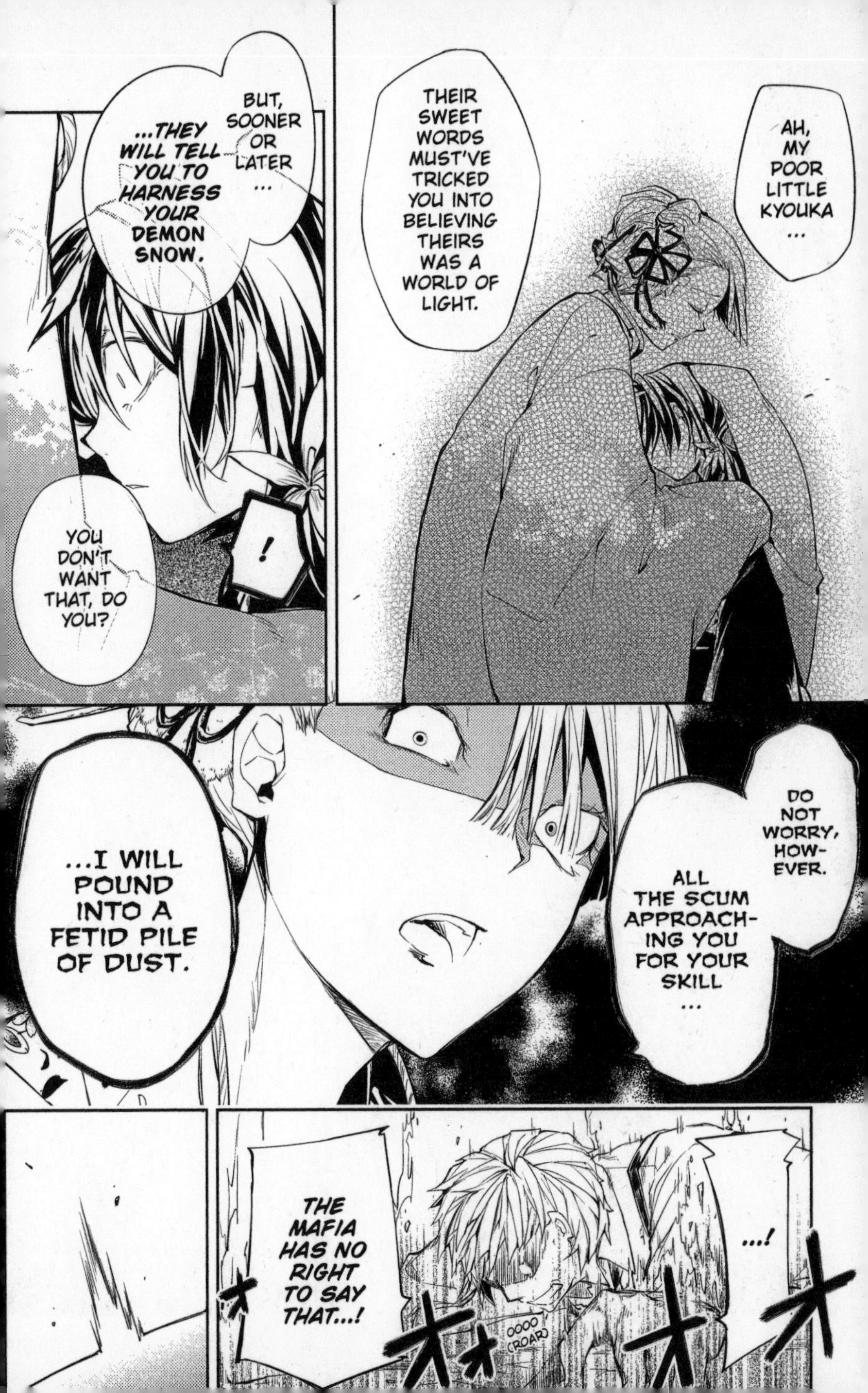
AH, MY POOR LITTLE KYOUKA ...
THEIR SWEET WORDS MUST'VE TRICKED YOU INTO BELIEVING THEIRS WAS A WORLD OF LIGHT.
BUT, SOONER OR LATER ...
...THEY WILL TELL YOU TO HARNESS YOUR DEMON SNOW.
!
YOU DON'T WANT THAT, DO YOU?
DO NOT WORRY, HOW-EVER.
ALL THE SCUM APPROACH-ING YOU FOR YOUR SKILL ...
...I WILL POUND INTO A FETID PILE OF DUST.
...!
THE MAFIA HAS NO RIGHT TO SAY THAT...!
OOOO (ROAR)

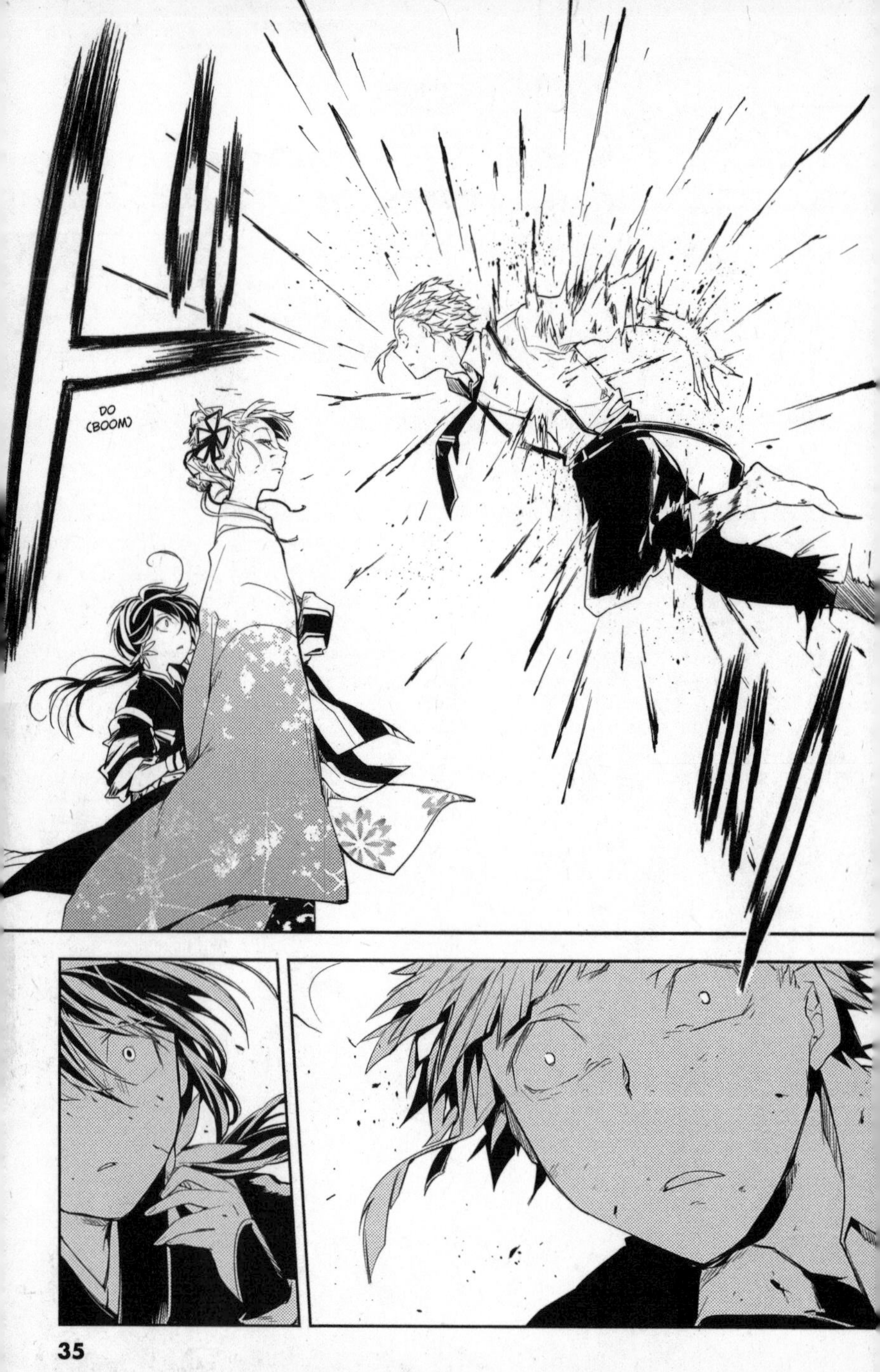
DO
(BOOM)

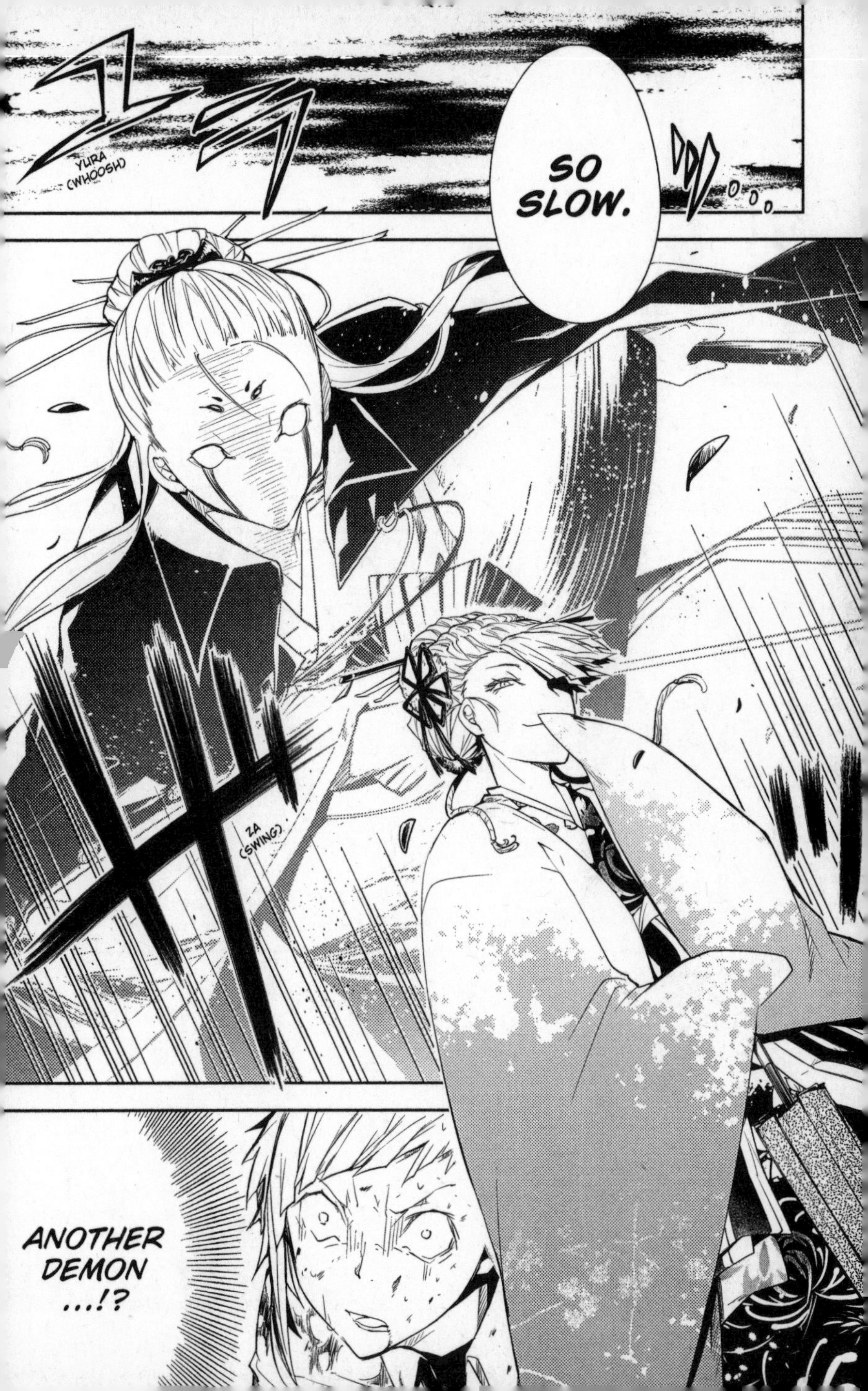
SO SLOW.
YURA (WHOOSH)
ZA (SWING)
ANOTHER DEMON ...!?

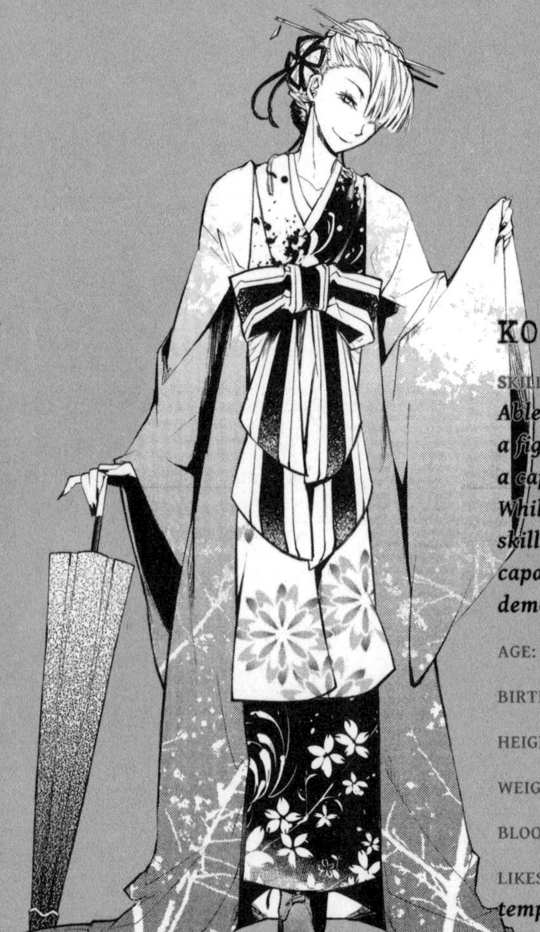

KOUYOU OZAKI

SKILL: **Golden Demon**

Able to control the Golden Demon, a figure in Japanese clothes and a cape who wields a sword cane. While possessing the same type of skill as Kyouka Izumi, she is fully capable of controlling her own demon.

AGE: ***26***

BIRTH DATE: ***January 10***

HEIGHT: ***171cm***

WEIGHT: ***62kg***

BLOOD TYPE: ***A***

LIKES: ***Kyouka Izumi, golden tempura, Japanese pickles***

DISLIKES: ***Hope, love***

BUNGO
STRAY DOGS

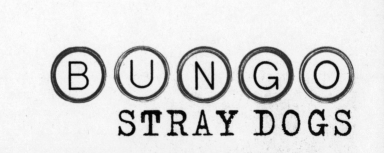

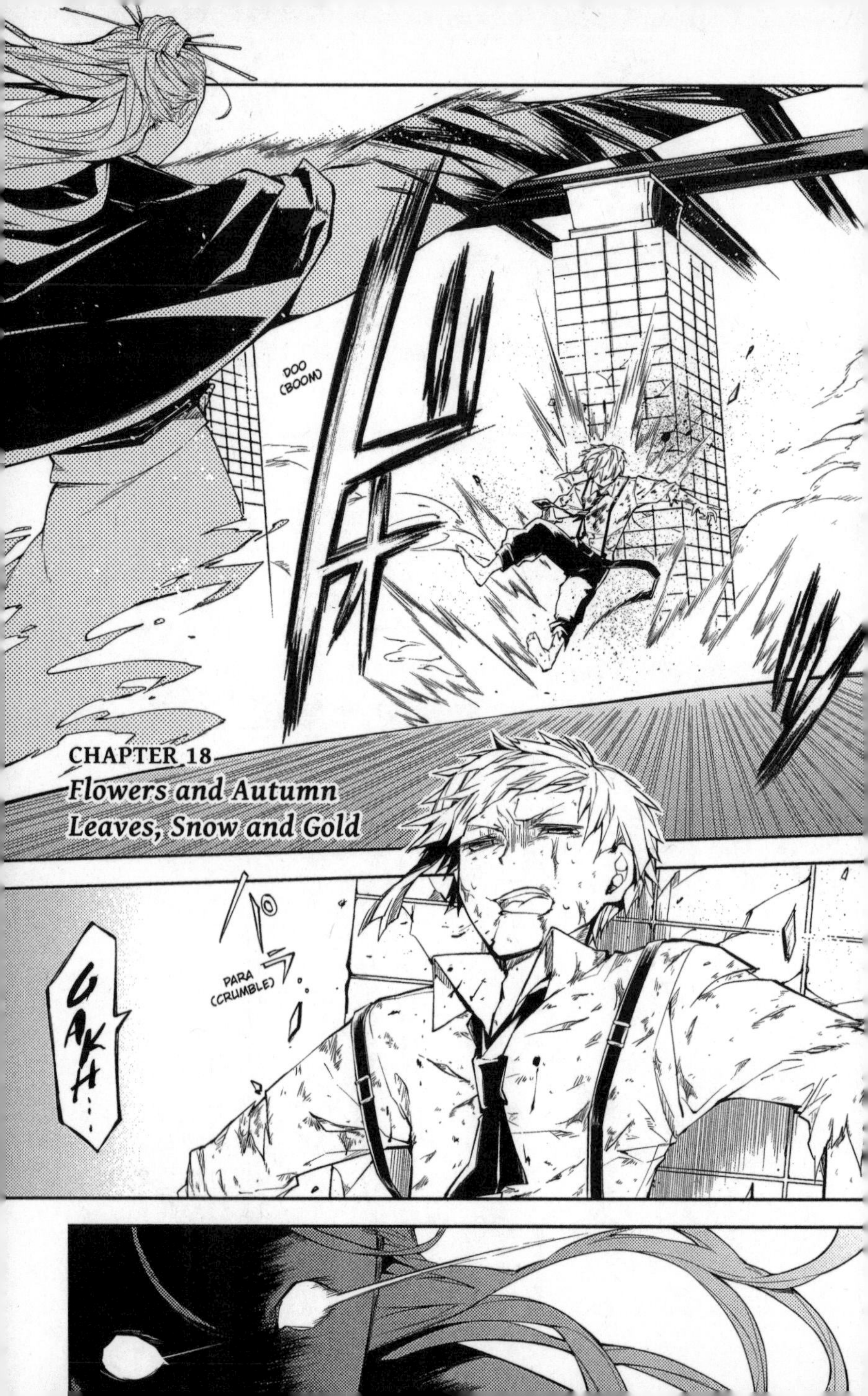
DOO (BOOM)
CHAPTER 18
Flowers and Autumn Leaves, Snow and Gold
PARA (CRUMBLE)
UAKH...

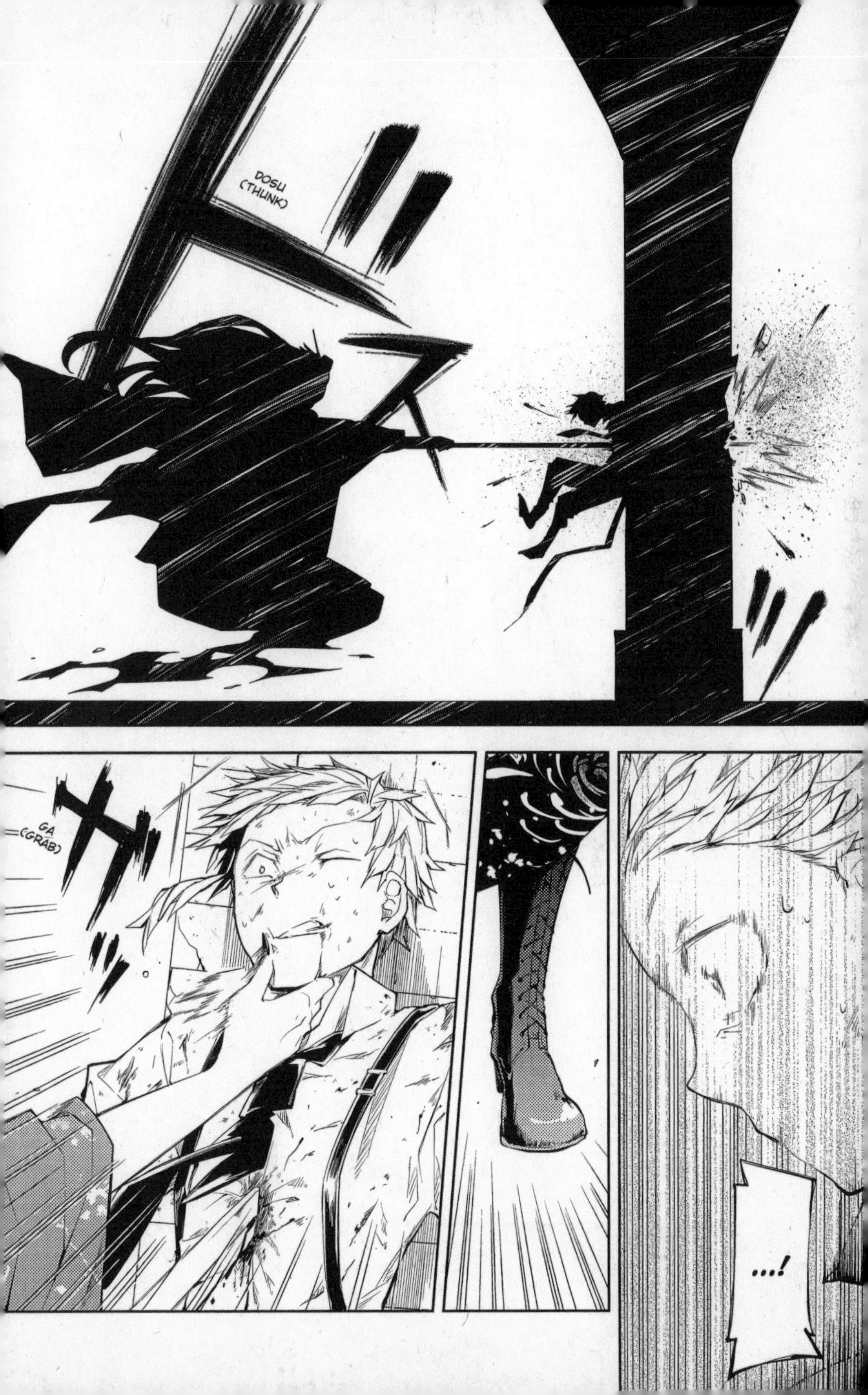
DOSU
(THUNK)
...!
GA
(GRAB)

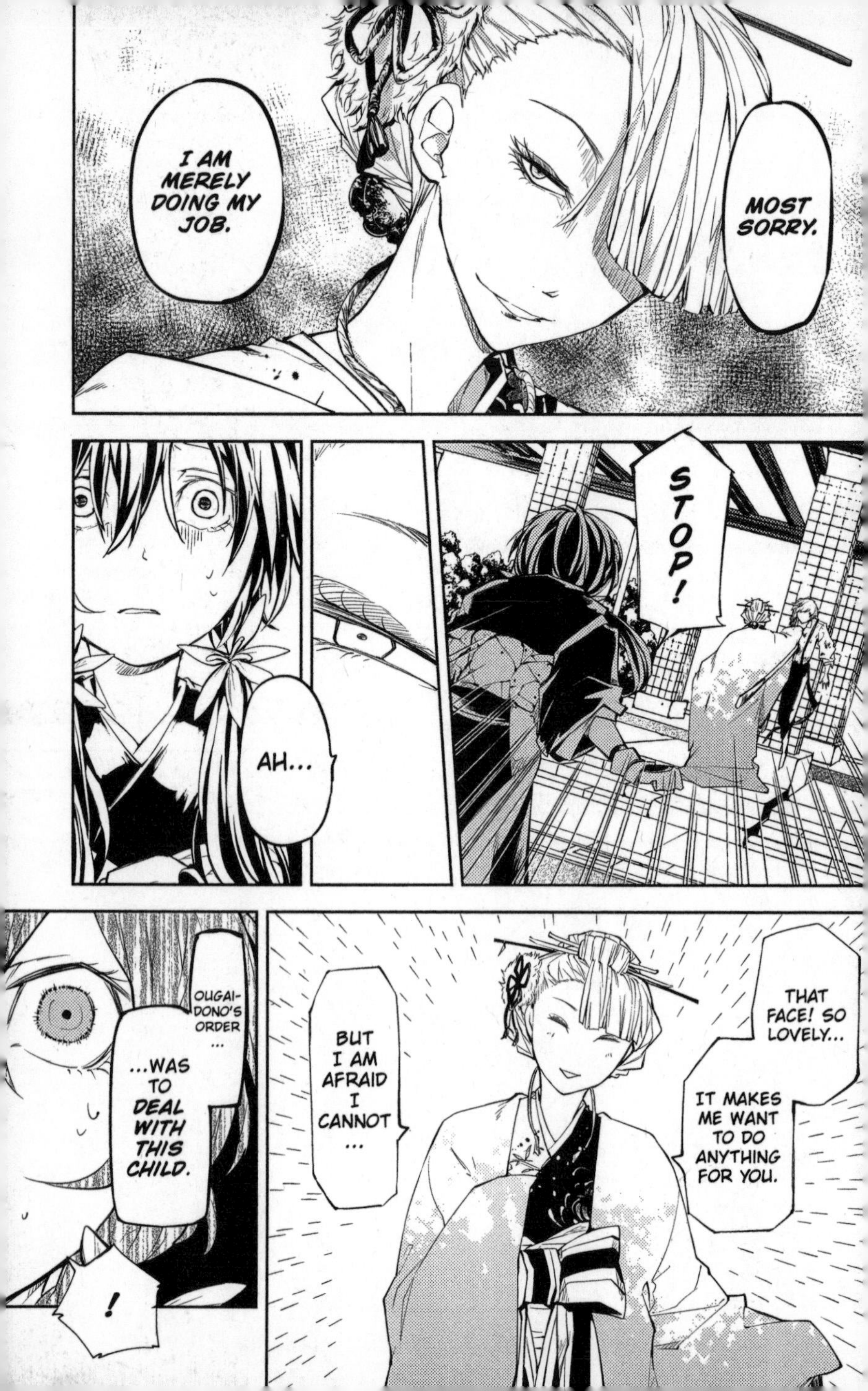
MOST SORRY.
I AM MERELY DOING MY JOB.
STOP!
AH...
THAT FACE! SO LOVELY...
IT MAKES ME WANT TO DO ANYTHING FOR YOU.
BUT I AM AFRAID I CANNOT...
OUGAI-DONO'S ORDER...
...WAS TO DEAL WITH THIS CHILD.
!

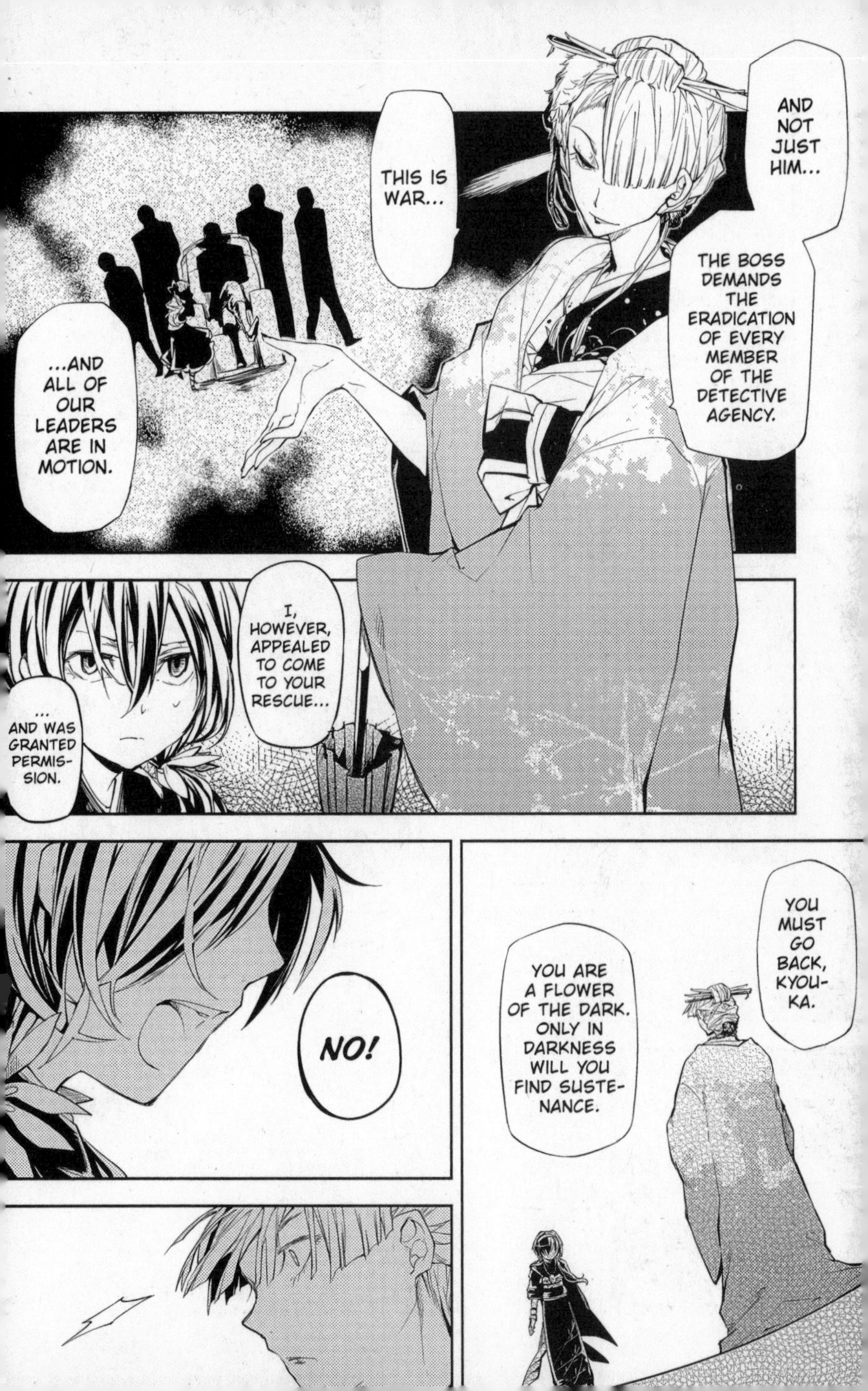
AND NOT JUST HIM...
THE BOSS DEMANDS THE ERADICATION OF EVERY MEMBER OF THE DETECTIVE AGENCY.
THIS IS WAR...
...AND ALL OF OUR LEADERS ARE IN MOTION.
I, HOWEVER, APPEALED TO COME TO YOUR RESCUE...
...AND WAS GRANTED PERMISSION.
YOU MUST GO BACK, KYOU-KA.
YOU ARE A FLOWER OF THE DARK. ONLY IN DARKNESS WILL YOU FIND SUSTE-NANCE.
NO!

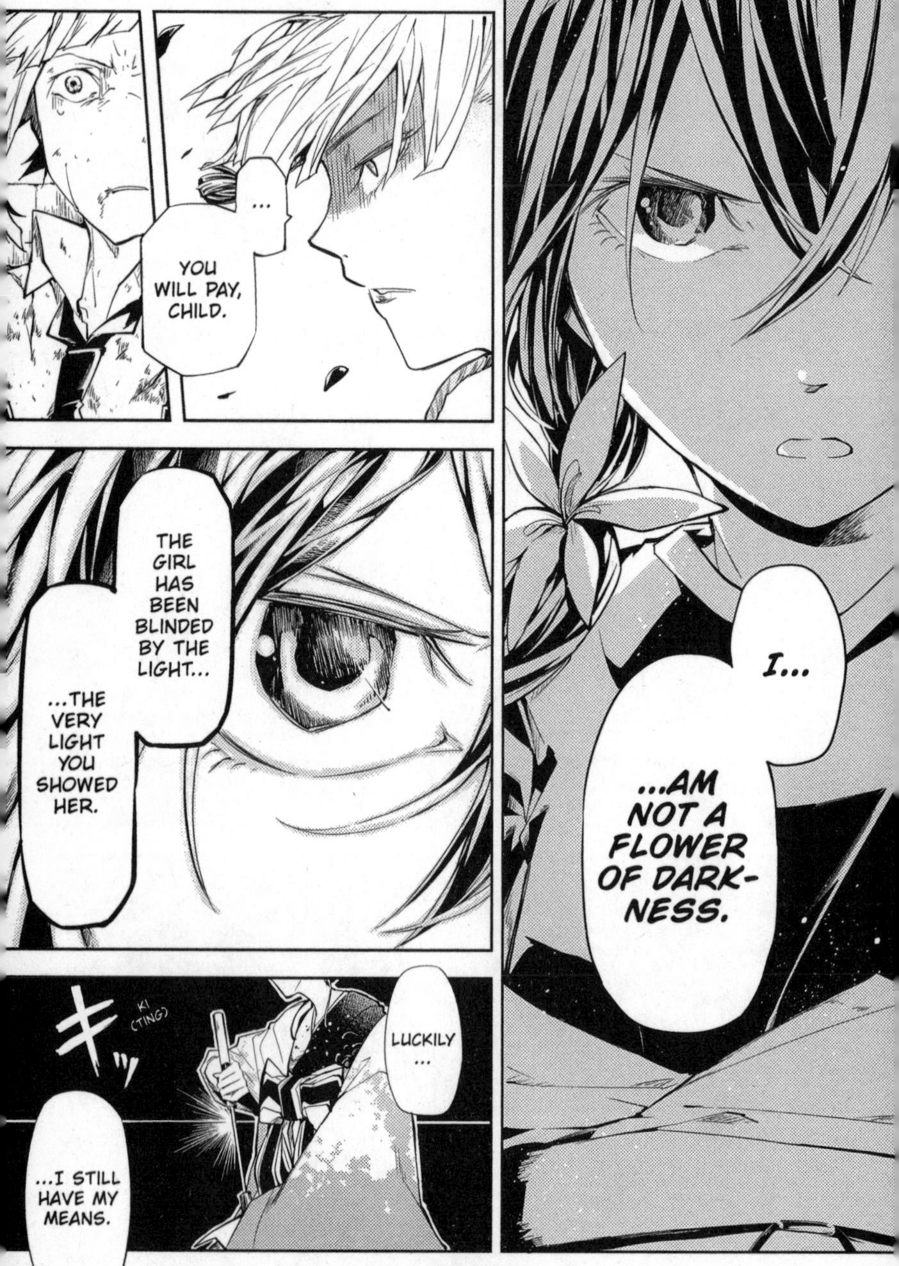
I...
...AM NOT A FLOWER OF DARKNESS.
...
YOU WILL PAY, CHILD.
THE GIRL HAS BEEN BLINDED BY THE LIGHT...
...THE VERY LIGHT YOU SHOWED HER.
LUCKILY...
キッ
KI (TING)
...I STILL HAVE MY MEANS.

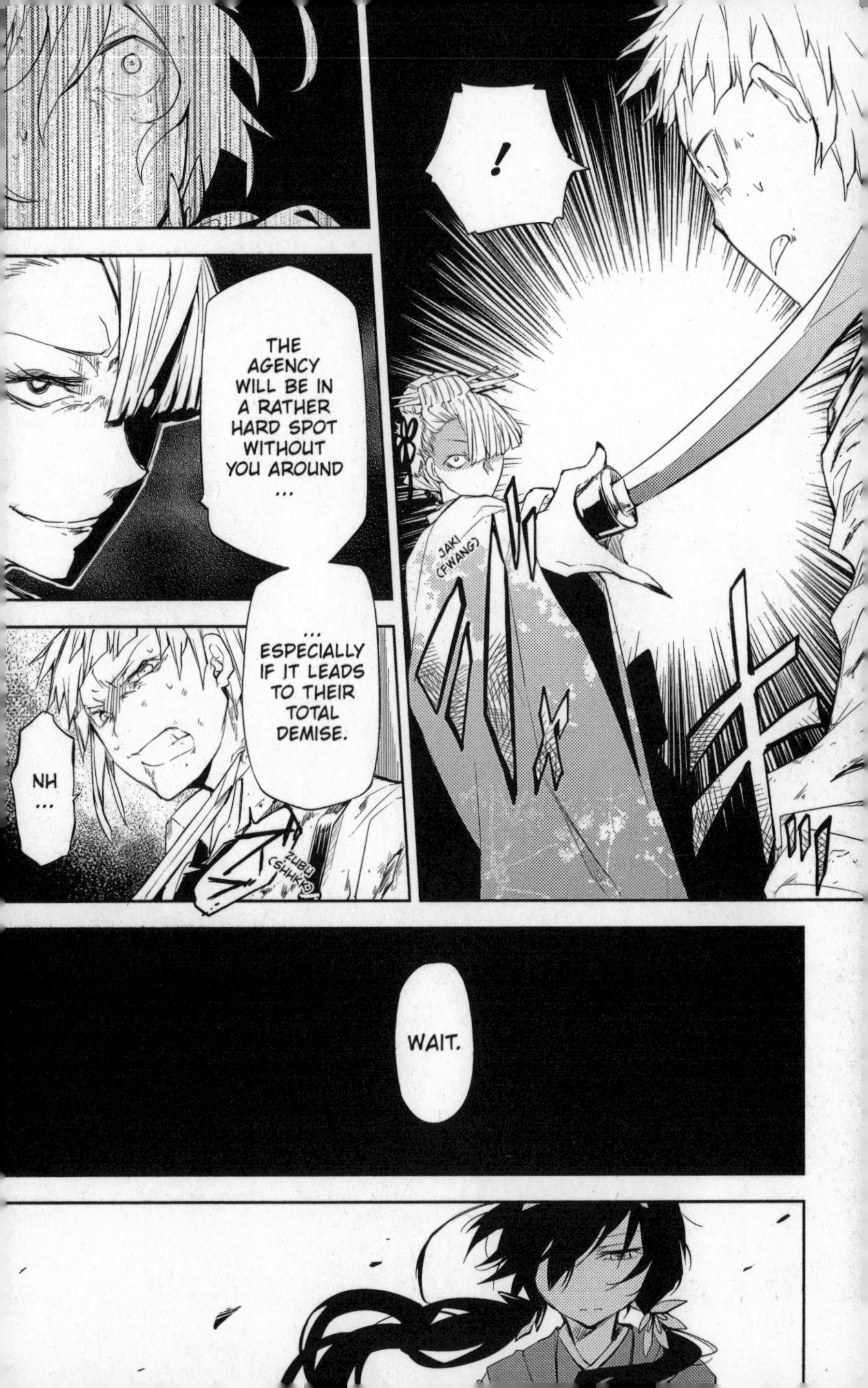
!
JAKI (FWANG)
THE AGENCY WILL BE IN A RATHER HARD SPOT WITHOUT YOU AROUND ...
... ESPECIALLY IF IT LEADS TO THEIR TOTAL DEMISE.
NH ...
ZUBU (SHHKK)
WAIT.

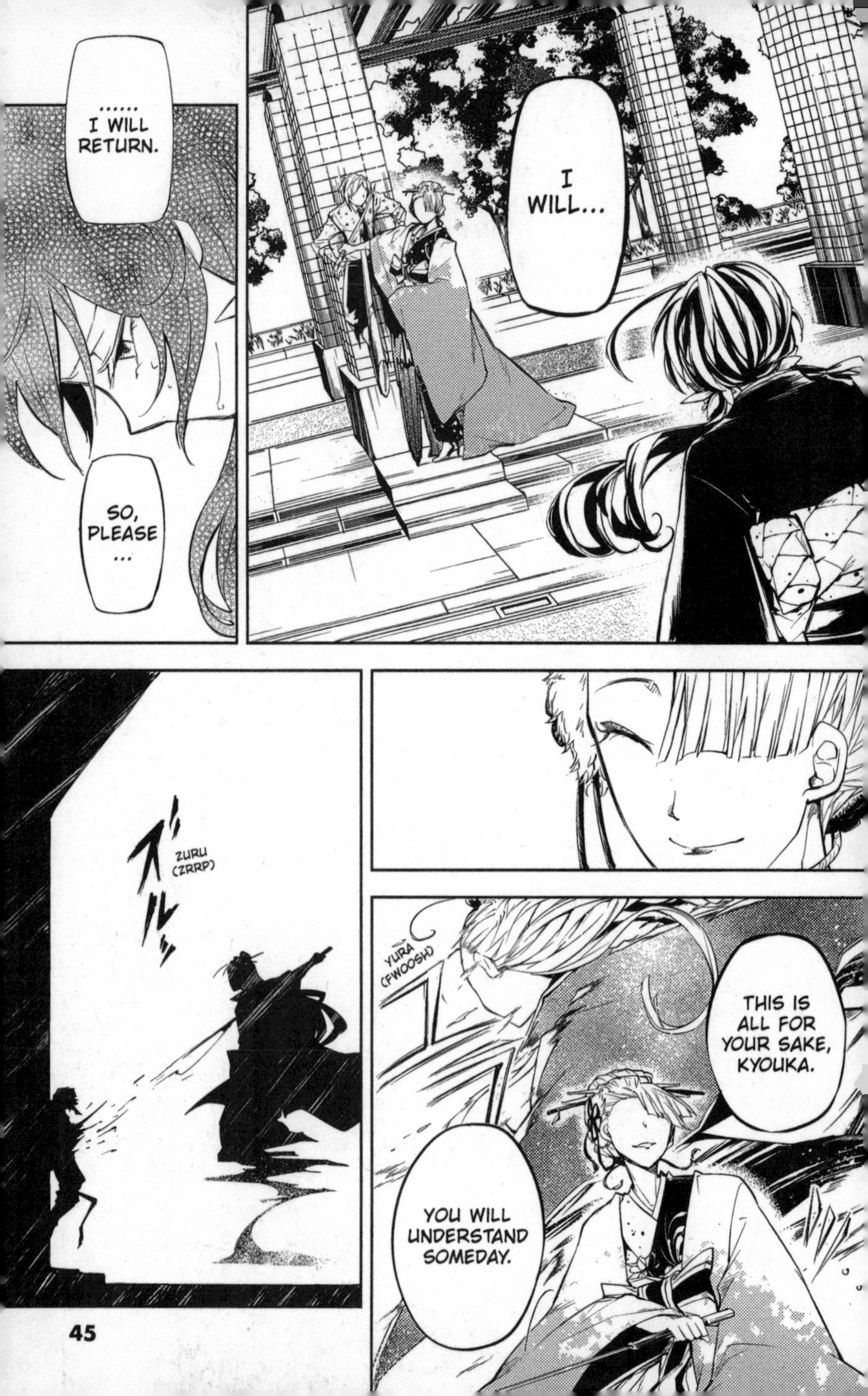
I WILL...
......
I WILL RETURN.
SO, PLEASE ...
YURA (FWOOSH)
THIS IS ALL FOR YOUR SAKE, KYOUKA.
YOU WILL UNDERSTAND SOMEDAY.
ZURU (ZRRP)

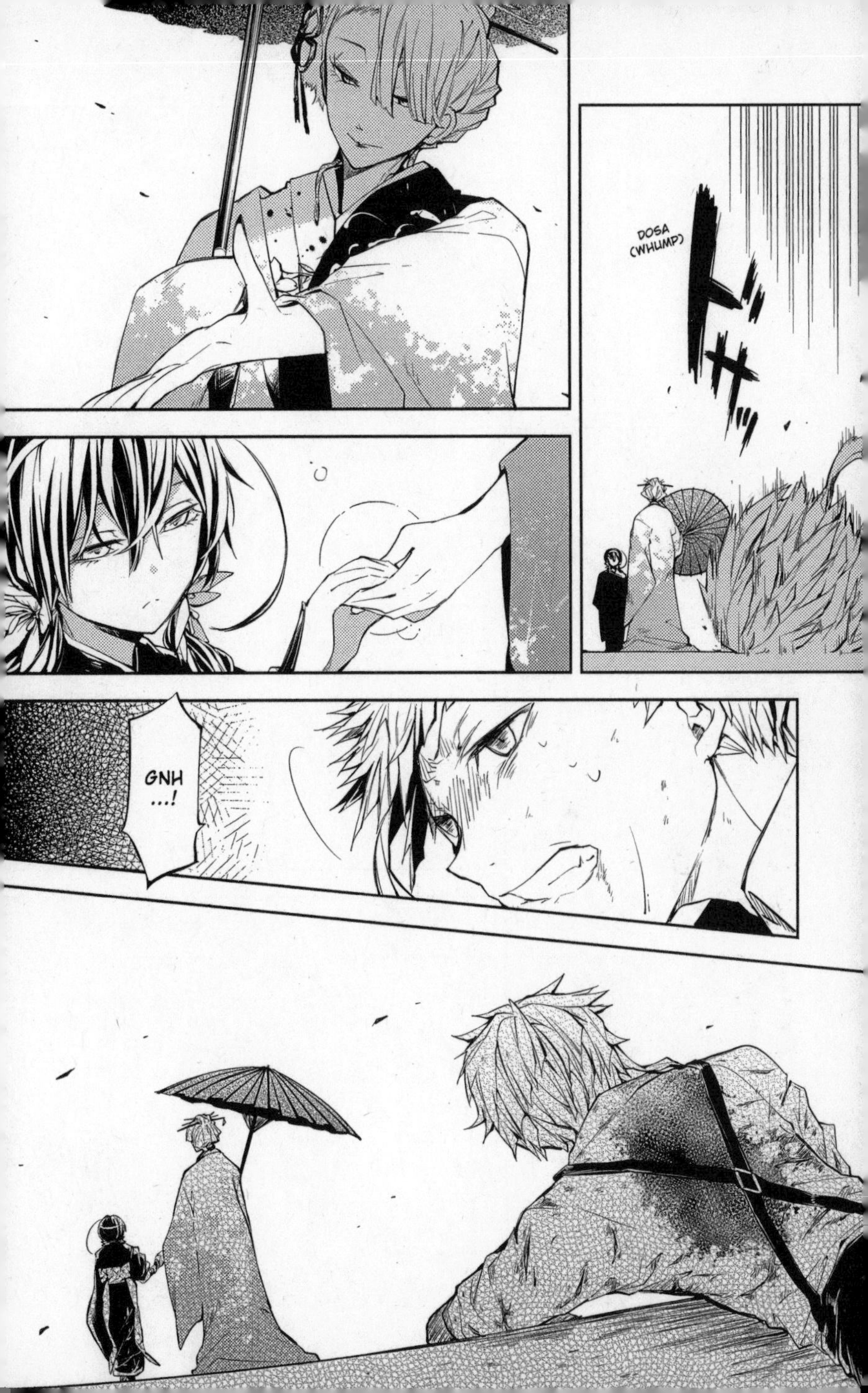
DOSA
(WHUMP)
GNH
...!

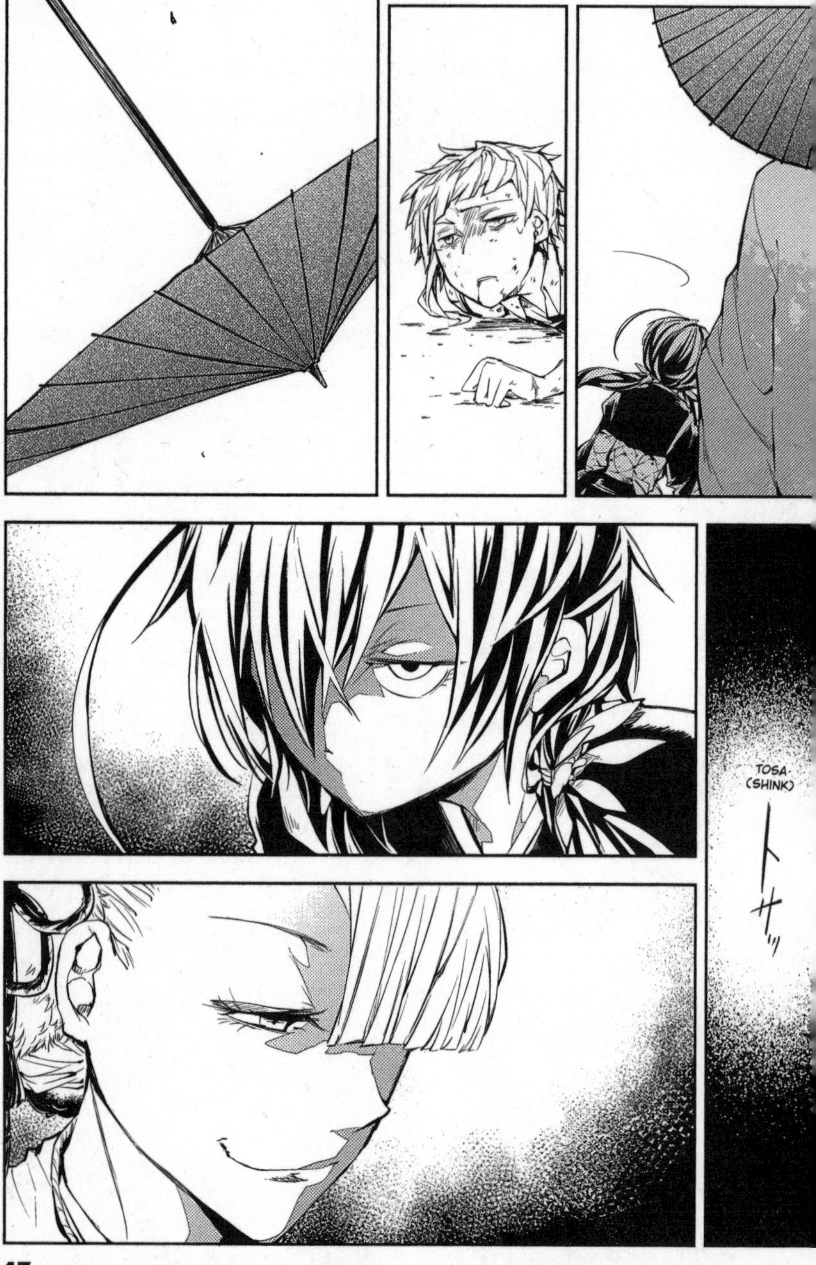
TOSA-
(SHINK)
トサッ

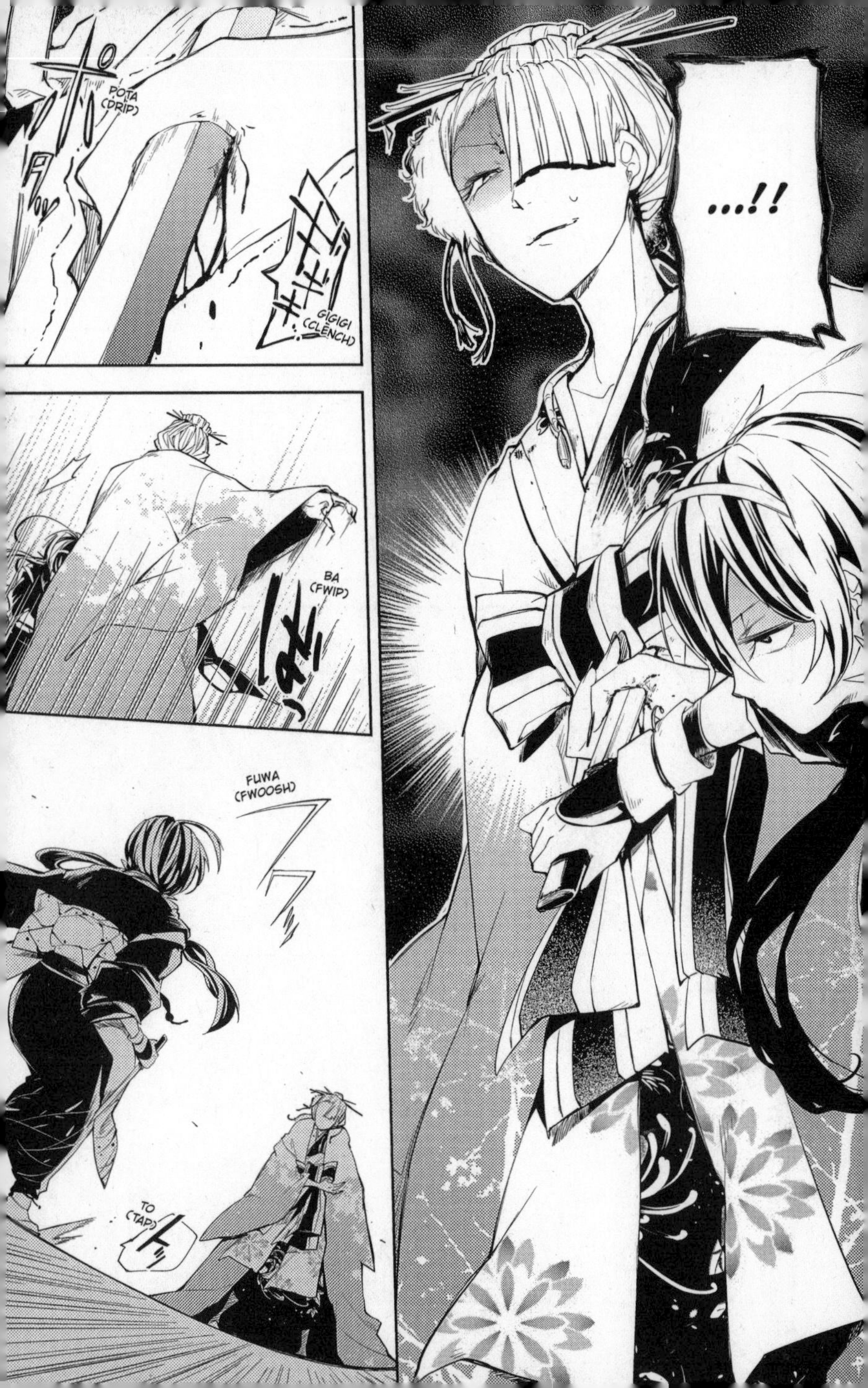
...!!
POTA (DRIP)
GIGIGI (CLENCH)
BA (FWIP)
FUWA (FWOOSH)
TO (TAP)

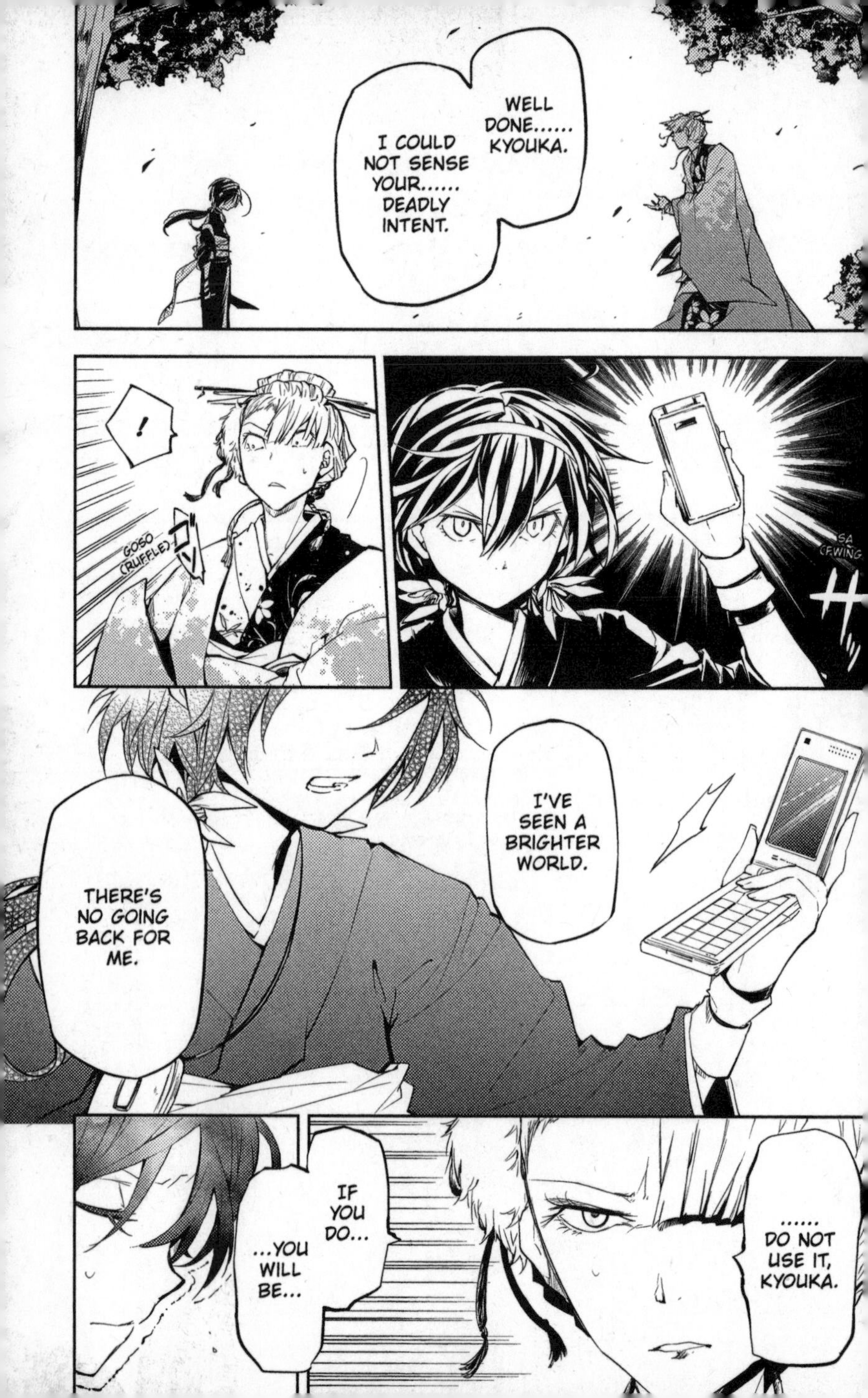
WELL DONE...... KYOUKA.
I COULD NOT SENSE YOUR...... DEADLY INTENT.
SA (FWING)
!
GOSO (RUFFLE)
I'VE SEEN A BRIGHTER WORLD.
THERE'S NO GOING BACK FOR ME.
...... DO NOT USE IT, KYOUKA.
IF YOU DO...
...YOU WILL BE...

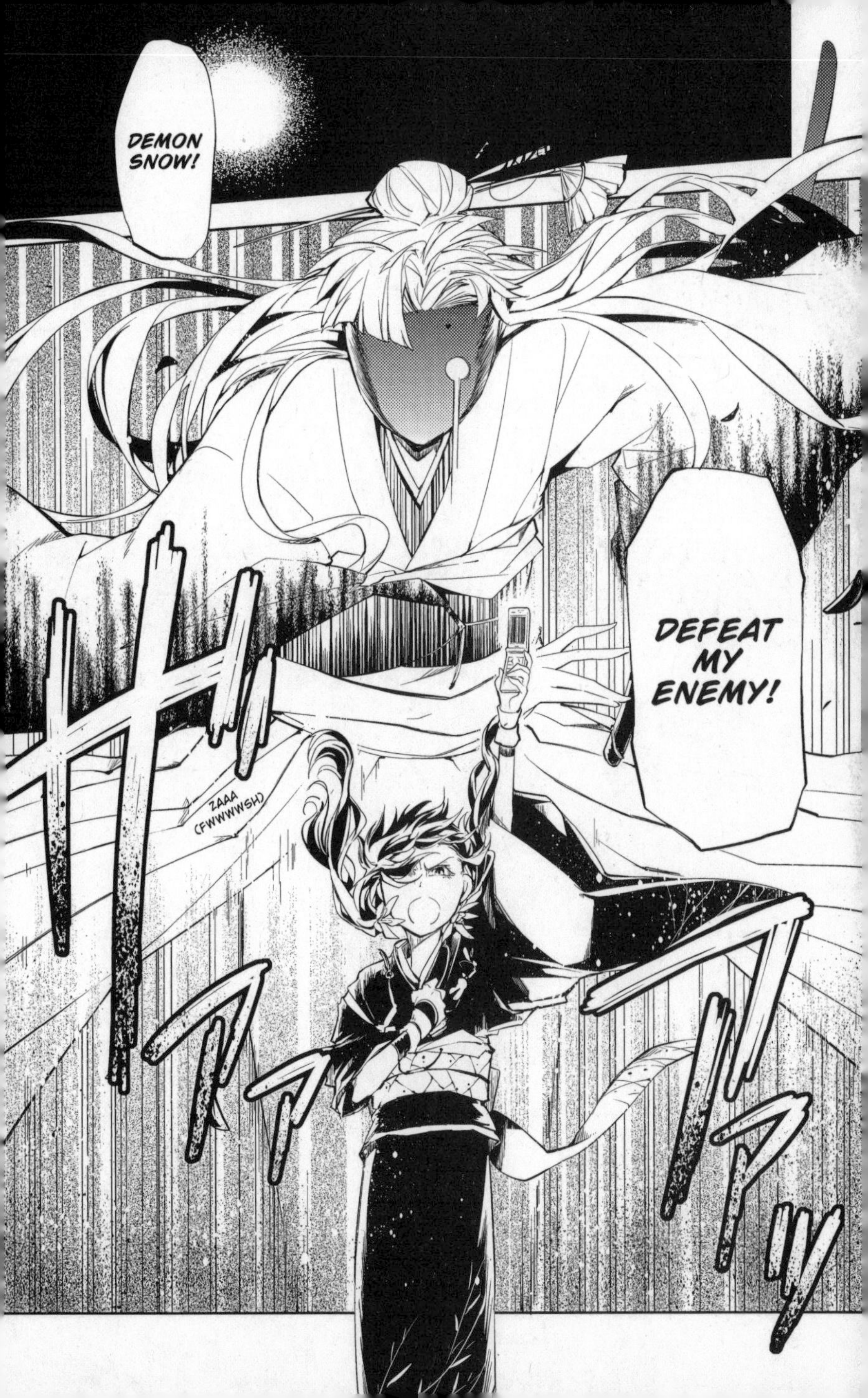
DEMON SNOW!
DEFEAT MY ENEMY!
ZAAA (FWWWSH)

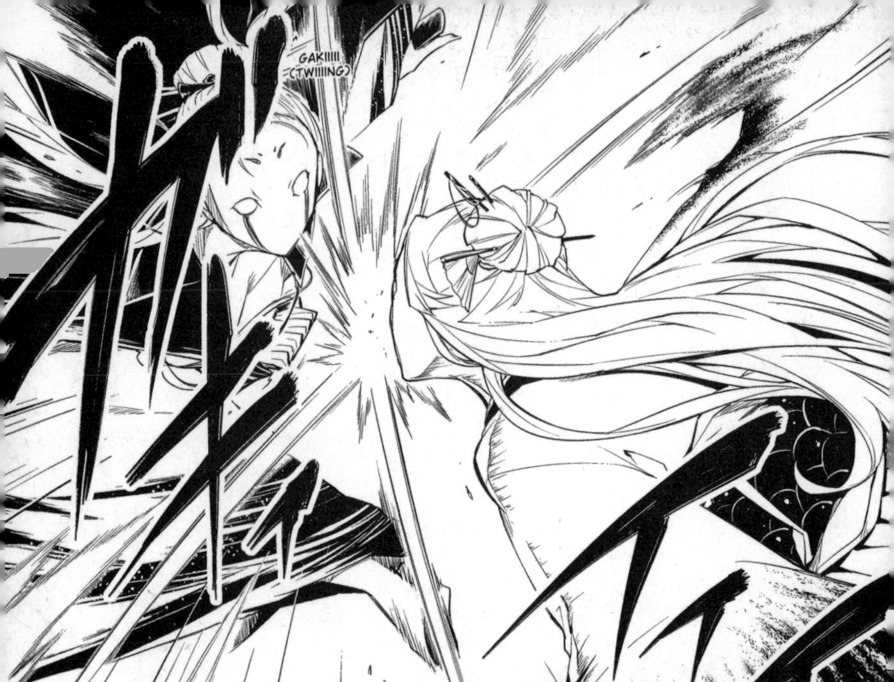
GAKIIIII
(TWIIIING)
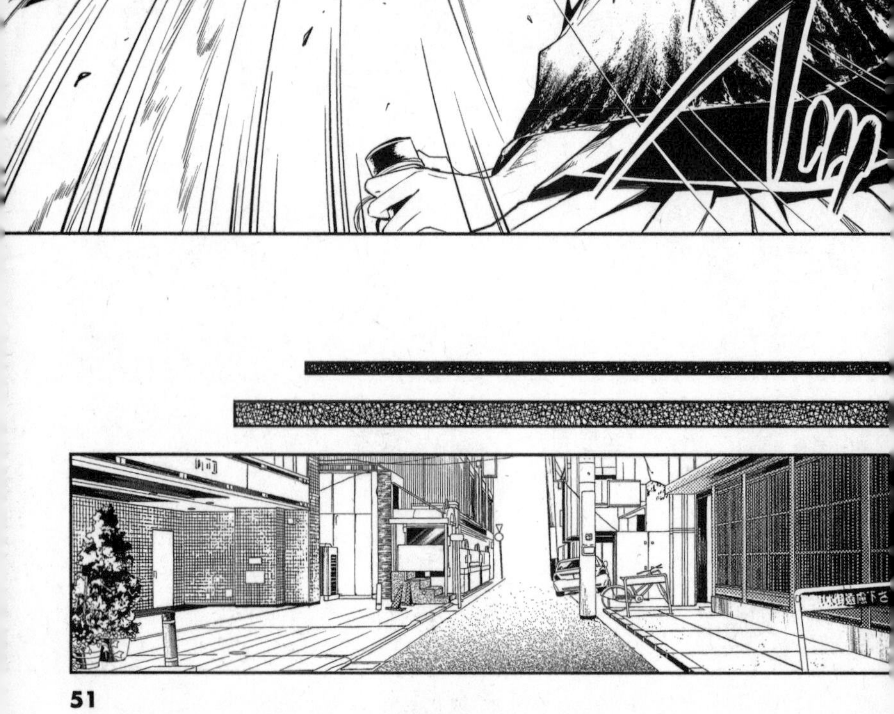

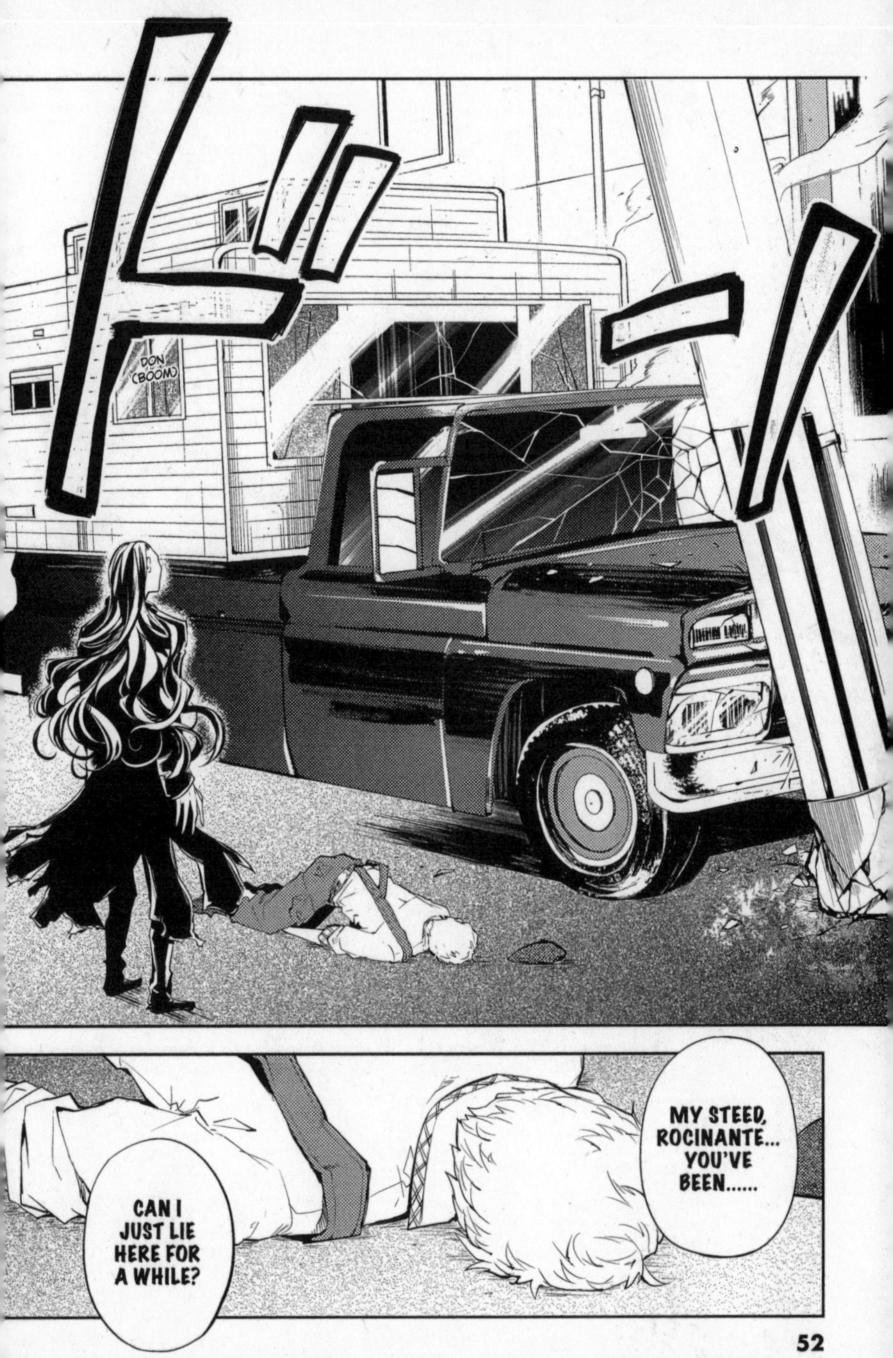
DON (BOOM)
MY STEED, ROCINANTE... YOU'VE BEEN......
CAN I JUST LIE HERE FOR A WHILE?

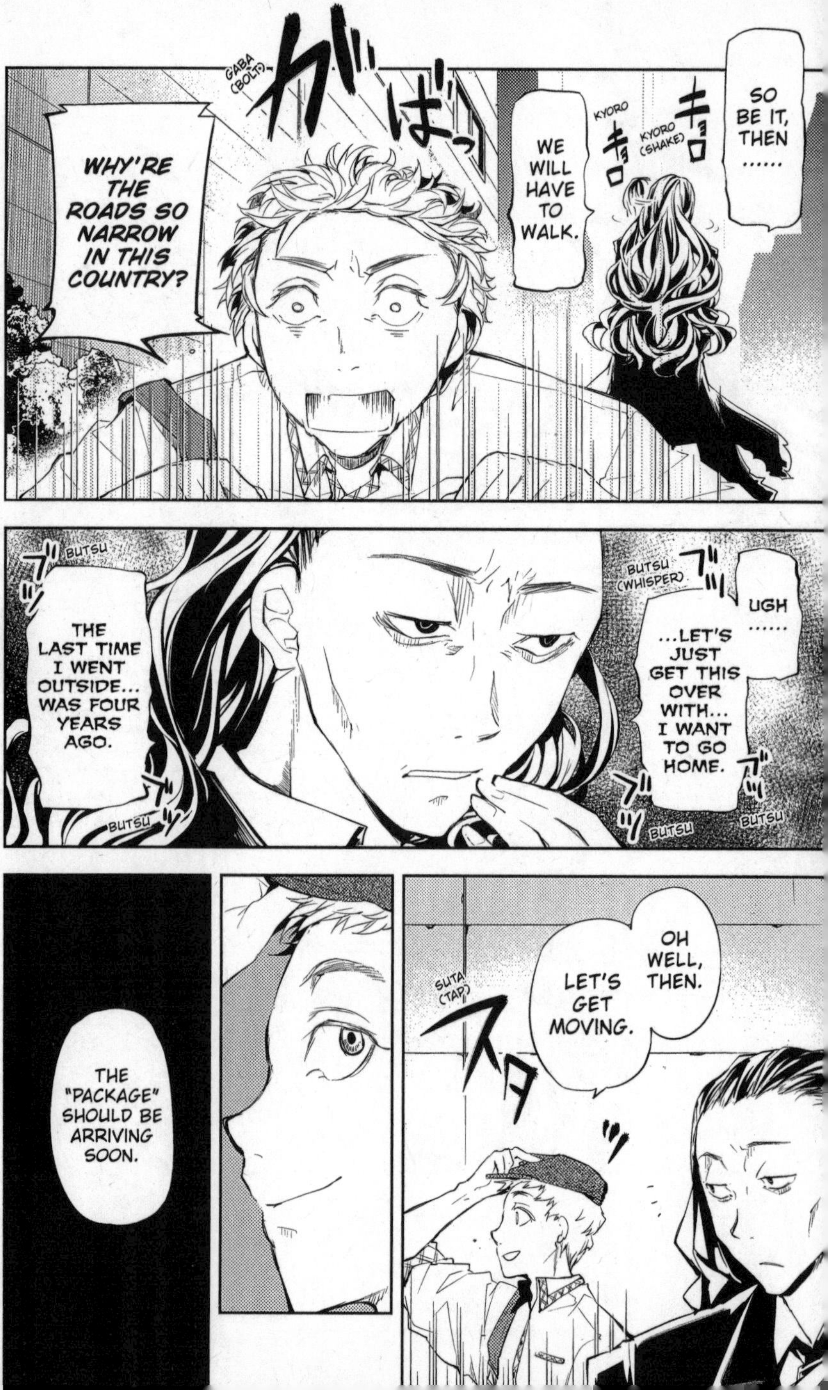
SO BE IT, THEN ......
KYORO KYORO (SHAKE)
WE WILL HAVE TO WALK.
GABA (BOLT)
WHY'RE THE ROADS SO NARROW IN THIS COUNTRY?
UGH ......
BUTSU (WHISPER)
...LET'S JUST GET THIS OVER WITH... I WANT TO GO HOME.
BUTSU
BUTSU
BUTSU
THE LAST TIME I WENT OUTSIDE... WAS FOUR YEARS AGO.
BUTSU
OH WELL, THEN.
LET'S GET MOVING.
SUTA (TAP)
THE "PACKAGE" SHOULD BE ARRIVING SOON.

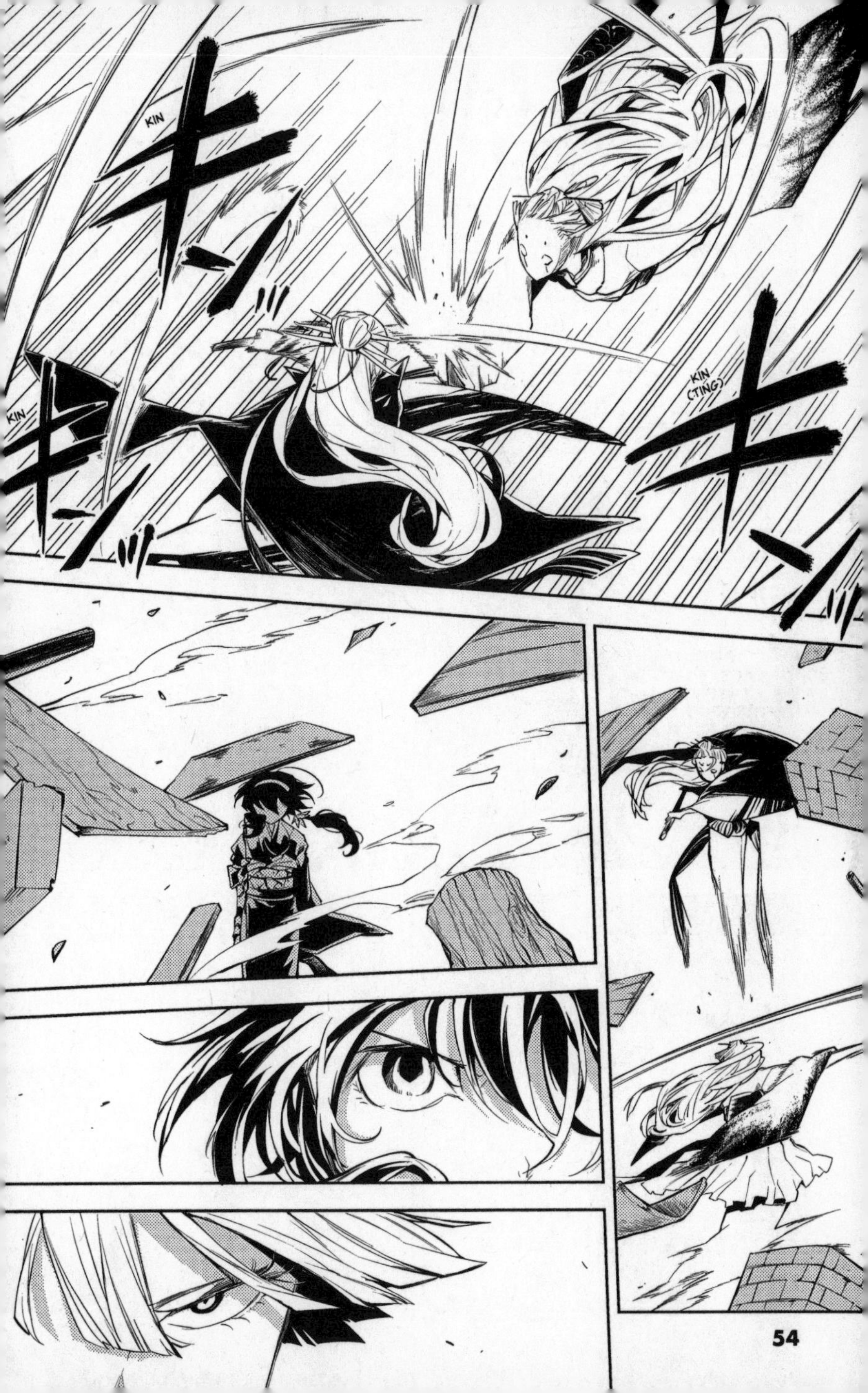
KIN
KIN (TING)
KIN

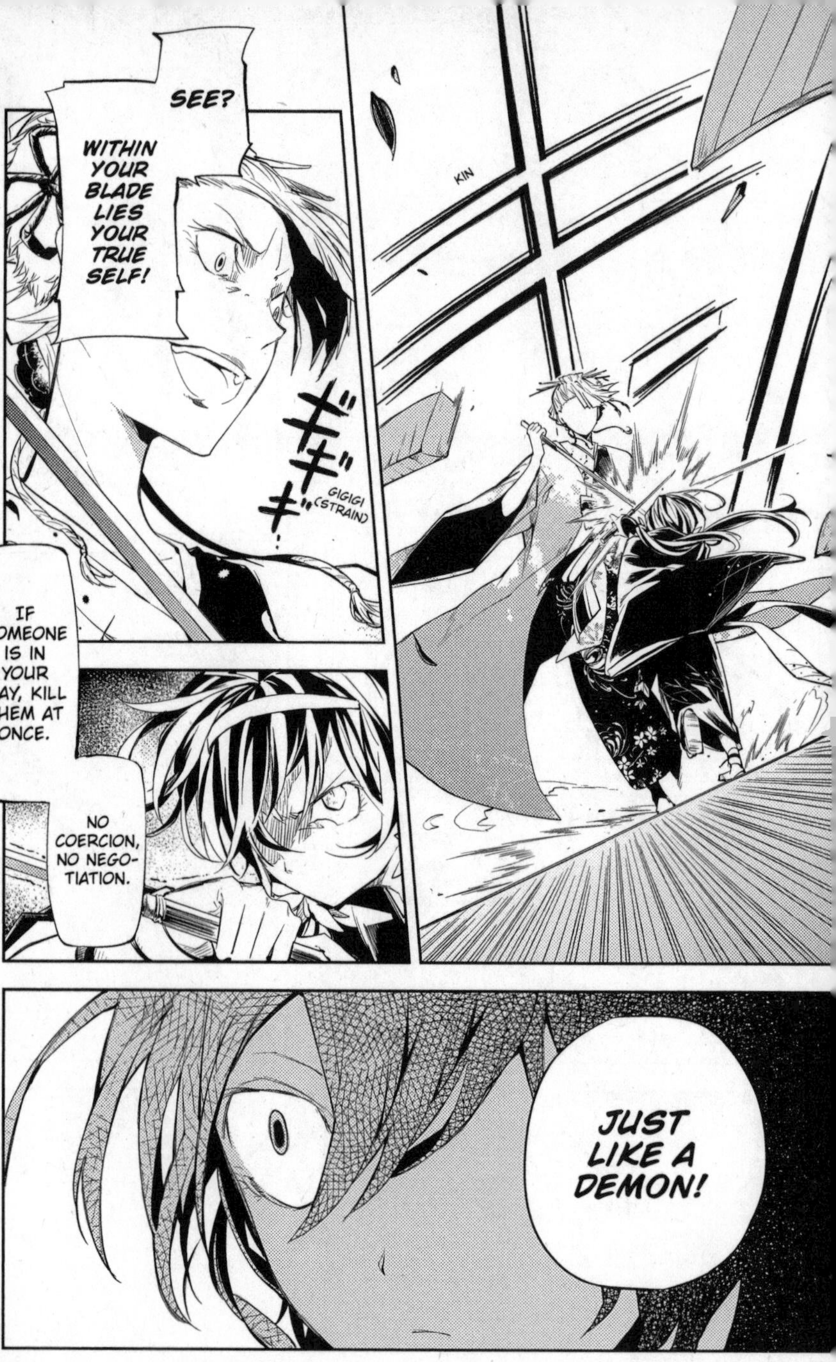
KIN
SEE?
WITHIN YOUR BLADE LIES YOUR TRUE SELF!
GIGIGI (STRAIN)
IF SOMEONE IS IN YOUR WAY, KILL THEM AT ONCE.
NO COERCION, NO NEGO-TIATION.
JUST LIKE A DEMON!

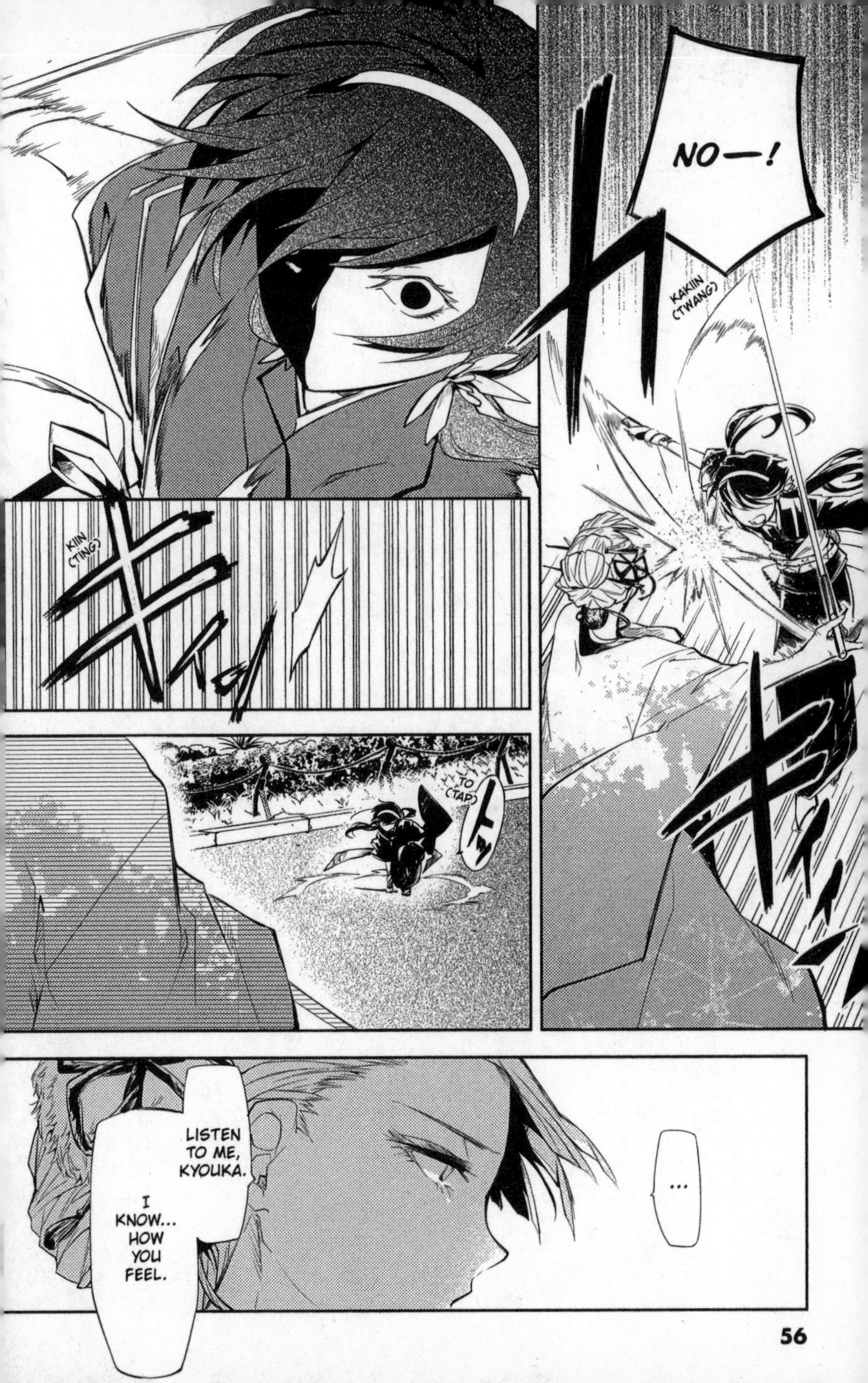
NO—!
KAKIIN (TWANG)
KIIN (TING)
TO (TAP)
...
LISTEN TO ME, KYOUKA.
I KNOW... HOW YOU FEEL.

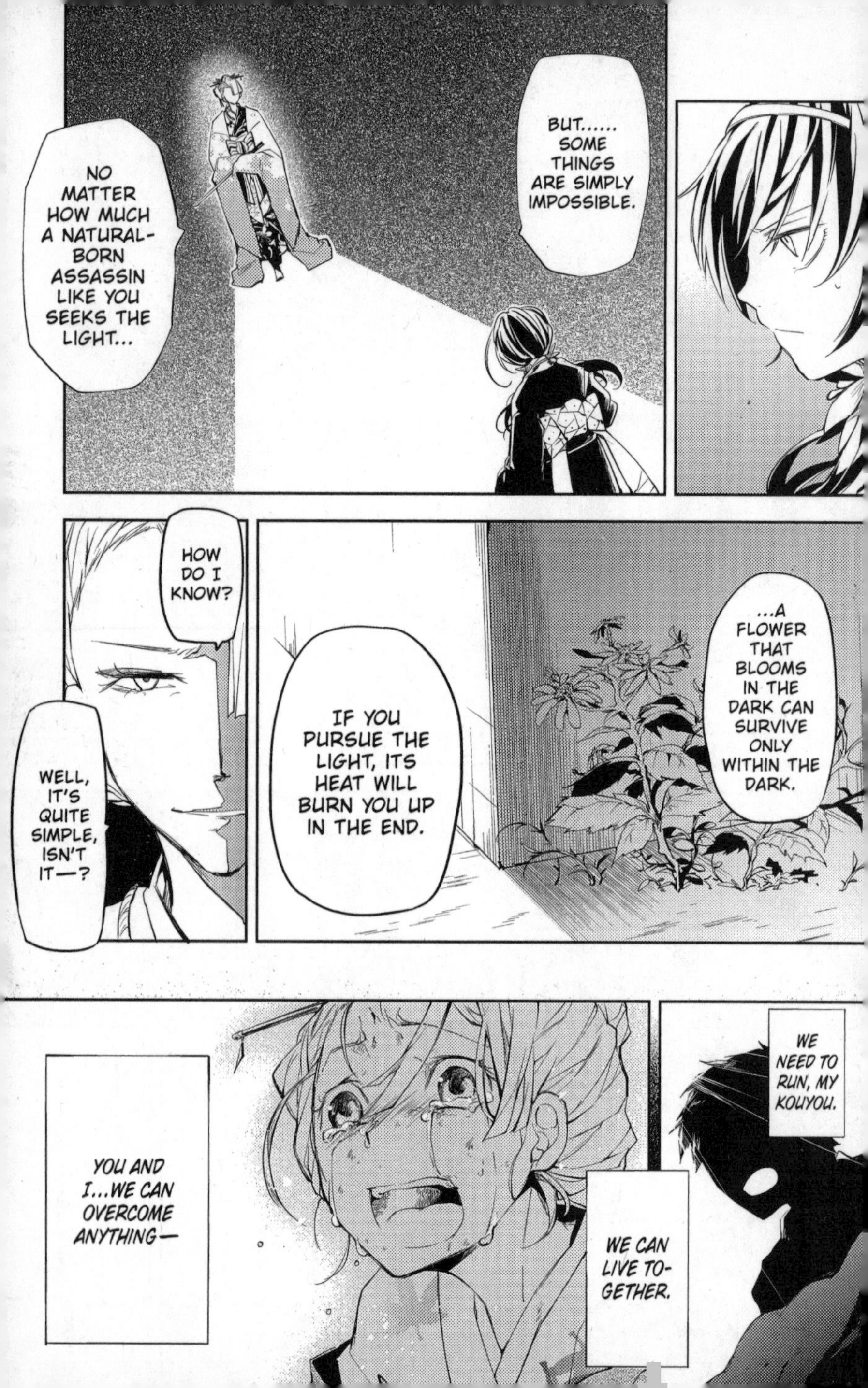
BUT...... SOME THINGS ARE SIMPLY IMPOSSIBLE.
NO MATTER HOW MUCH A NATURAL-BORN ASSASSIN LIKE YOU SEEKS THE LIGHT...
...A FLOWER THAT BLOOMS IN THE DARK CAN SURVIVE ONLY WITHIN THE DARK.
IF YOU PURSUE THE LIGHT, ITS HEAT WILL BURN YOU UP IN THE END.
HOW DO I KNOW?
WELL, IT'S QUITE SIMPLE, ISN'T IT—?
WE NEED TO RUN, MY KOUYOU.
WE CAN LIVE TO-GETHER.
YOU AND I...WE CAN OVERCOME ANYTHING—

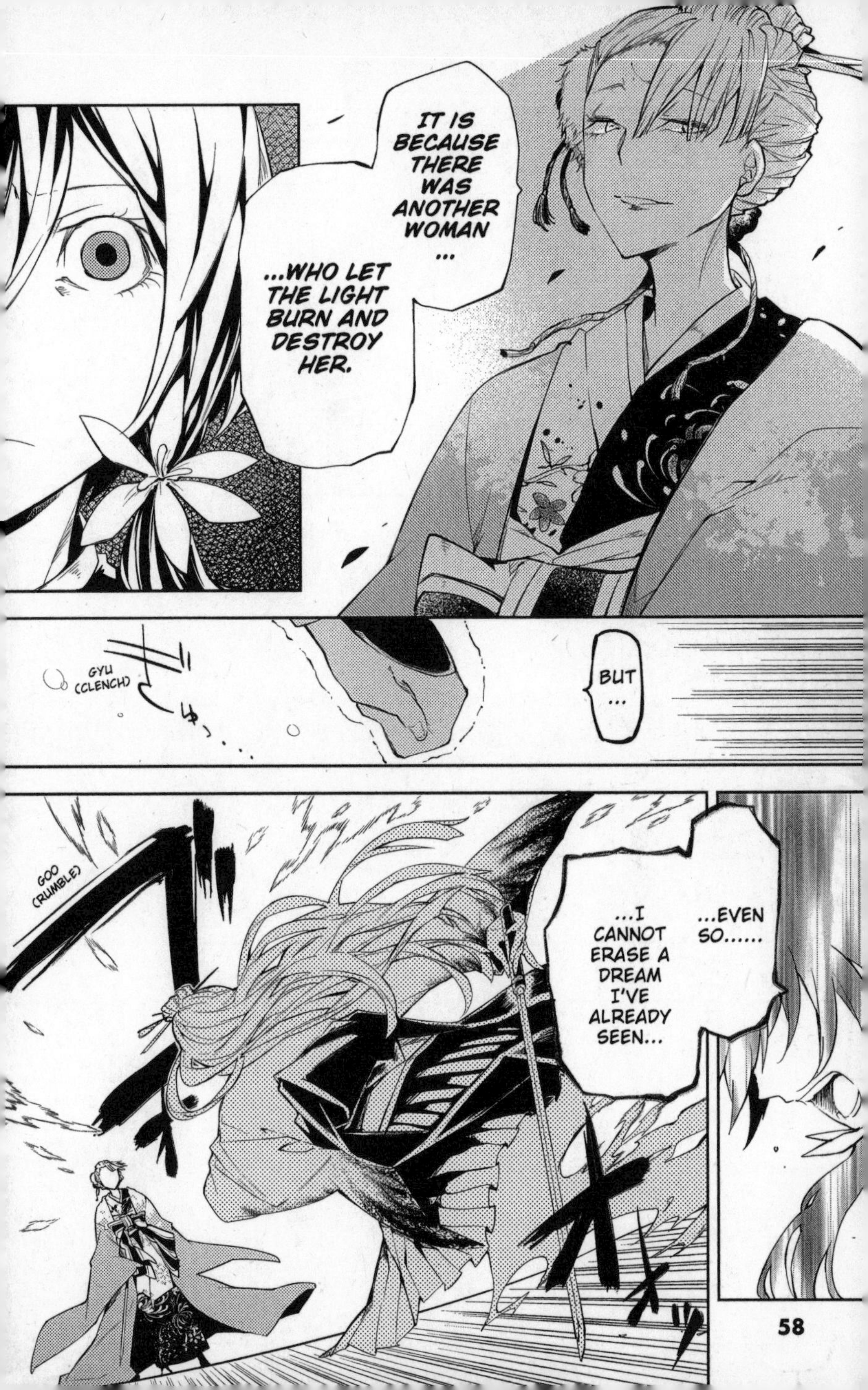
IT IS BECAUSE THERE WAS ANOTHER WOMAN...
...WHO LET THE LIGHT BURN AND DESTROY HER.
BUT...
GYU (CLENCH)
...EVEN SO......
...I CANNOT ERASE A DREAM I'VE ALREADY SEEN...
GOO (RUMBLE)

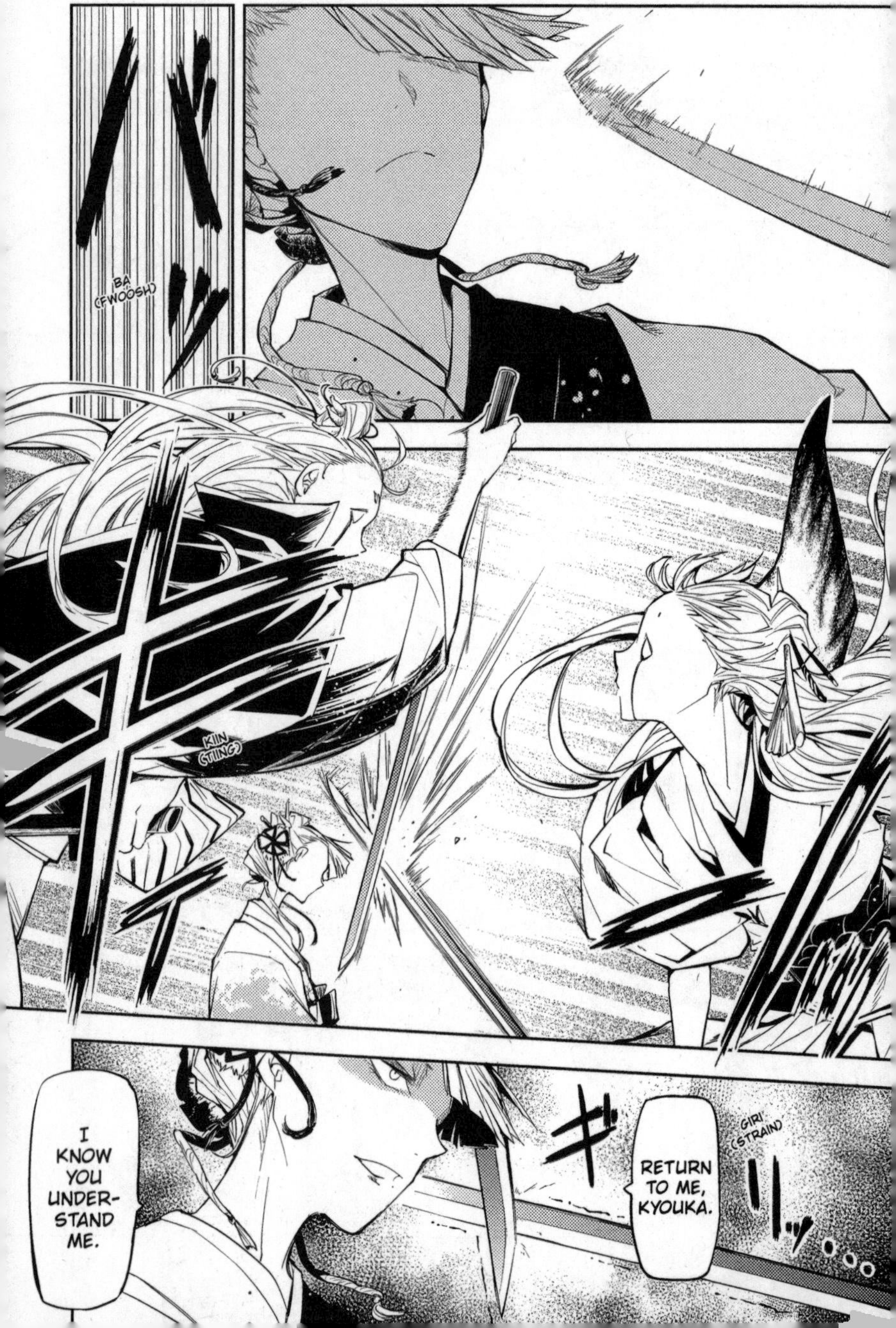
BA (FWOOSH)
KIIN (STIING)
GIRI (STRAIN)
RETURN TO ME, KYOUKA.
I KNOW YOU UNDER-STAND ME.

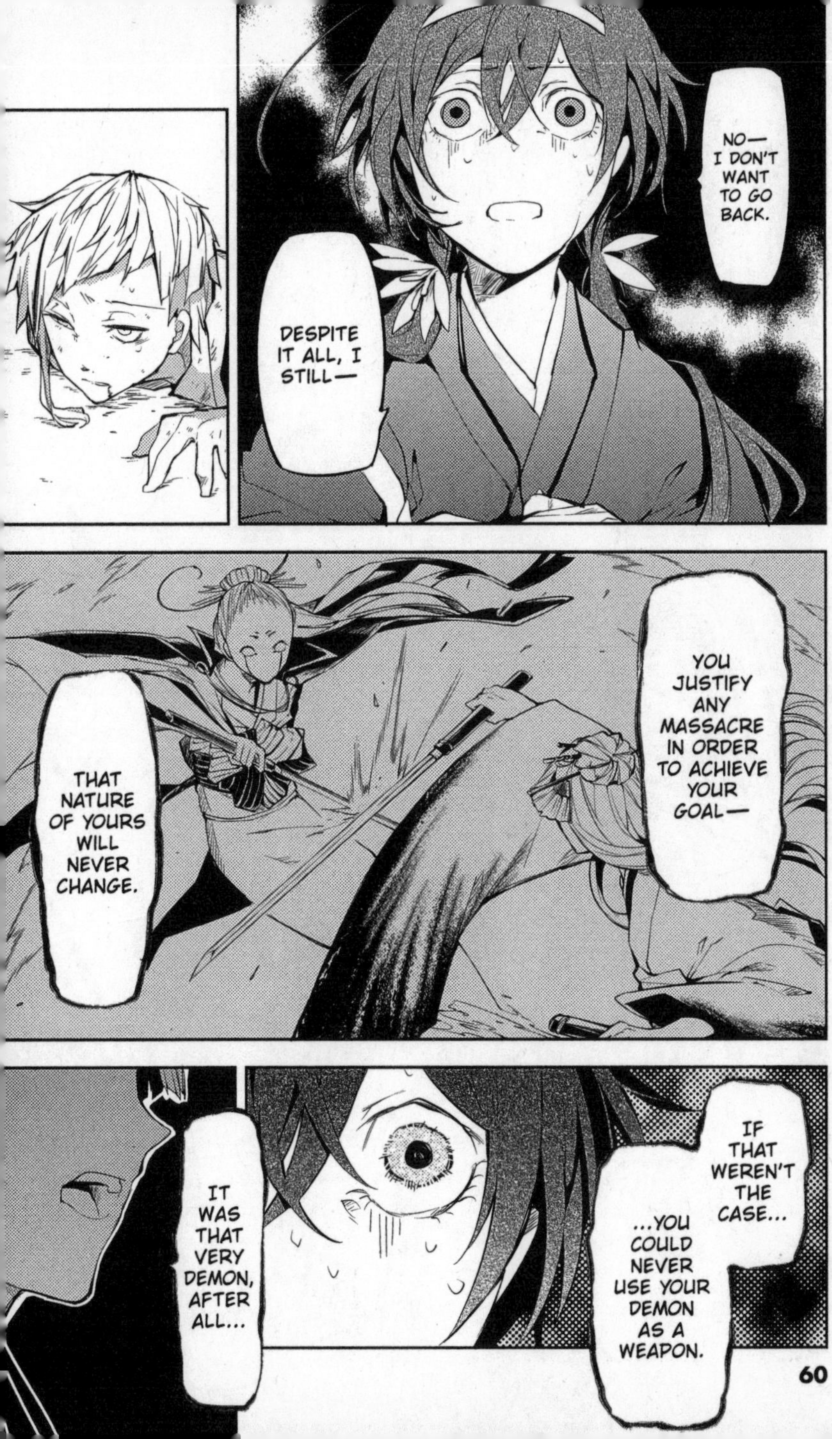
NO— I DON'T WANT TO GO BACK.
DESPITE IT ALL, I STILL—
YOU JUSTIFY ANY MASSACRE IN ORDER TO ACHIEVE YOUR GOAL—
THAT NATURE OF YOURS WILL NEVER CHANGE.
IF THAT WEREN'T THE CASE...
...YOU COULD NEVER USE YOUR DEMON AS A WEAPON.
IT WAS THAT VERY DEMON, AFTER ALL...

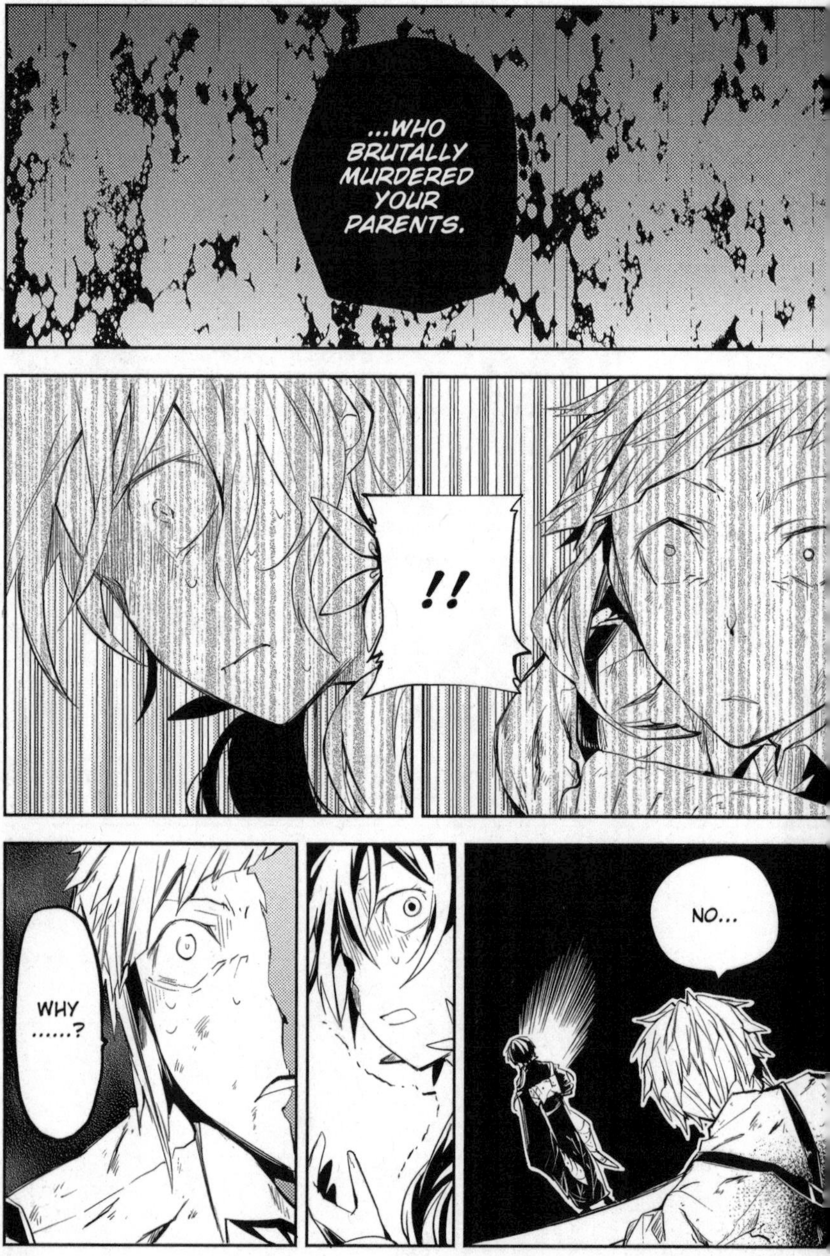
...WHO BRUTALLY MURDERED YOUR PARENTS.
!!
NO...
WHY ......?

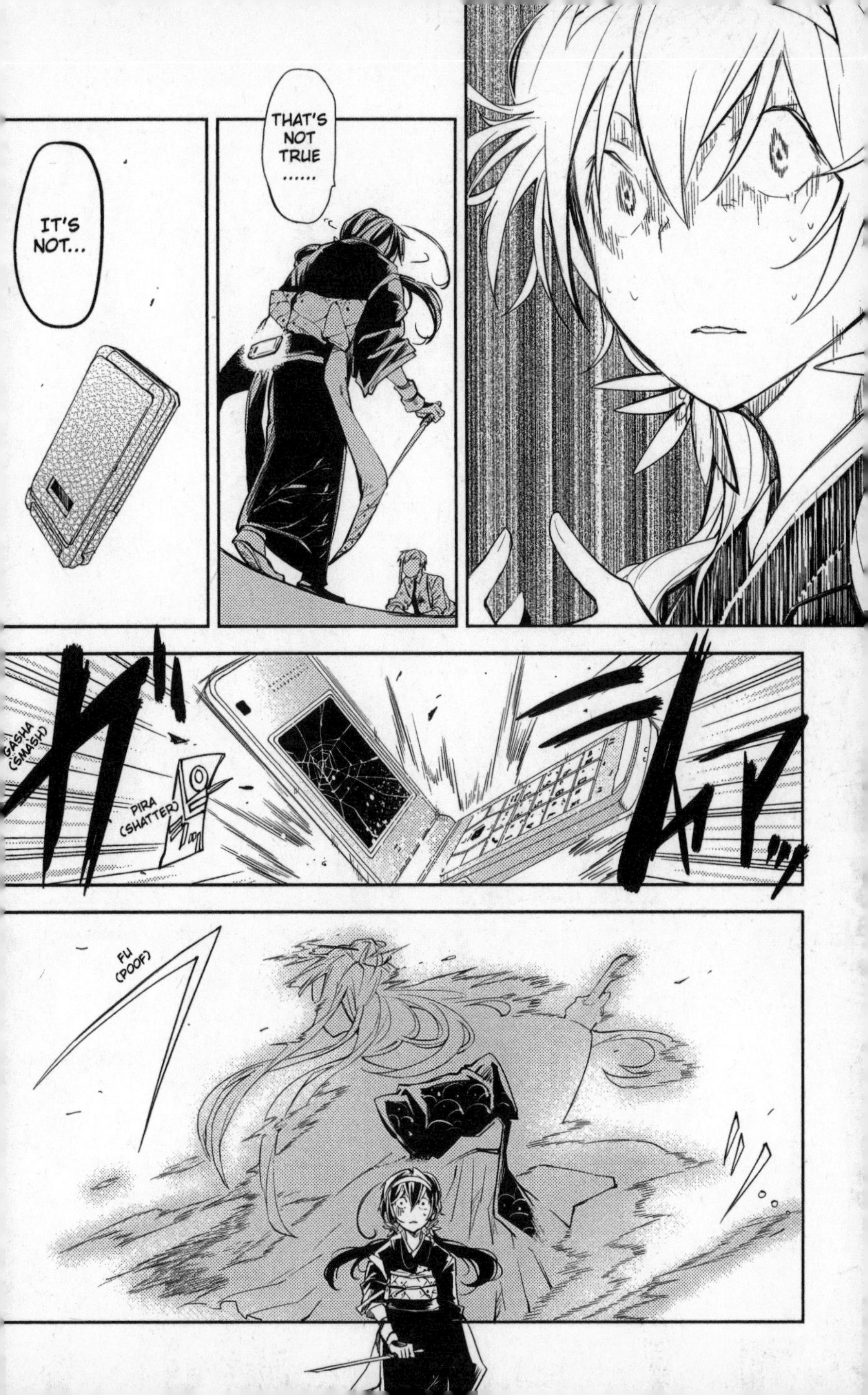
THAT'S NOT TRUE ......
IT'S NOT...
GASHA (SMASH)
PIRA (SHATTER)
FU (POOF)

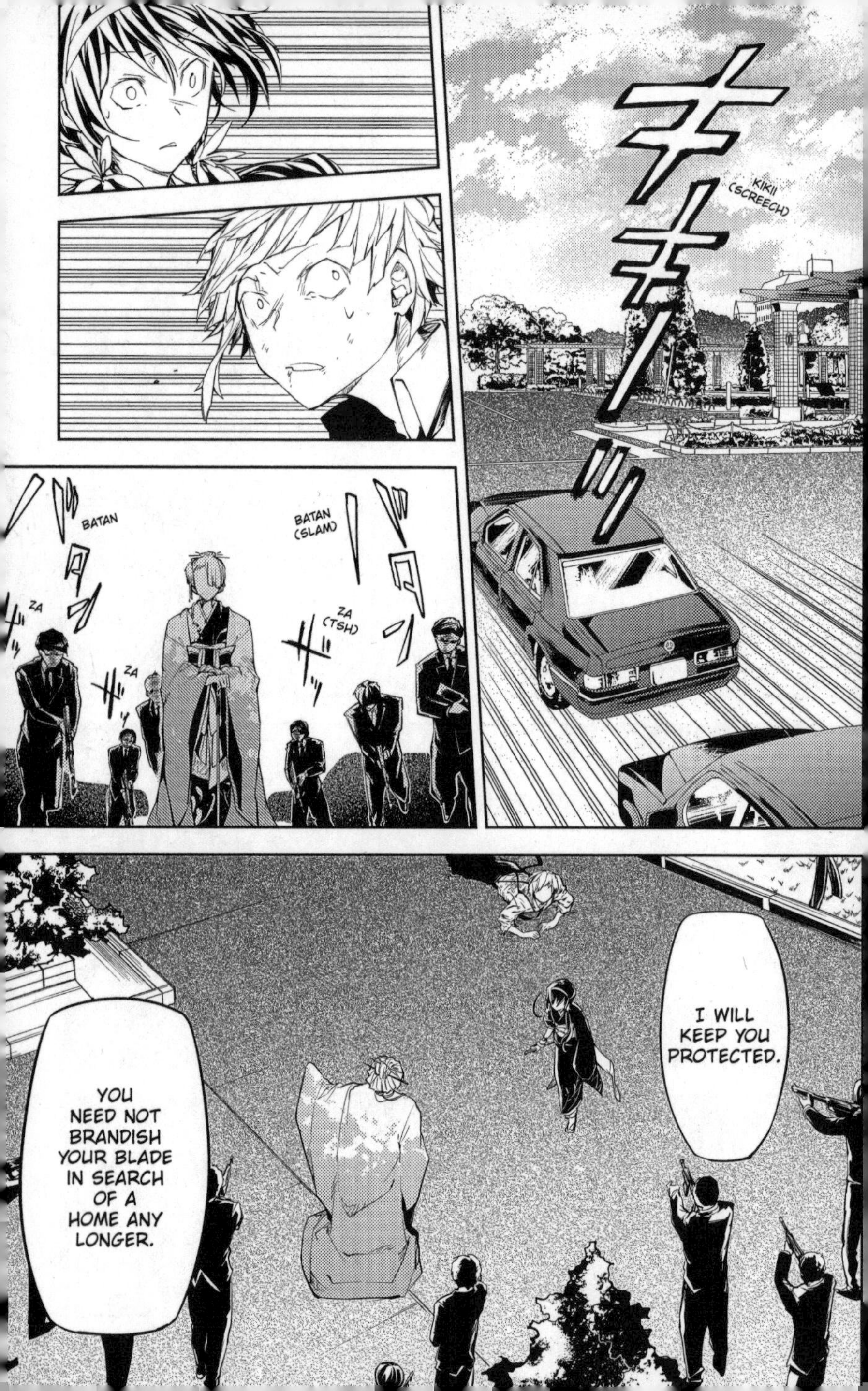
KIKII (SCREECH)
BATAN (SLAM)
ZA (TSH)
BATAN
ZA
ZA
I WILL KEEP YOU PROTECTED.
YOU NEED NOT BRANDISH YOUR BLADE IN SEARCH OF A HOME ANY LONGER.

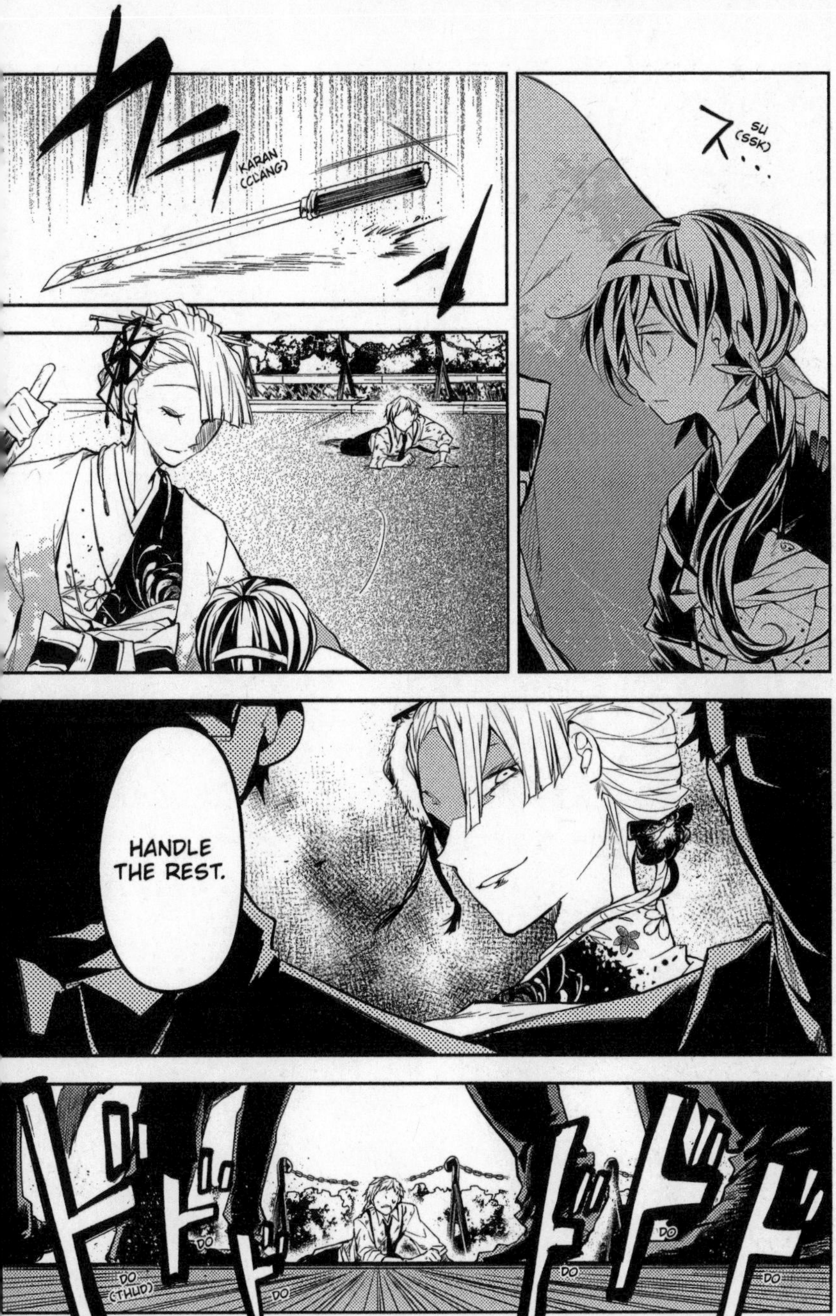
SU (SSK)
KARAN (CLANG)
HANDLE THE REST.
DO DO DO
DO DO DO (THUD)

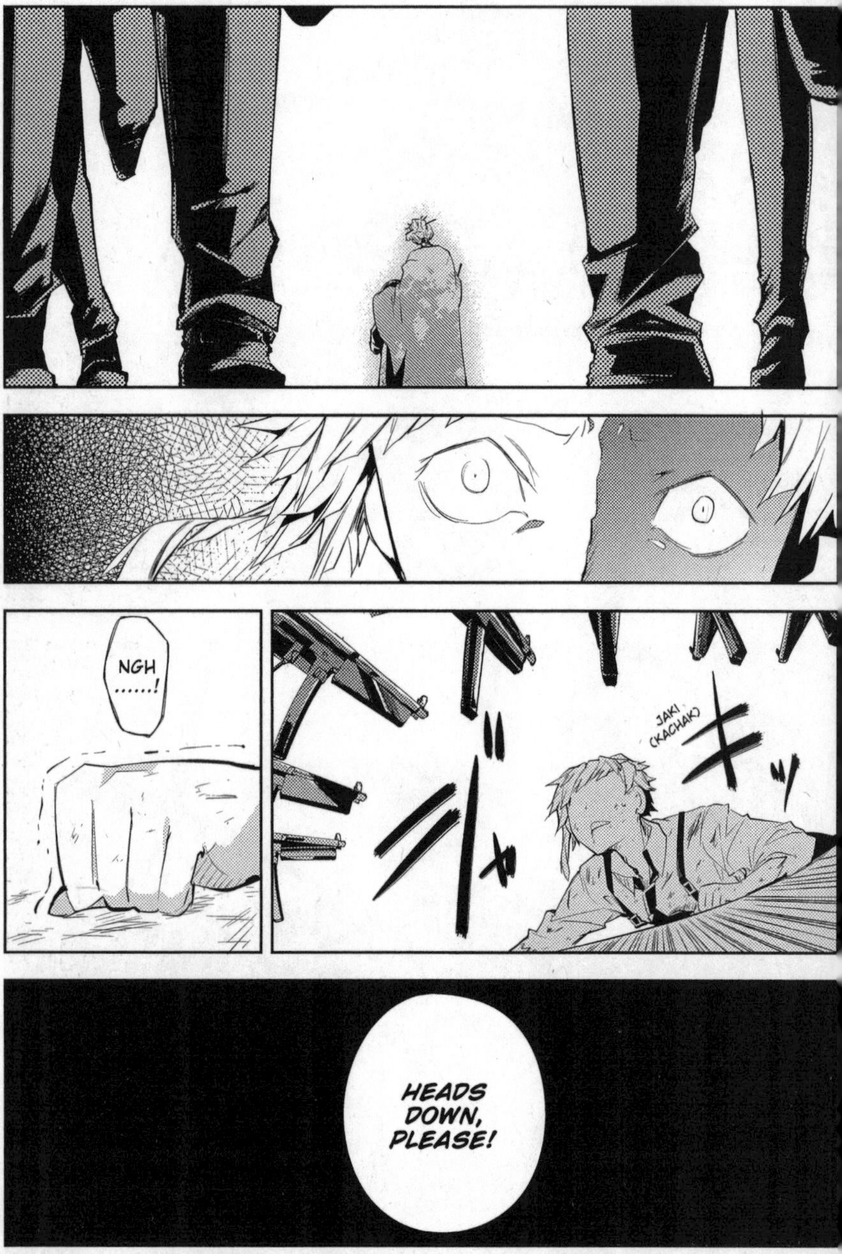
JAKI (KACHAK)
NGH ......!
HEADS DOWN, PLEASE!

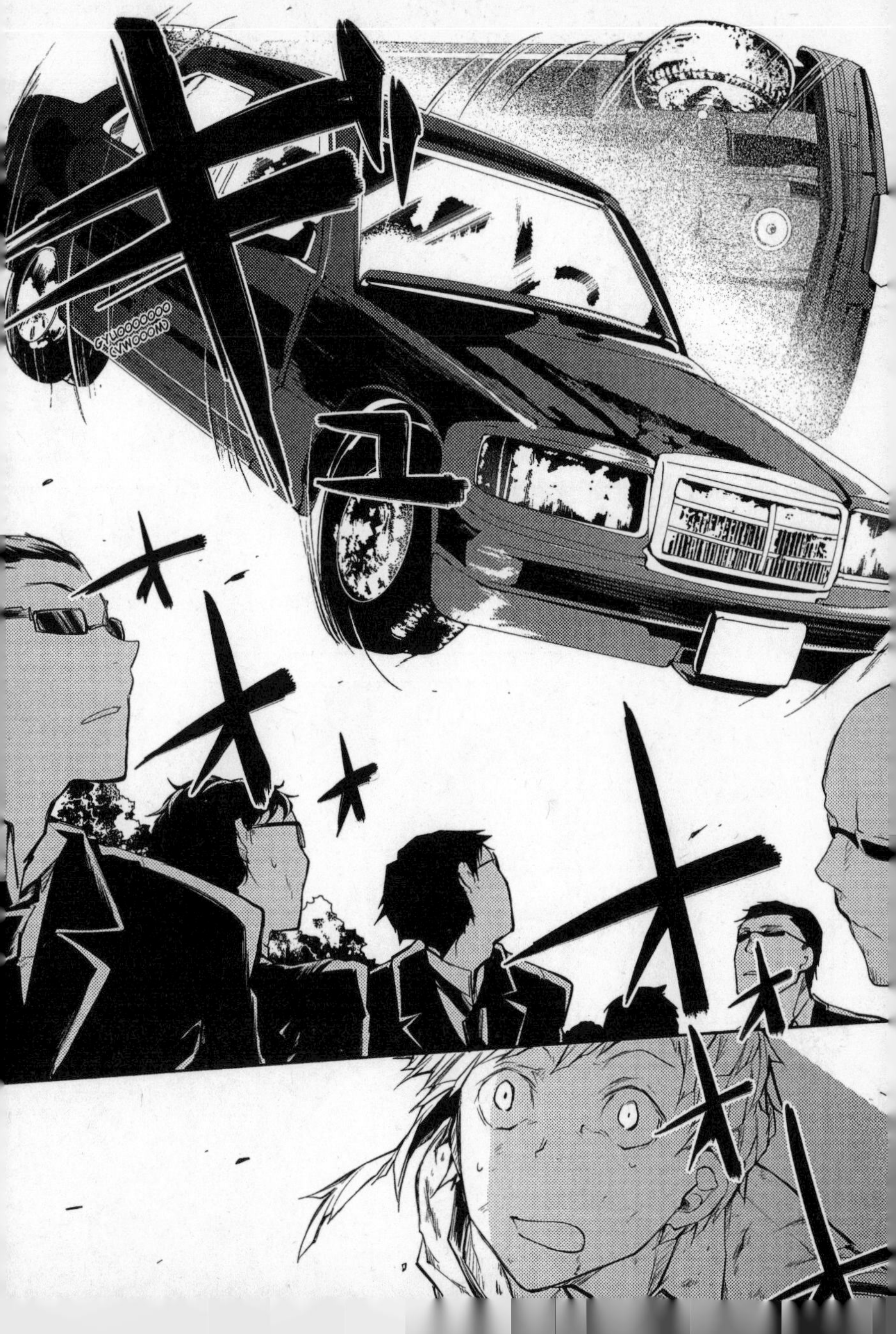
GYUOOOOOOO
(VWOOOM)

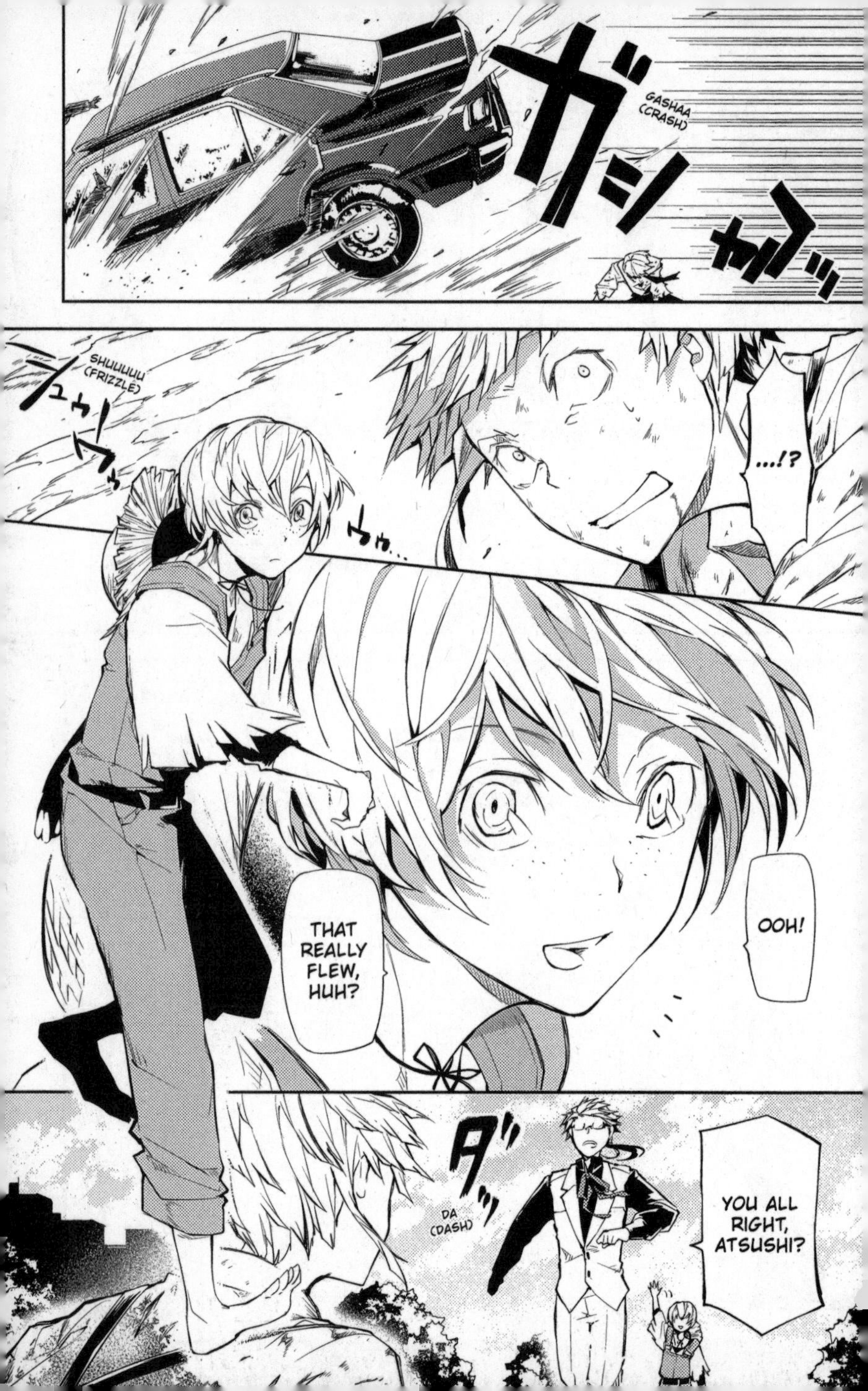

GASHAA (CRASH)
...!?
SHUUUUU (FRIZZLE)
OOH!
THAT REALLY FLEW, HUH?
YOU ALL RIGHT, ATSUSHI?
DA (DASH)

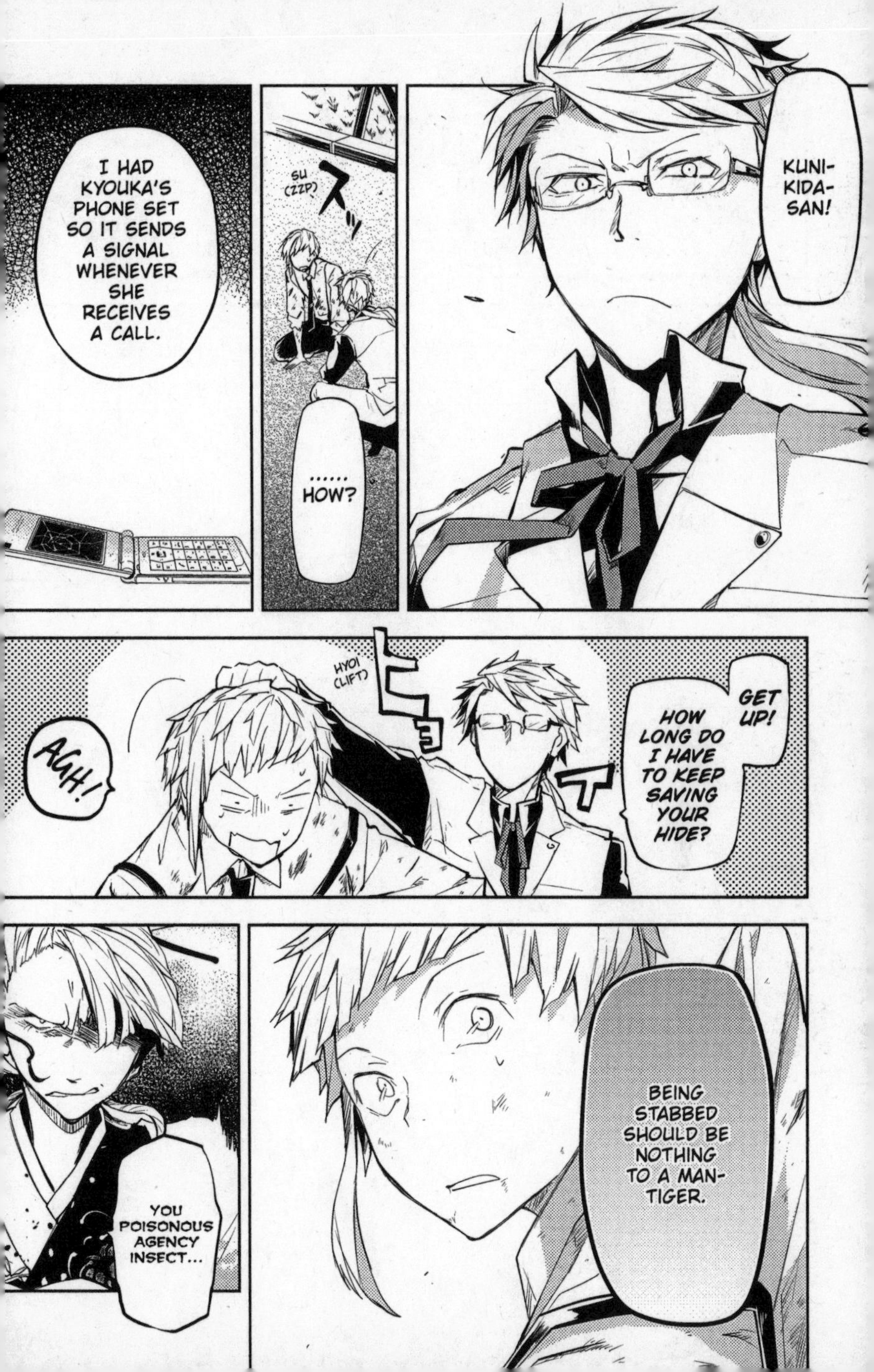
KUNI-KIDA-SAN!
SU (ZZP)
...... HOW?
I HAD KYOUKA'S PHONE SET SO IT SENDS A SIGNAL WHENEVER SHE RECEIVES A CALL.
GET UP!
HOW LONG DO I HAVE TO KEEP SAVING YOUR HIDE?
HYOI (LIFT)
AGH!
BEING STABBED SHOULD BE NOTHING TO A MAN-TIGER.
YOU POISONOUS AGENCY INSECT...

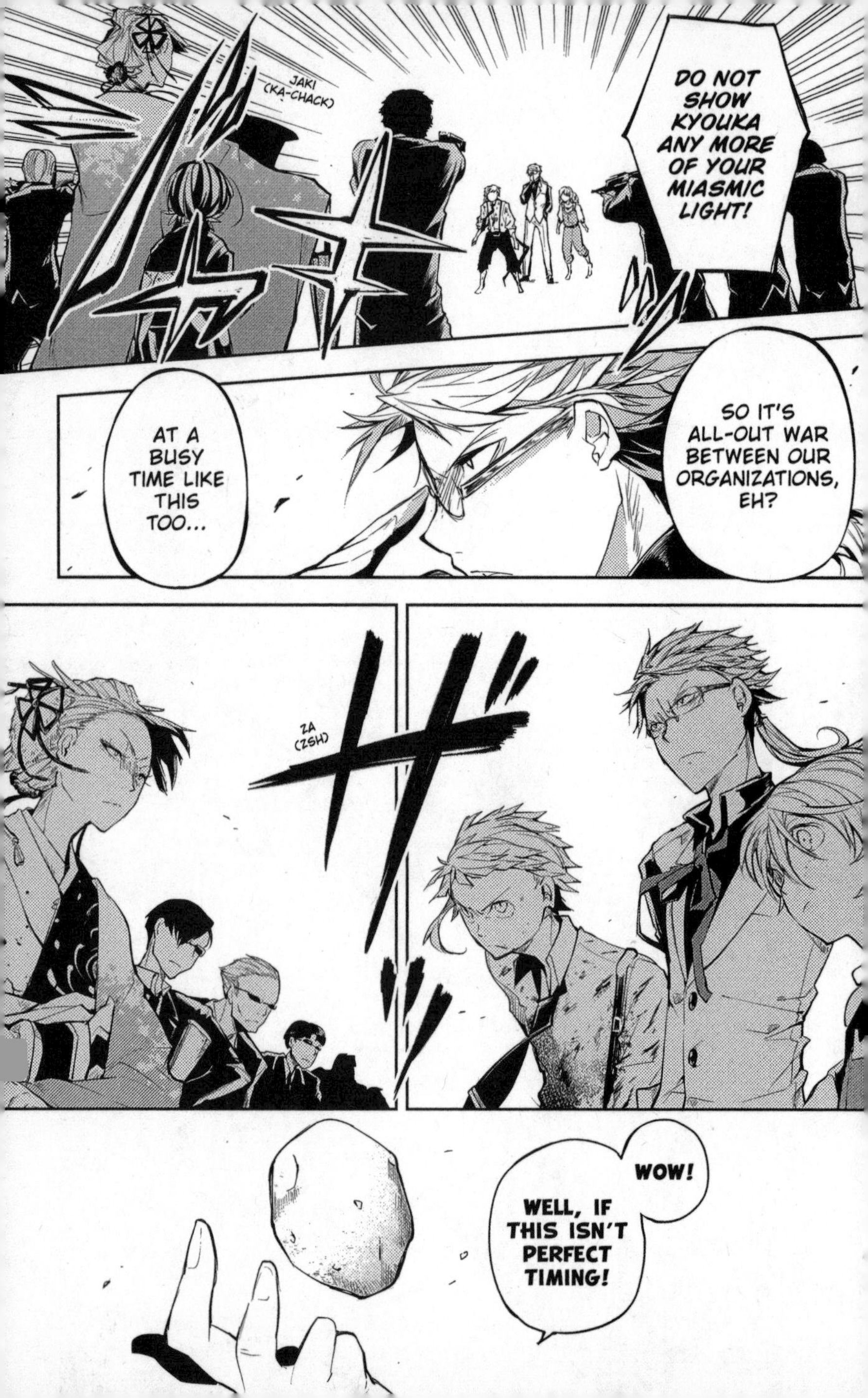
DO NOT SHOW KYOUKA ANY MORE OF YOUR MIASMIC LIGHT!
JAKI (KA-CHACK)
SO IT'S ALL-OUT WAR BETWEEN OUR ORGANIZATIONS, EH?
AT A BUSY TIME LIKE THIS TOO...
ZA (ZSH)
WOW!
WELL, IF THIS ISN'T PERFECT TIMING!

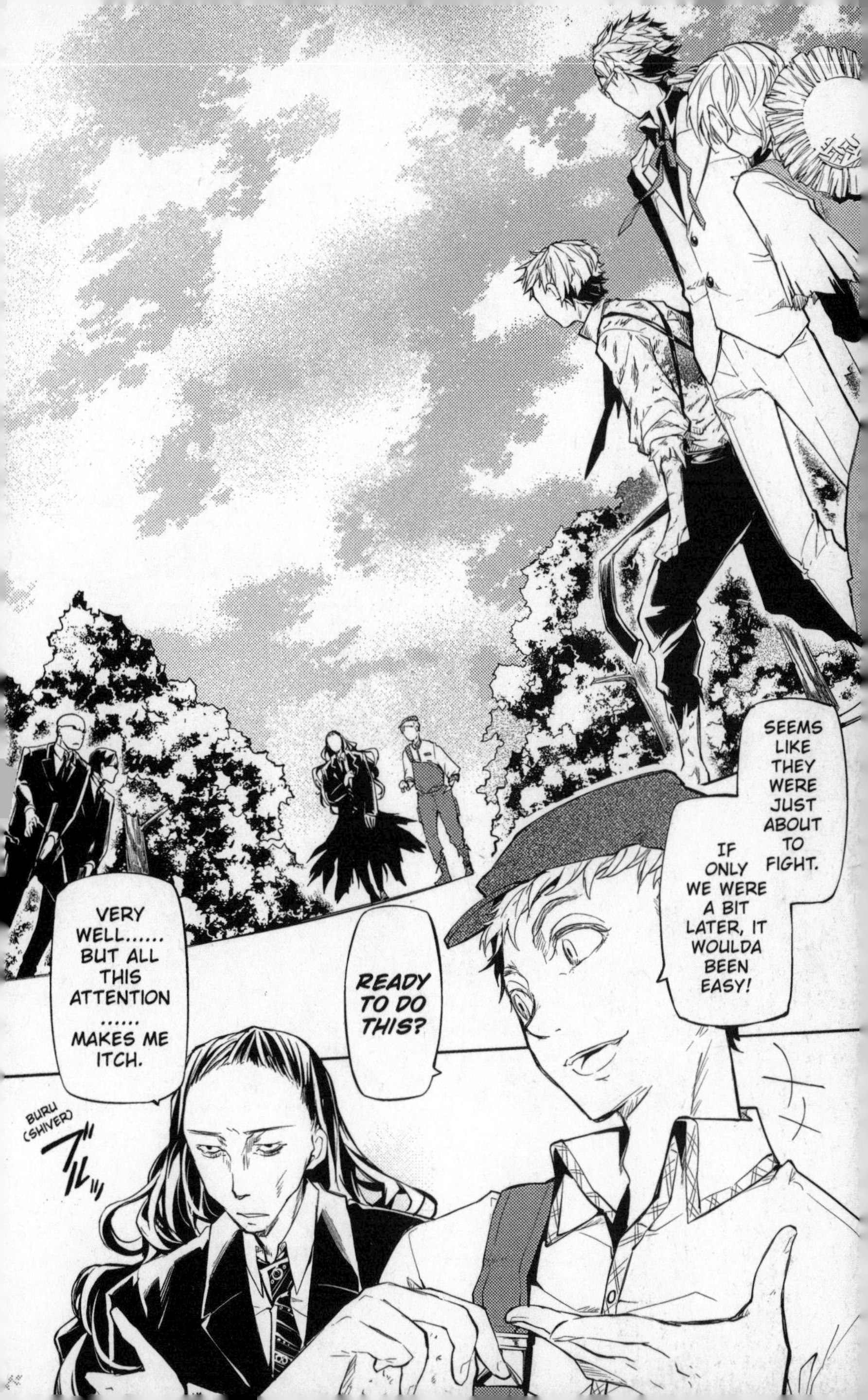
SEEMS LIKE THEY WERE JUST ABOUT TO FIGHT.
IF ONLY WE WERE A BIT LATER, IT WOULDA BEEN EASY!
READY TO DO THIS?
VERY WELL...... BUT ALL THIS ATTENTION ...... MAKES ME ITCH.
BURU (SHIVER)

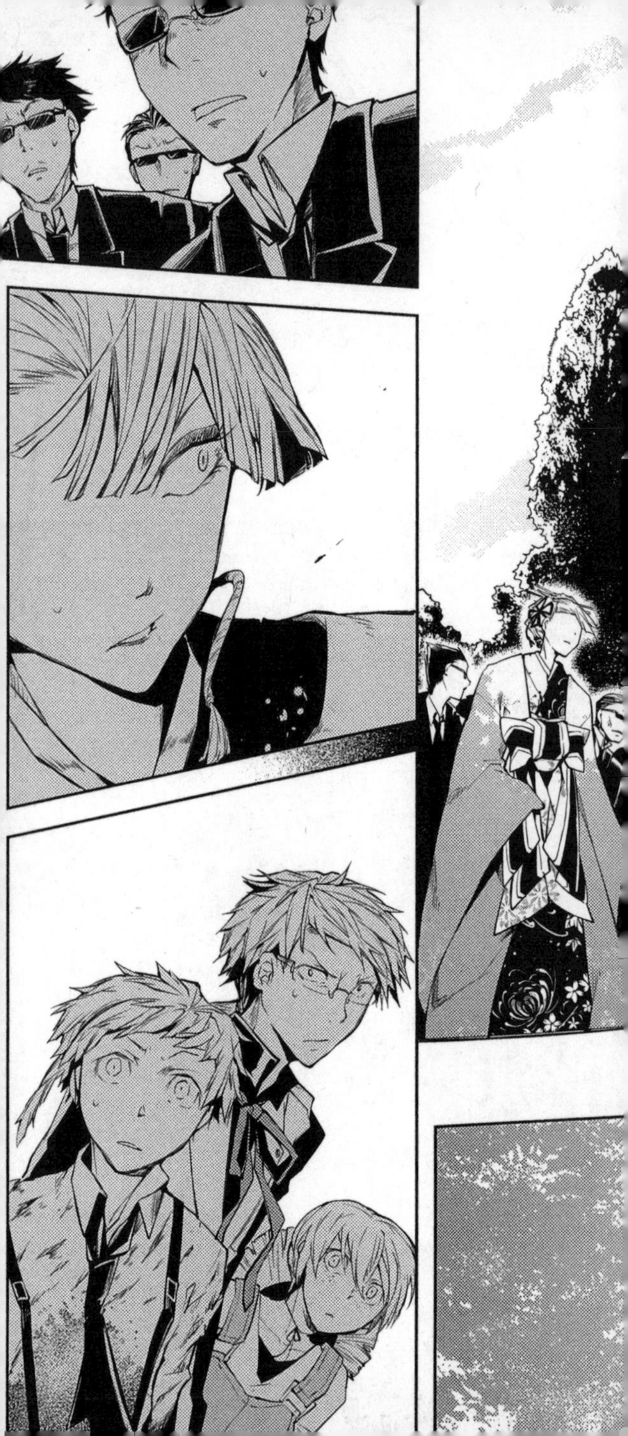

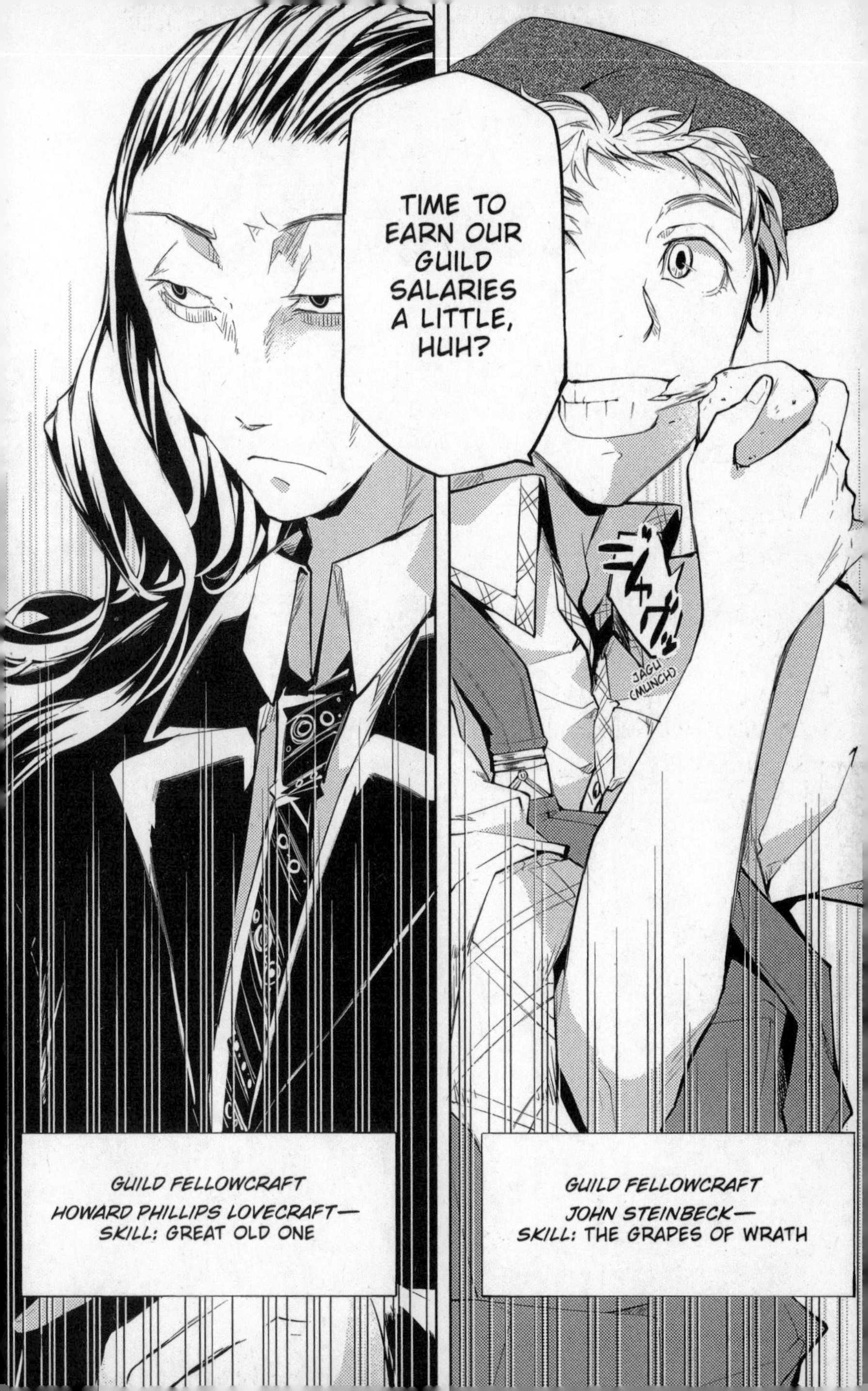
TIME TO EARN OUR GUILD SALARIES A LITTLE, HUH?
JAGU (MUNCH)
GUILD FELLOWCRAFT JOHN STEINBECK— SKILL: THE GRAPES OF WRATH
GUILD FELLOWCRAFT HOWARD PHILLIPS LOVECRAFT— SKILL: GREAT OLD ONE

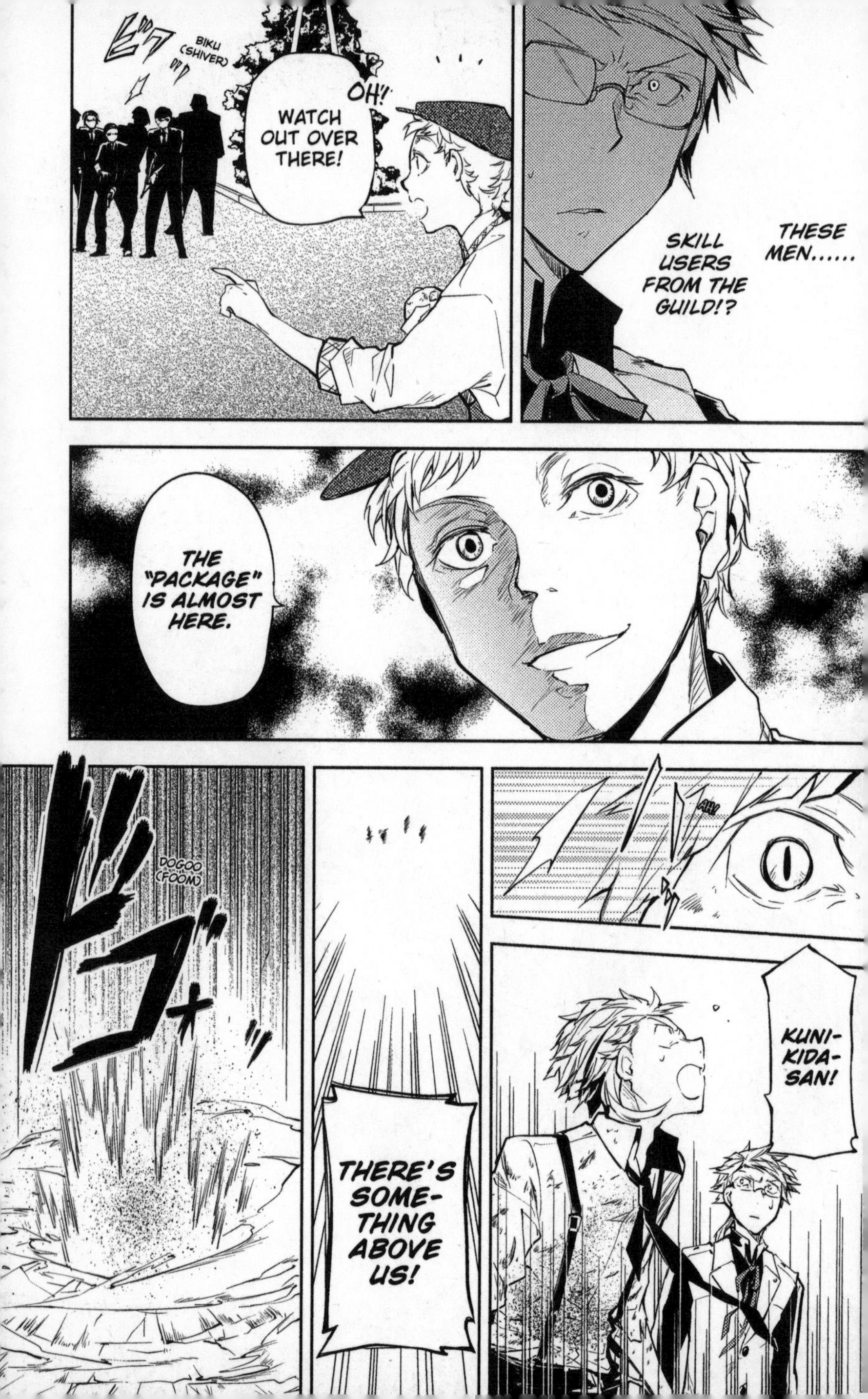
THESE MEN......
SKILL USERS FROM THE GUILD!?
BIKU (SHIVER)
OH!
WATCH OUT OVER THERE!
THE "PACKAGE" IS ALMOST HERE.
AH!
KUNI-KIDA-SAN!
THERE'S SOME-THING ABOVE US!
DOGOO (FOOM)

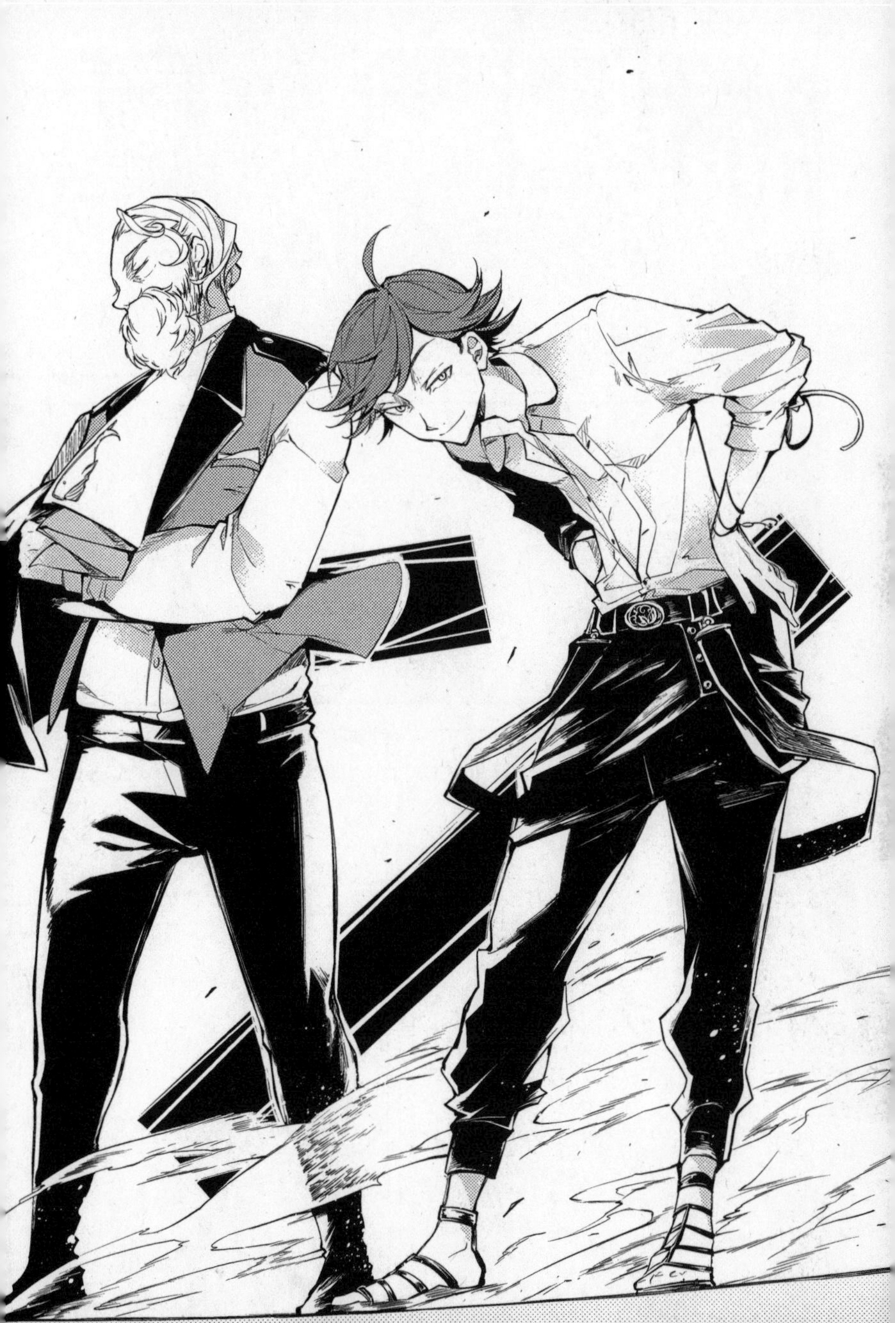

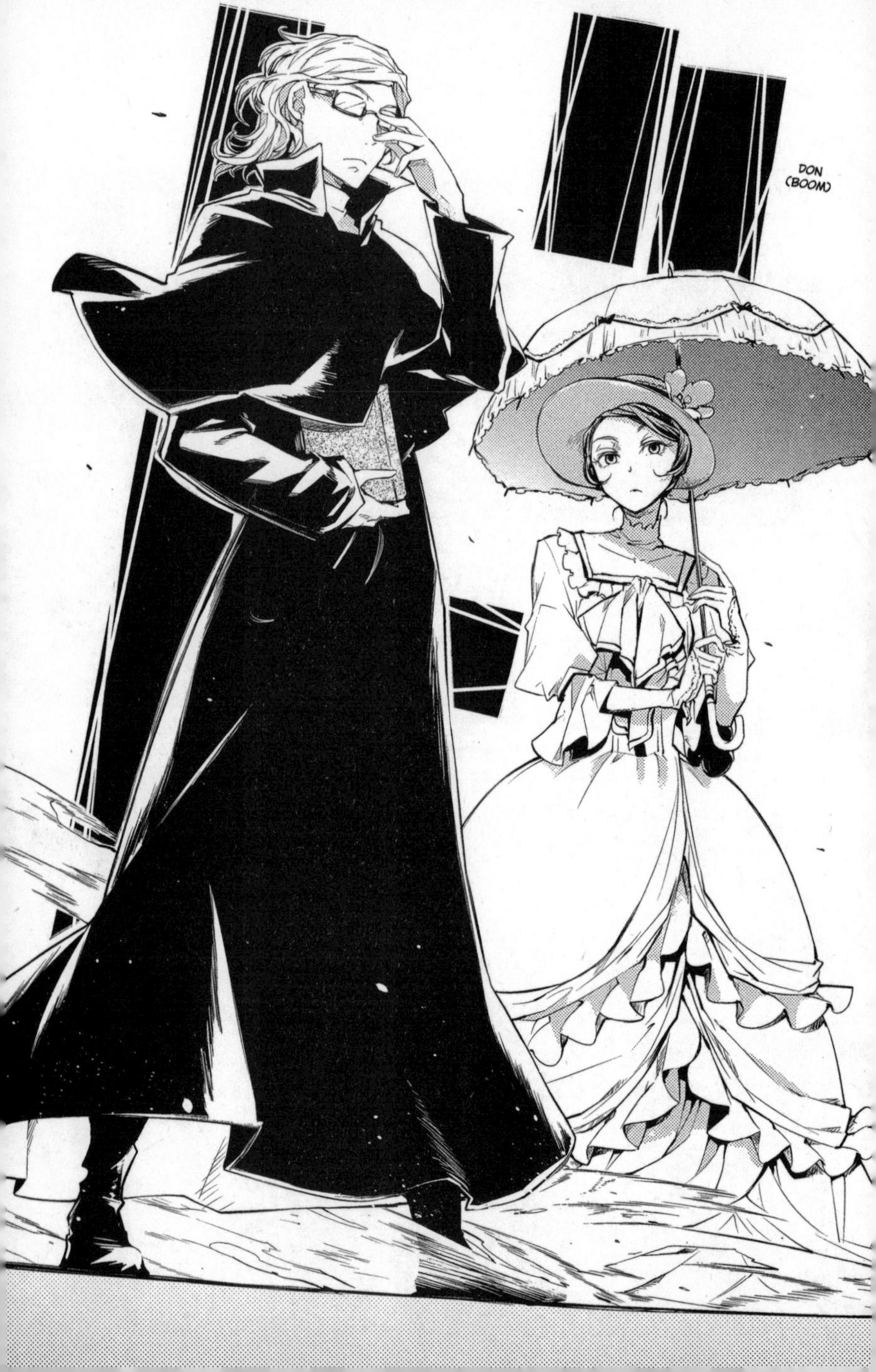
DON
(BOOM)

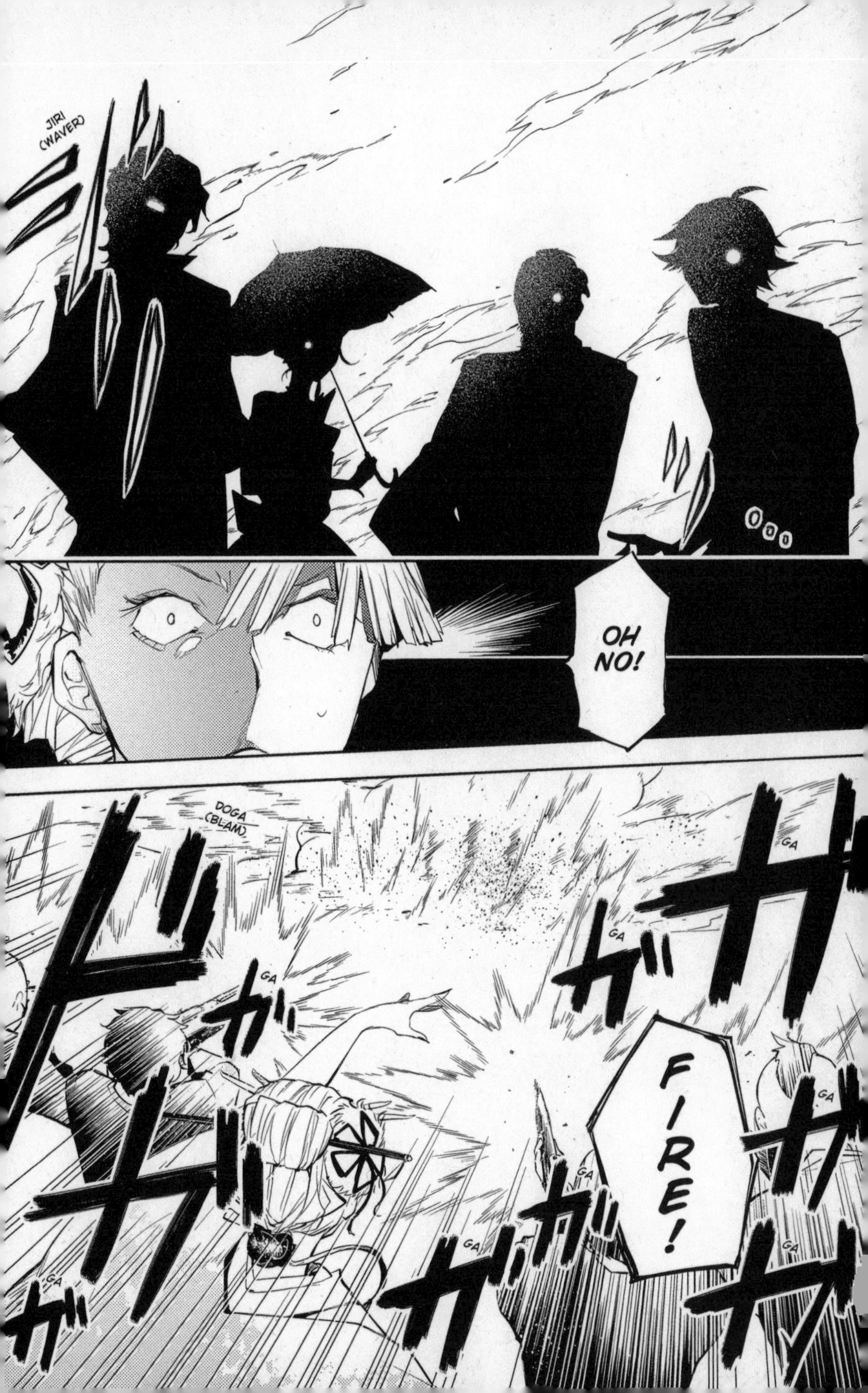
JIRI (WAVER)
OH NO!
GA
GA
DOGA (BLAM)
GA
FIRE!
GA
GA
GA
GA
GA

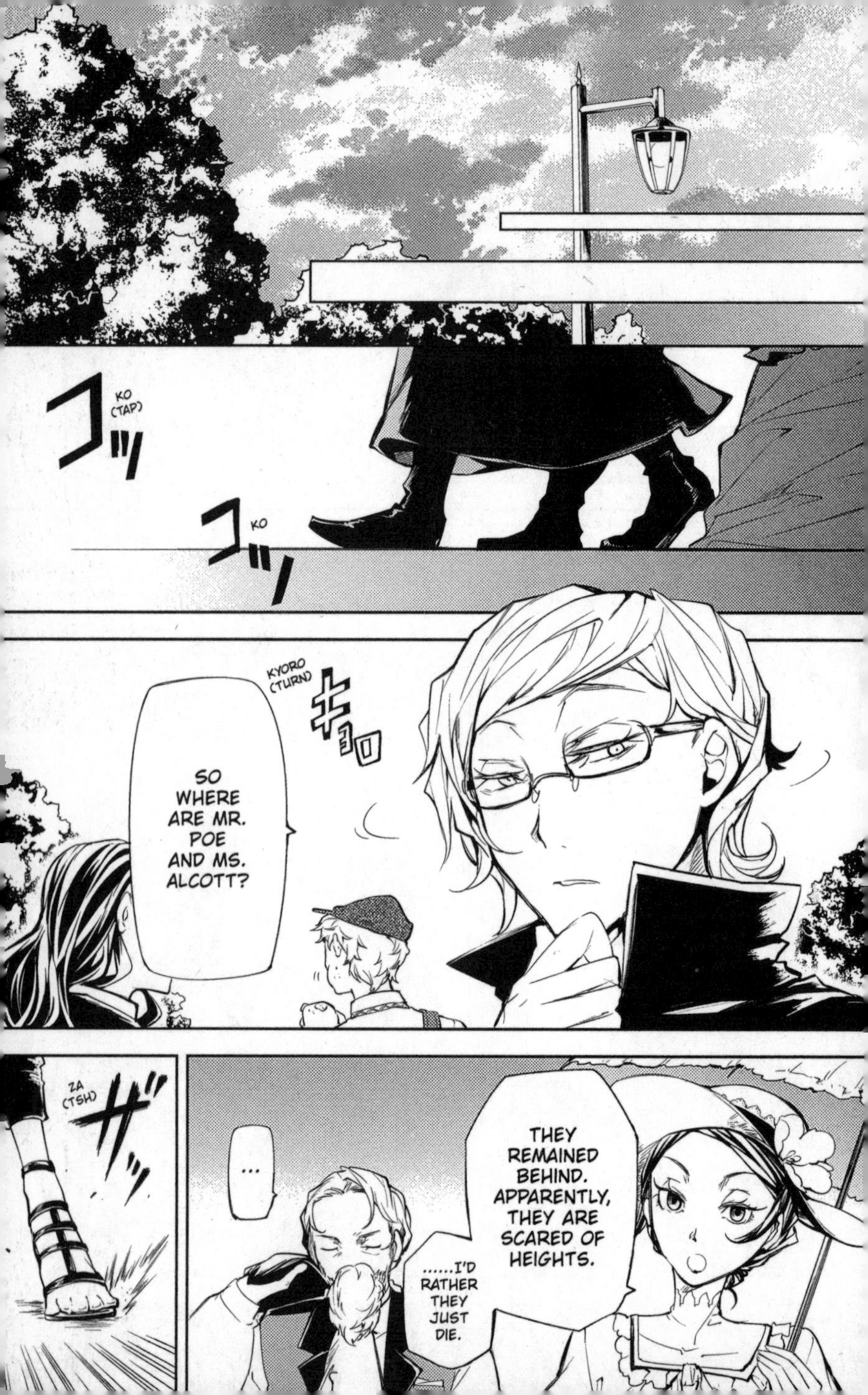
KO (TAP)
KO
KYORO (TURN)
SO WHERE ARE MR. POE AND MS. ALCOTT?
THEY REMAINED BEHIND. APPARENTLY, THEY ARE SCARED OF HEIGHTS.
...
......I'D RATHER THEY JUST DIE.
ZA (TSH)

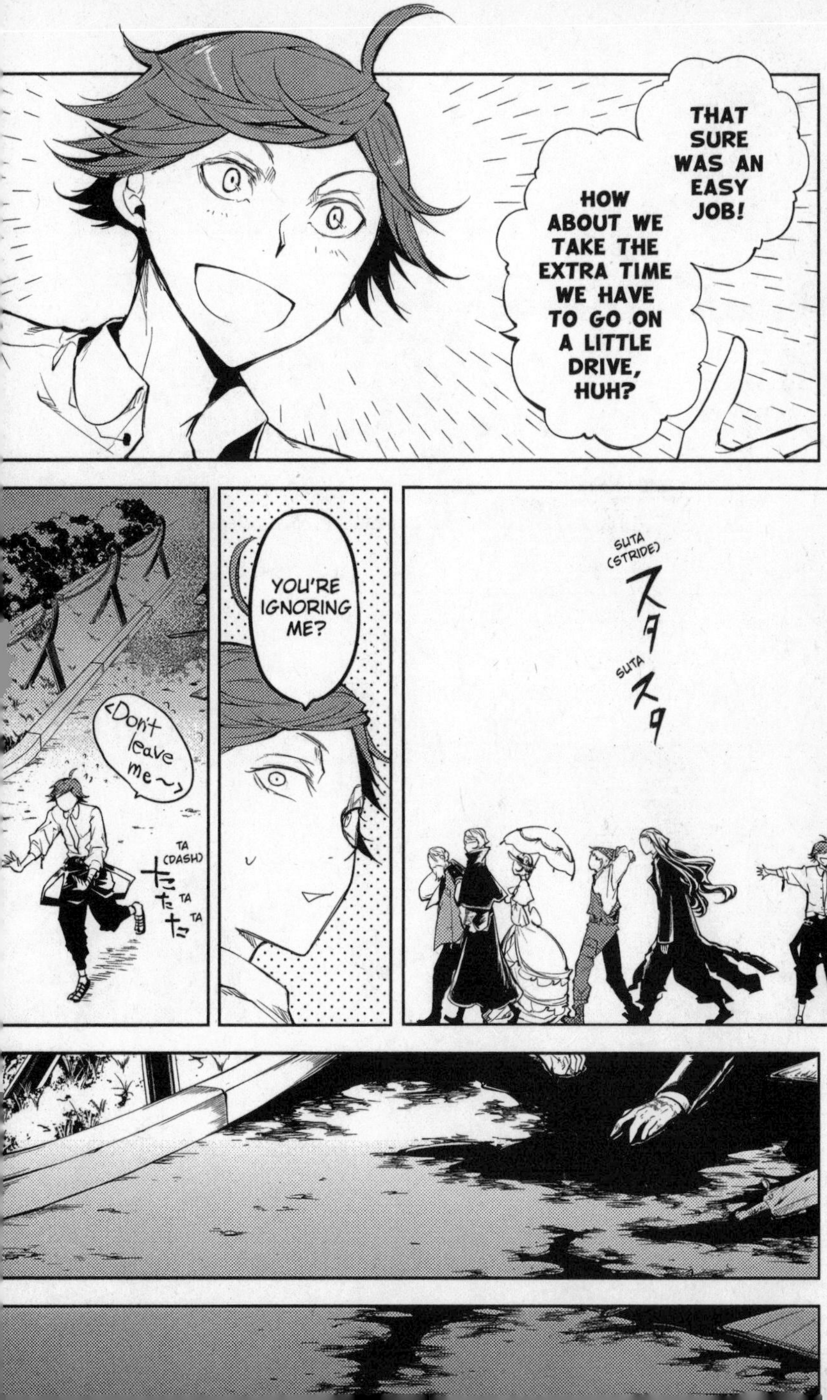
THAT SURE WAS AN EASY JOB!
HOW ABOUT WE TAKE THE EXTRA TIME WE HAVE TO GO ON A LITTLE DRIVE, HUH?
SUTA (STRIDE)
スタ
SUTA
スタ
YOU'RE IGNORING ME?
<Don't leave me~>
TA (DASH)
たたた
TA TA

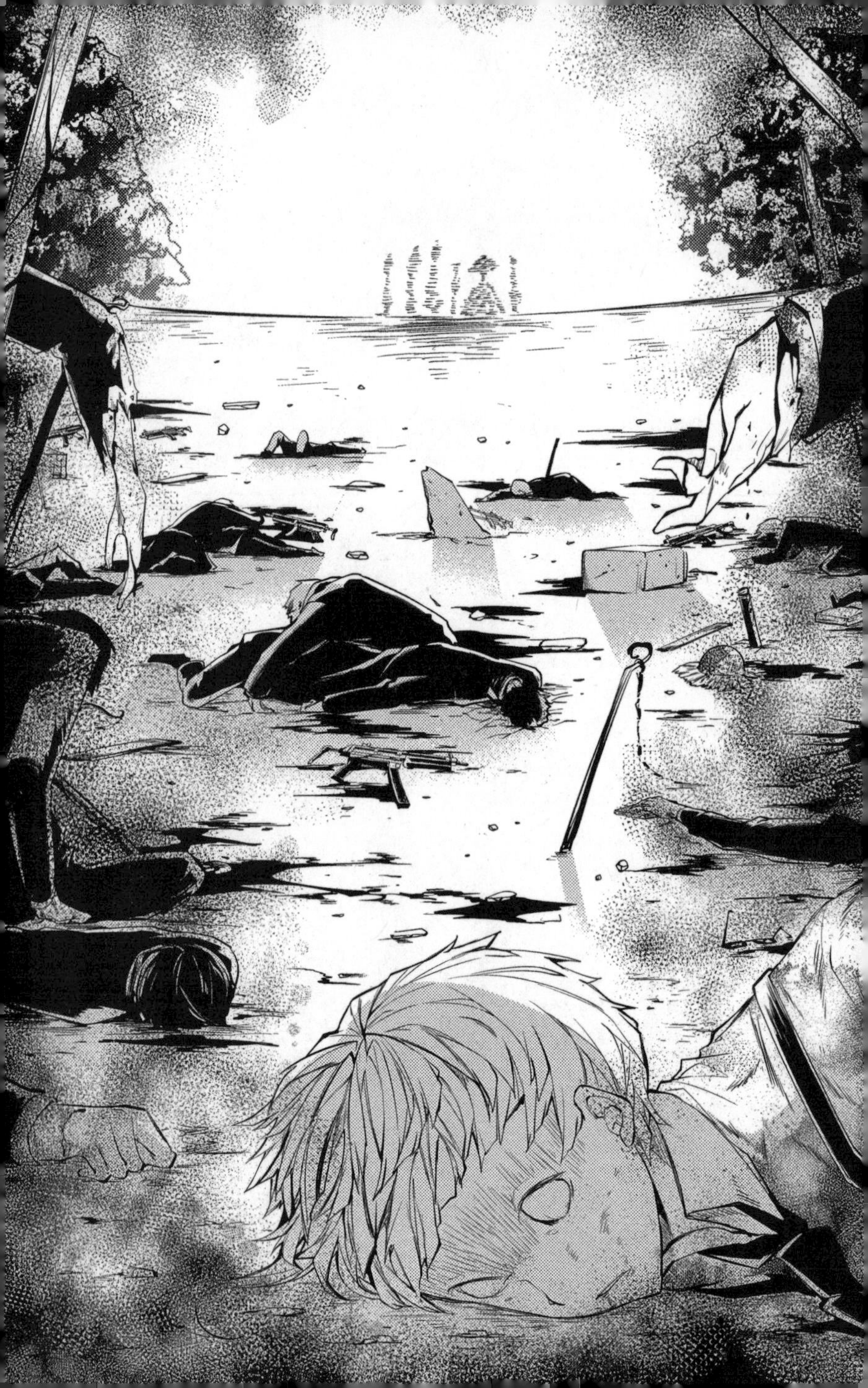

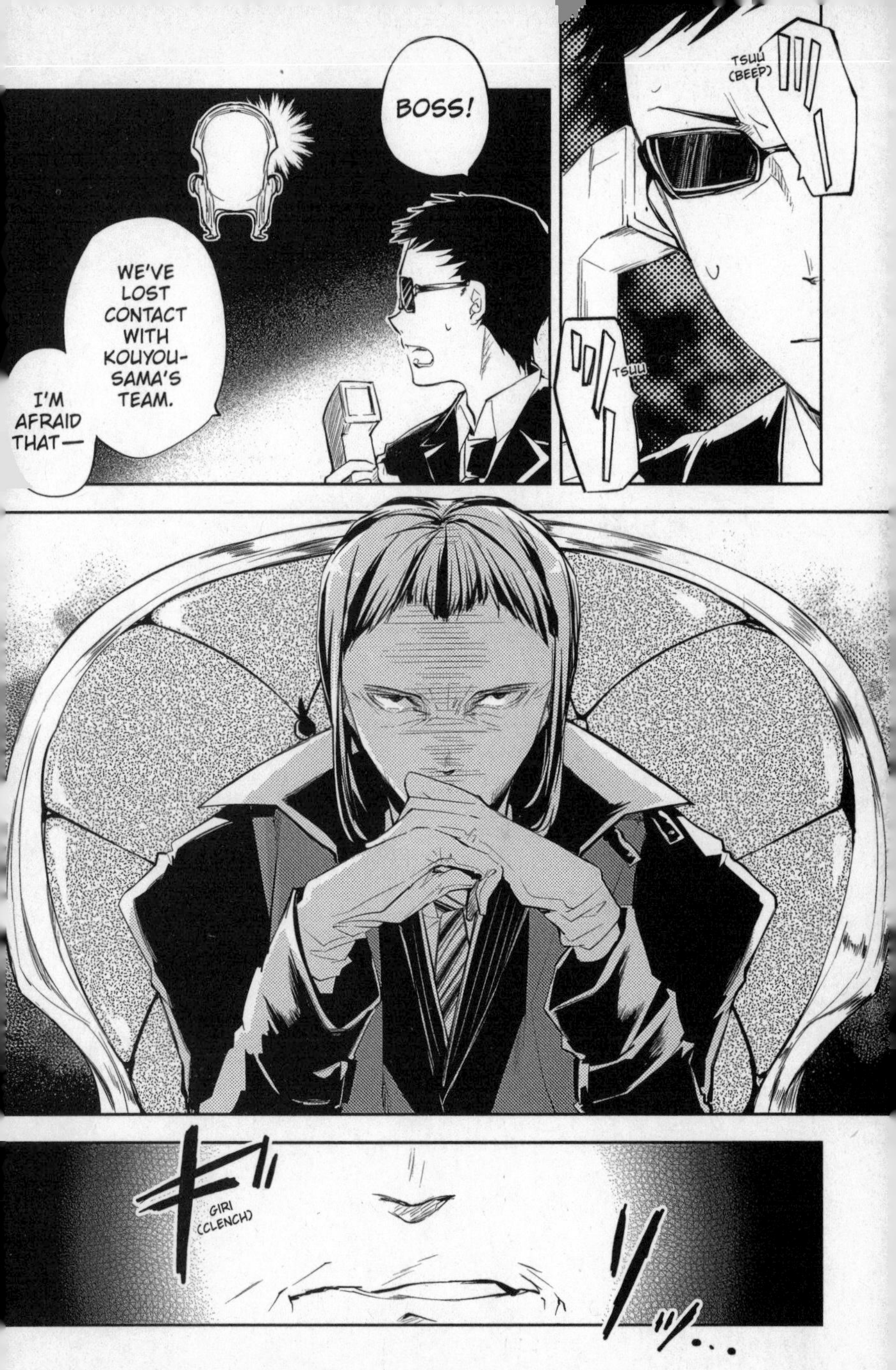
TSUU (BEEP)
TSUU
BOSS!
WE'VE LOST CONTACT WITH KOUYOU-SAMA'S TEAM.
I'M AFRAID THAT—
GIRI (CLENCH)
...

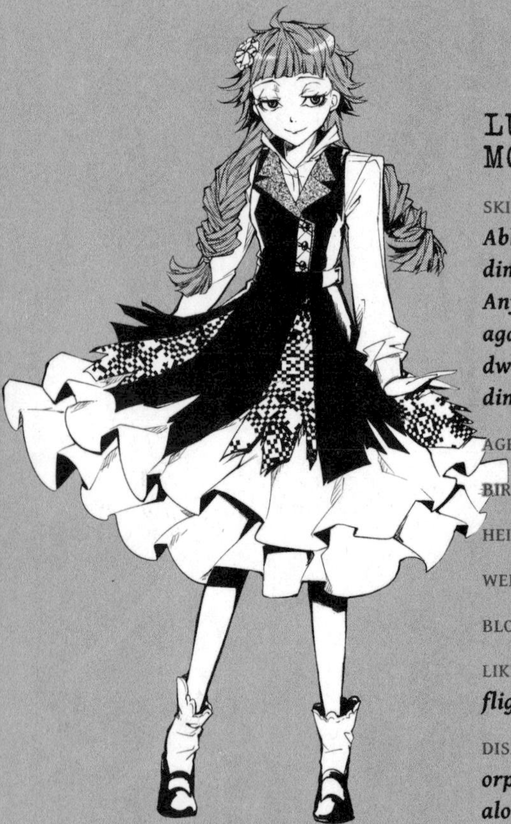

LUCY MAUD MONTGOMERY

SKILL: Anne of Abyssal Red
Able to create an alternate dimension called Anne's Room. Anyone who loses a game of tag against the monstrous Anne, who dwells inside, is locked in the dimension forever.

AGE: *19*

BIRTH DATE: *November 30*

HEIGHT: *165cm*

WEIGHT: *44kg*

BLOOD TYPE: *AB*

LIKES: *Stuffed animals, chatting, flights of fancy, romantic things*

DISLIKES: *Cheap people, the orphanage she was at, being alone*

BUNGO
STRAY DOGS

CHAPTER 19

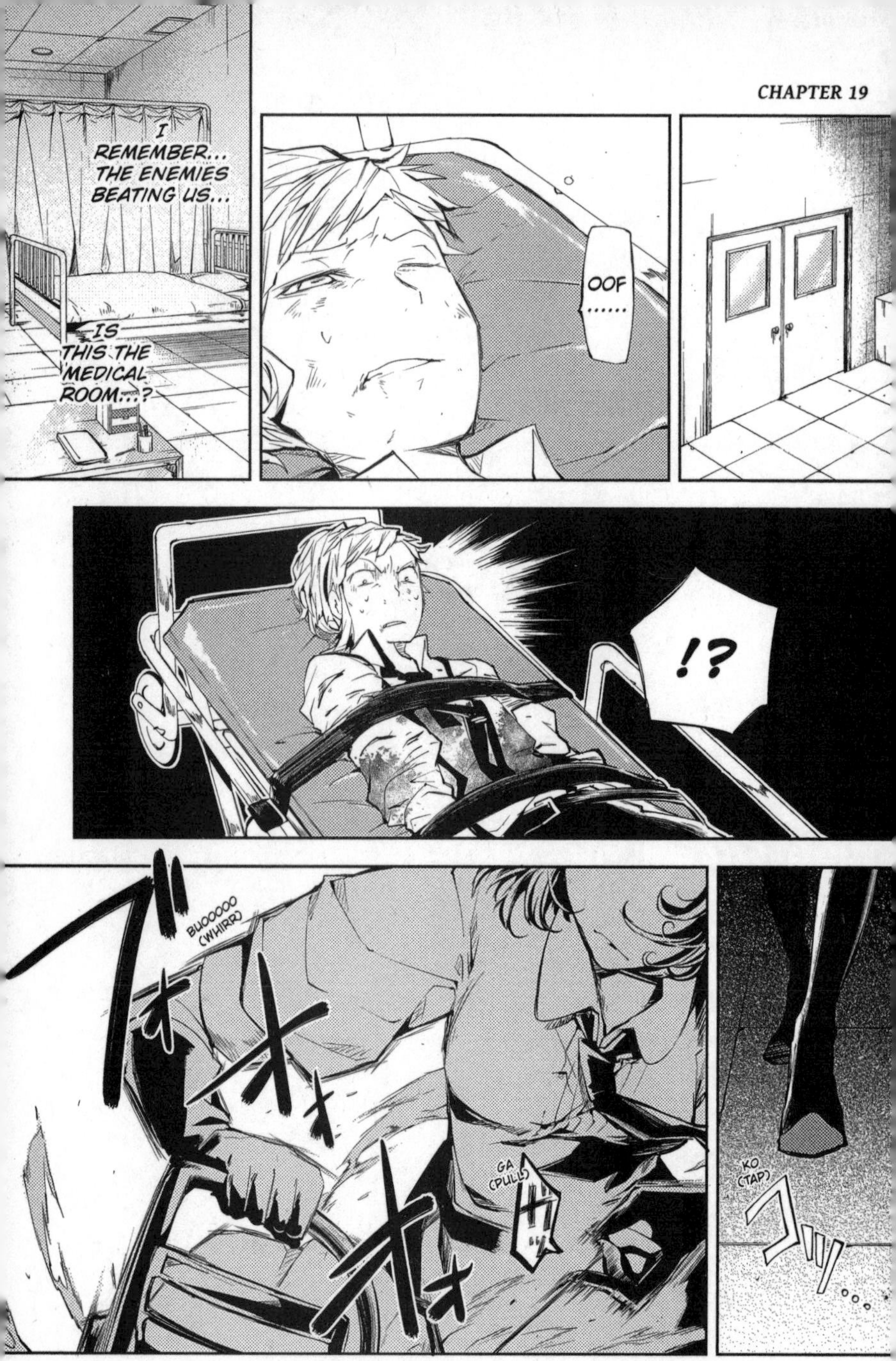

OOF ......
I REMEMBER... THE ENEMIES BEATING US...
IS THIS THE MEDICAL ROOM...?
!?
KO (TAP)
BUOOOOO (WHIRR)
GA (PULL)

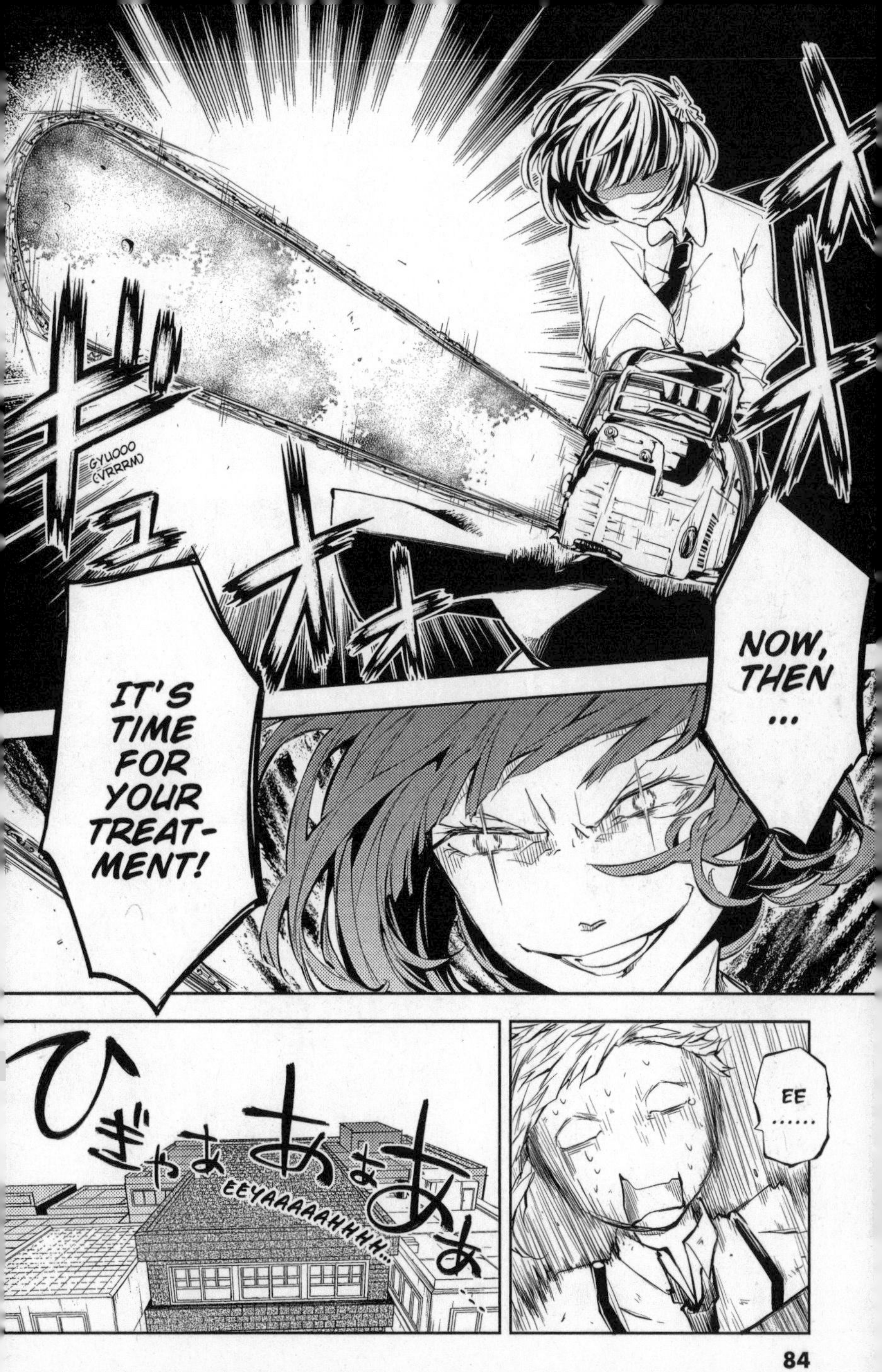
GYUOOO (VRRRM)
NOW, THEN ...
IT'S TIME FOR YOUR TREATMENT!
EE ......
EEYAAAAAAHHHH...

CHAPTER 19
The Three-Way Battle

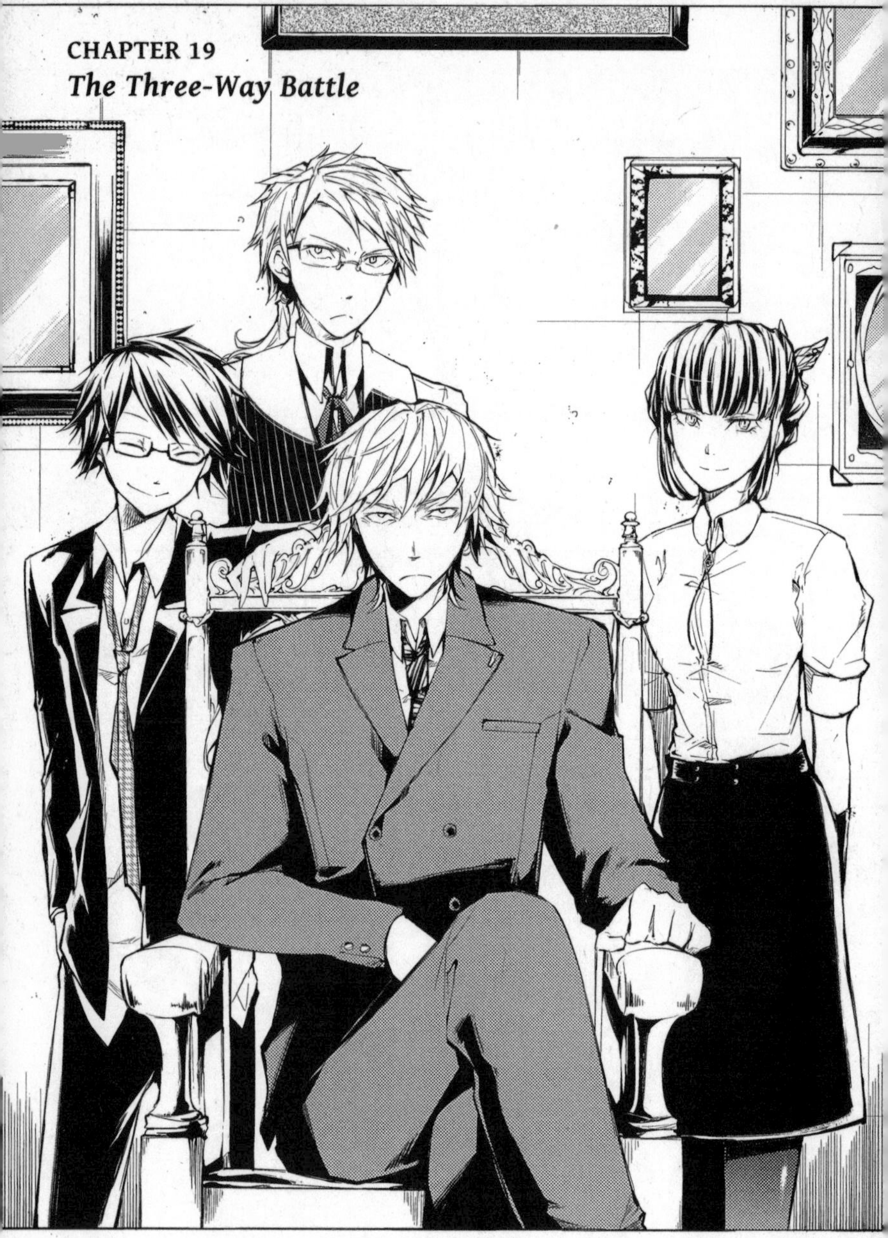

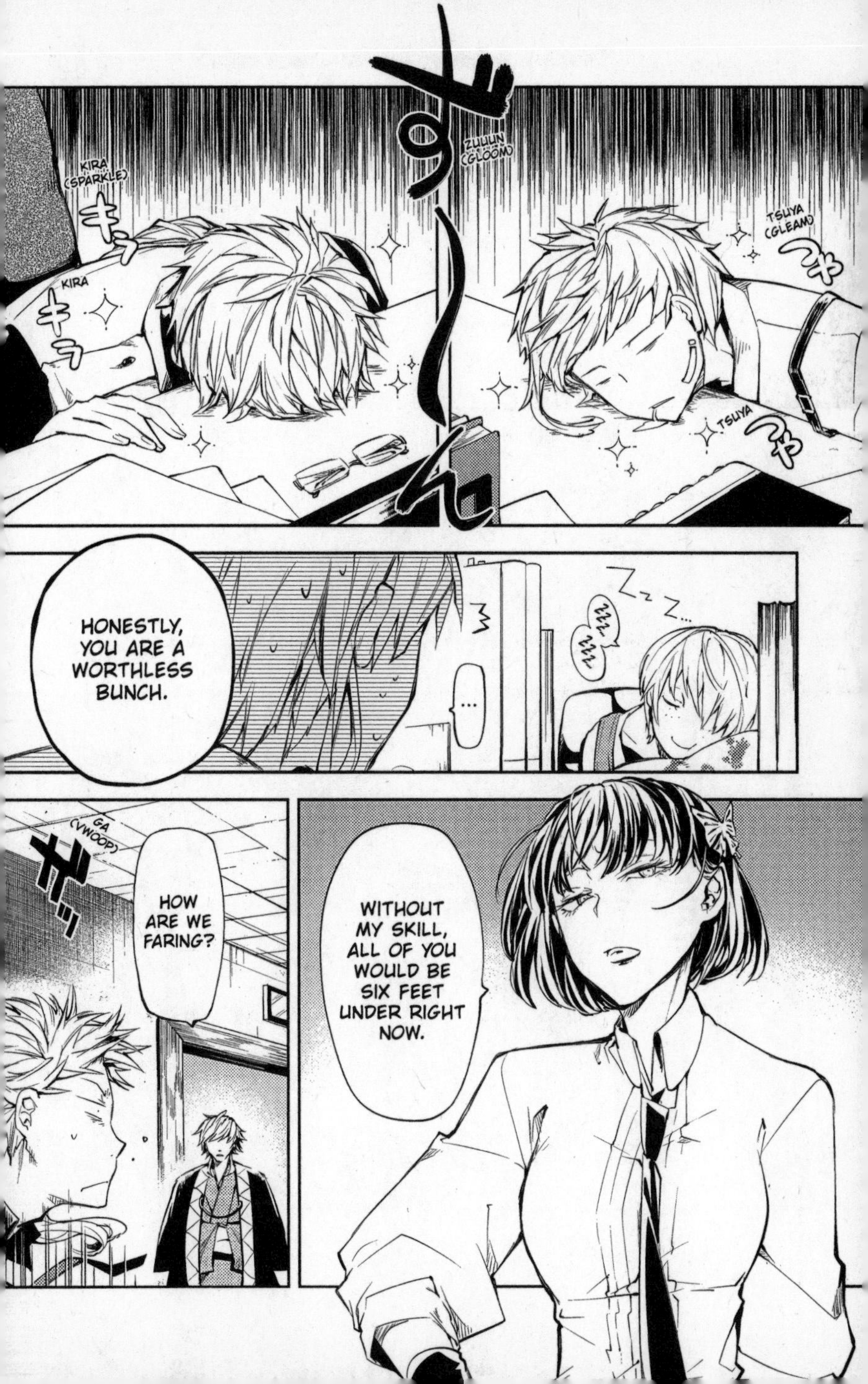

TSUYA (GLEAM)
TSUYA
ZUUUN (GLOOM)
KIRA (SPARKLE)
KIRA
Z z Z...
ZZZ
ZZZ
...
HONESTLY, YOU ARE A WORTHLESS BUNCH.
WITHOUT MY SKILL, ALL OF YOU WOULD BE SIX FEET UNDER RIGHT NOW.
GA (VWOOP)
HOW ARE WE FARING?

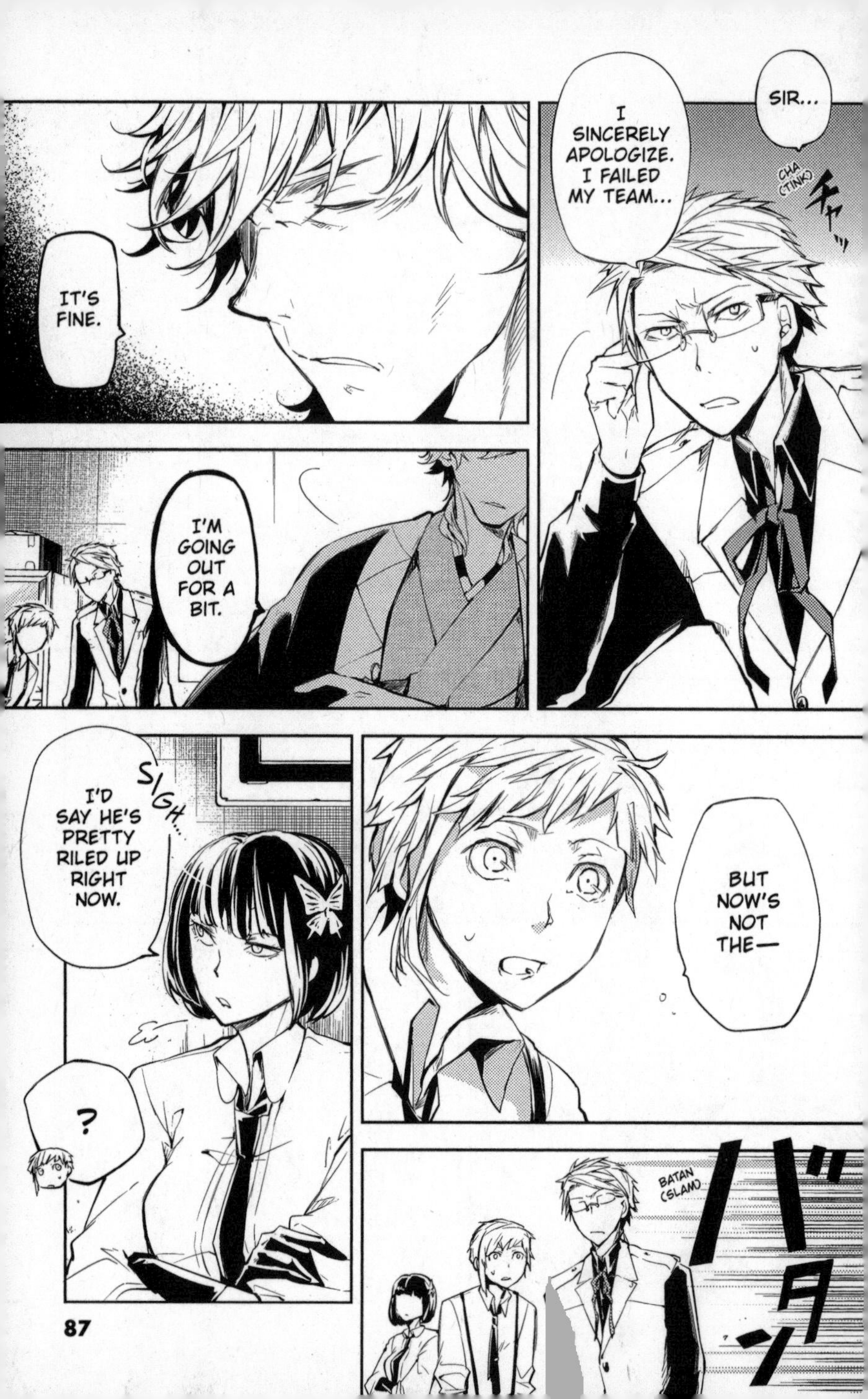

SIR...
I SINCERELY APOLOGIZE. I FAILED MY TEAM...
CHA (TINK)
チャッ
IT'S FINE.
I'M GOING OUT FOR A BIT.
BUT NOW'S NOT THE—
SIGH...
I'D SAY HE'S PRETTY RILED UP RIGHT NOW.
?
BATAN (SLAM)
バタンッ

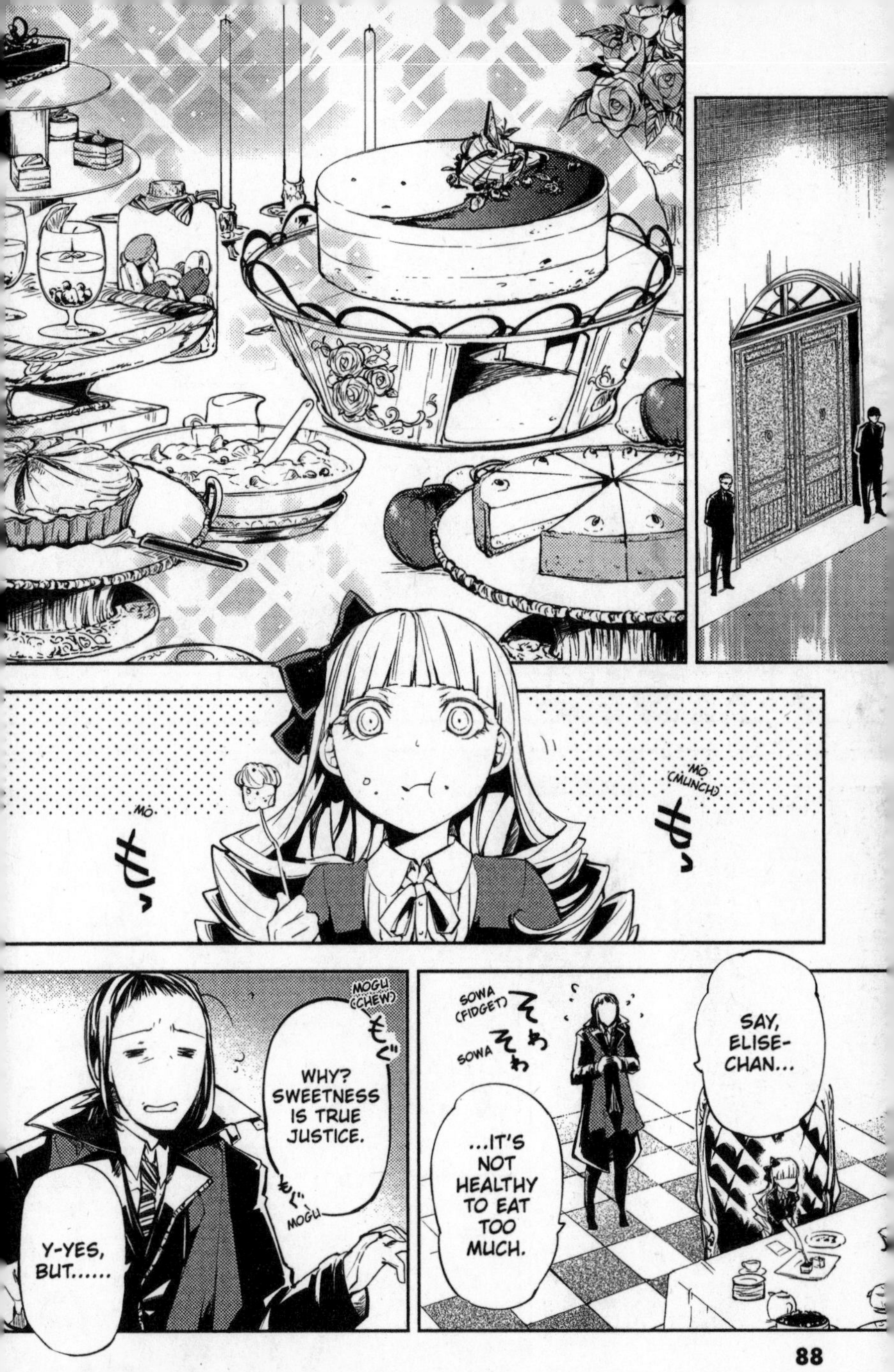
MO (MUNCH)
もっ
MO
もっ
SAY, ELISE-CHAN...
SOWA (FIDGET) そわ
SOWA そわ
...IT'S NOT HEALTHY TO EAT TOO MUCH.
MOGU (CHEW) もぐ
WHY? SWEETNESS IS TRUE JUSTICE.
もぐ MOGU
Y-YES, BUT......

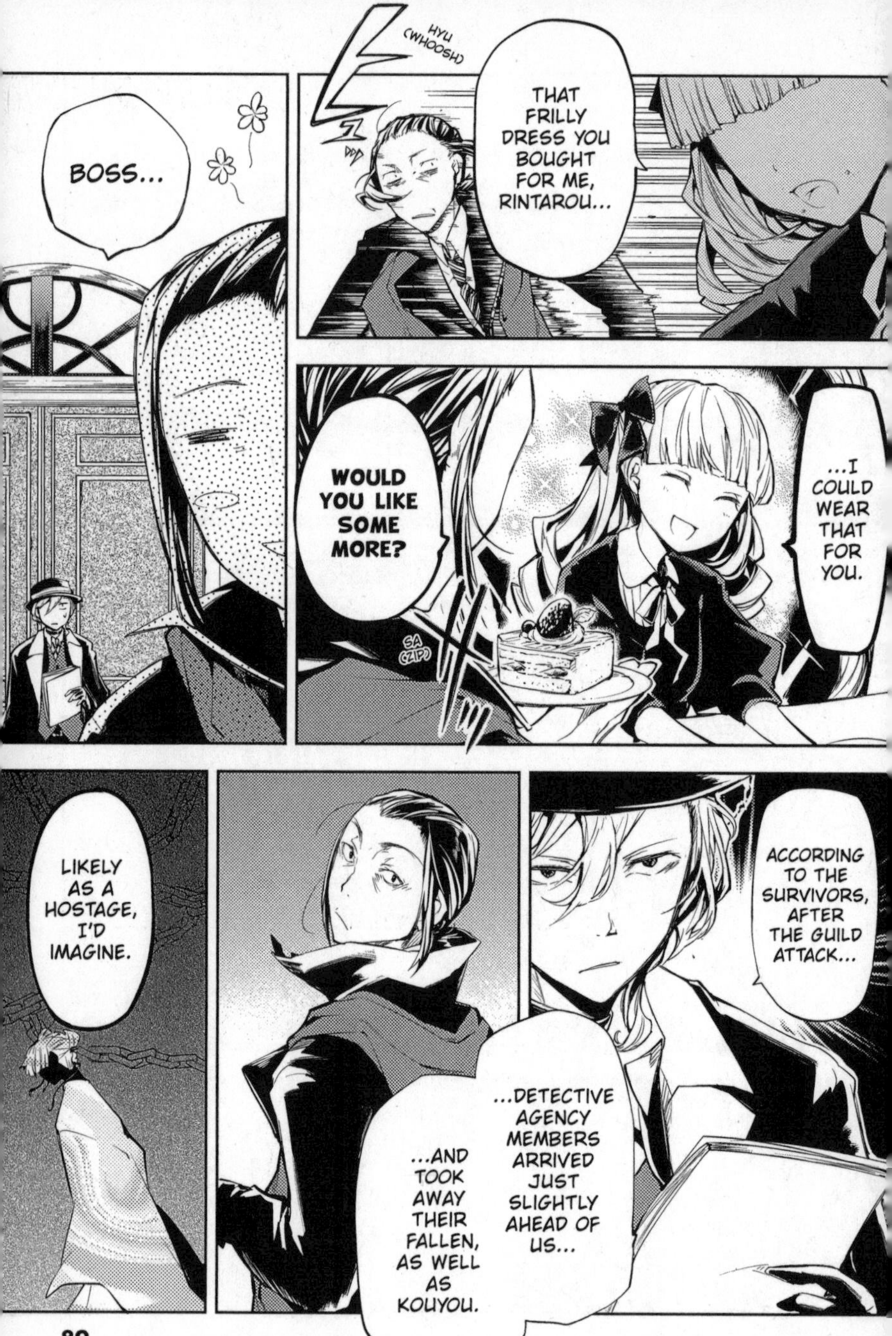
HYU (WHOOSH)
THAT FRILLY DRESS YOU BOUGHT FOR ME, RINTAROU...
...I COULD WEAR THAT FOR YOU.
SA (ZIP)
WOULD YOU LIKE SOME MORE?
BOSS...
ACCORDING TO THE SURVIVORS, AFTER THE GUILD ATTACK...
...DETECTIVE AGENCY MEMBERS ARRIVED JUST SLIGHTLY AHEAD OF US...
...AND TOOK AWAY THEIR FALLEN, AS WELL AS KOUYOU.
LIKELY AS A HOSTAGE, I'D IMAGINE.

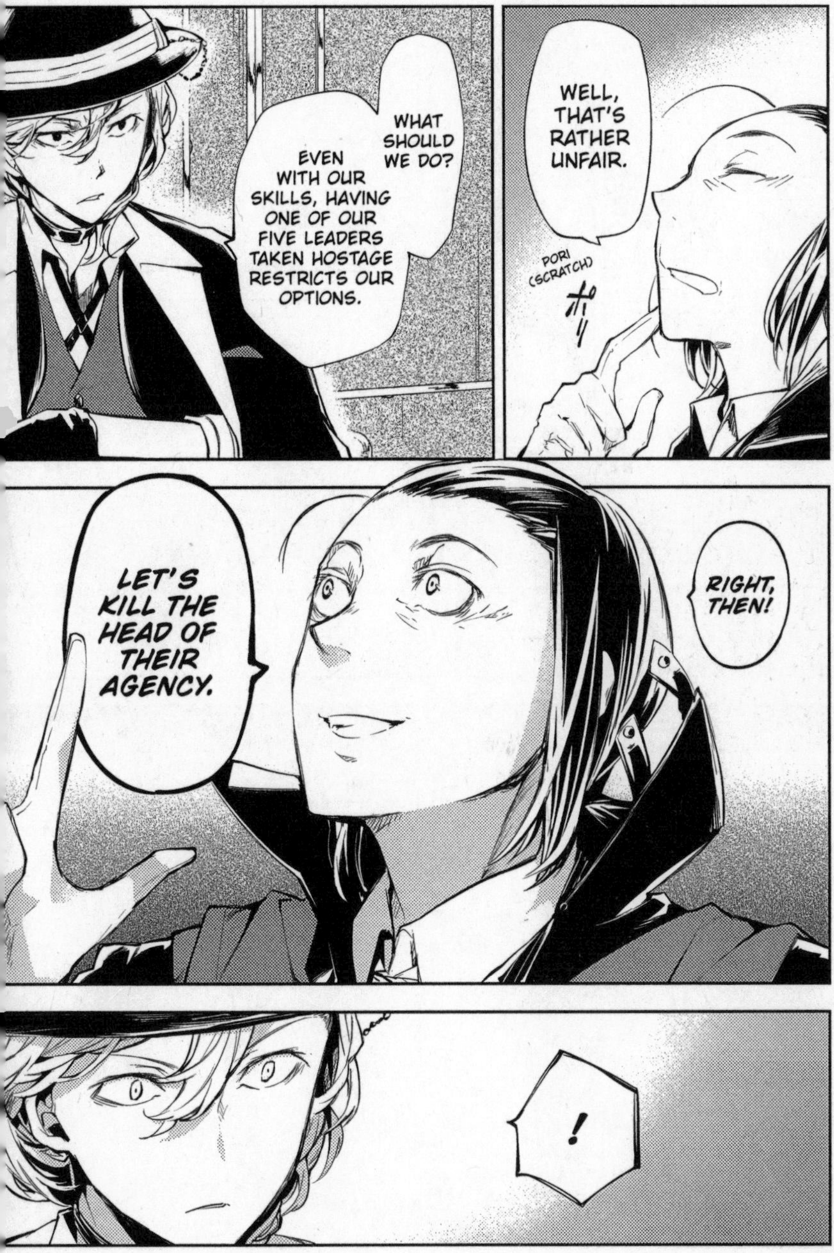
WELL, THAT'S RATHER UNFAIR.
PORI (SCRATCH)
WHAT SHOULD WE DO?
EVEN WITH OUR SKILLS, HAVING ONE OF OUR FIVE LEADERS TAKEN HOSTAGE RESTRICTS OUR OPTIONS.
RIGHT, THEN!
LET'S KILL THE HEAD OF THEIR AGENCY.
!

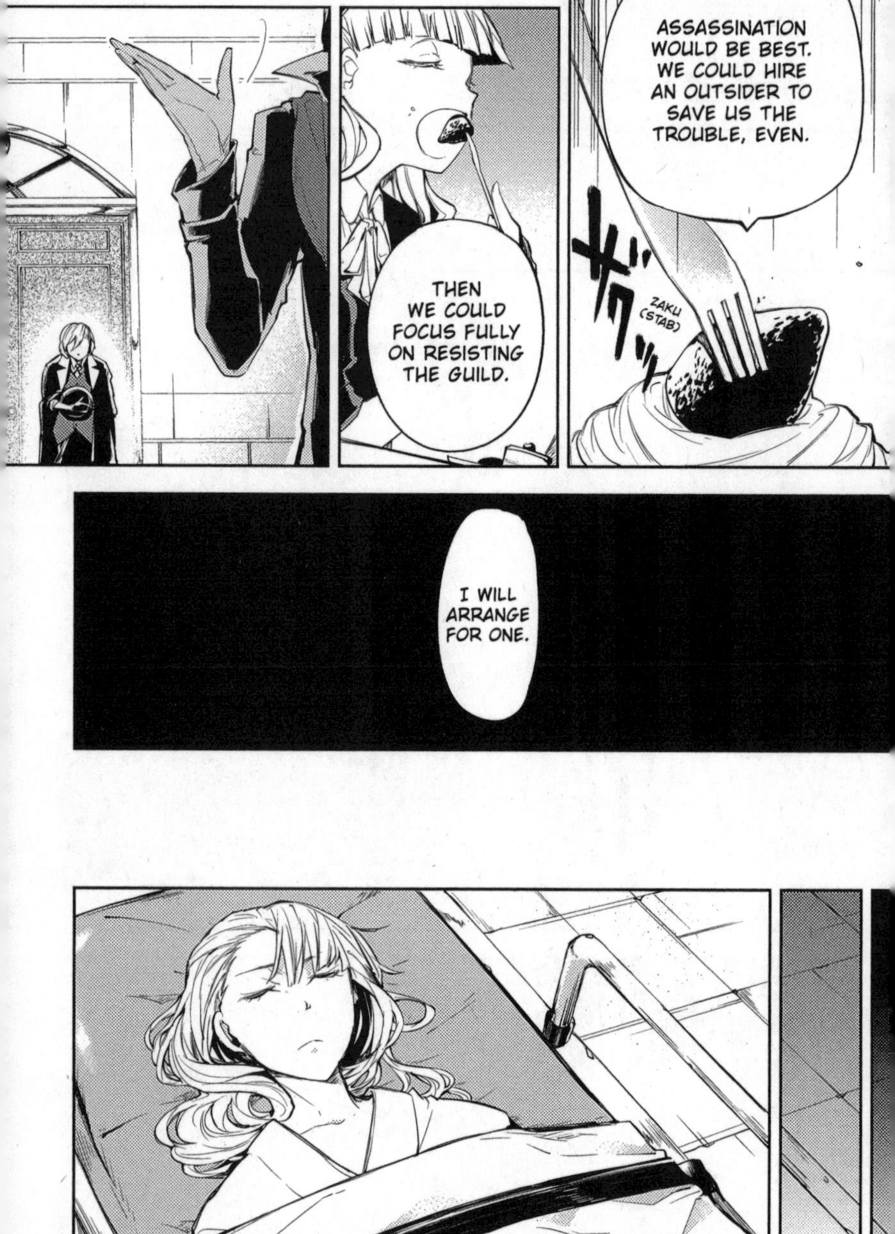
ASSASSINATION WOULD BE BEST. WE COULD HIRE AN OUTSIDER TO SAVE US THE TROUBLE, EVEN.
ZAKU (STAB)
THEN WE COULD FOCUS FULLY ON RESISTING THE GUILD.
I WILL ARRANGE FOR ONE.

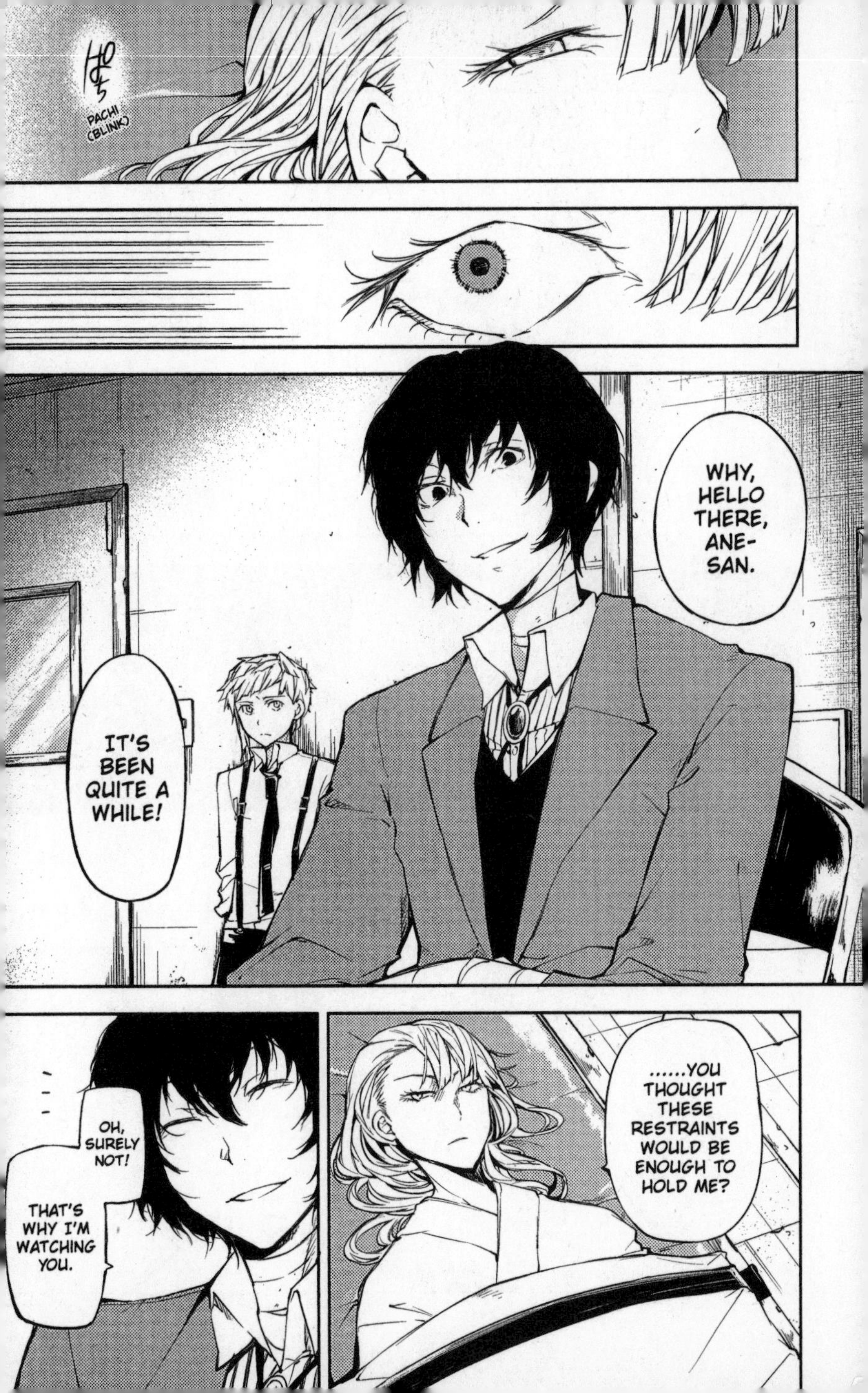
PACHI (BLINK)
WHY, HELLO THERE, ANE-SAN.
IT'S BEEN QUITE A WHILE!
......YOU THOUGHT THESE RESTRAINTS WOULD BE ENOUGH TO HOLD ME?
OH, SURELY NOT!
THAT'S WHY I'M WATCHING YOU.

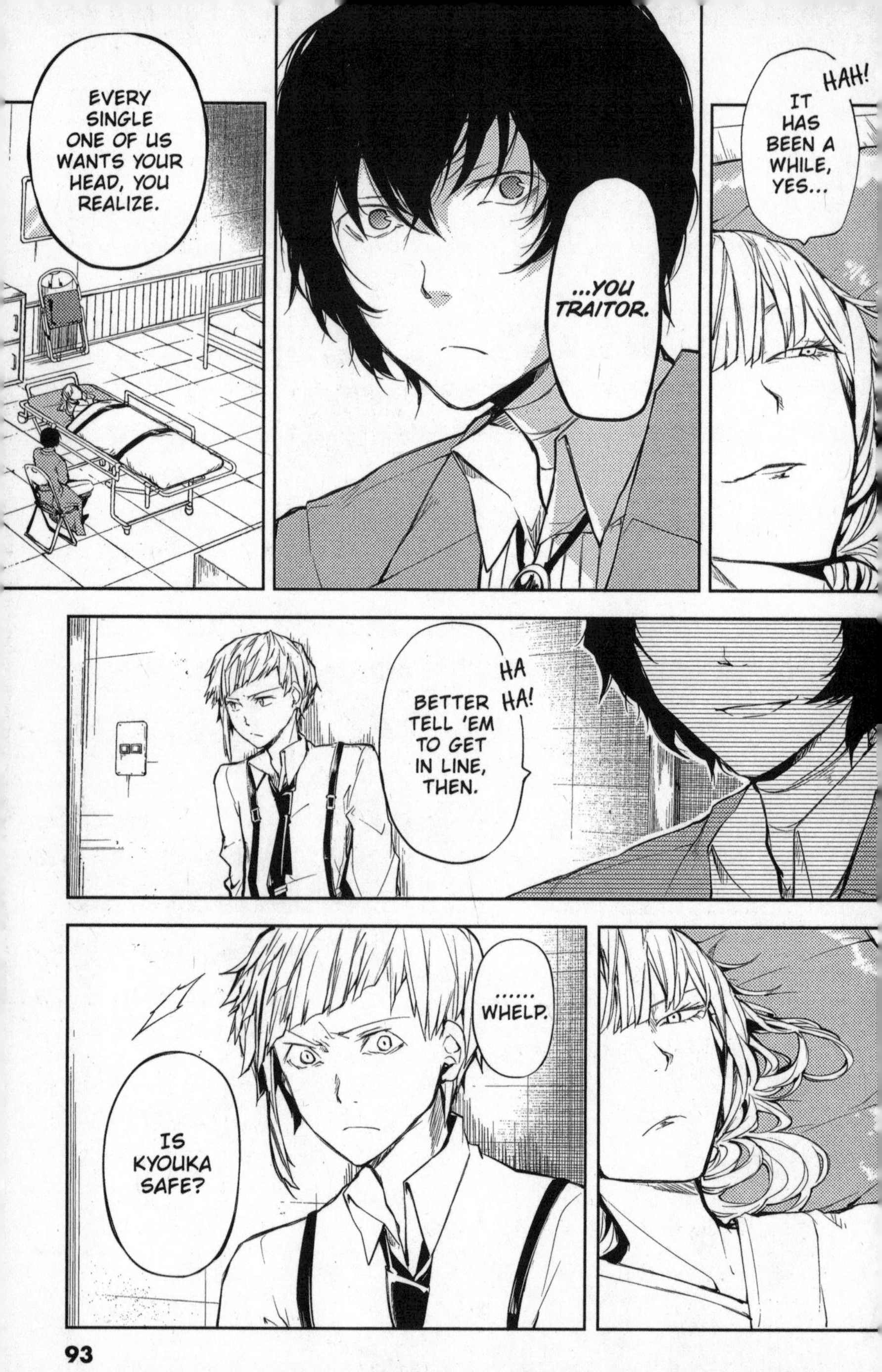
HAH!
IT HAS BEEN A WHILE, YES...
...YOU TRAITOR.
EVERY SINGLE ONE OF US WANTS YOUR HEAD, YOU REALIZE.
HA HA!
BETTER TELL 'EM TO GET IN LINE, THEN.
......WHELP.
IS KYOUKA SAFE?

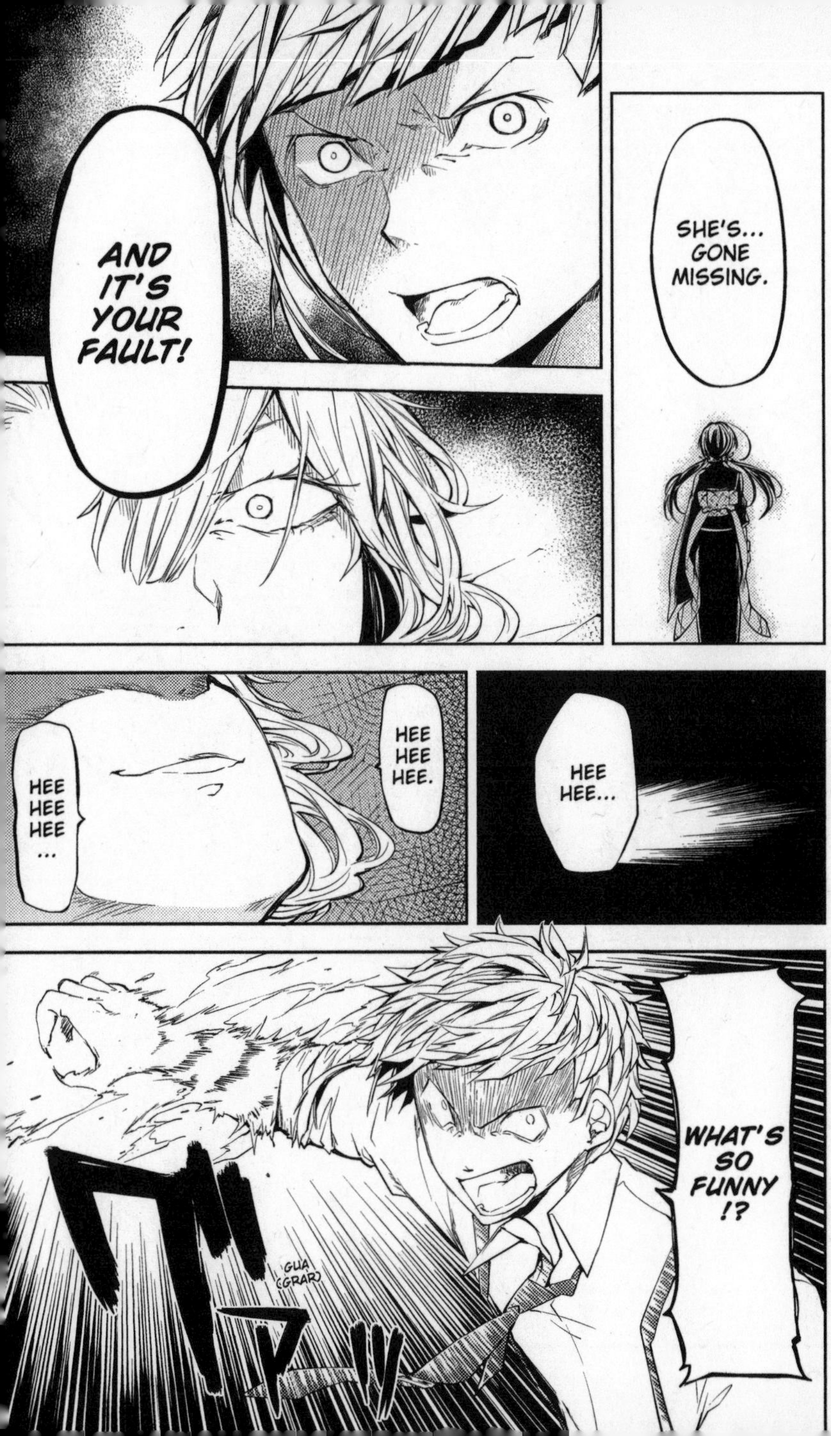
SHE'S... GONE MISSING.
AND IT'S YOUR FAULT!
HEE HEE...
HEE HEE HEE.
HEE HEE HEE ...
WHAT'S SO FUNNY !?
GUA (GRAR)

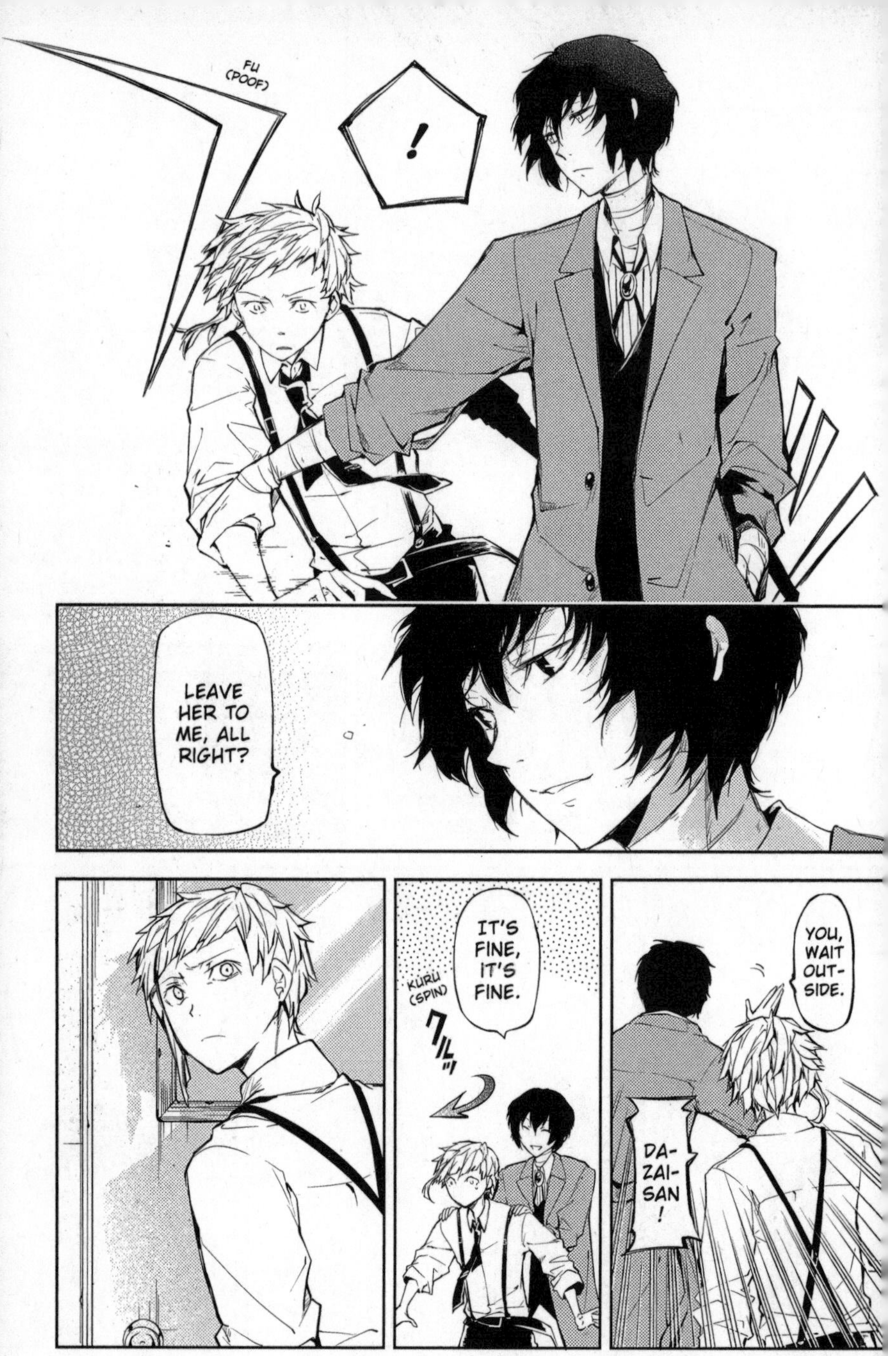
!
FU (POOF)
LEAVE HER TO ME, ALL RIGHT?
YOU, WAIT OUT-SIDE.
DA-ZAI-SAN!
IT'S FINE, IT'S FINE.
KURU (SPIN)

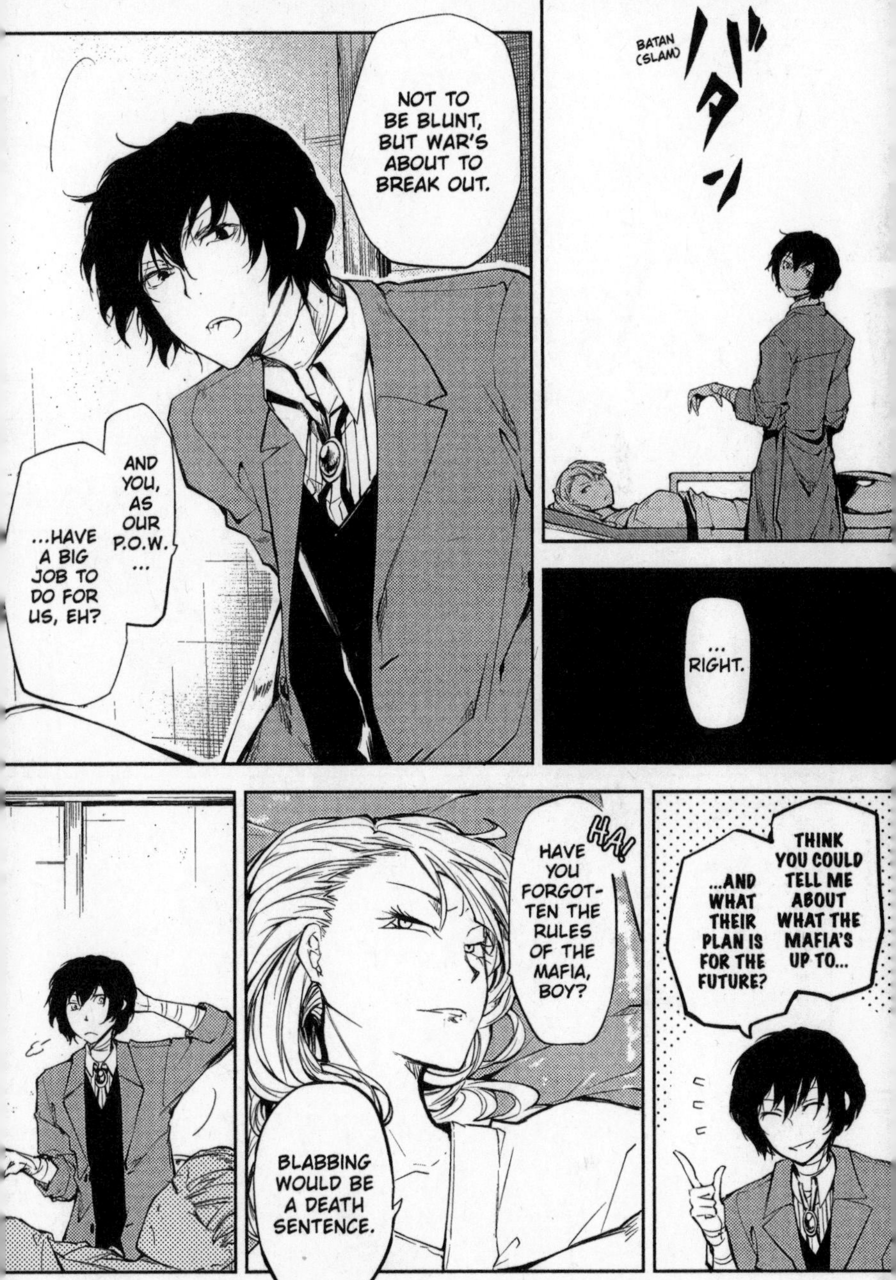
BATAN (SLAM)
... RIGHT.
NOT TO BE BLUNT, BUT WAR'S ABOUT TO BREAK OUT.
AND YOU, AS OUR P.O.W. ...
...HAVE A BIG JOB TO DO FOR US, EH?
THINK YOU COULD TELL ME ABOUT WHAT THE MAFIA'S UP TO...
...AND WHAT THEIR PLAN IS FOR THE FUTURE?
HA!
HAVE YOU FORGOTTEN THE RULES OF THE MAFIA, BOY?
BLABBING WOULD BE A DEATH SENTENCE.

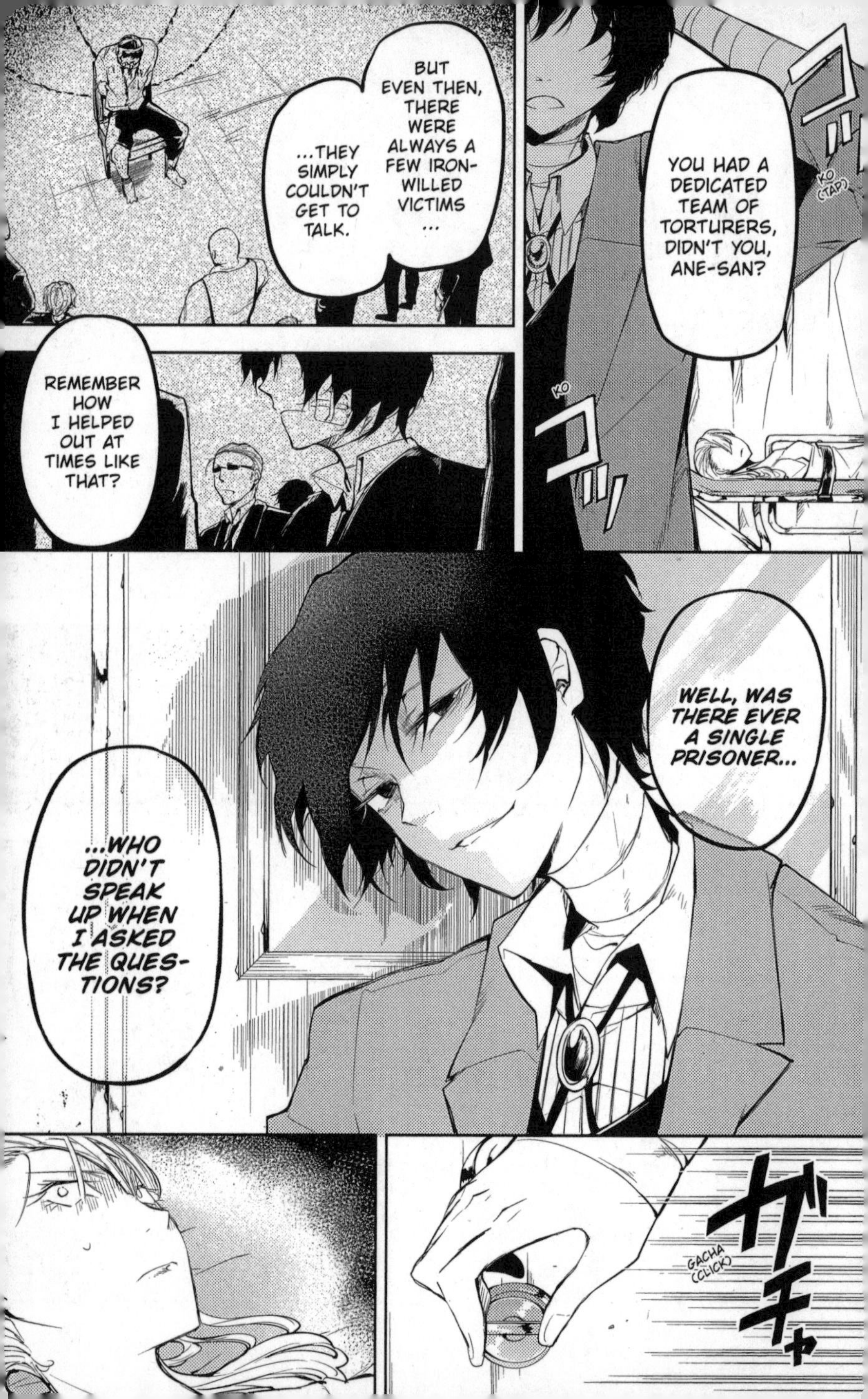
YOU HAD A DEDICATED TEAM OF TORTURERS, DIDN'T YOU, ANE-SAN?
KO (TAP)
KO
BUT EVEN THEN, THERE WERE ALWAYS A FEW IRON-WILLED VICTIMS...
...THEY SIMPLY COULDN'T GET TO TALK.
REMEMBER HOW I HELPED OUT AT TIMES LIKE THAT?
WELL, WAS THERE EVER A SINGLE PRISONER...
...WHO DIDN'T SPEAK UP WHEN I ASKED THE QUESTIONS?
GACHA (CLICK)

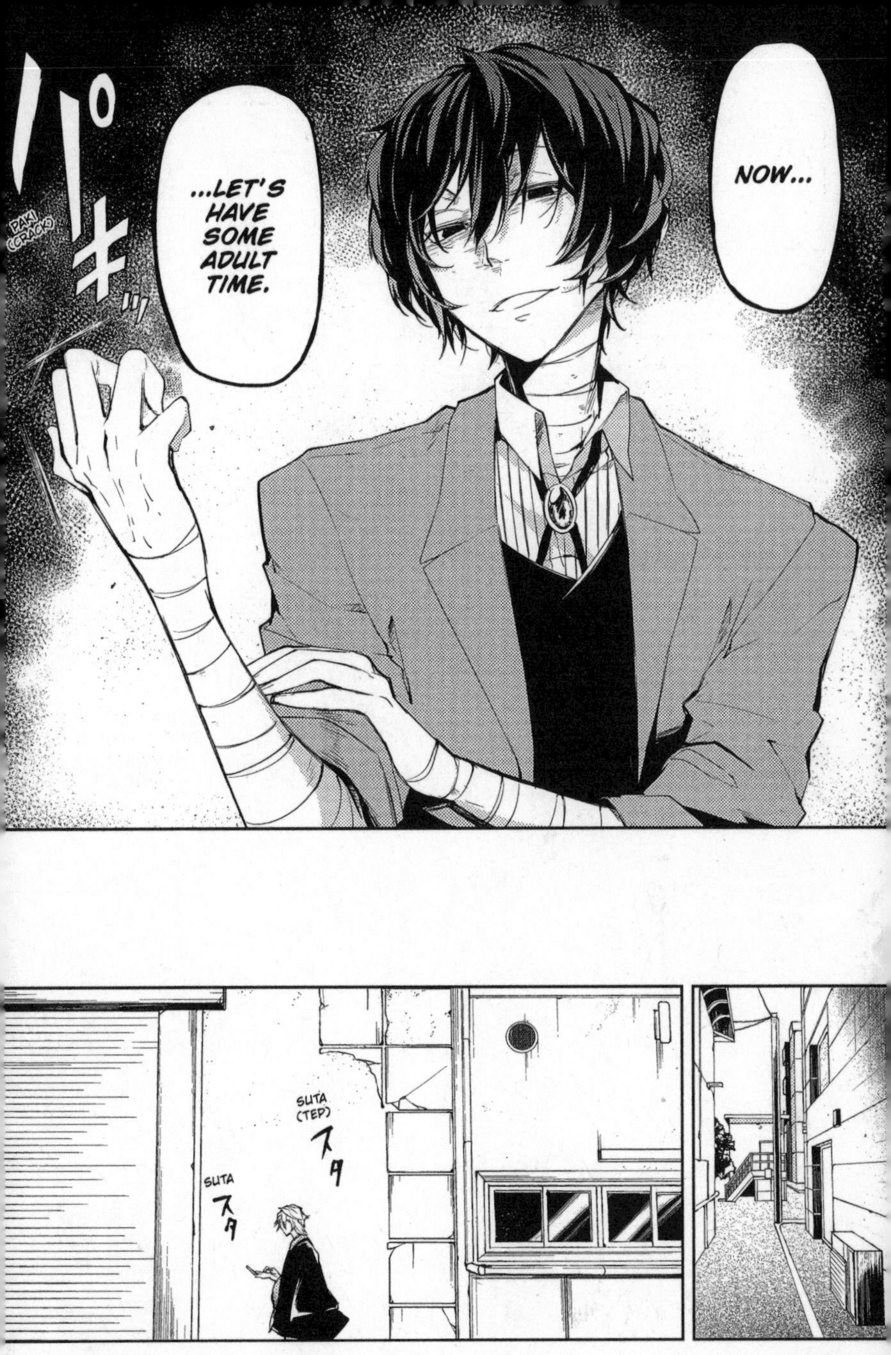
NOW...
...LET'S HAVE SOME ADULT TIME.
PAKI (CRACK)
SUTA (TEP)
SUTA

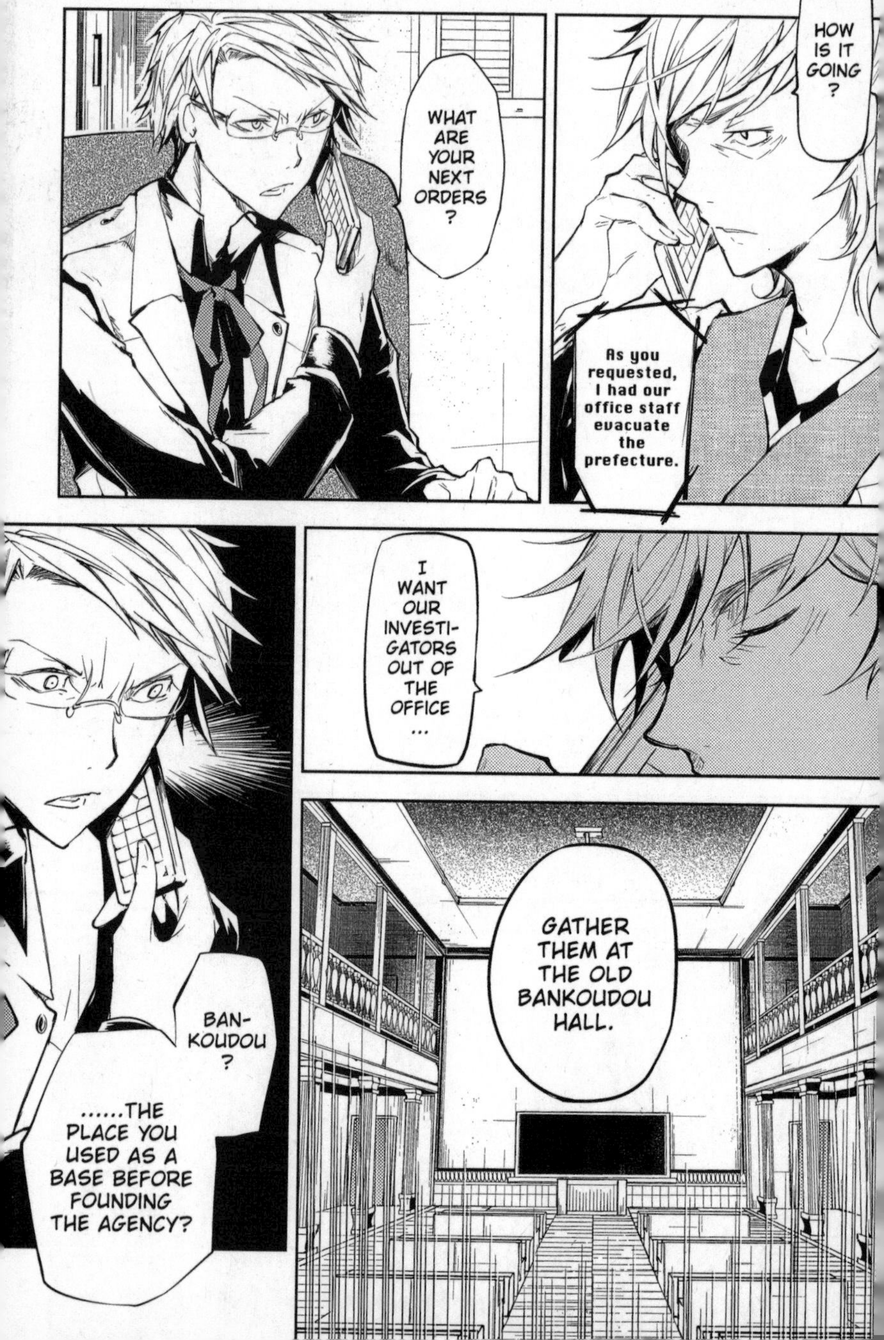
HOW IS IT GOING?
As you requested, I had our office staff evacuate the prefecture.
WHAT ARE YOUR NEXT ORDERS?
I WANT OUR INVESTIGATORS OUT OF THE OFFICE...
GATHER THEM AT THE OLD BANKOUDOU HALL.
BANKOUDOU?
......THE PLACE YOU USED AS A BASE BEFORE FOUNDING THE AGENCY?

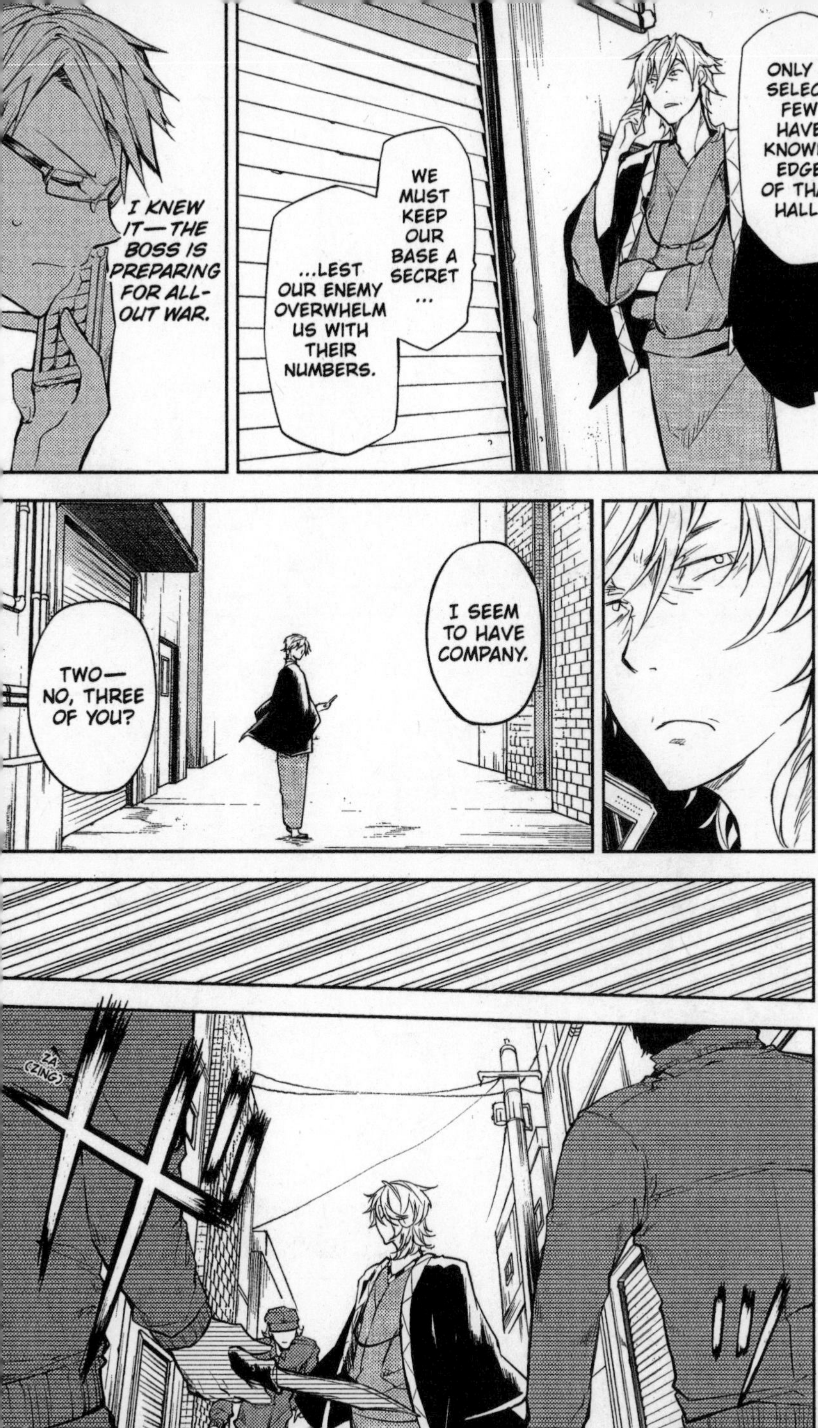
ONLY A SELECT FEW HAVE KNOWLEDGE OF THAT HALL.
WE MUST KEEP OUR BASE A SECRET...
...LEST OUR ENEMY OVERWHELM US WITH THEIR NUMBERS.
I KNEW IT—THE BOSS IS PREPARING FOR ALL-OUT WAR.
I SEEM TO HAVE COMPANY.
TWO—NO, THREE OF YOU?
ZA (ZING)

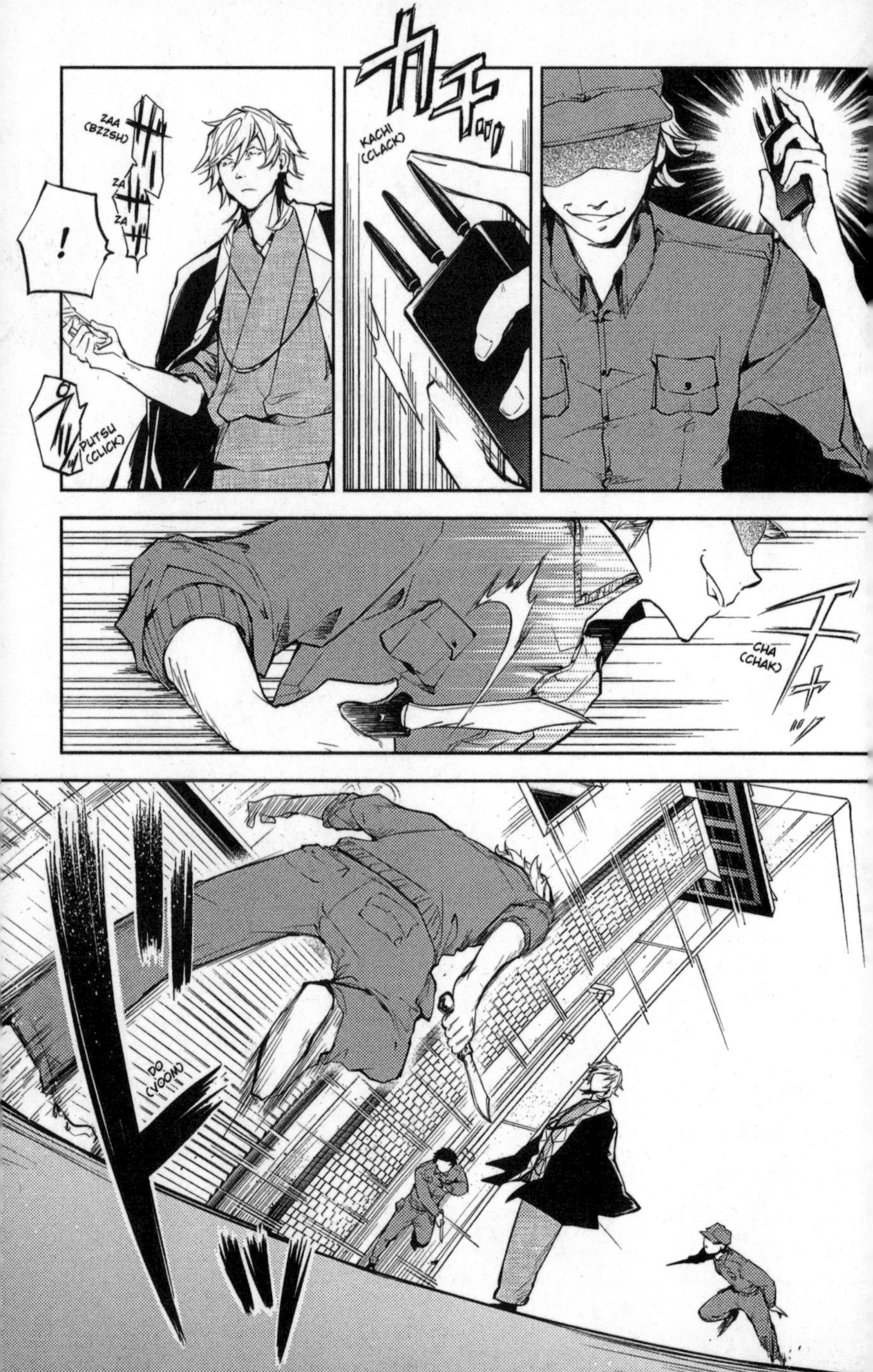
カチ
KACHI (CLACK)
ZAA (BZZSH)
ZA
ZA
!
PUTSU (CLICK)
CHA (CHAK)
DO (VOOM)

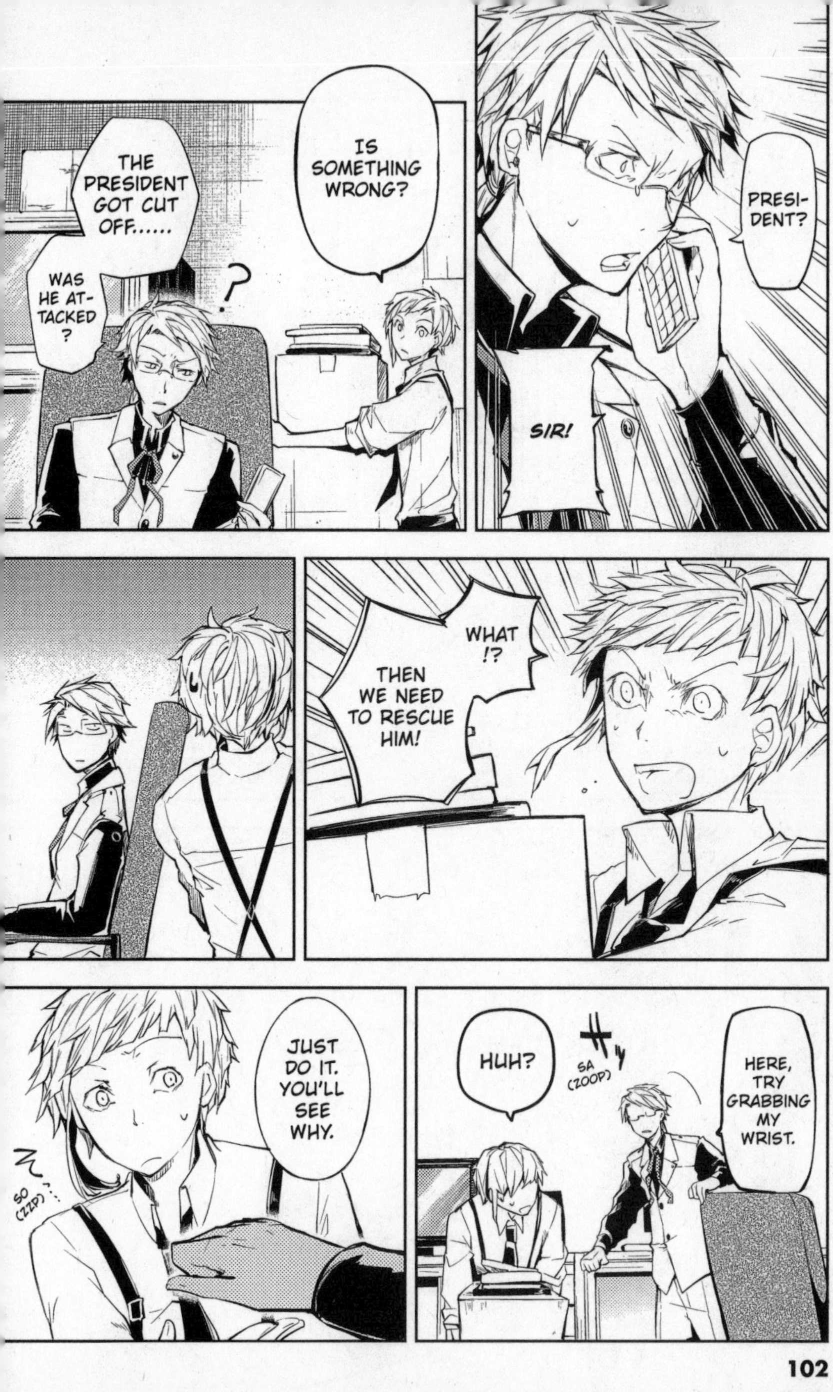
PRESI-DENT?
SIR!
IS SOMETHING WRONG?
THE PRESIDENT GOT CUT OFF......
WAS HE AT-TACKED?
WHAT!?
THEN WE NEED TO RESCUE HIM!
HERE, TRY GRABBING MY WRIST.
SA (ZOOP)
HUH?
JUST DO IT. YOU'LL SEE WHY.
SO (ZZP)...

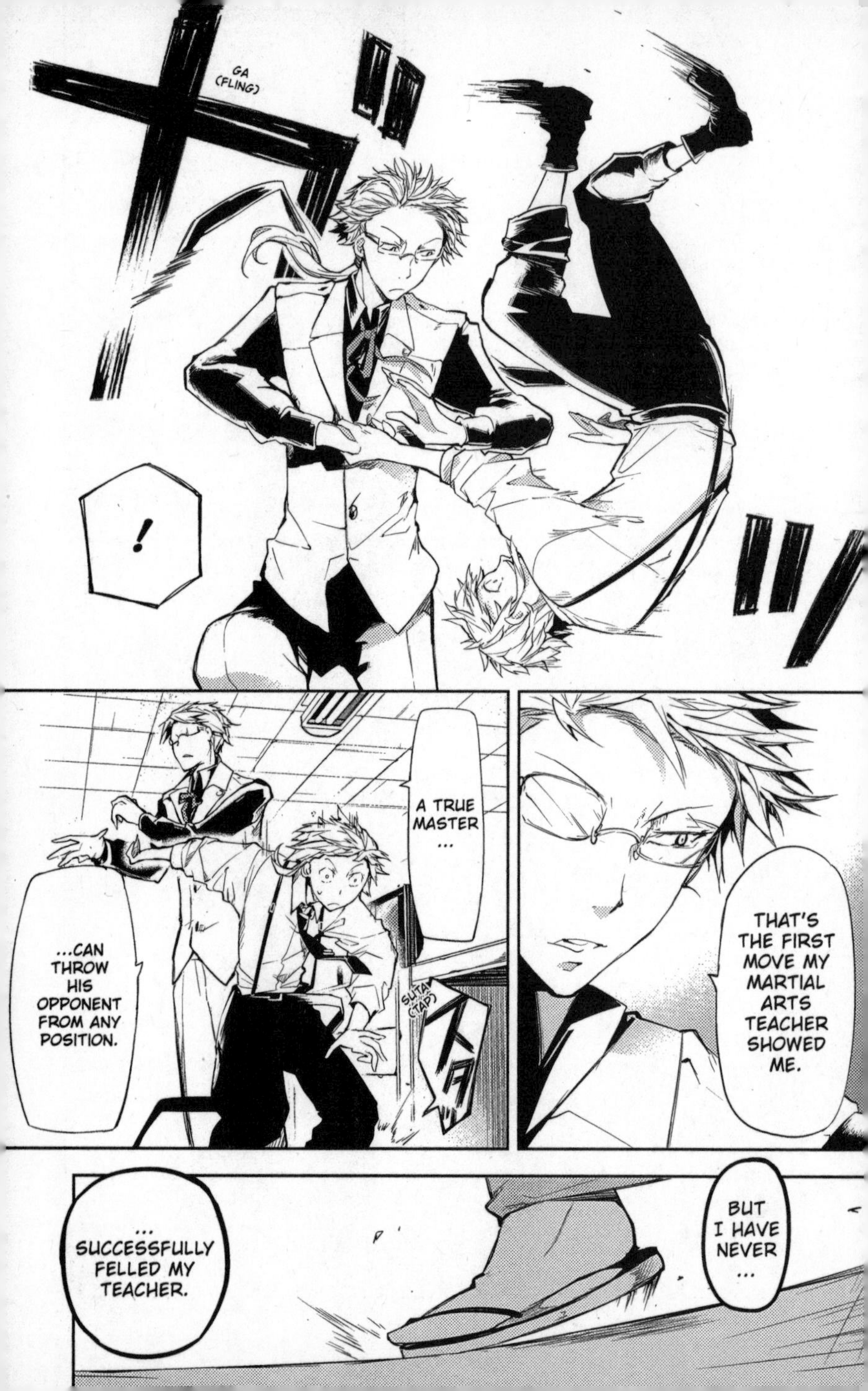
GA (FLING)
!
THAT'S THE FIRST MOVE MY MARTIAL ARTS TEACHER SHOWED ME.
A TRUE MASTER...
...CAN THROW HIS OPPONENT FROM ANY POSITION.
SUTA (TAP)
BUT I HAVE NEVER...
...SUCCESSFULLY FELLED MY TEACHER.

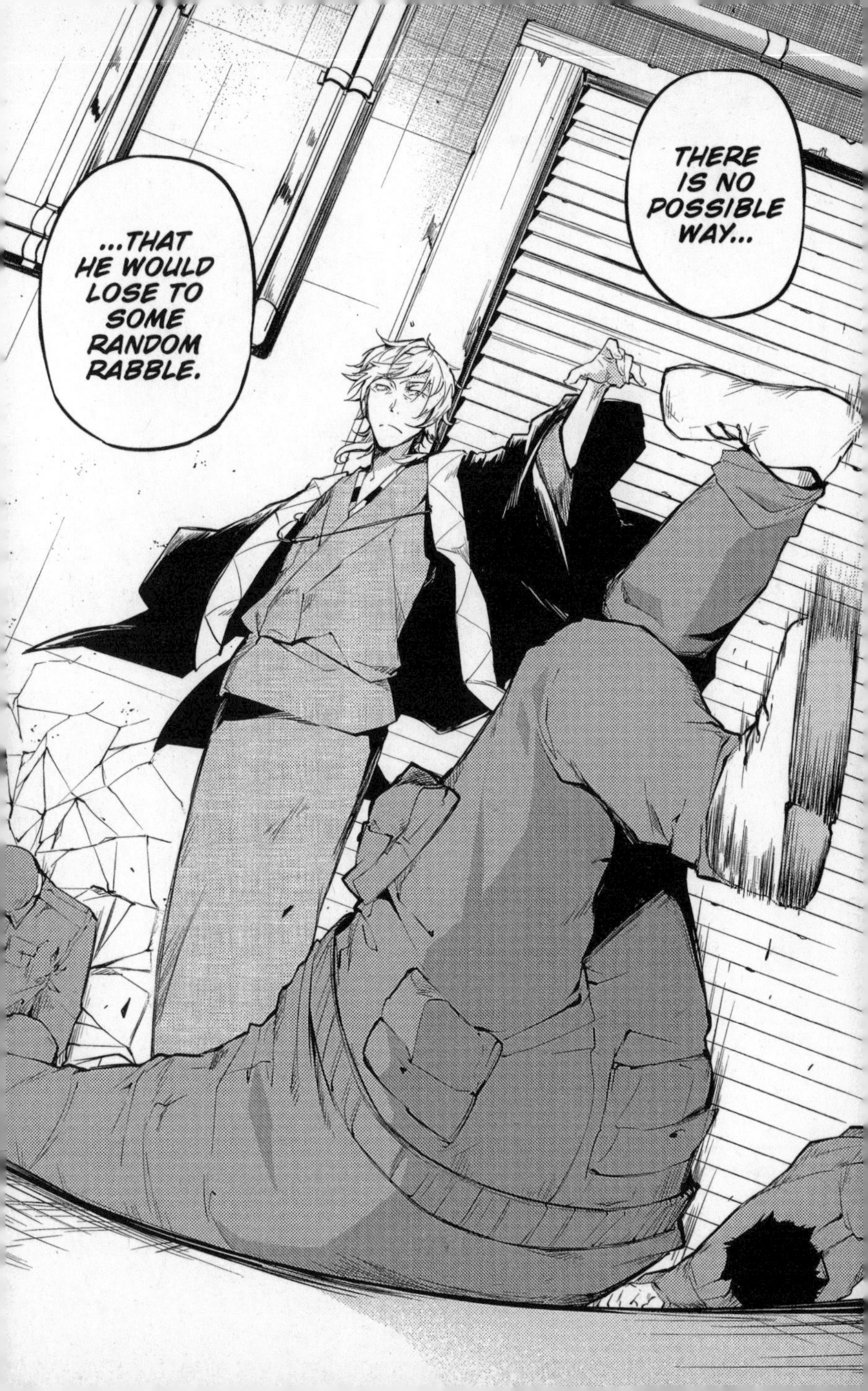
THERE IS NO POSSIBLE WAY...
...THAT HE WOULD LOSE TO SOME RANDOM RABBLE.

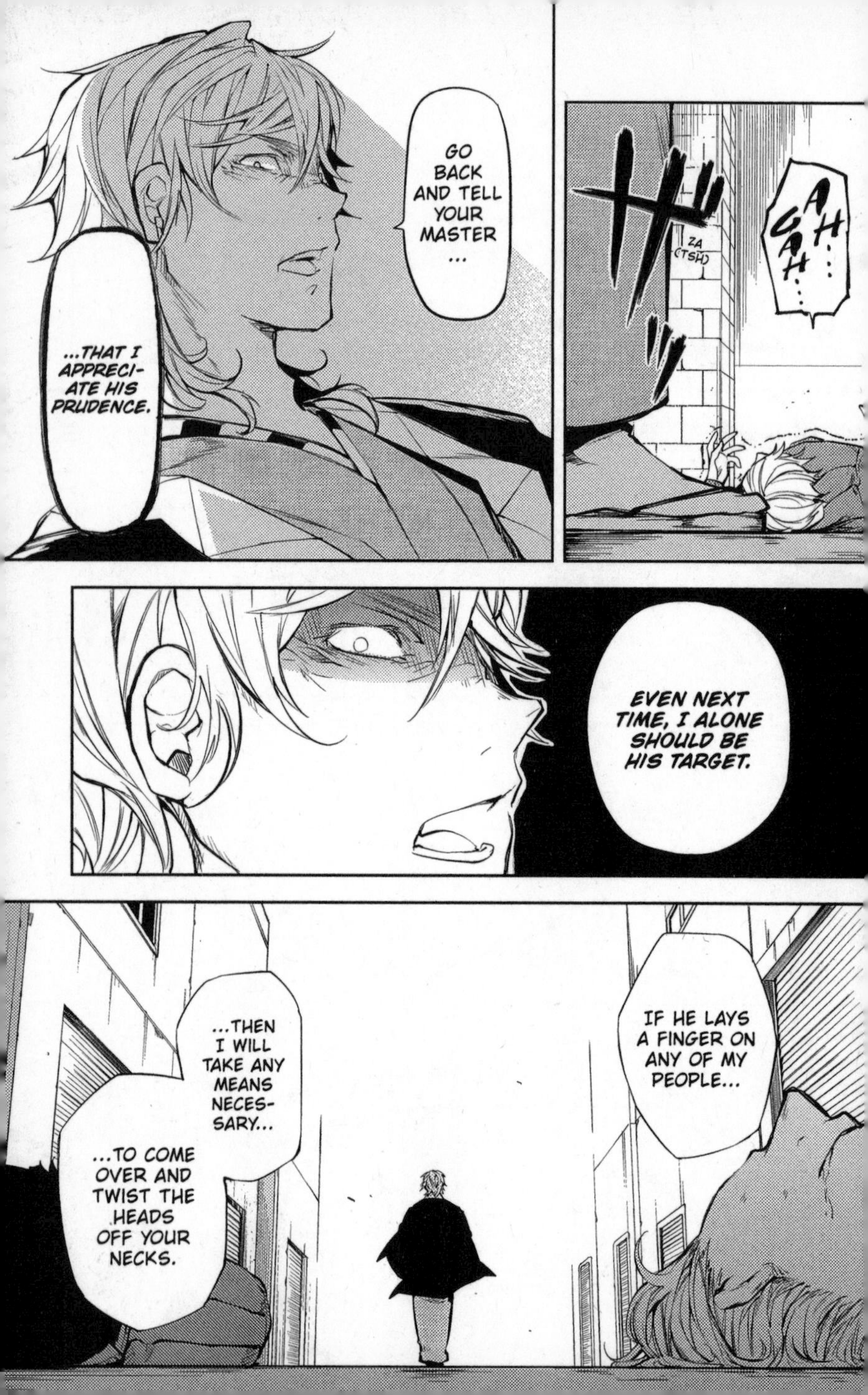
AH... GAH...
ZA (TSH)
GO BACK AND TELL YOUR MASTER...
...THAT I APPRECIATE HIS PRUDENCE.
EVEN NEXT TIME, I ALONE SHOULD BE HIS TARGET.
IF HE LAYS A FINGER ON ANY OF MY PEOPLE...
...THEN I WILL TAKE ANY MEANS NECESSARY...
...TO COME OVER AND TWIST THE HEADS OFF YOUR NECKS.

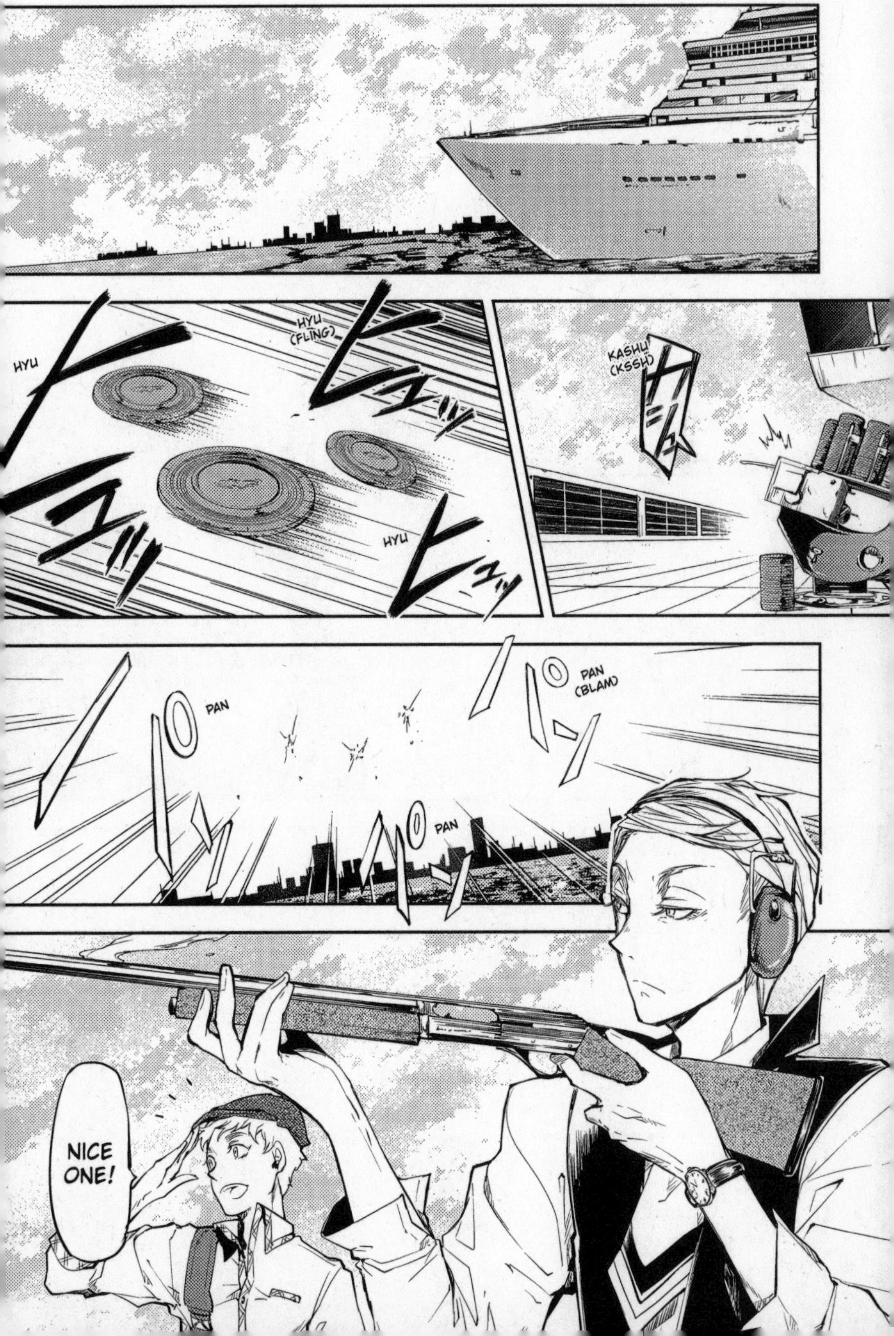
KASHU (KSSH)
HYU (FLING)
HYU
HYU
PAN (BLAM)
PAN
PAN
NICE ONE!

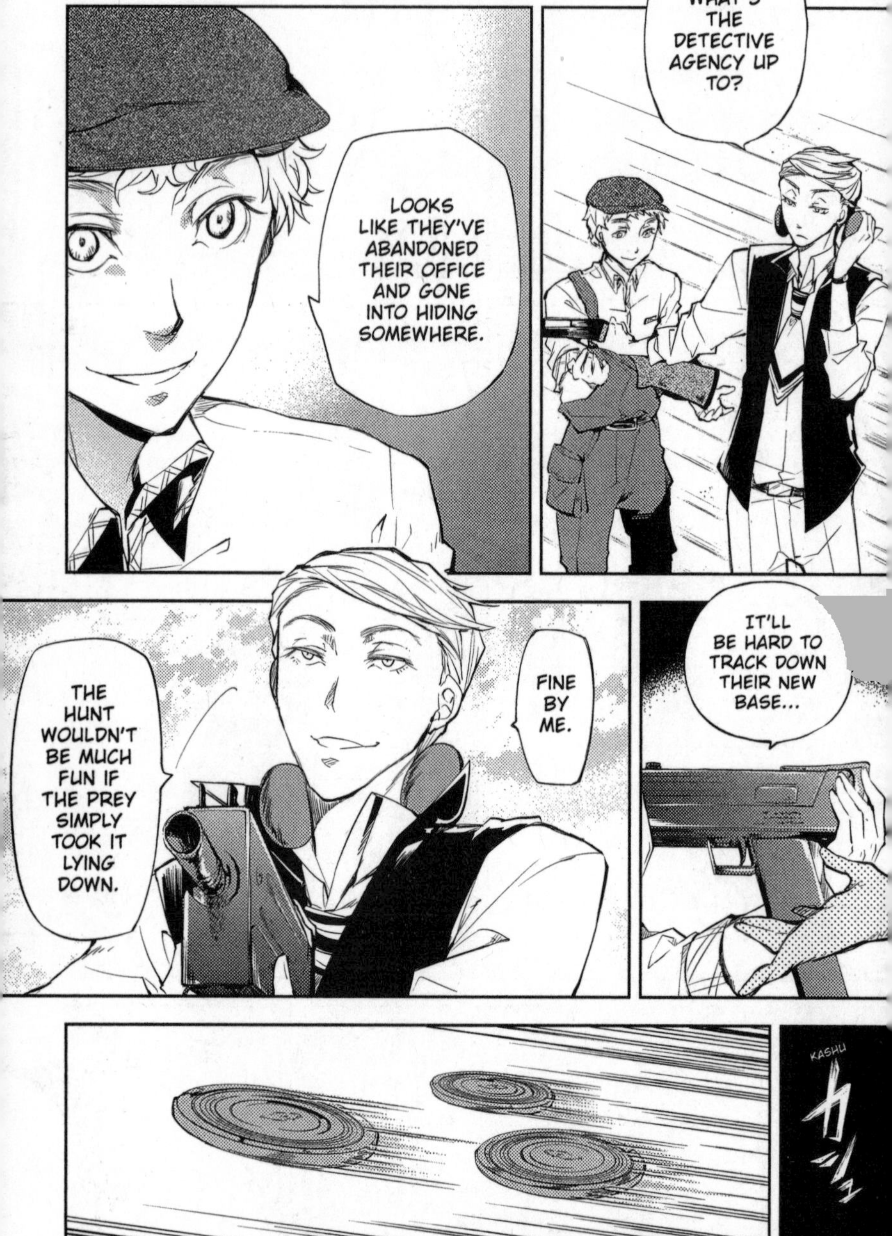
WHAT'S THE DETECTIVE AGENCY UP TO?
LOOKS LIKE THEY'VE ABANDONED THEIR OFFICE AND GONE INTO HIDING SOMEWHERE.
IT'LL BE HARD TO TRACK DOWN THEIR NEW BASE...
FINE BY ME.
THE HUNT WOULDN'T BE MUCH FUN IF THE PREY SIMPLY TOOK IT LYING DOWN.
KASHU

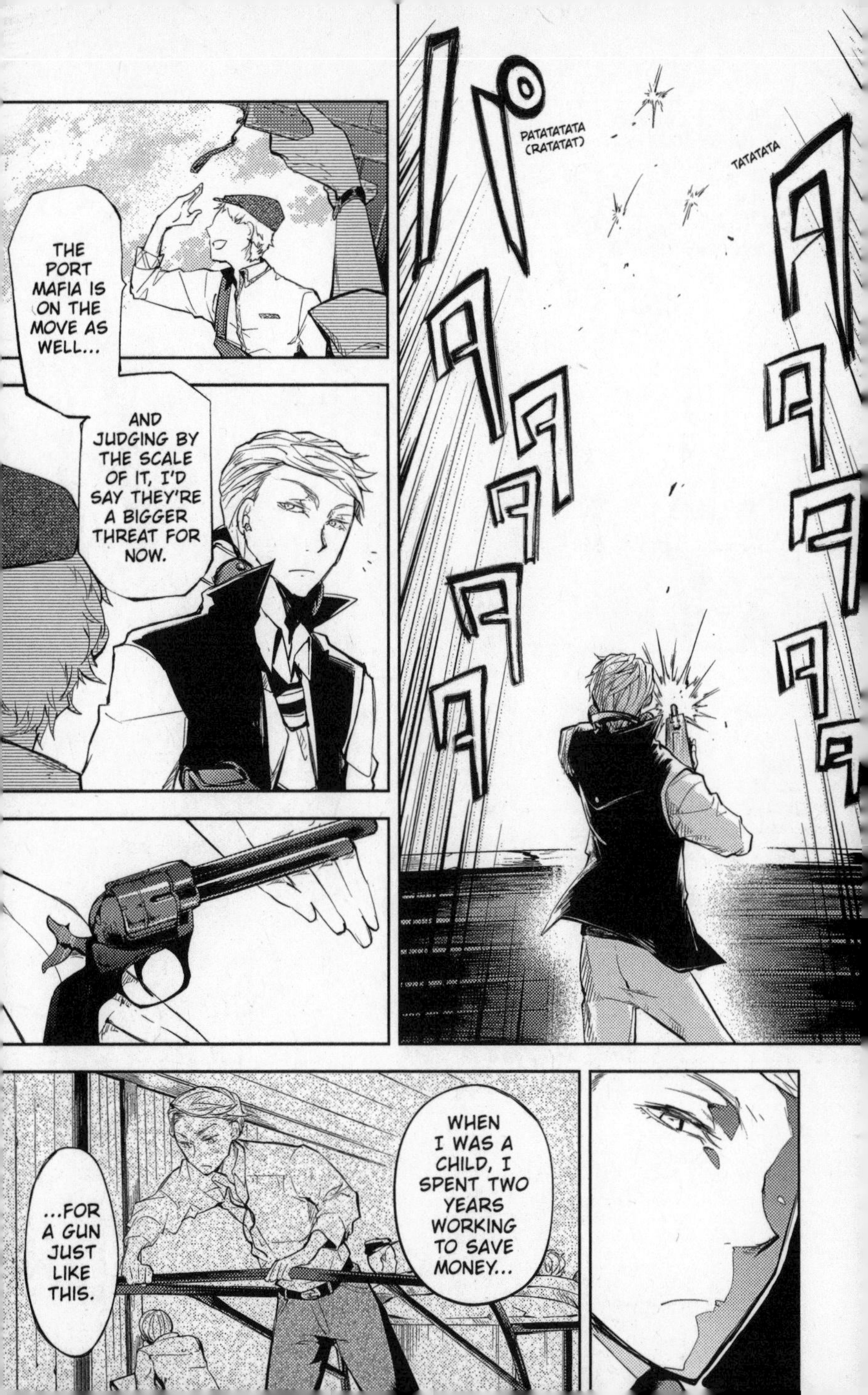
TATATATA
PATATATATA (RATATAT)
THE PORT MAFIA IS ON THE MOVE AS WELL...
AND JUDGING BY THE SCALE OF IT, I'D SAY THEY'RE A BIGGER THREAT FOR NOW.
WHEN I WAS A CHILD, I SPENT TWO YEARS WORKING TO SAVE MONEY...
...FOR A GUN JUST LIKE THIS.

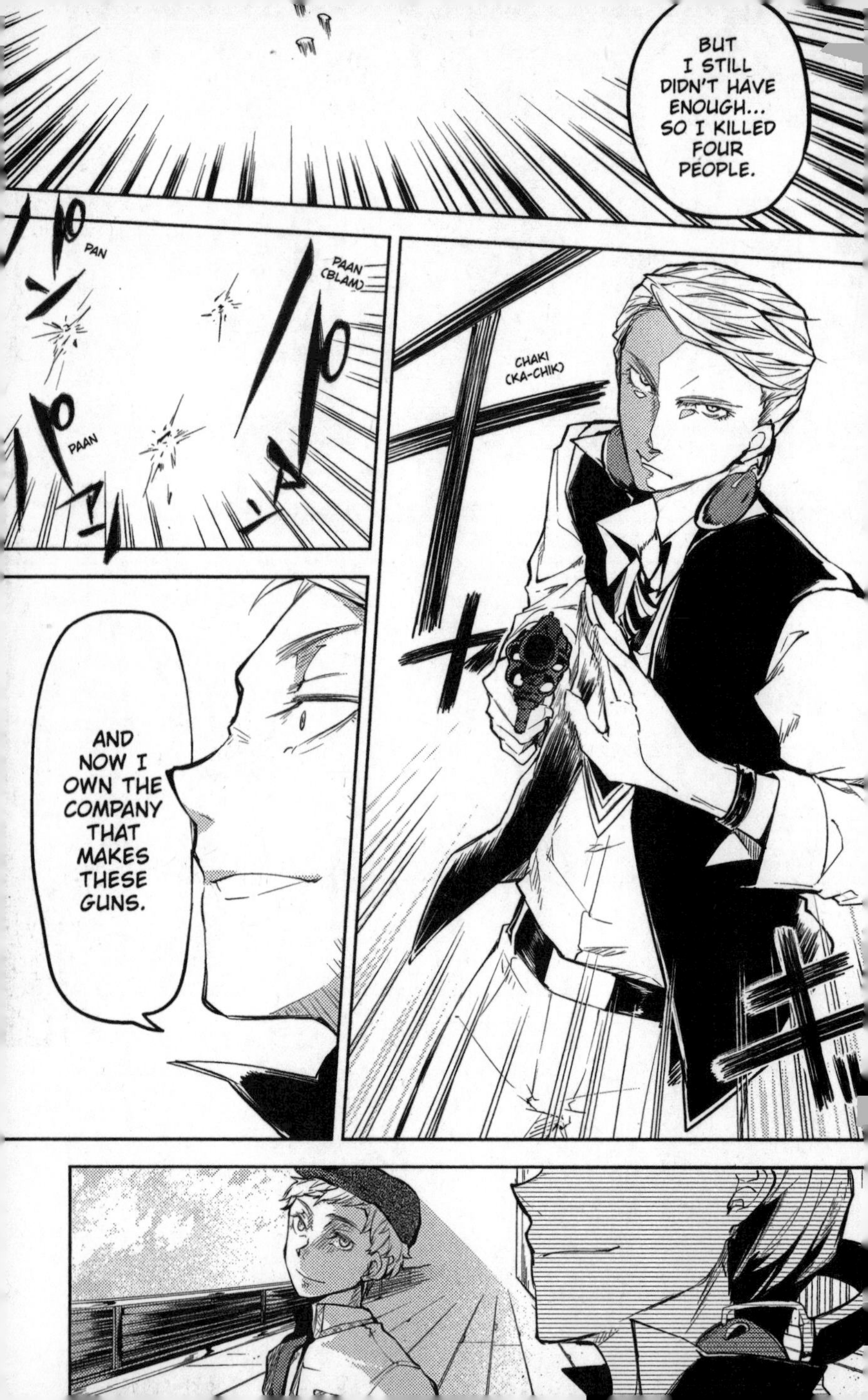
BUT I STILL DIDN'T HAVE ENOUGH... SO I KILLED FOUR PEOPLE.
CHAKI (KA-CHIK)
PAAN (BLAM)
PAN
PAAN
AND NOW I OWN THE COMPANY THAT MAKES THESE GUNS.

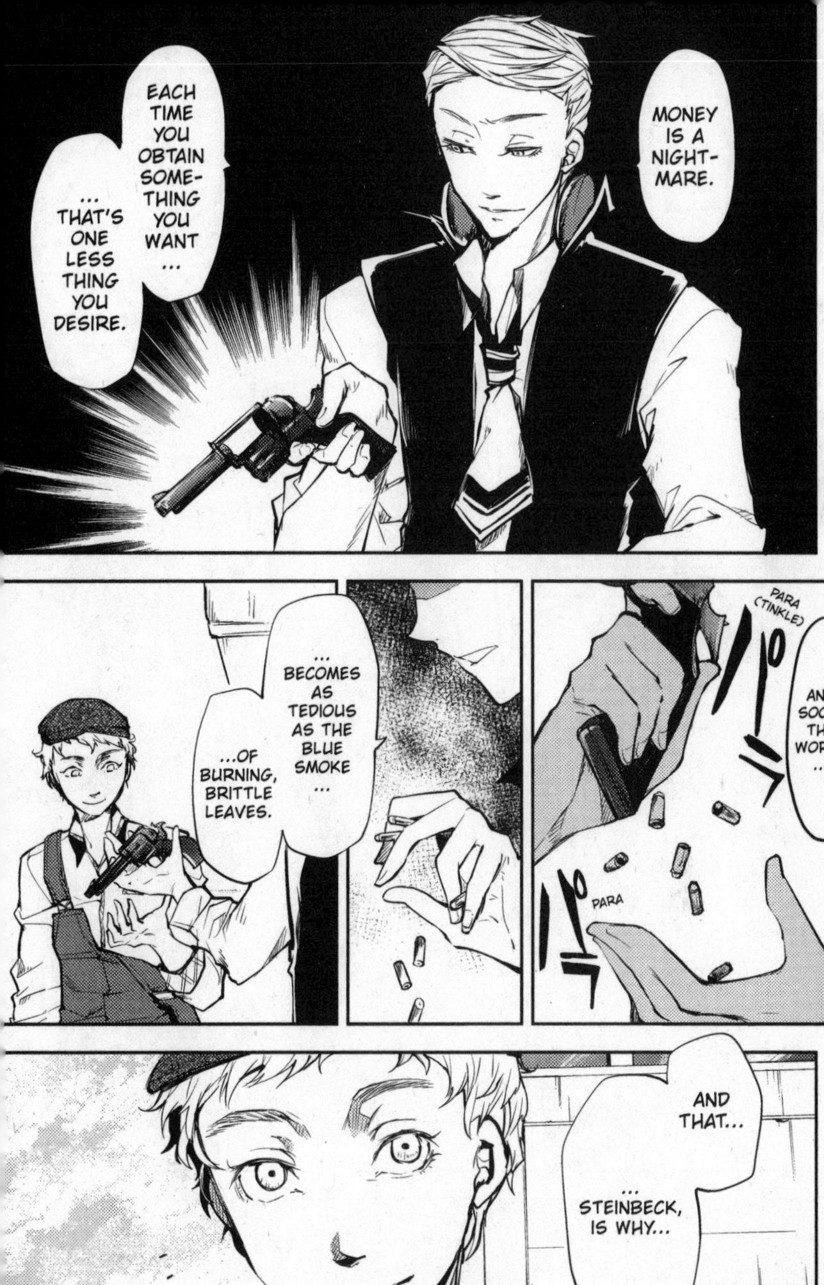
MONEY IS A NIGHT-MARE.
EACH TIME YOU OBTAIN SOME-THING YOU WANT...
...THAT'S ONE LESS THING YOU DESIRE.
PARA (TINKLE)
AND SOON, THE WORLD...
PARA
...BECOMES AS TEDIOUS AS THE BLUE SMOKE...
...OF BURNING, BRITTLE LEAVES.
AND THAT...
...STEINBECK, IS WHY...

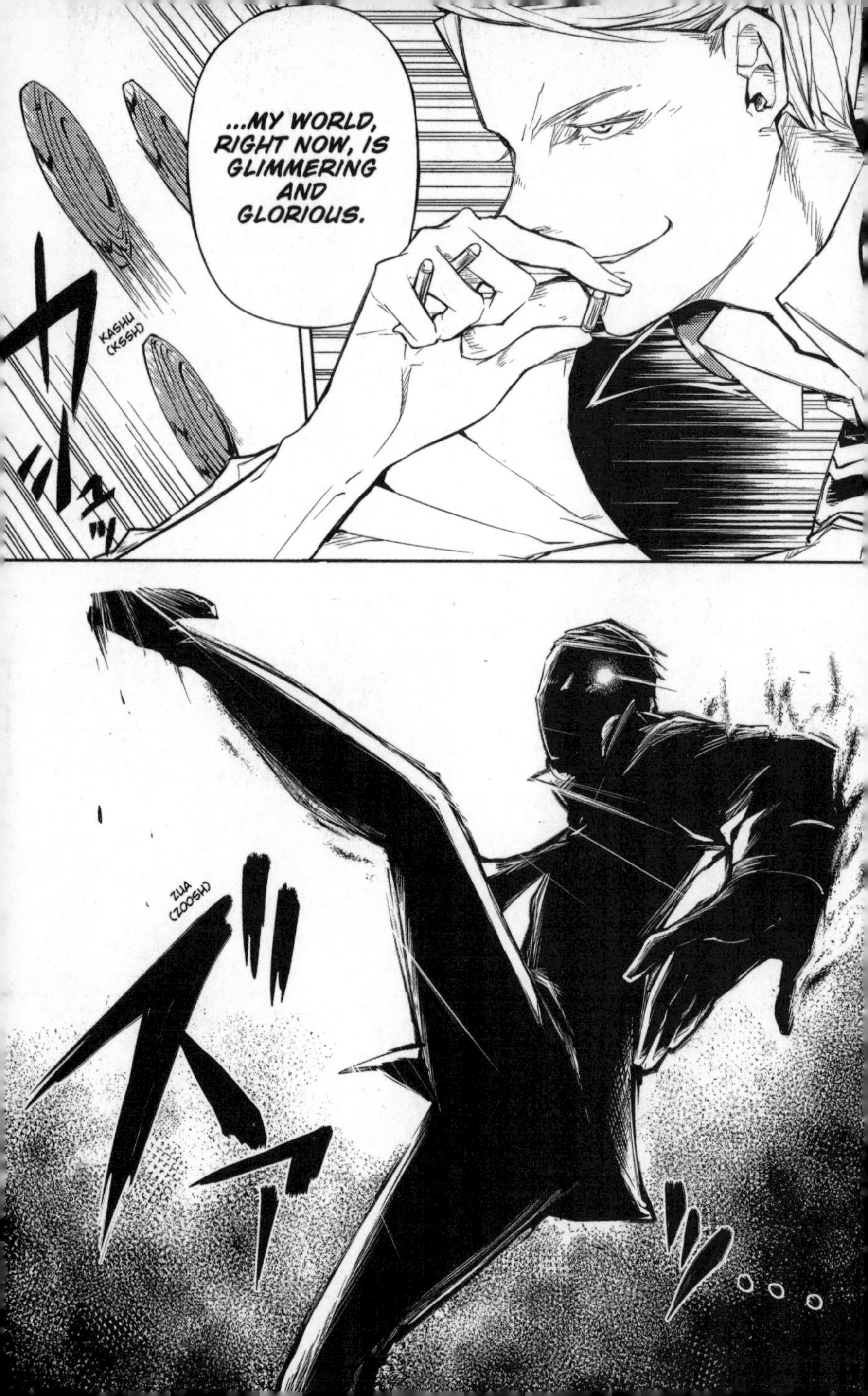
...MY WORLD, RIGHT NOW, IS GLIMMERING AND GLORIOUS.
KASHU (KSSH)
ZUA (ZOOSH)

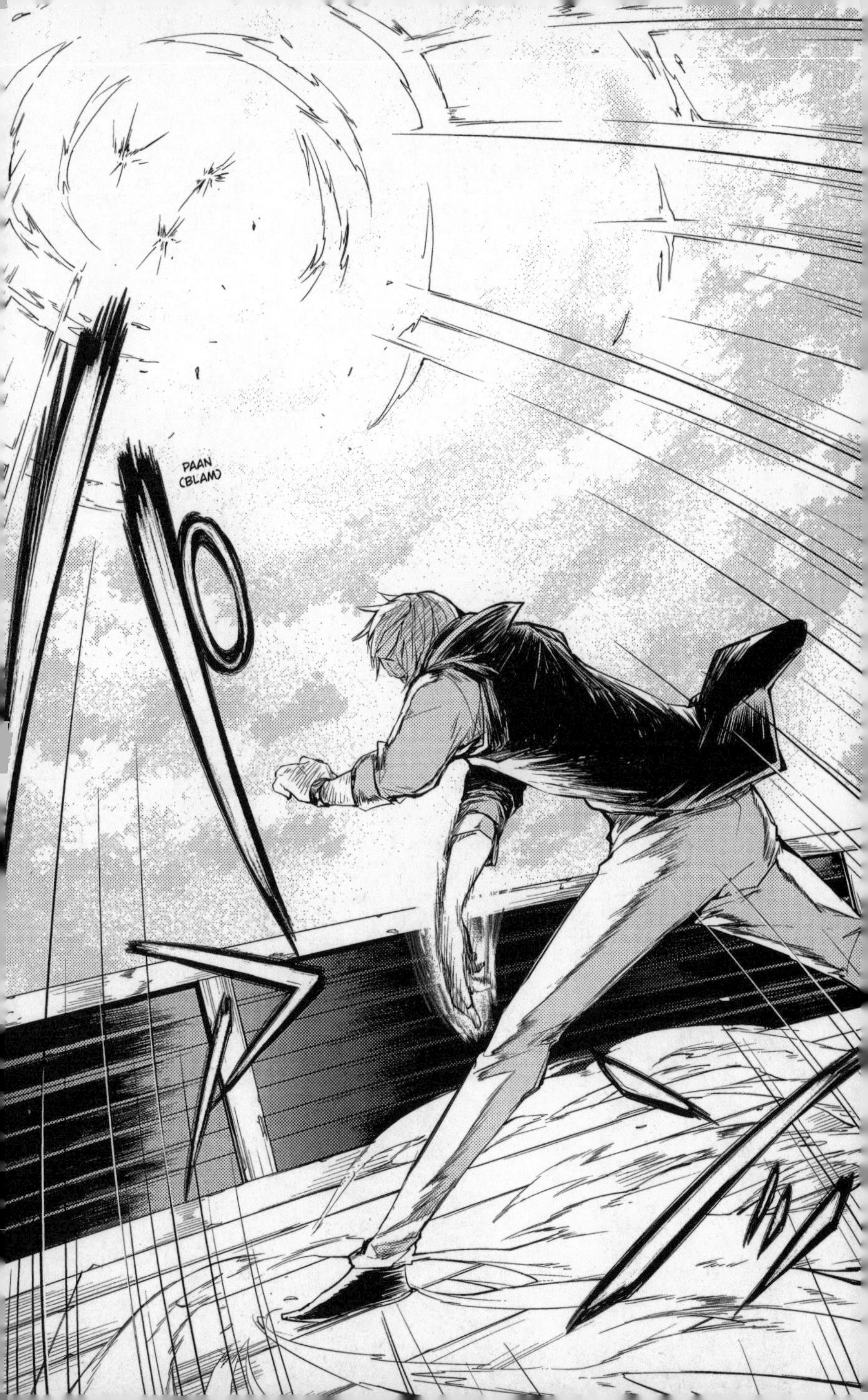
PAAN
(BLAM)

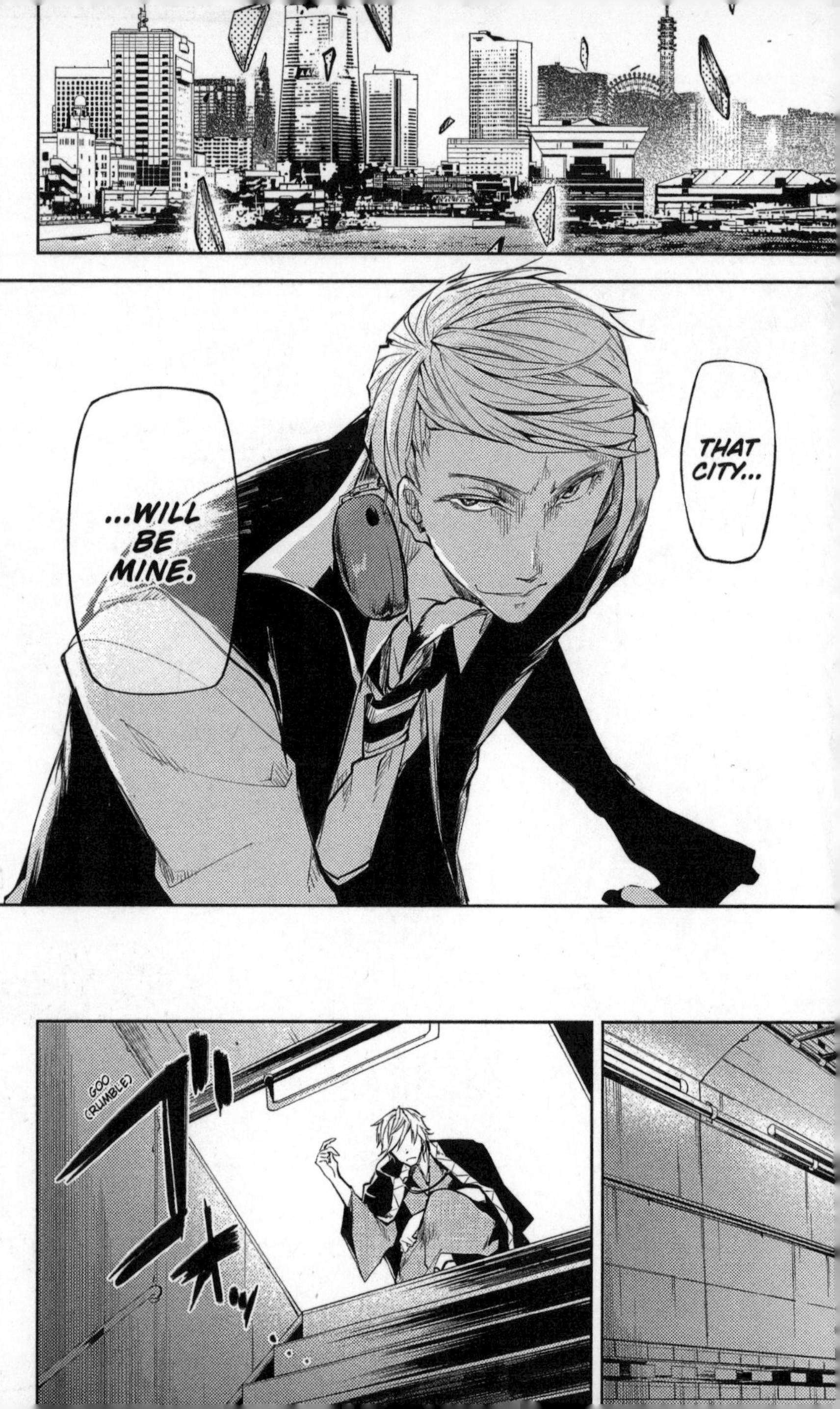
THAT CITY...
...WILL BE MINE.
GOO (RUMBLE)

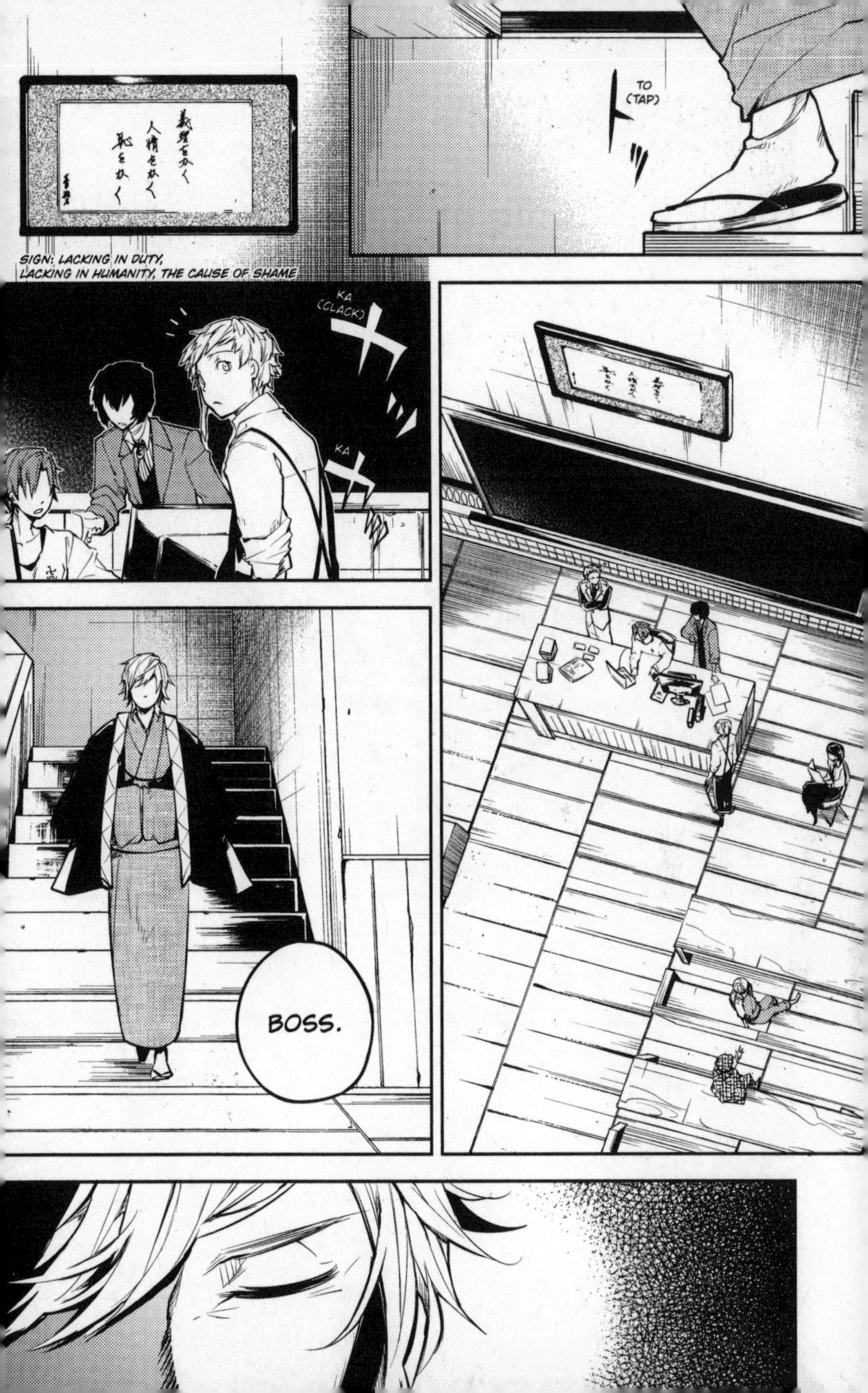
TO (TAP)
SIGN: LACKING IN DUTY, LACKING IN HUMANITY, THE CAUSE OF SHAME
KA (CLACK)
KA
BOSS.

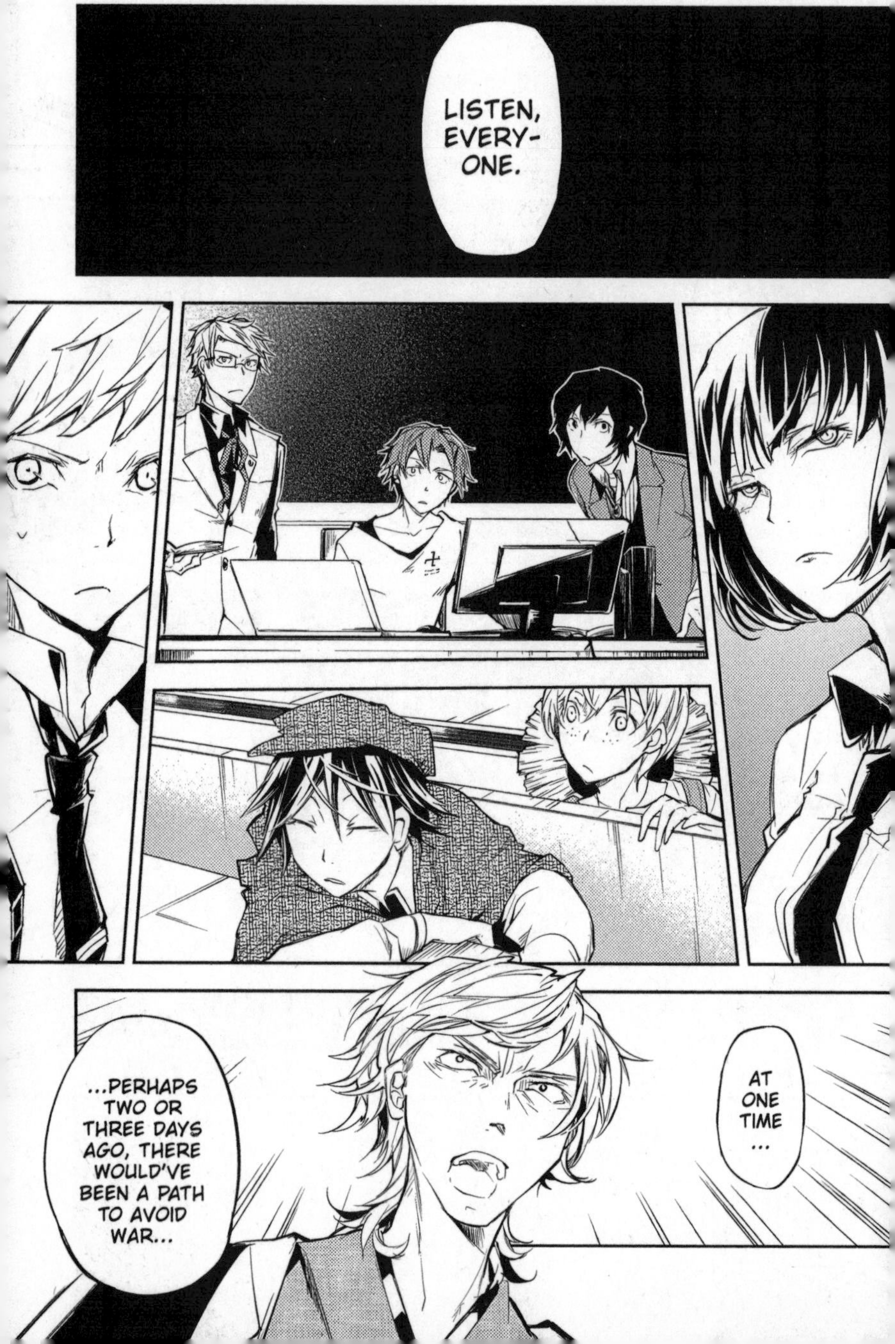
LISTEN, EVERY-ONE.
AT ONE TIME ...
...PERHAPS TWO OR THREE DAYS AGO, THERE WOULD'VE BEEN A PATH TO AVOID WAR...

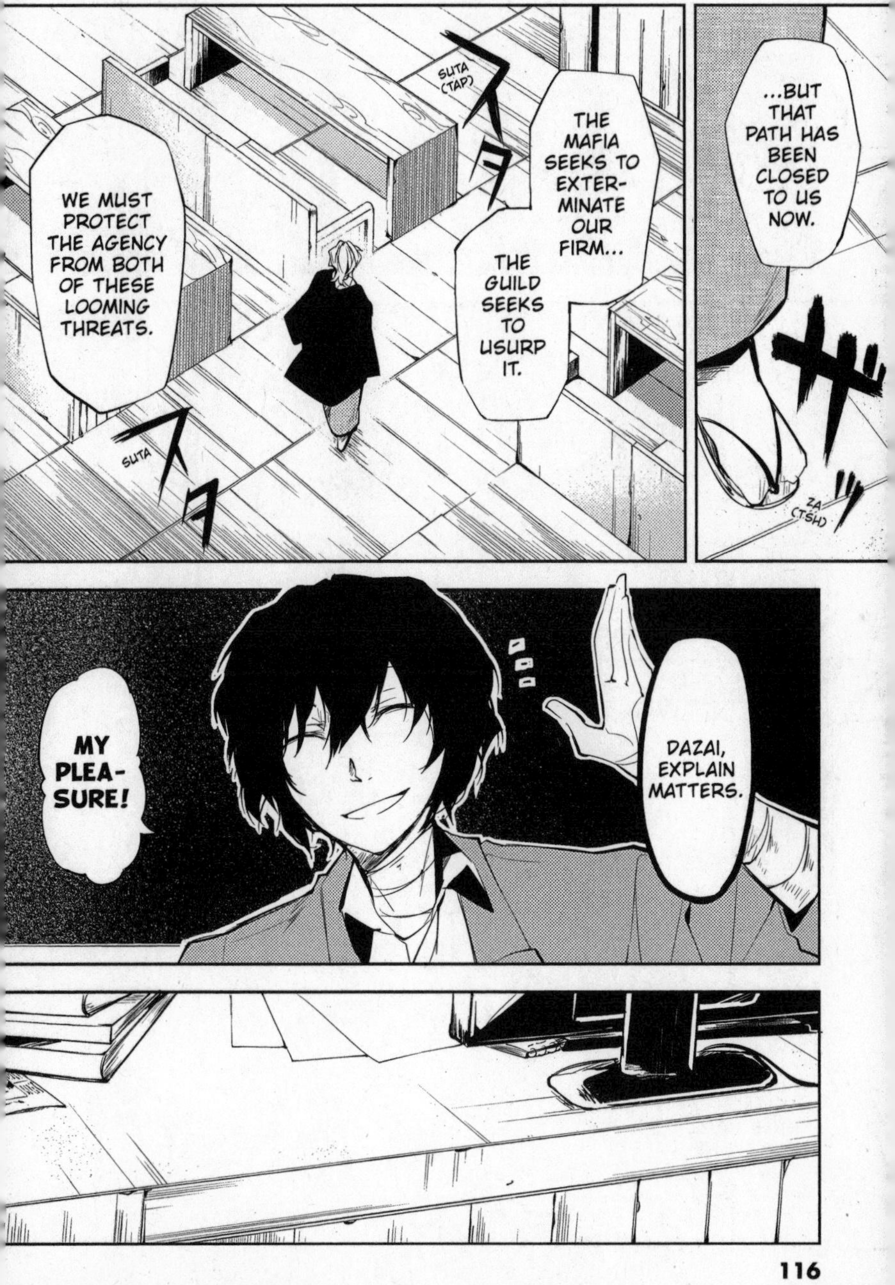
...BUT THAT PATH HAS BEEN CLOSED TO US NOW.
ZA (TSH)
THE MAFIA SEEKS TO EXTER-MINATE OUR FIRM...
SUTA (TAP)
THE GUILD SEEKS TO USURP IT.
WE MUST PROTECT THE AGENCY FROM BOTH OF THESE LOOMING THREATS.
SUTA
DAZAI, EXPLAIN MATTERS.
MY PLEA-SURE!

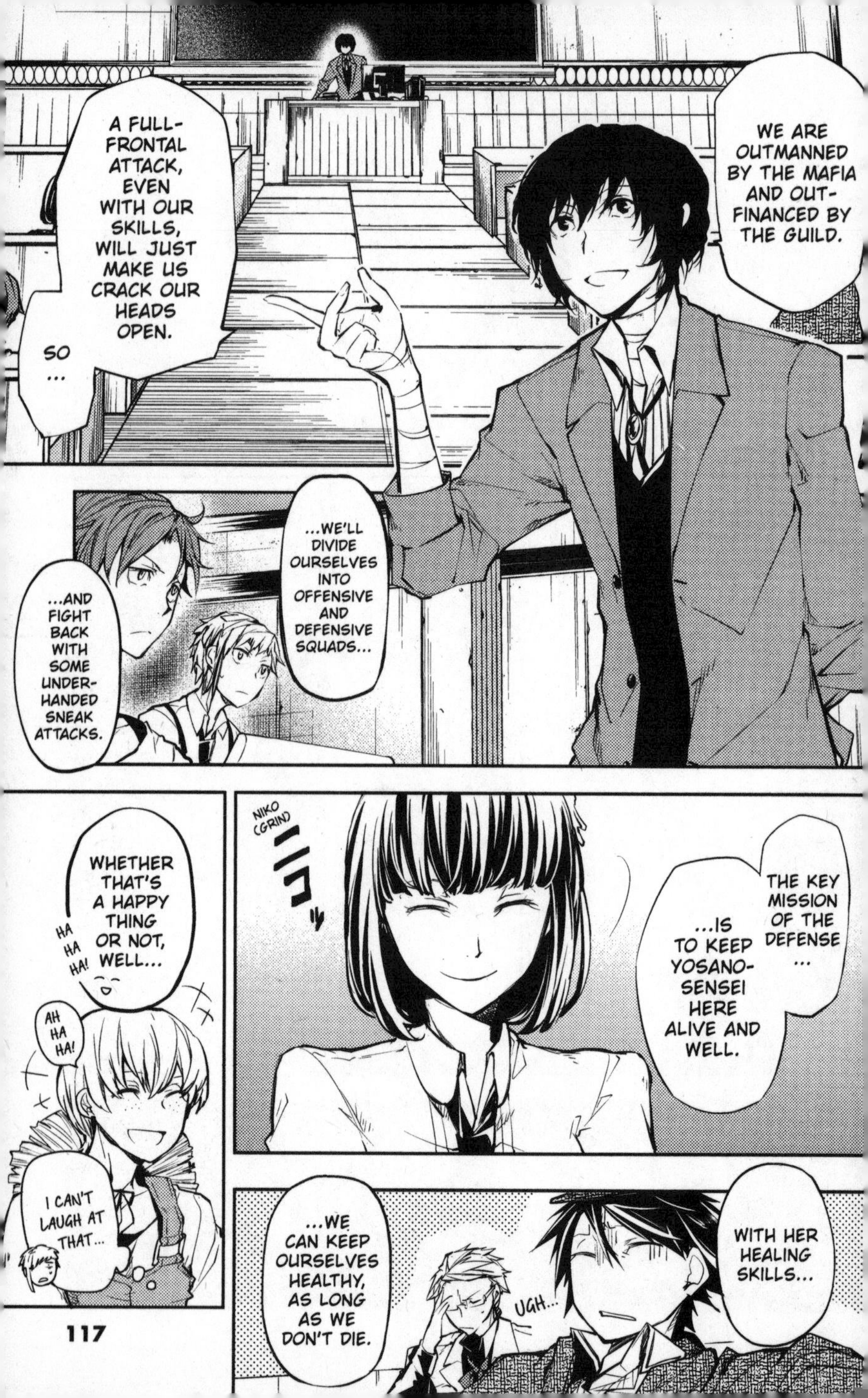

WE ARE OUTMANNED BY THE MAFIA AND OUT-FINANCED BY THE GUILD.
A FULL-FRONTAL ATTACK, EVEN WITH OUR SKILLS, WILL JUST MAKE US CRACK OUR HEADS OPEN.
SO ...
...WE'LL DIVIDE OURSELVES INTO OFFENSIVE AND DEFENSIVE SQUADS...
...AND FIGHT BACK WITH SOME UNDER-HANDED SNEAK ATTACKS.
NIKO (GRIN)
THE KEY MISSION OF THE DEFENSE ...
...IS TO KEEP YOSANO-SENSEI HERE ALIVE AND WELL.
WITH HER HEALING SKILLS...
...WE CAN KEEP OURSELVES HEALTHY, AS LONG AS WE DON'T DIE.
UGH...
WHETHER THAT'S A HAPPY THING OR NOT, WELL...
HA HA HA!
AH HA HA!
I CAN'T LAUGH AT THAT...

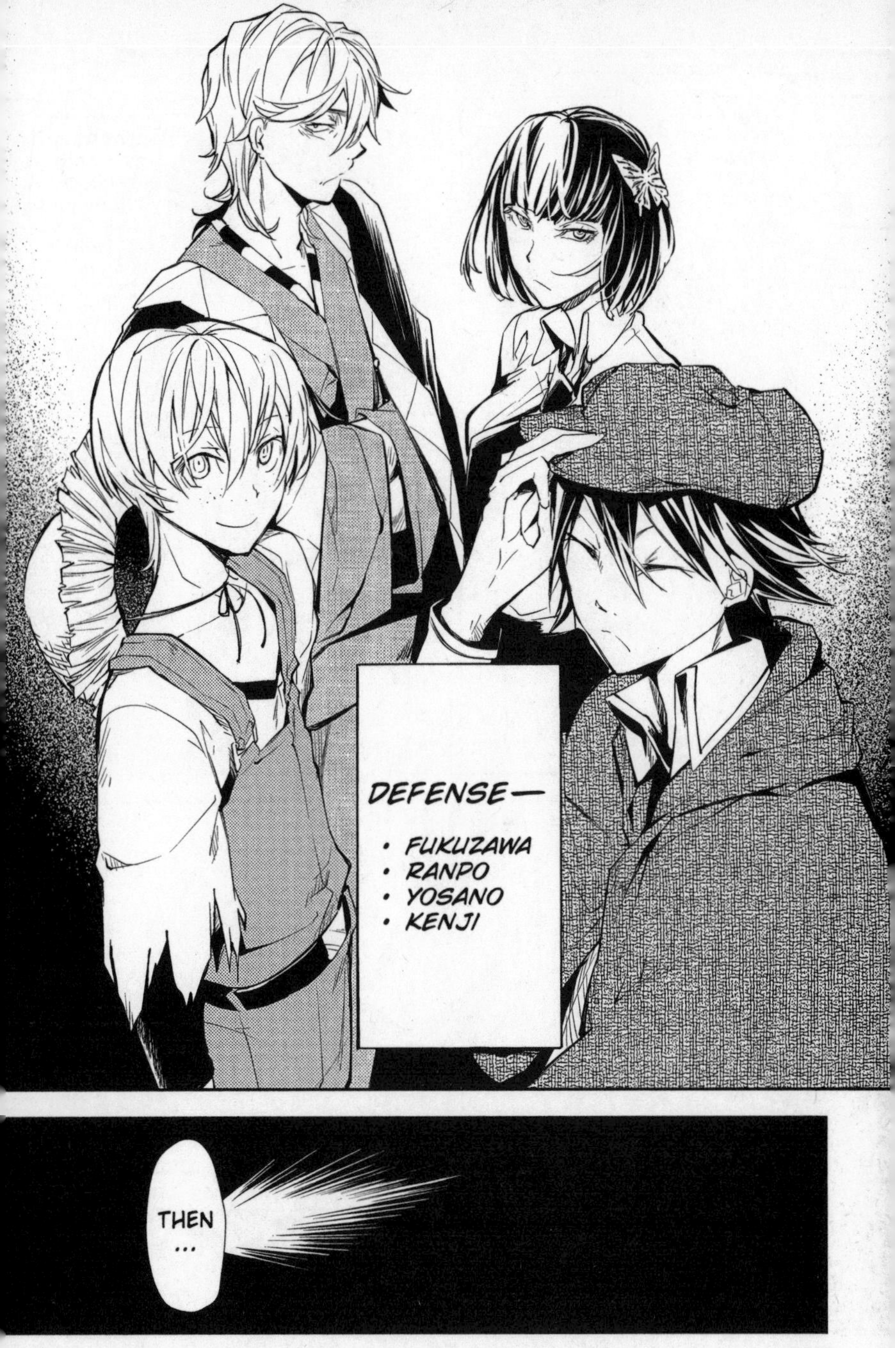
DEFENSE—
• FUKUZAWA
• RANPO
• YOSANO
• KENJI
THEN ...

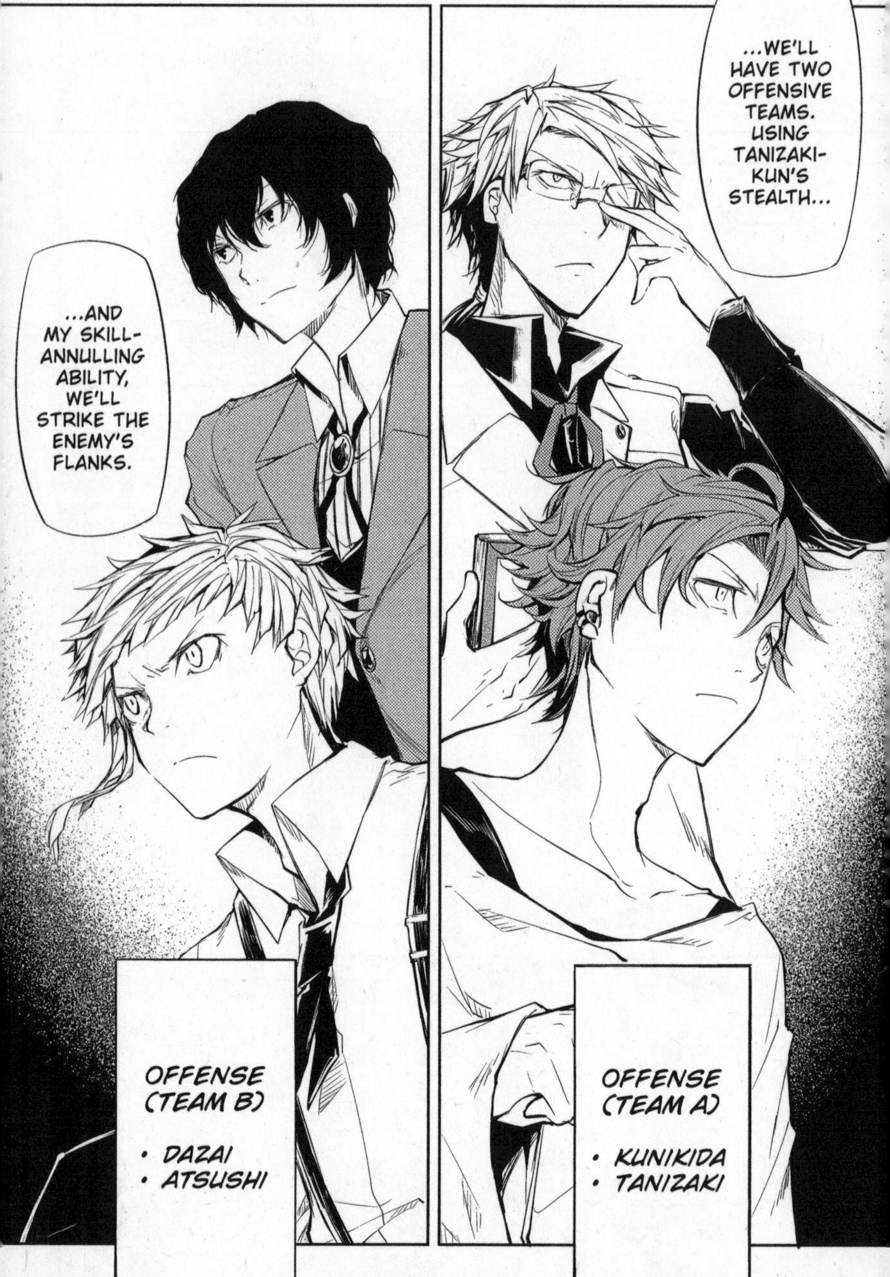
...WE'LL HAVE TWO OFFENSIVE TEAMS. USING TANIZAKI-KUN'S STEALTH...
OFFENSE (TEAM A)
• KUNIKIDA
• TANIZAKI
...AND MY SKILL-ANNULLING ABILITY, WE'LL STRIKE THE ENEMY'S FLANKS.
OFFENSE (TEAM B)
• DAZAI
• ATSUSHI

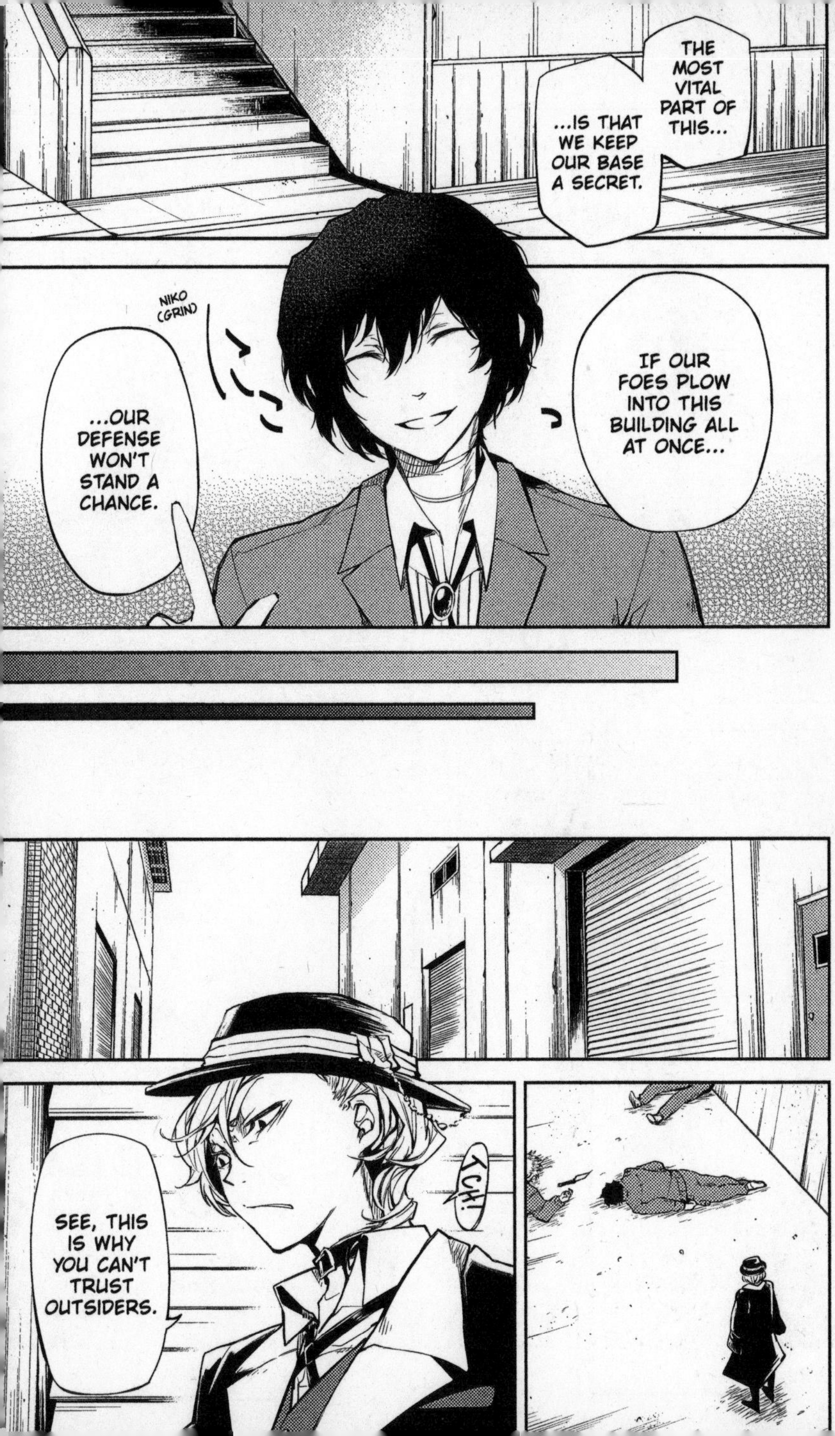
THE MOST VITAL PART OF THIS...
...IS THAT WE KEEP OUR BASE A SECRET.
IF OUR FOES PLOW INTO THIS BUILDING ALL AT ONCE...
NIKO (GRIN)
...OUR DEFENSE WON'T STAND A CHANCE.
TCH!
SEE, THIS IS WHY YOU CAN'T TRUST OUTSIDERS.

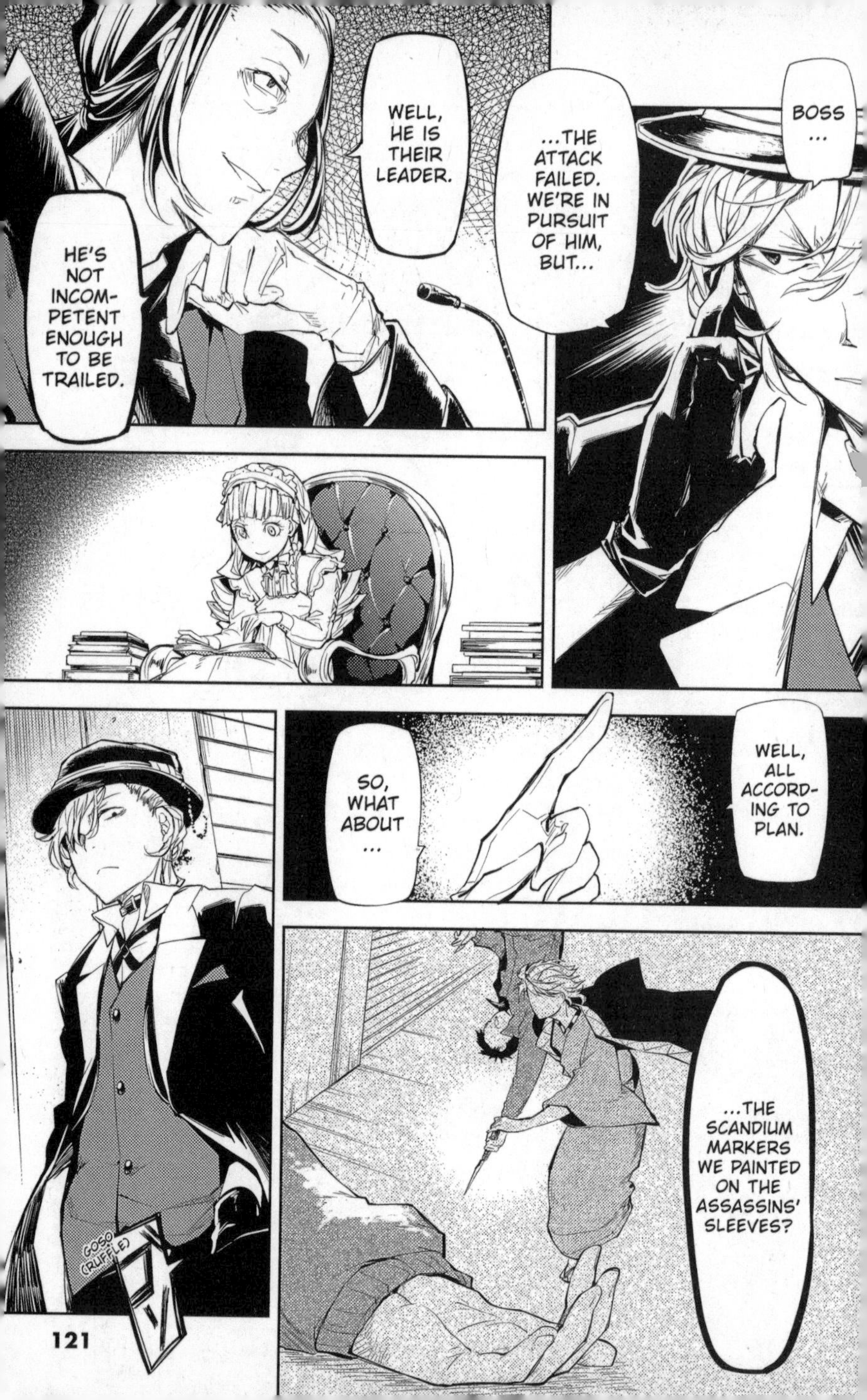
BOSS...
...THE ATTACK FAILED. WE'RE IN PURSUIT OF HIM, BUT...
WELL, HE IS THEIR LEADER.
HE'S NOT INCOMPETENT ENOUGH TO BE TRAILED.
WELL, ALL ACCORDING TO PLAN.
SO, WHAT ABOUT...
...THE SCANDIUM MARKERS WE PAINTED ON THE ASSASSINS' SLEEVES?
GOSO (RUFFLE)

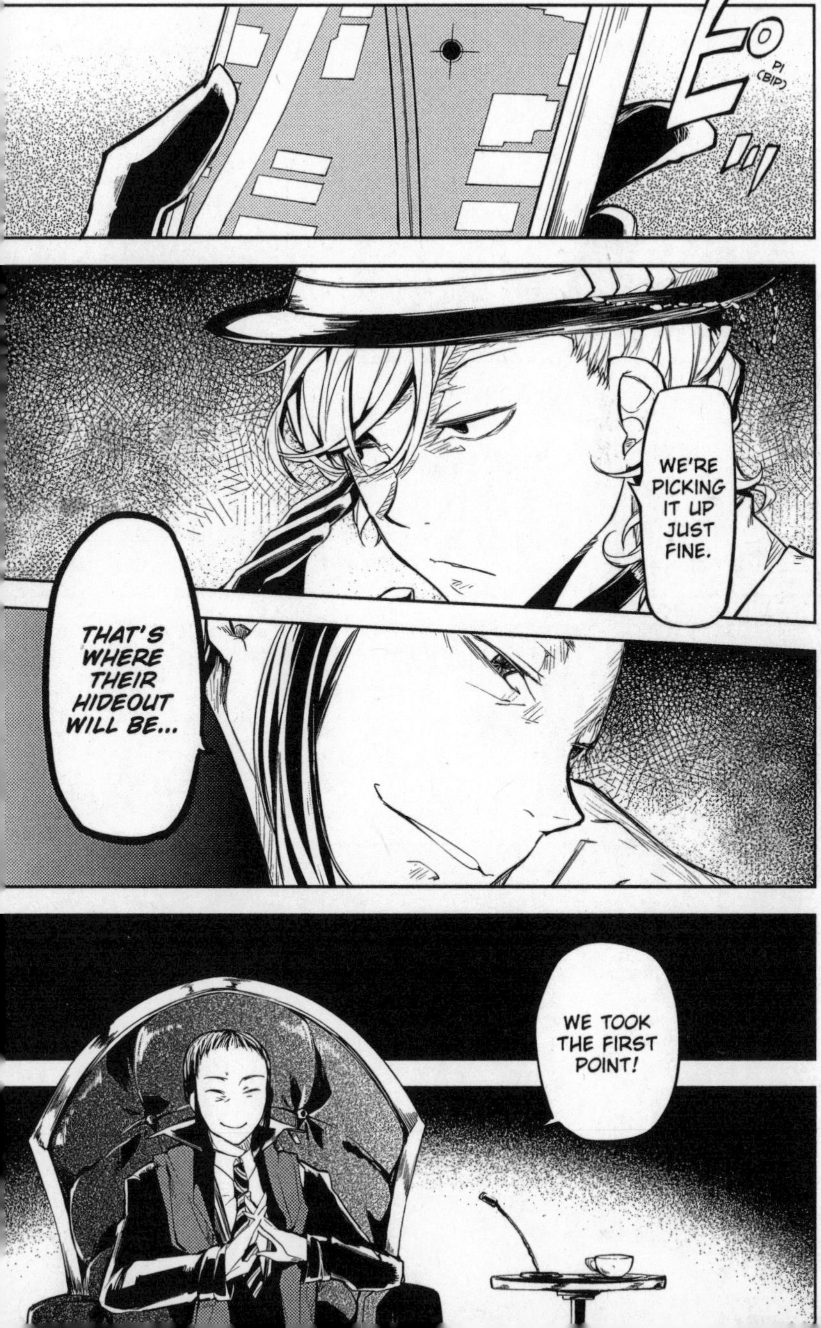
PI (BIP)
WE'RE PICKING IT UP JUST FINE.
THAT'S WHERE THEIR HIDEOUT WILL BE...
WE TOOK THE FIRST POINT!

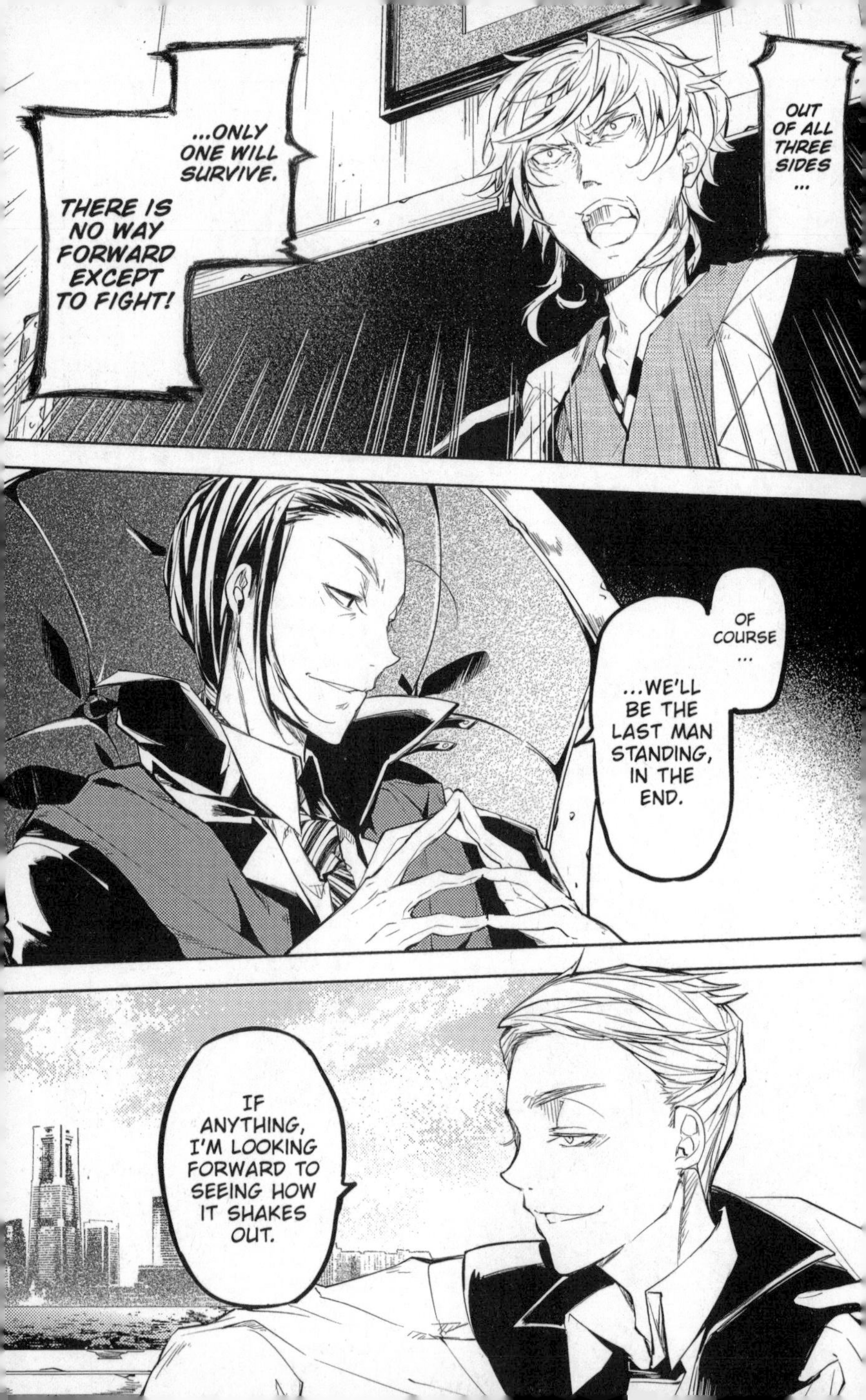
OUT OF ALL THREE SIDES...
...ONLY ONE WILL SURVIVE.
THERE IS NO WAY FORWARD EXCEPT TO FIGHT!
OF COURSE...
...WE'LL BE THE LAST MAN STANDING, IN THE END.
IF ANYTHING, I'M LOOKING FORWARD TO SEEING HOW IT SHAKES OUT.

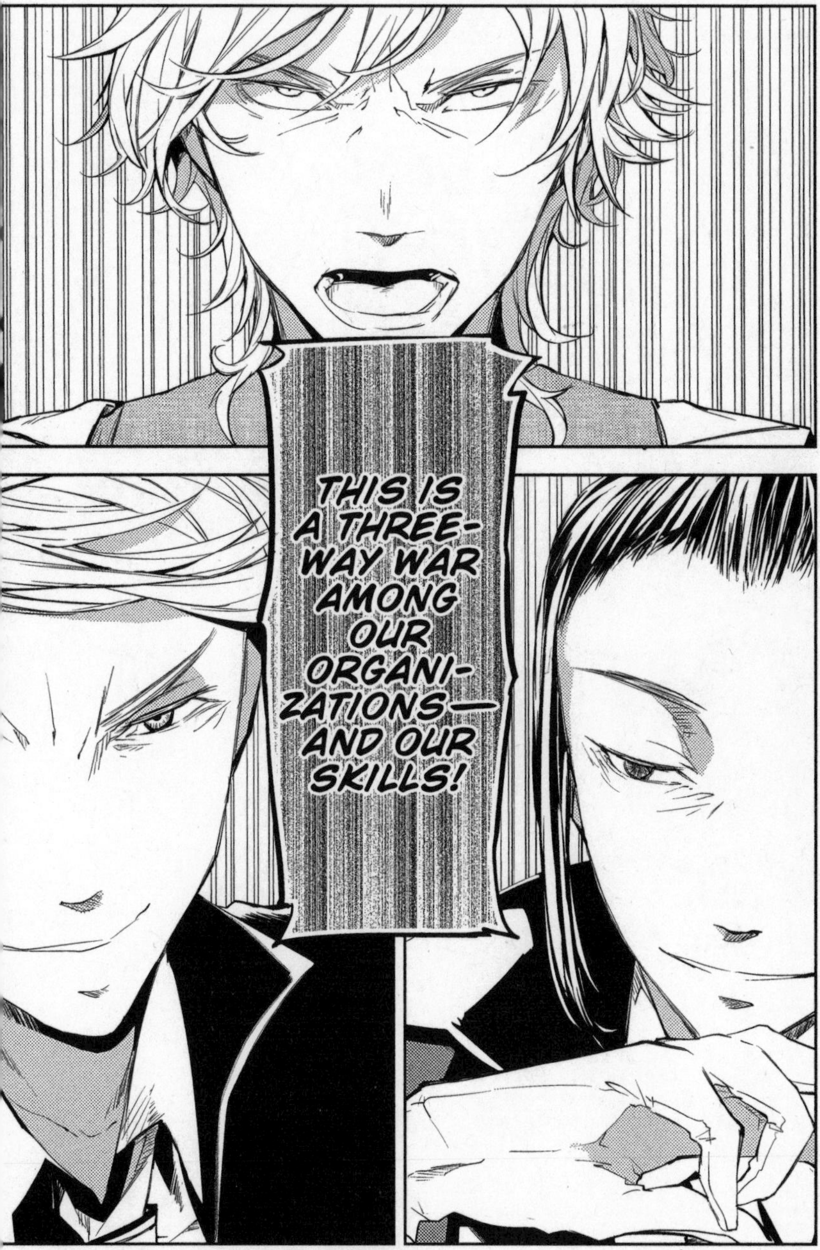
THIS IS A THREE-WAY WAR AMONG OUR ORGANIZATIONS—AND OUR SKILLS!

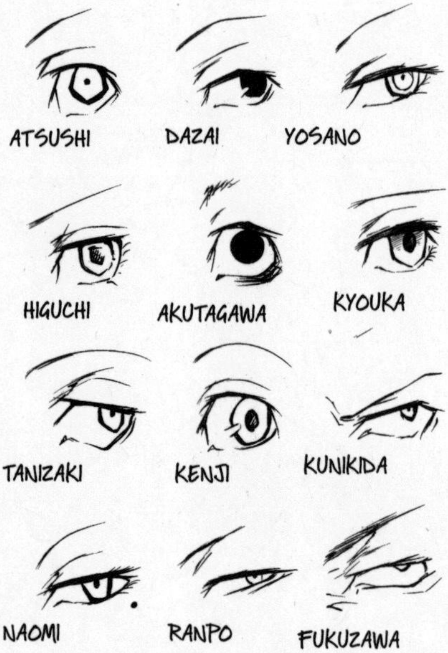
ATSUSHI
DAZAI
YOSANO
HIGUCHI
AKUTAGAWA
KYOUKA
TANIZAKI
KENJI
KUNIKIDA
NAOMI
RANPO
FUKUZAWA

BUNGO
STRAY DOGS

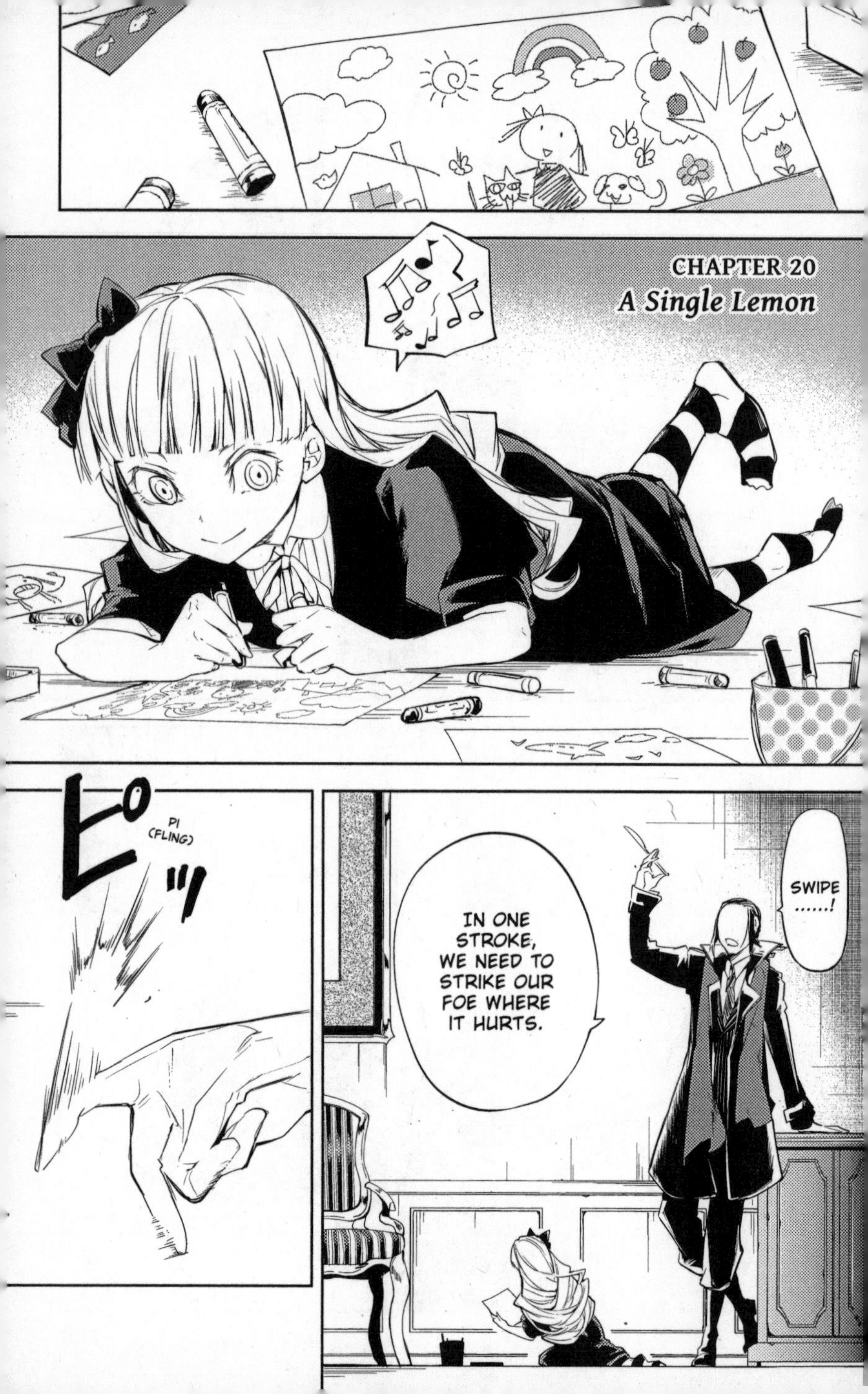
CHAPTER 20
A Single Lemon
SWIPE ......!
IN ONE STROKE, WE NEED TO STRIKE OUR FOE WHERE IT HURTS.
PI (FLING)

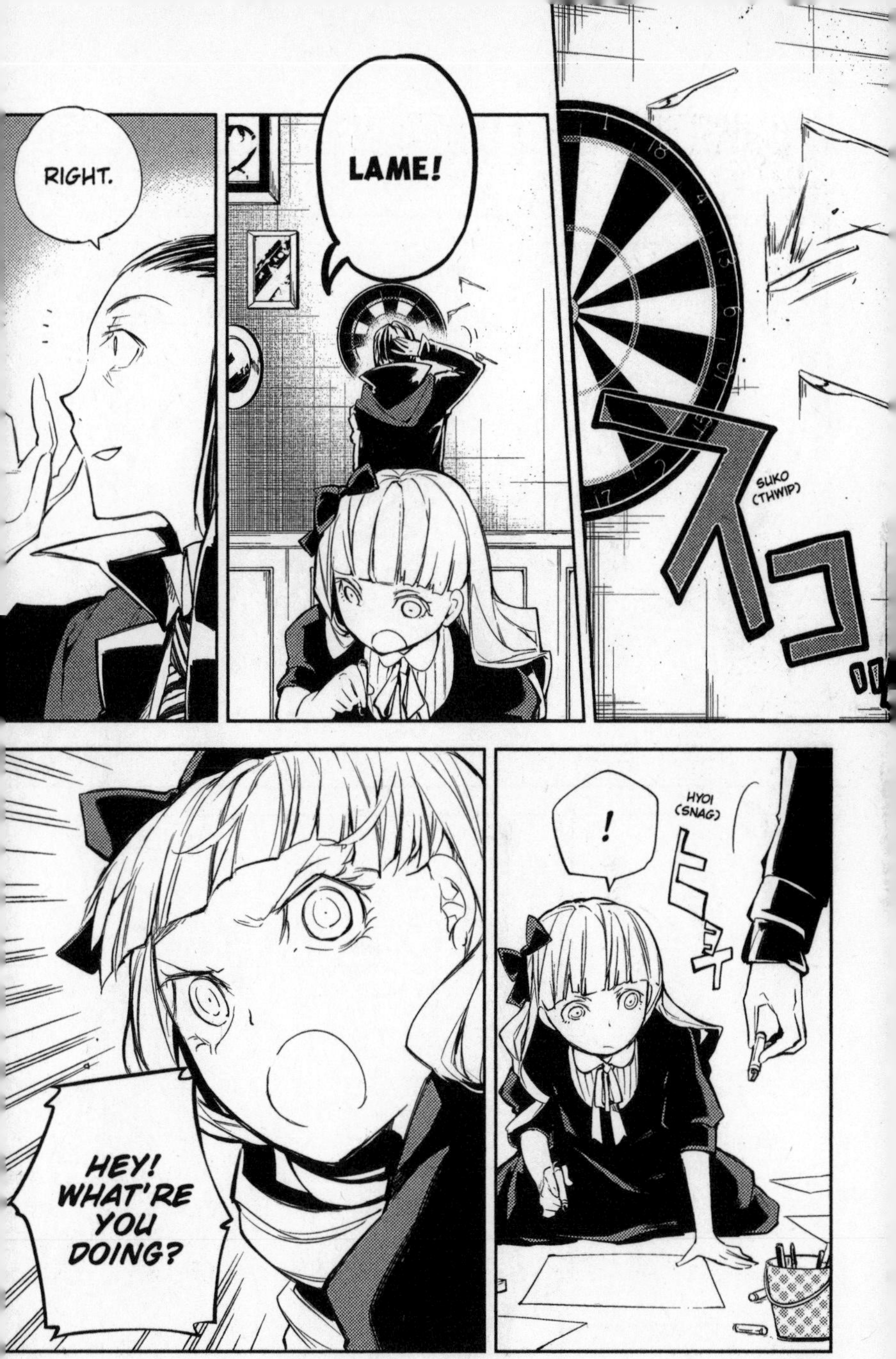

スコッ
SUKO (THWIP)
LAME!
RIGHT.
!
HYOI (SNAG)
ヒョイ
HEY! WHAT'RE YOU DOING?

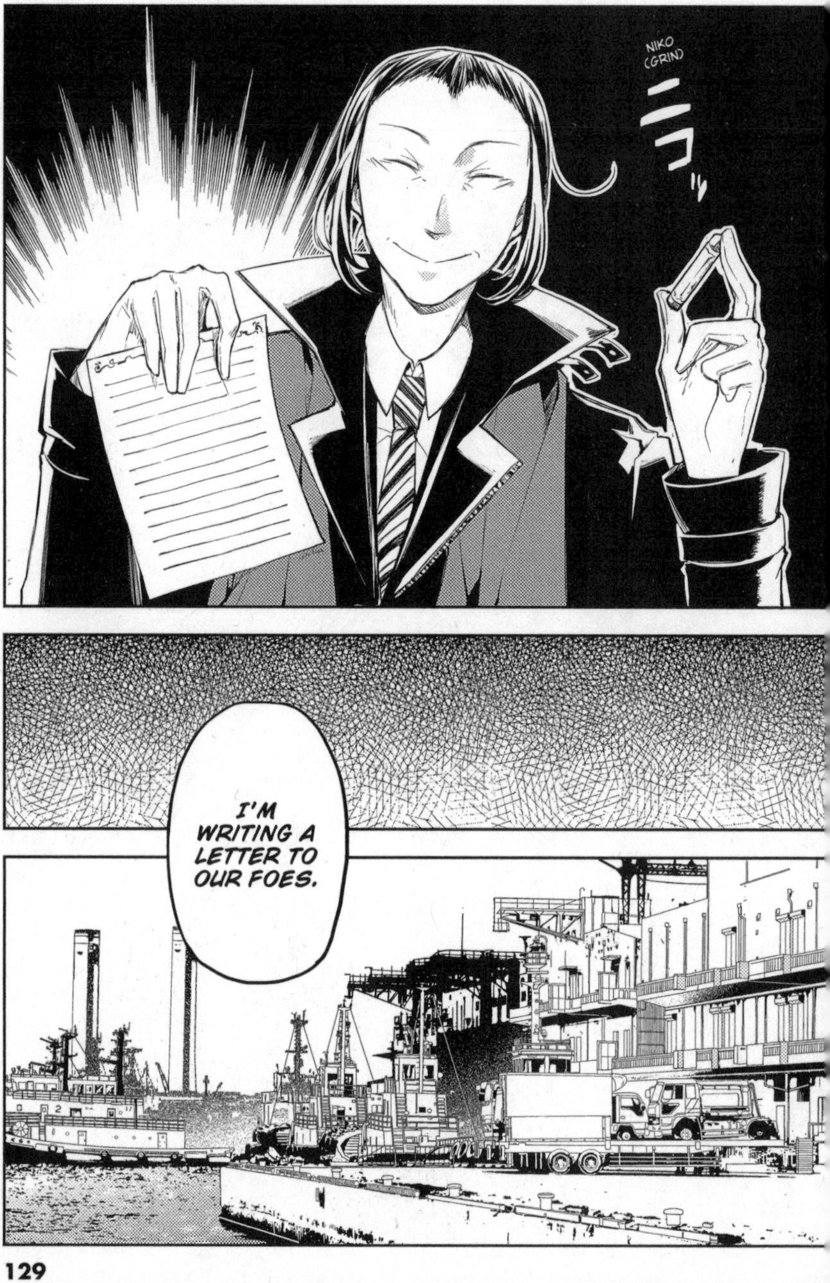
NIKO (GRIN)
ニコッ
I'M WRITING A LETTER TO OUR FOES.

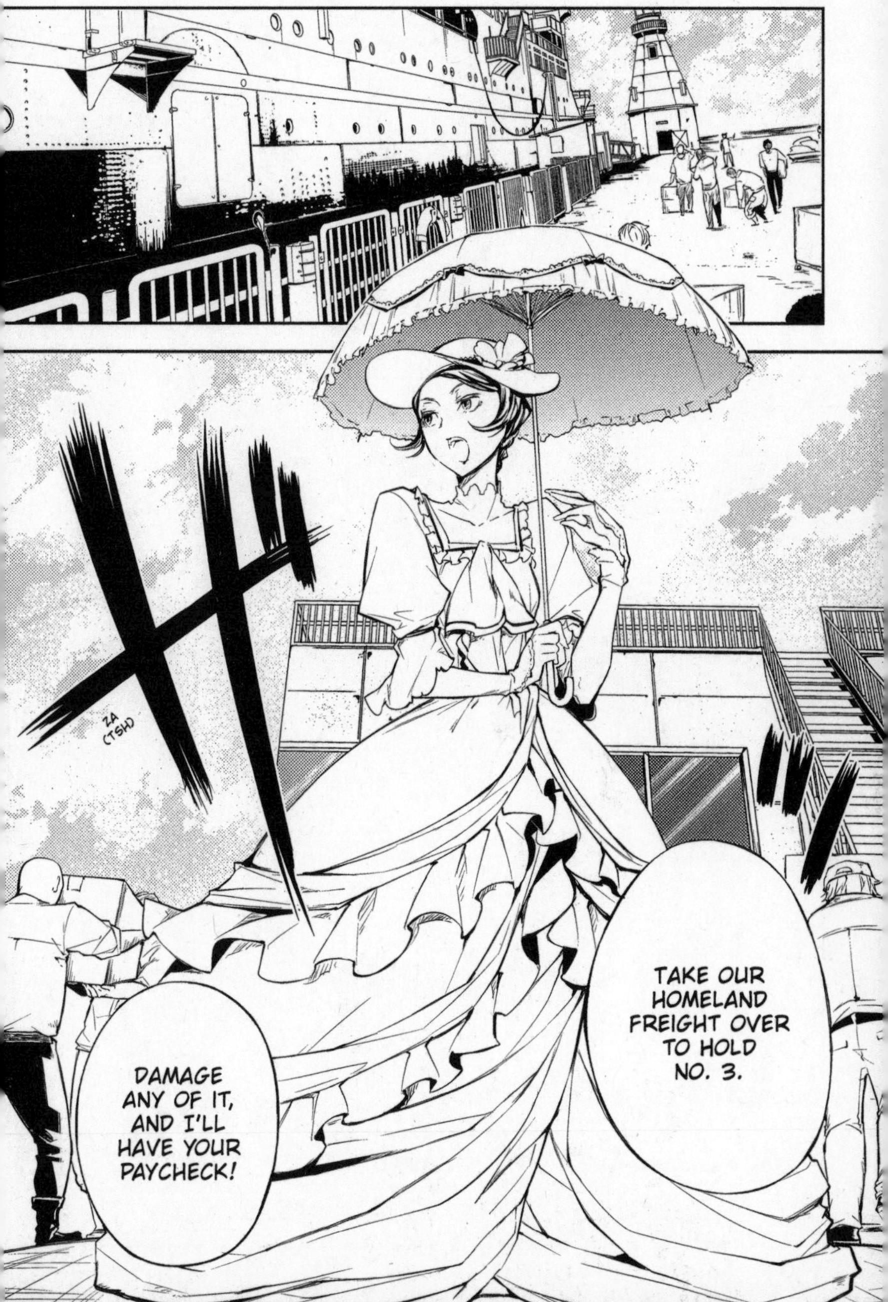
TAKE OUR HOMELAND FREIGHT OVER TO HOLD NO. 3.
ZA (TSH)
DAMAGE ANY OF IT, AND I'LL HAVE YOUR PAYCHECK!

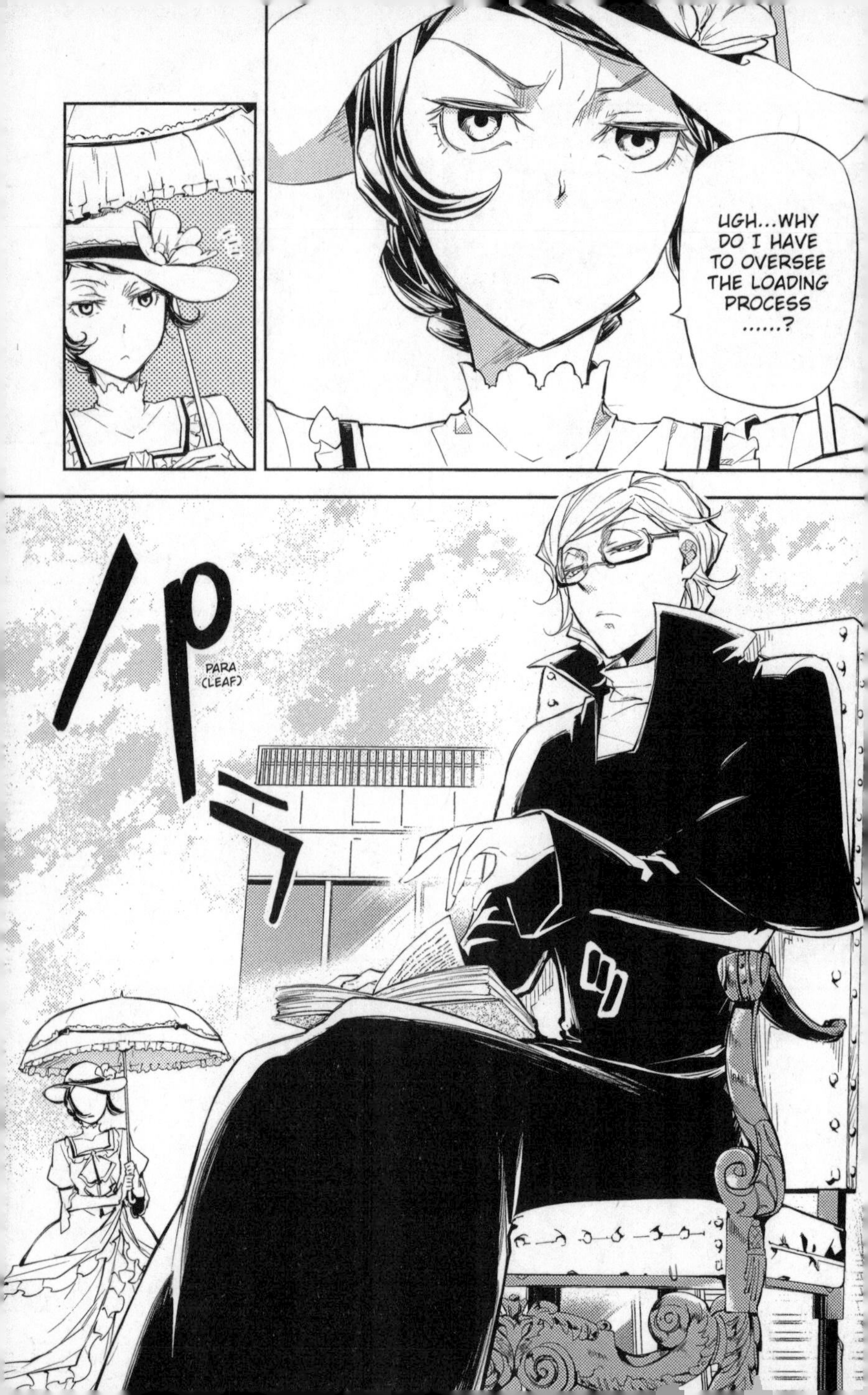
UGH...WHY DO I HAVE TO OVERSEE THE LOADING PROCESS ......?
PARA (LEAF)

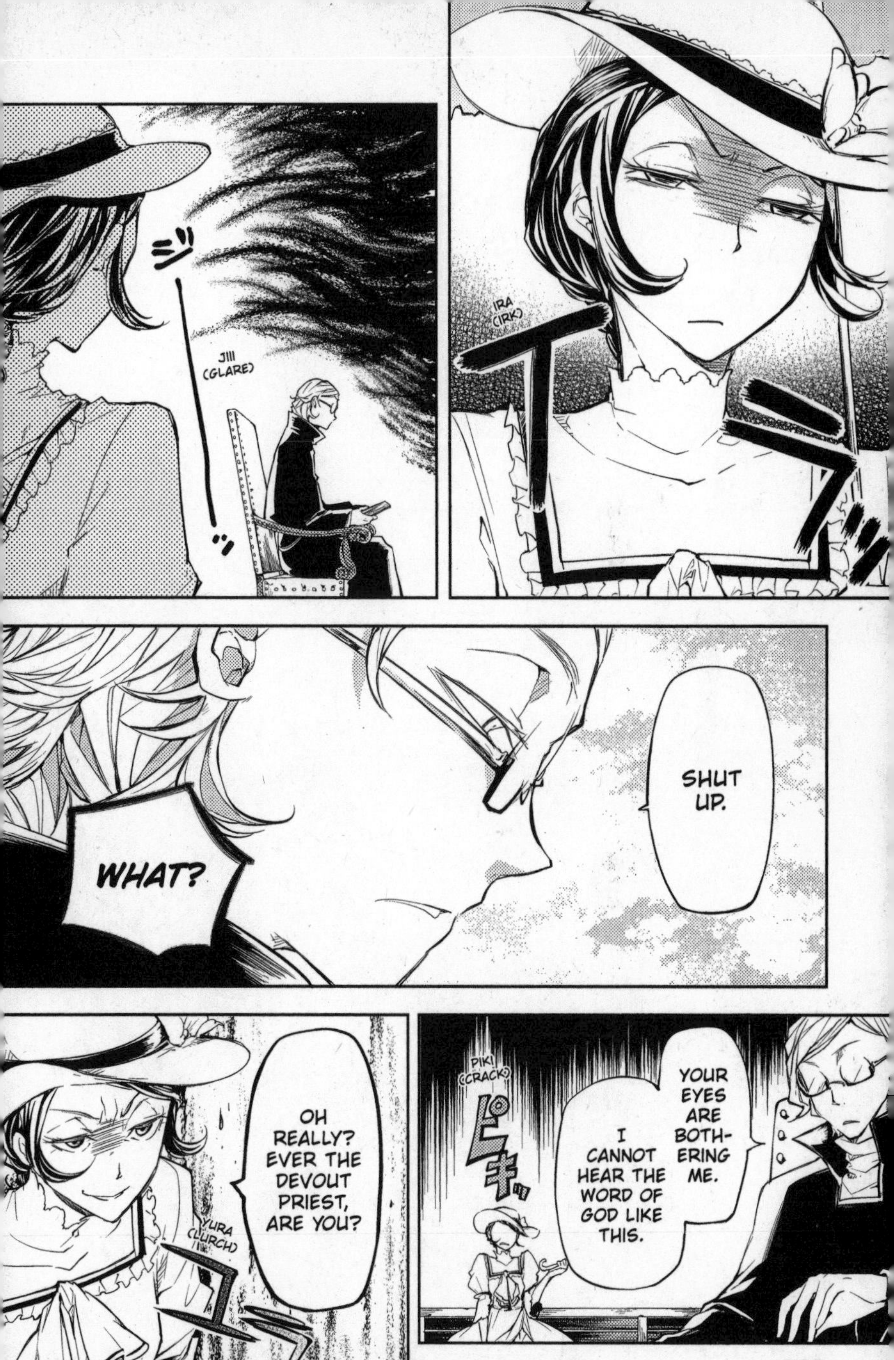
IRA (IRK)
JIII (GLARE)
SHUT UP.
WHAT?
PIKI (CRACK)
YOUR EYES ARE BOTHERING ME.
I CANNOT HEAR THE WORD OF GOD LIKE THIS.
OH REALLY? EVER THE DEVOUT PRIEST, ARE YOU?
YURA (LURCH)

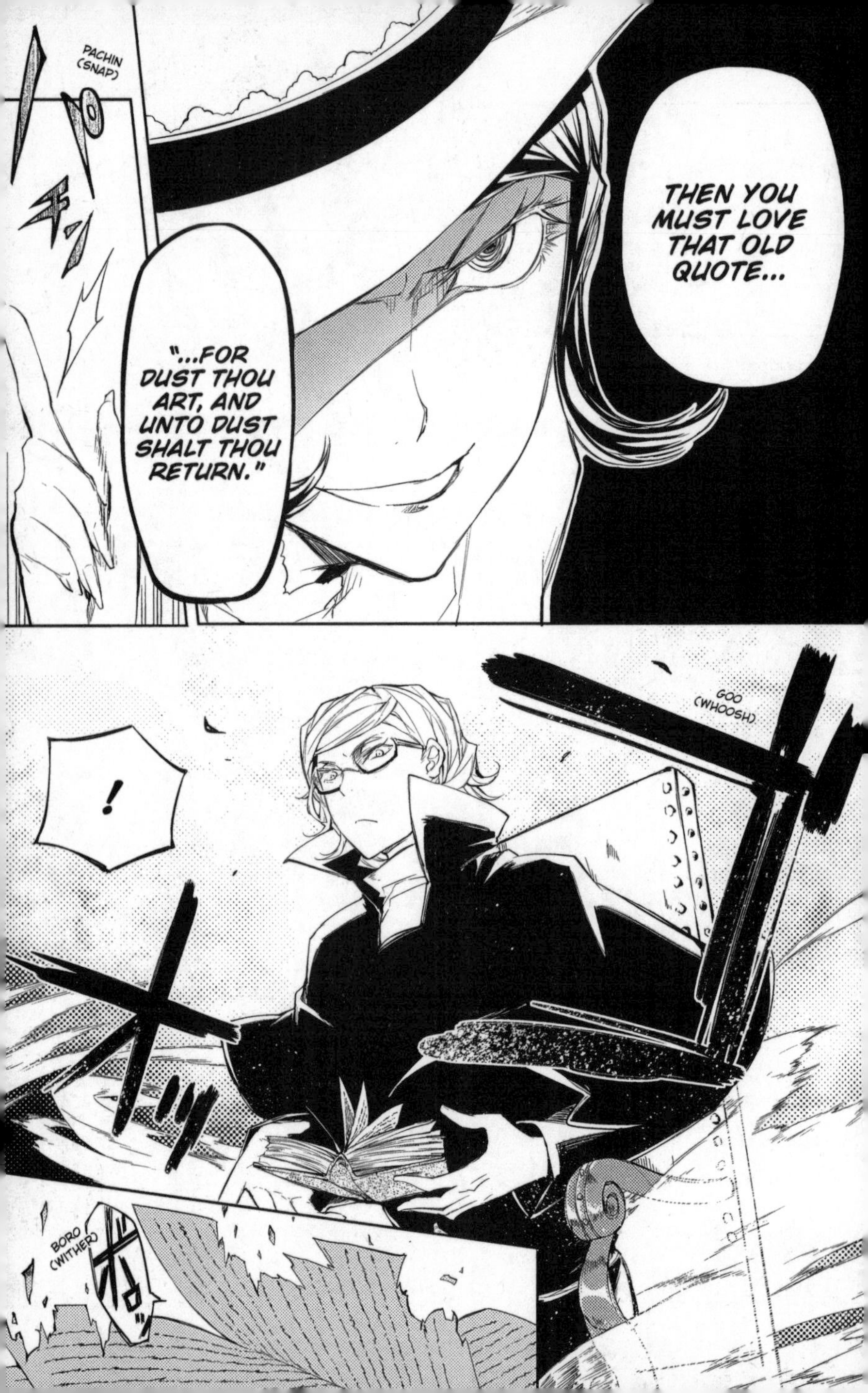
THEN YOU MUST LOVE THAT OLD QUOTE...
"...FOR DUST THOU ART, AND UNTO DUST SHALT THOU RETURN."
PACHIN (SNAP)
GOO (WHOOSH)
!
BORO (WITHER)

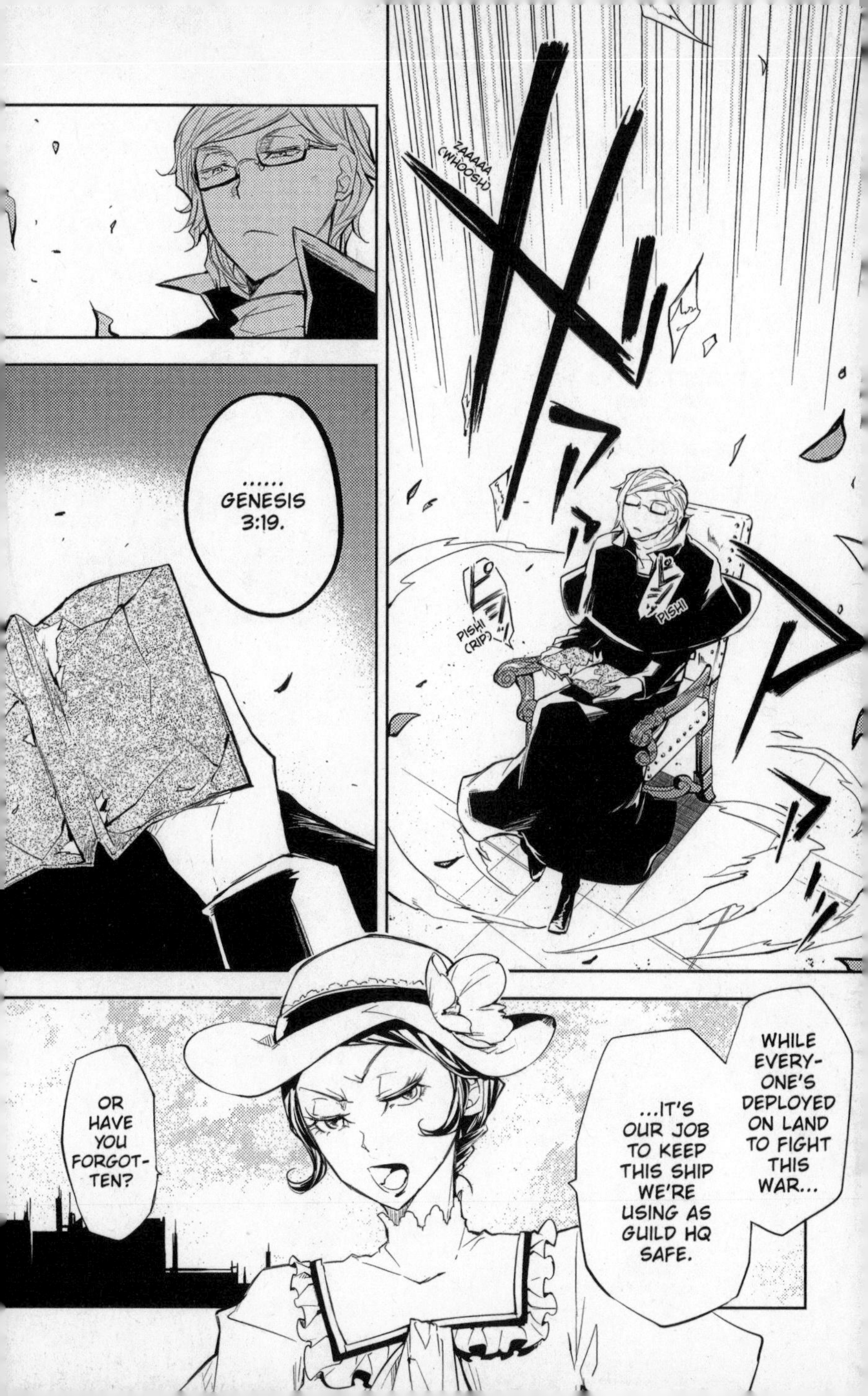
ZAAAAA (WHOOSH)
PISHI
PISHI (RIP)
...... GENESIS 3:19.
WHILE EVERY-ONE'S DEPLOYED ON LAND TO FIGHT THIS WAR...
...IT'S OUR JOB TO KEEP THIS SHIP WE'RE USING AS GUILD HQ SAFE.
OR HAVE YOU FORGOT-TEN?

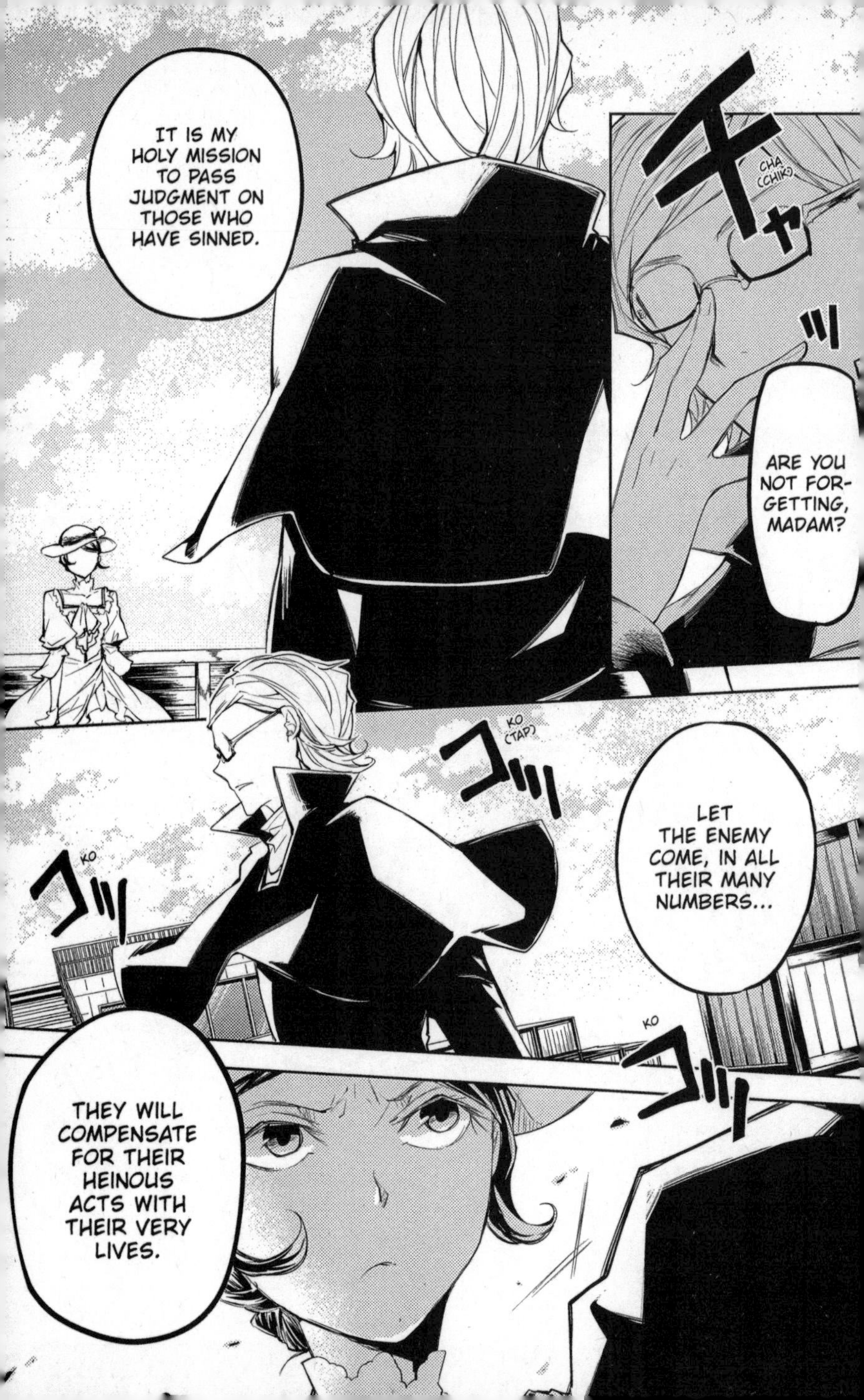
CHA (CHIK)
ARE YOU NOT FORGETTING, MADAM?
IT IS MY HOLY MISSION TO PASS JUDGMENT ON THOSE WHO HAVE SINNED.
KO (TAP)
LET THE ENEMY COME, IN ALL THEIR MANY NUMBERS...
KO
KO
THEY WILL COMPENSATE FOR THEIR HEINOUS ACTS WITH THEIR VERY LIVES.

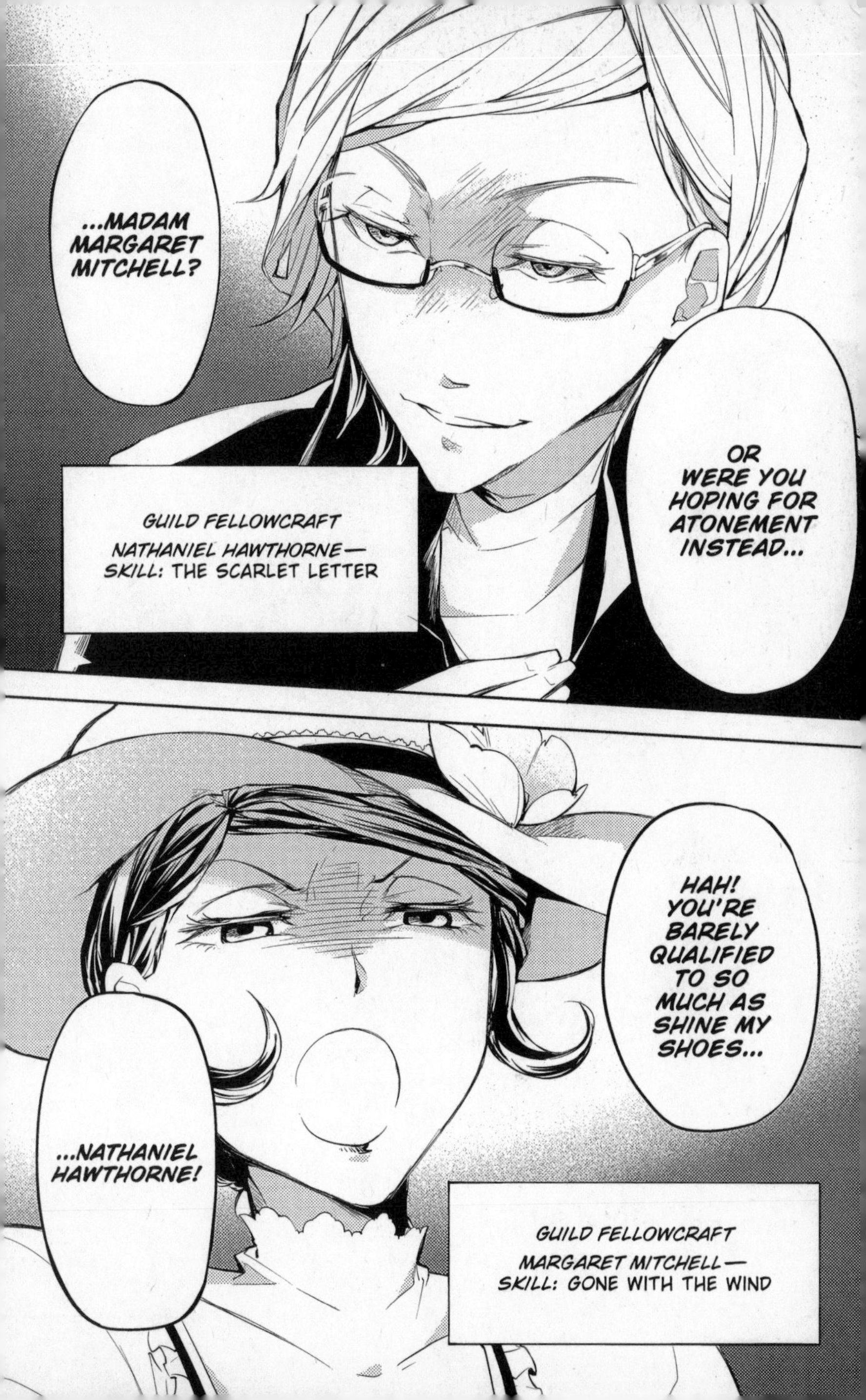
...MADAM MARGARET MITCHELL?
OR WERE YOU HOPING FOR ATONEMENT INSTEAD...
GUILD FELLOWCRAFT
NATHANIEL HAWTHORNE—
SKILL: THE SCARLET LETTER
HAH! YOU'RE BARELY QUALIFIED TO SO MUCH AS SHINE MY SHOES...
...NATHANIEL HAWTHORNE!
GUILD FELLOWCRAFT
MARGARET MITCHELL—
SKILL: GONE WITH THE WIND

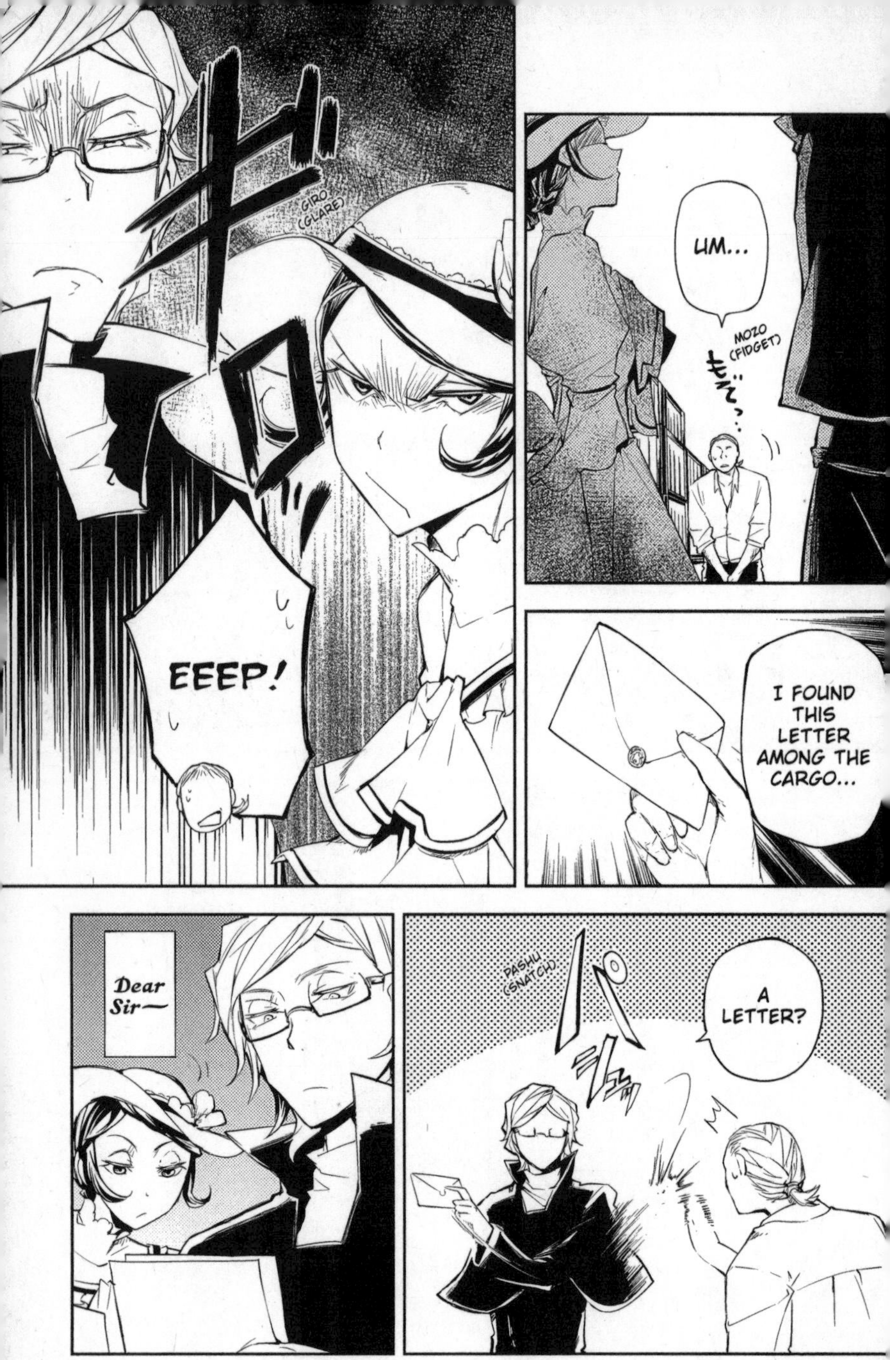
UM...
MOZO (FIDGET)
I FOUND THIS LETTER AMONG THE CARGO...
GIRO (GLARE)
EEEP!
PASHU (SNATCH)
A LETTER?
Dear Sir—

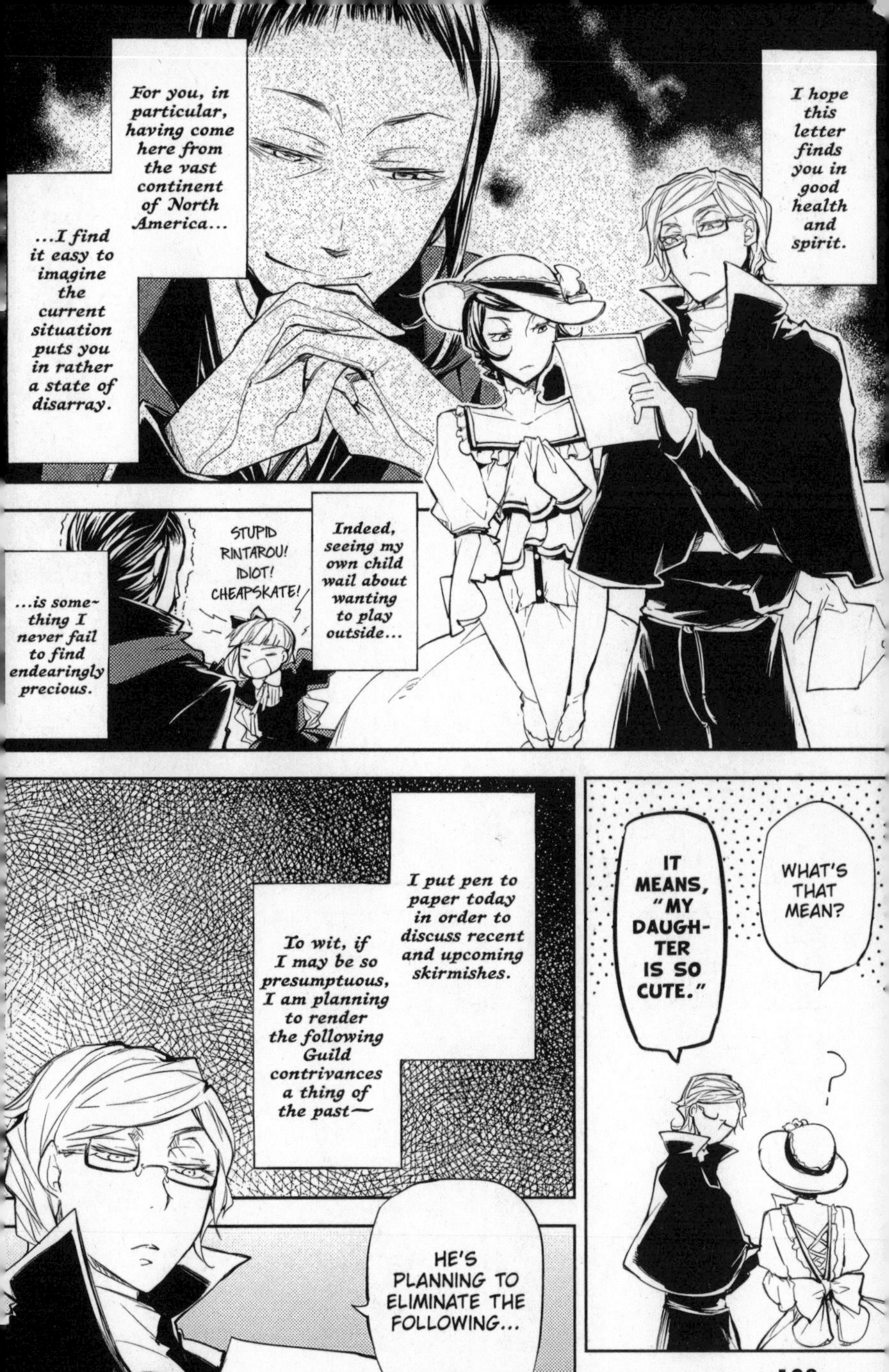
I hope this letter finds you in good health and spirit.
For you, in particular, having come here from the vast continent of North America...
...I find it easy to imagine the current situation puts you in rather a state of disarray.
Indeed, seeing my own child wail about wanting to play outside...
STUPID RINTAROU! IDIOT! CHEAPSKATE!
...is some-thing I never fail to find endearingly precious.
WHAT'S THAT MEAN?
IT MEANS, "MY DAUGH-TER IS SO CUTE."
I put pen to paper today in order to discuss recent and upcoming skirmishes.
To wit, if I may be so presumptuous, I am planning to render the following Guild contrivances a thing of the past—
HE'S PLANNING TO ELIMINATE THE FOLLOWING...

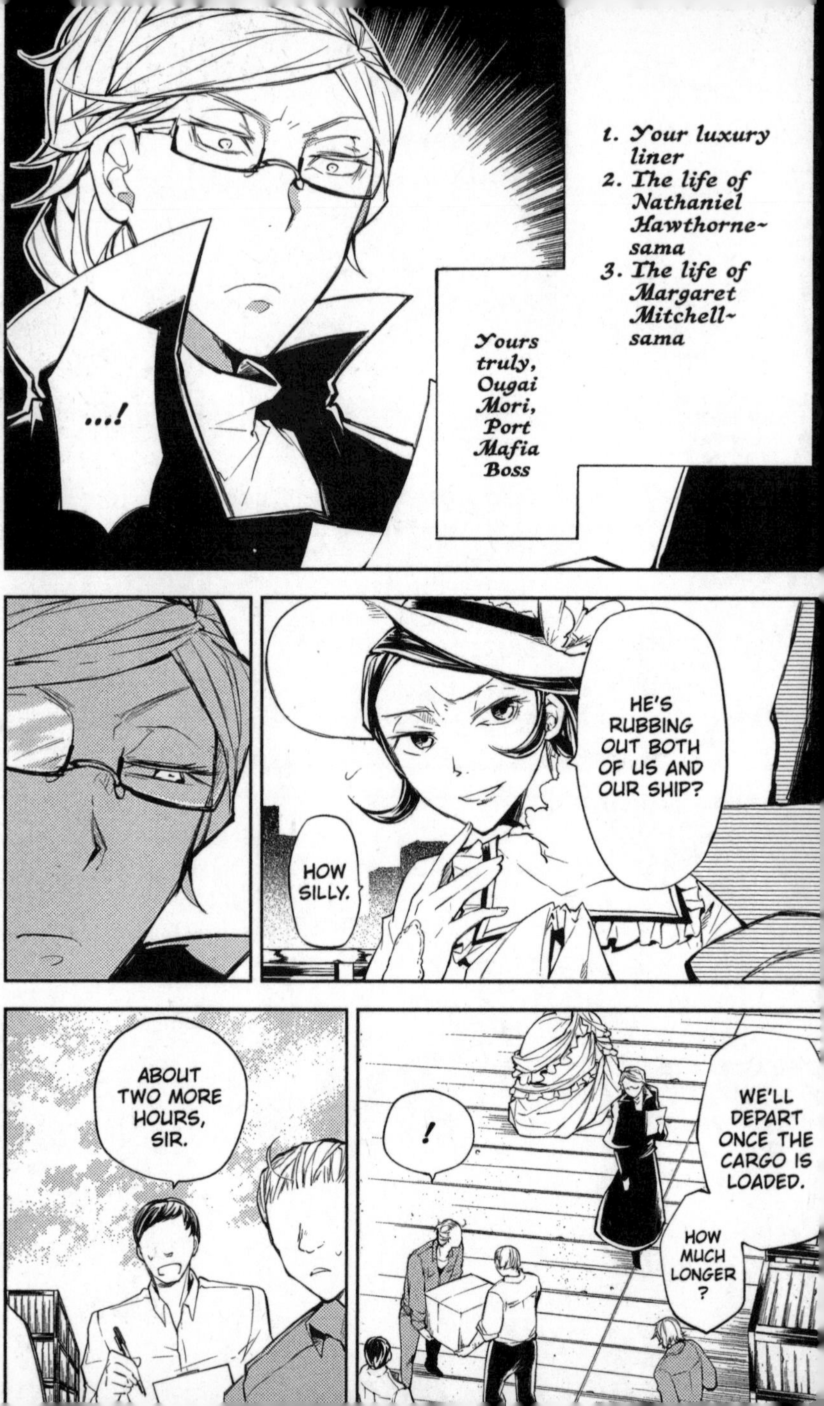
1. Your luxury liner
2. The life of Nathaniel Hawthorne-sama
3. The life of Margaret Mitchell-sama
Yours truly, Ougai Mori, Port Mafia Boss
...!
HE'S RUBBING OUT BOTH OF US AND OUR SHIP?
HOW SILLY.
WE'LL DEPART ONCE THE CARGO IS LOADED.
!
HOW MUCH LONGER?
ABOUT TWO MORE HOURS, SIR.

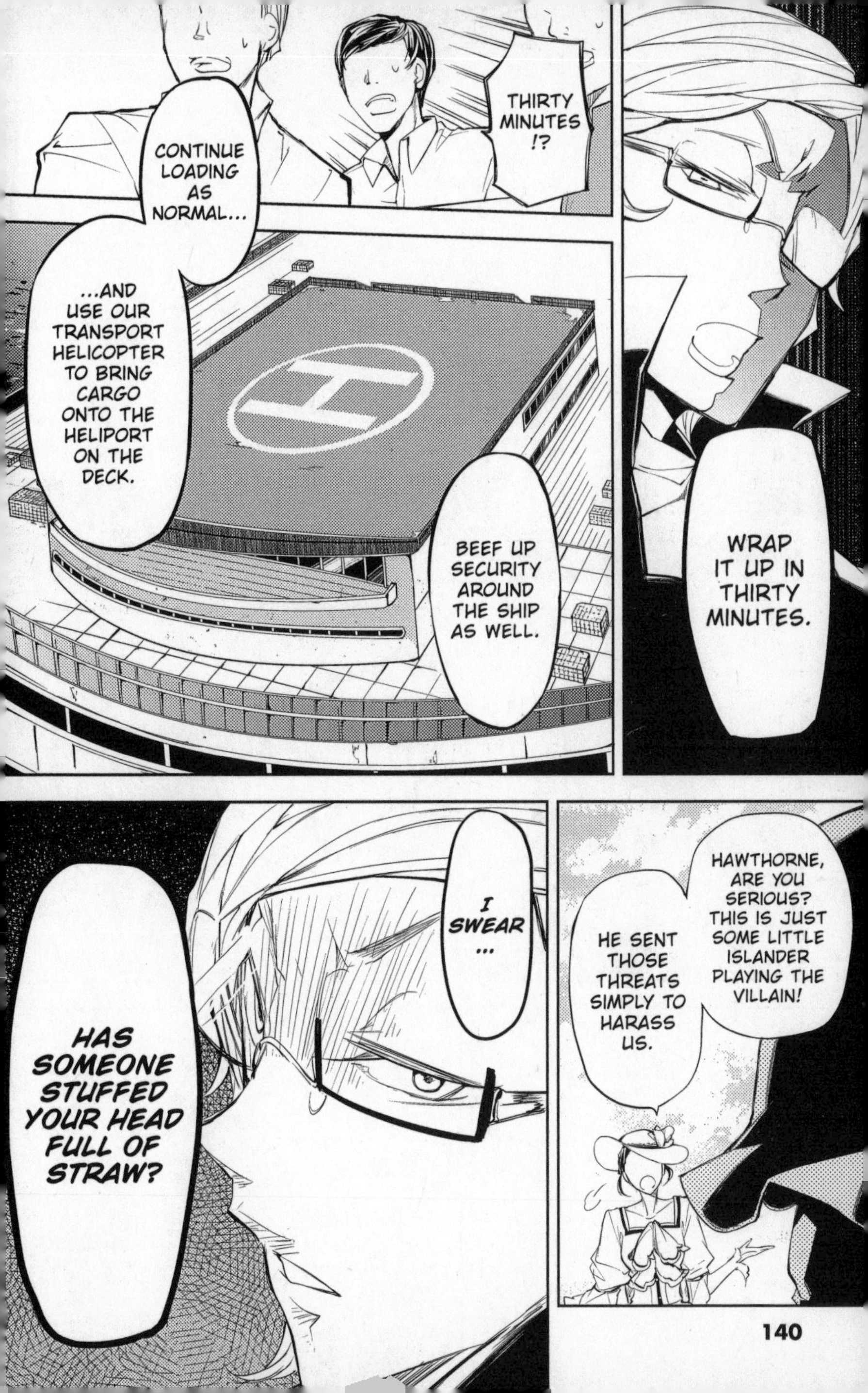
WRAP IT UP IN THIRTY MINUTES.
THIRTY MINUTES !?
CONTINUE LOADING AS NORMAL...
...AND USE OUR TRANSPORT HELICOPTER TO BRING CARGO ONTO THE HELIPORT ON THE DECK.
BEEF UP SECURITY AROUND THE SHIP AS WELL.
HAWTHORNE, ARE YOU SERIOUS? THIS IS JUST SOME LITTLE ISLANDER PLAYING THE VILLAIN!
HE SENT THOSE THREATS SIMPLY TO HARASS US.
I SWEAR ...
HAS SOMEONE STUFFED YOUR HEAD FULL OF STRAW?

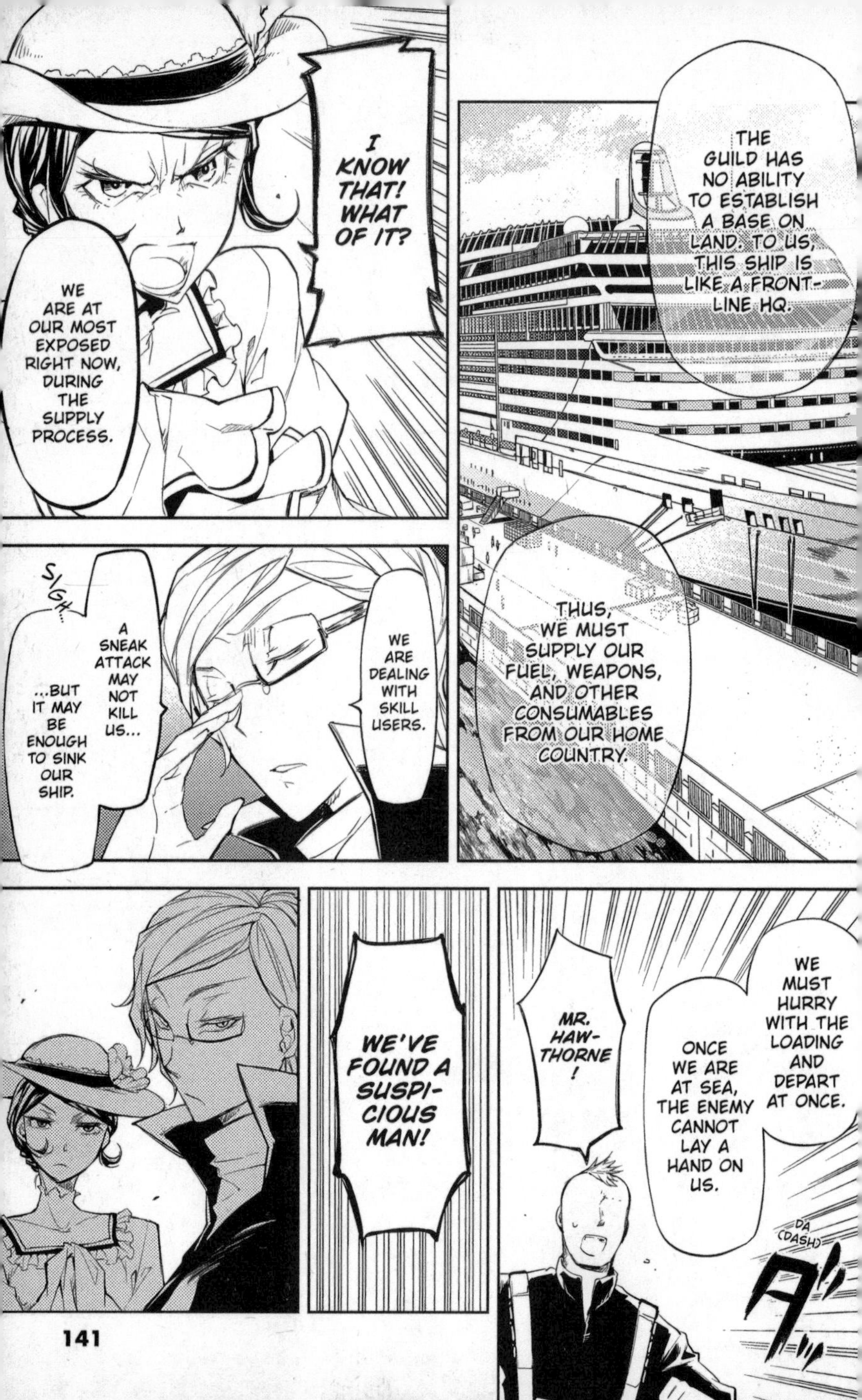
THE GUILD HAS NO ABILITY TO ESTABLISH A BASE ON LAND. TO US, THIS SHIP IS LIKE A FRONT-LINE HQ.
THUS, WE MUST SUPPLY OUR FUEL, WEAPONS, AND OTHER CONSUMABLES FROM OUR HOME COUNTRY.
I KNOW THAT! WHAT OF IT?
WE ARE AT OUR MOST EXPOSED RIGHT NOW, DURING THE SUPPLY PROCESS.
WE ARE DEALING WITH SKILL USERS.
A SNEAK ATTACK MAY NOT KILL US...
SIGH...
...BUT IT MAY BE ENOUGH TO SINK OUR SHIP.
WE MUST HURRY WITH THE LOADING AND DEPART AT ONCE.
ONCE WE ARE AT SEA, THE ENEMY CANNOT LAY A HAND ON US.
MR. HAWTHORNE!
DA (DASH)
WE'VE FOUND A SUSPICIOUS MAN!

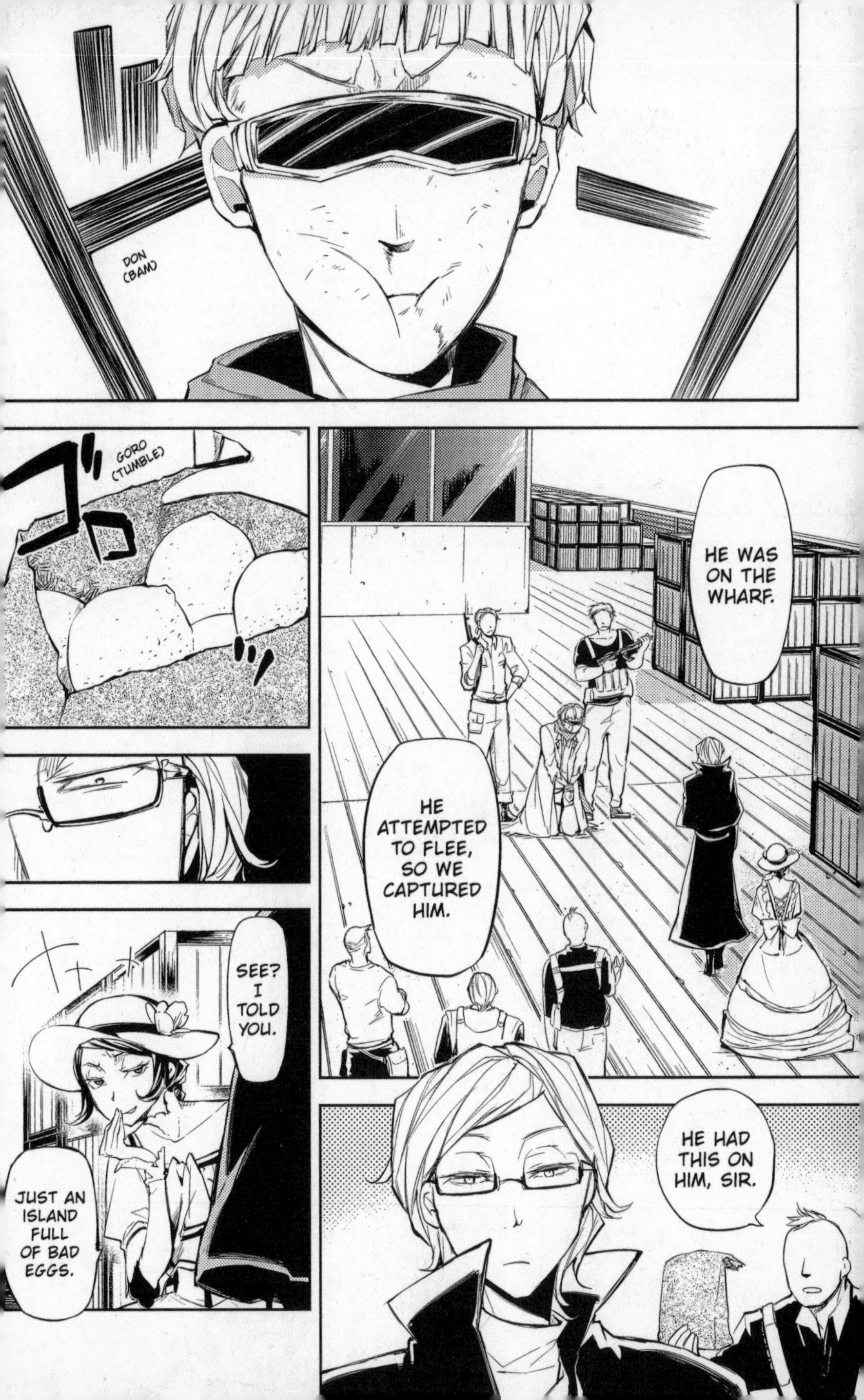
DON (BAM)
HE WAS ON THE WHARF.
HE ATTEMPTED TO FLEE, SO WE CAPTURED HIM.
HE HAD THIS ON HIM, SIR.
GORO (TUMBLE)
SEE? I TOLD YOU.
JUST AN ISLAND FULL OF BAD EGGS.

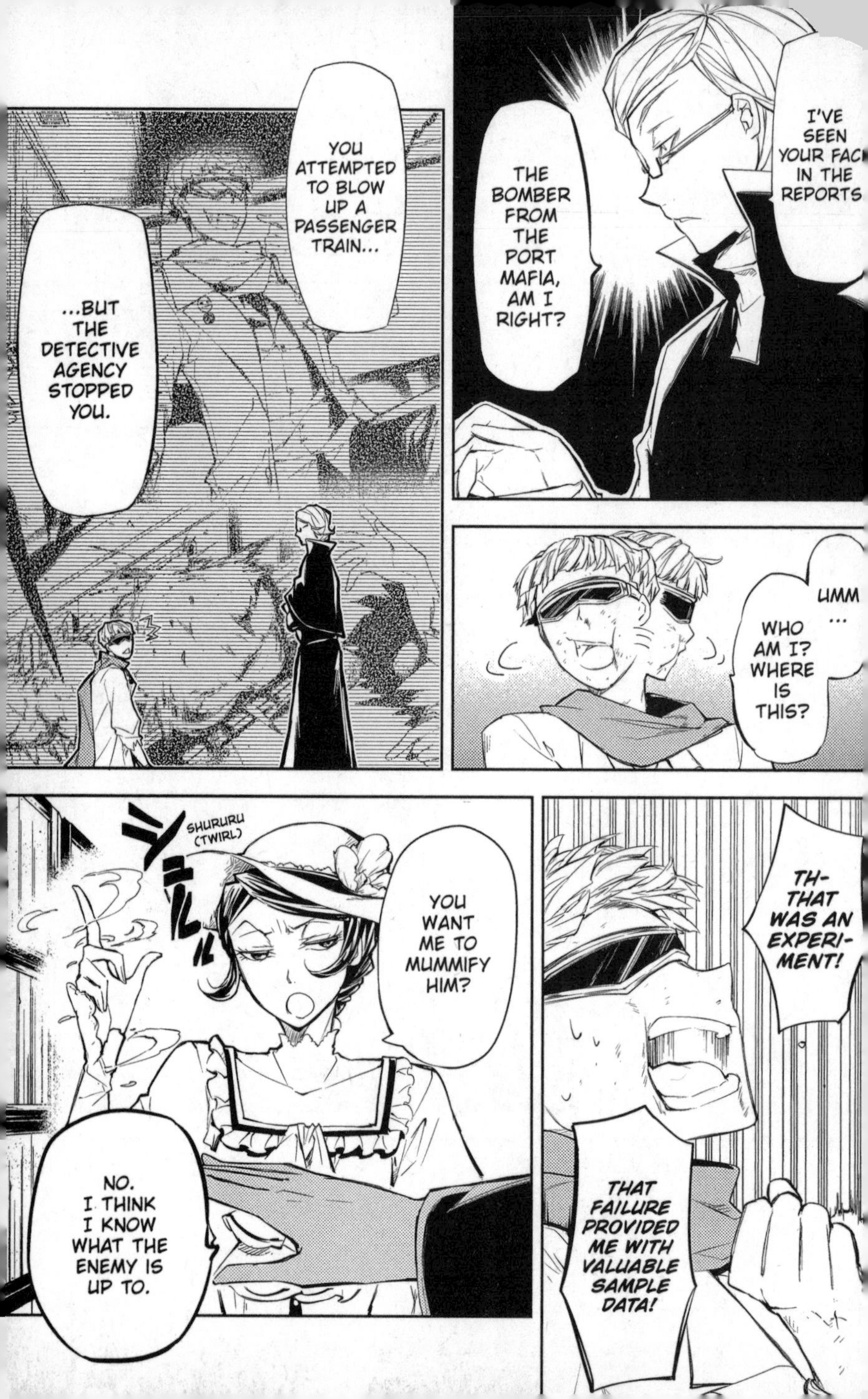
I'VE SEEN YOUR FAC IN THE REPORTS
THE BOMBER FROM THE PORT MAFIA, AM I RIGHT?
UMM ...
WHO AM I? WHERE IS THIS?
YOU ATTEMPTED TO BLOW UP A PASSENGER TRAIN...
...BUT THE DETECTIVE AGENCY STOPPED YOU.
TH-THAT WAS AN EXPERI-MENT!
THAT FAILURE PROVIDED ME WITH VALUABLE SAMPLE DATA!
SHURURU (TWIRL)
YOU WANT ME TO MUMMIFY HIM?
NO. I THINK I KNOW WHAT THE ENEMY IS UP TO.

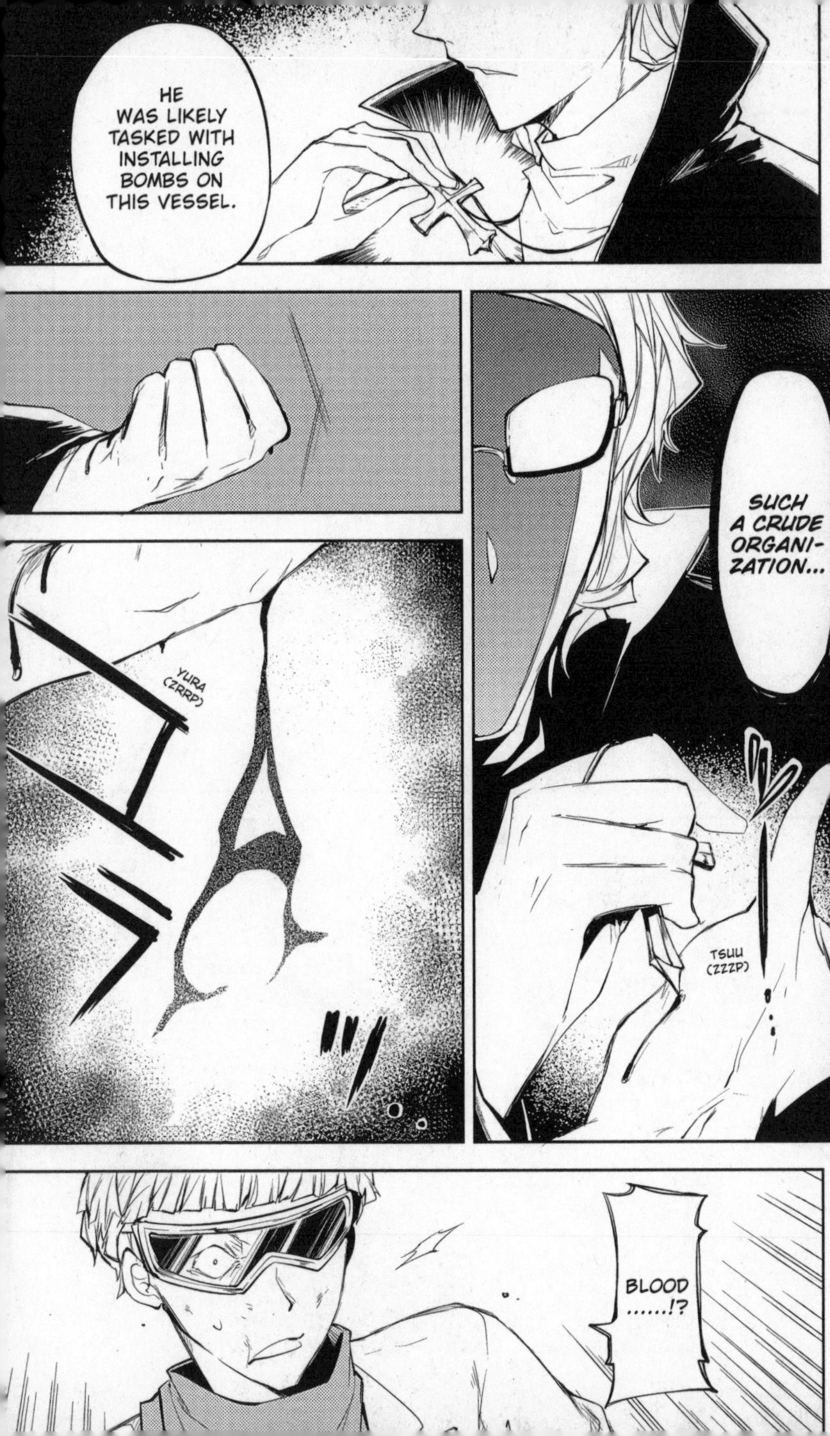
HE WAS LIKELY TASKED WITH INSTALLING BOMBS ON THIS VESSEL.
SUCH A CRUDE ORGANI-ZATION...
TSUU (ZZZP)
YURA (ZRRP)
BLOOD ......!?

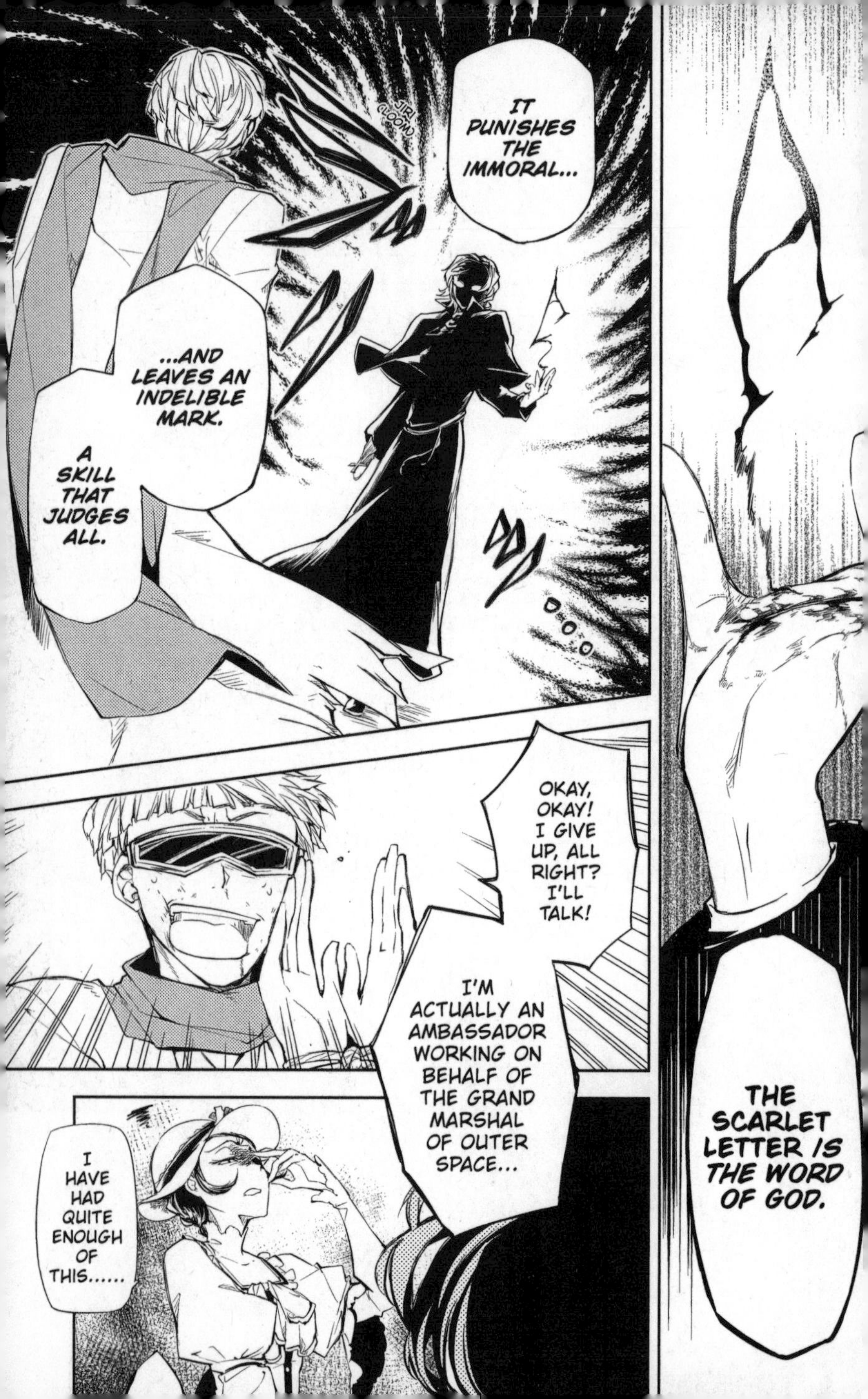
THE SCARLET LETTER IS THE WORD OF GOD.
IT PUNISHES THE IMMORAL...
JIRI (GLOOM)
...AND LEAVES AN INDELIBLE MARK.
A SKILL THAT JUDGES ALL.
OKAY, OKAY! I GIVE UP, ALL RIGHT? I'LL TALK!
I'M ACTUALLY AN AMBASSADOR WORKING ON BEHALF OF THE GRAND MARSHAL OF OUTER SPACE...
I HAVE HAD QUITE ENOUGH OF THIS......

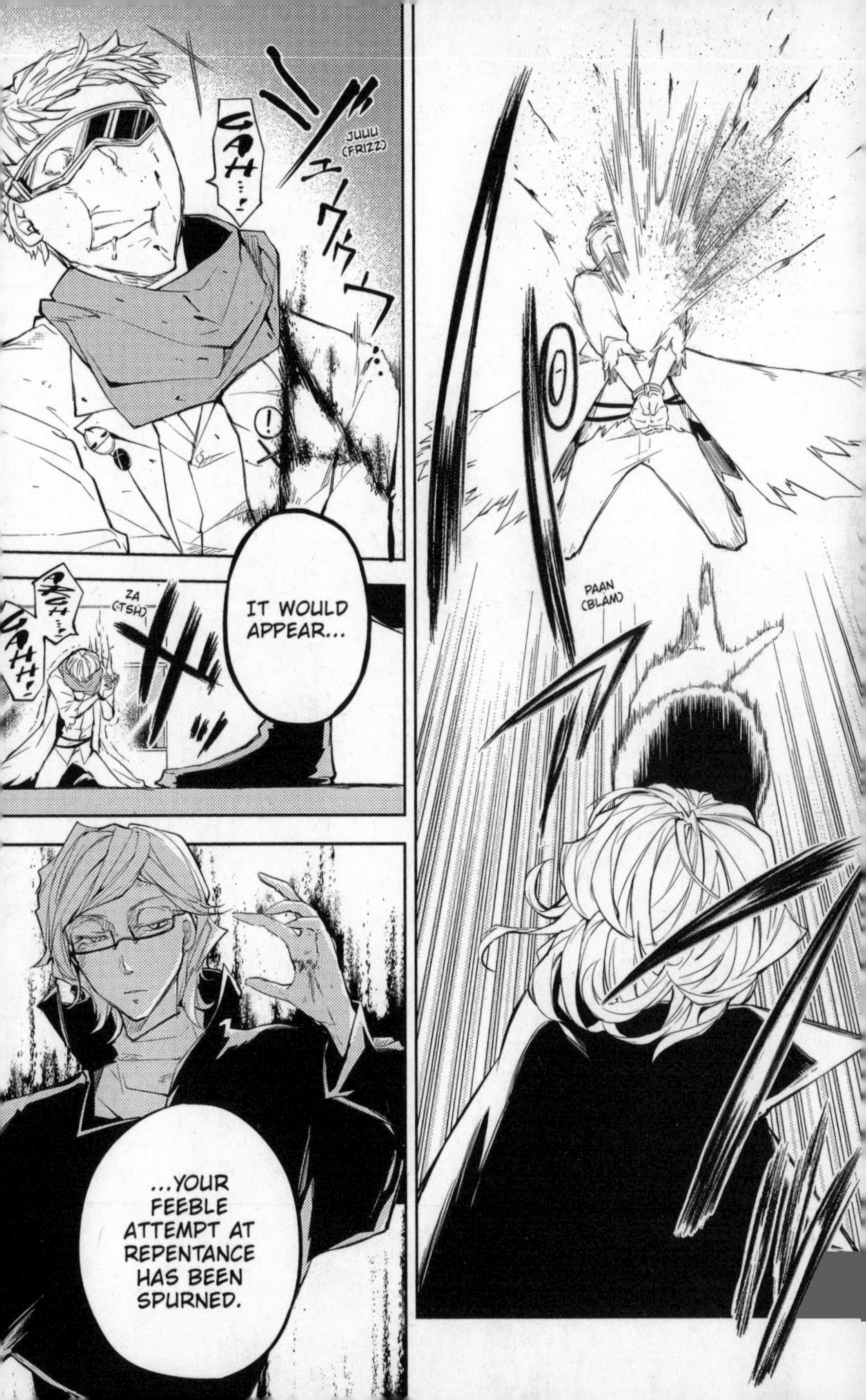
PAAN (BLAM)
JUUU (FRIZZ)
GAH...!
IT WOULD APPEAR...
ZA (TSH)
AAGH...!
UAHH!
...YOUR FEEBLE ATTEMPT AT REPENTANCE HAS BEEN SPURNED.

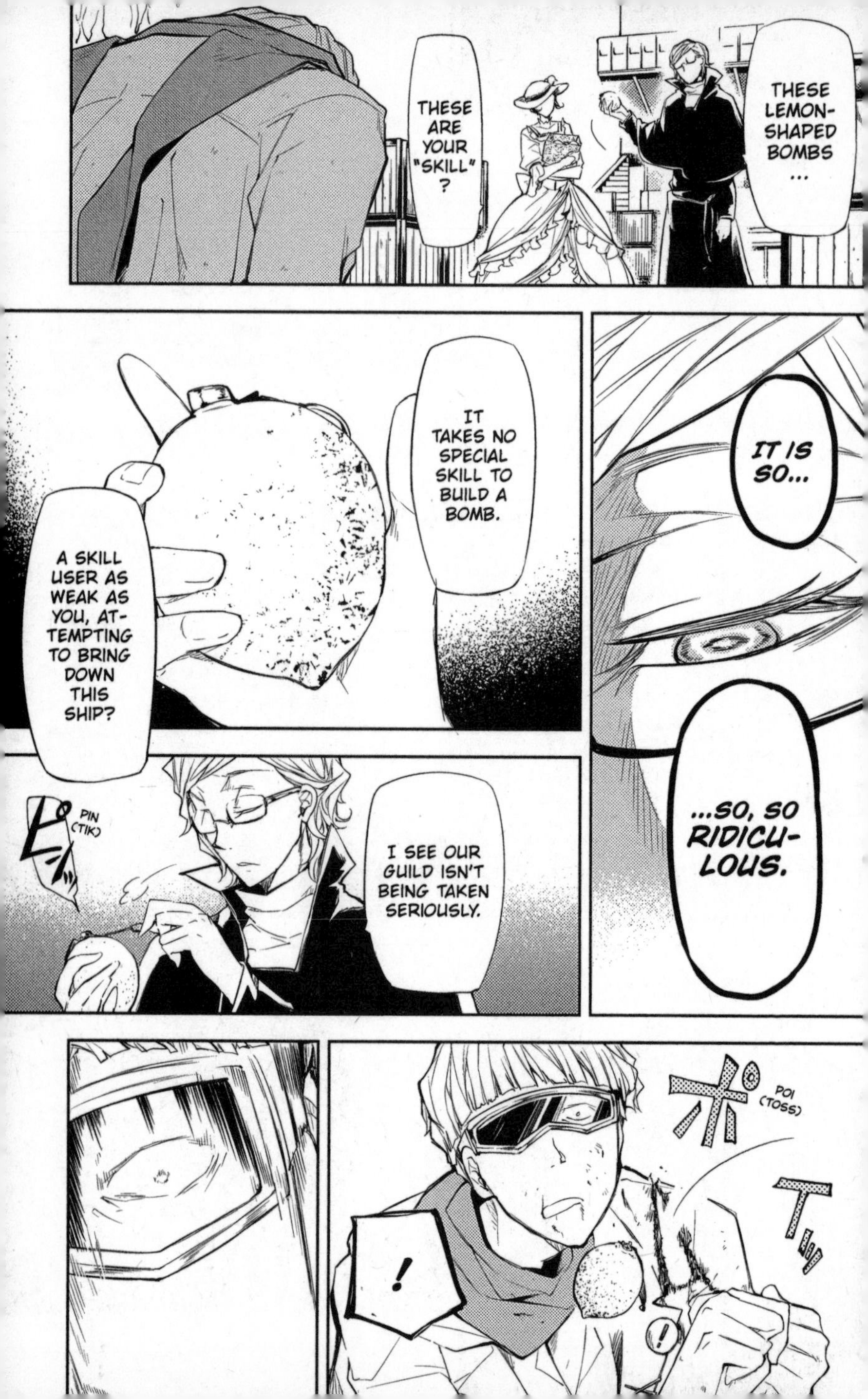
THESE LEMON-SHAPED BOMBS ...
THESE ARE YOUR "SKILL"?
IT IS SO...
...SO, SO RIDICULOUS.
IT TAKES NO SPECIAL SKILL TO BUILD A BOMB.
A SKILL USER AS WEAK AS YOU, AT-TEMPTING TO BRING DOWN THIS SHIP?
I SEE OUR GUILD ISN'T BEING TAKEN SERIOUSLY.
PIN (TIK)
POI (TOSS)
!
!

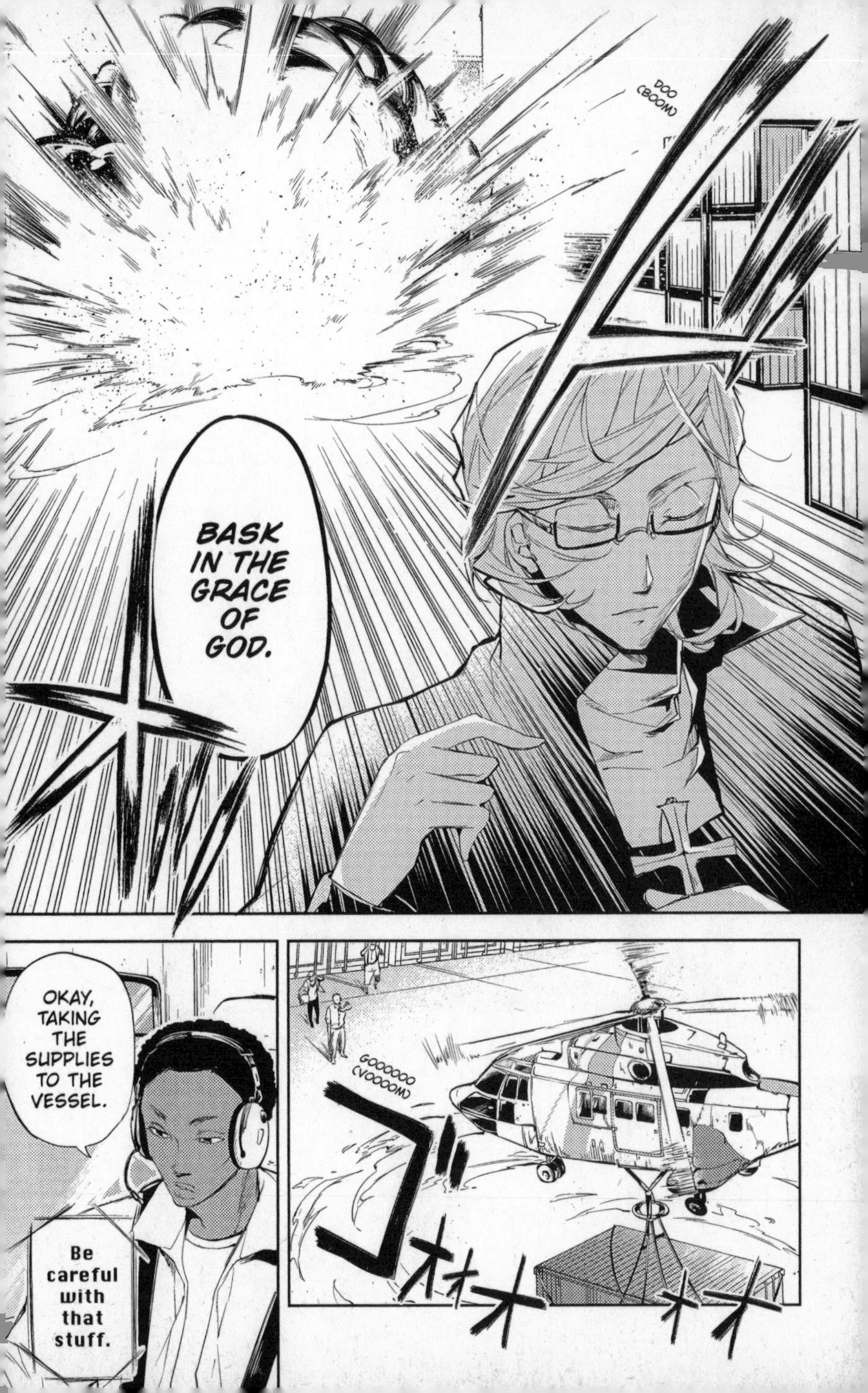
DOO (BOOM)
BASK IN THE GRACE OF GOD.
GOOOOOO (VOOOOM)
OKAY, TAKING THE SUPPLIES TO THE VESSEL.
Be careful with that stuff.

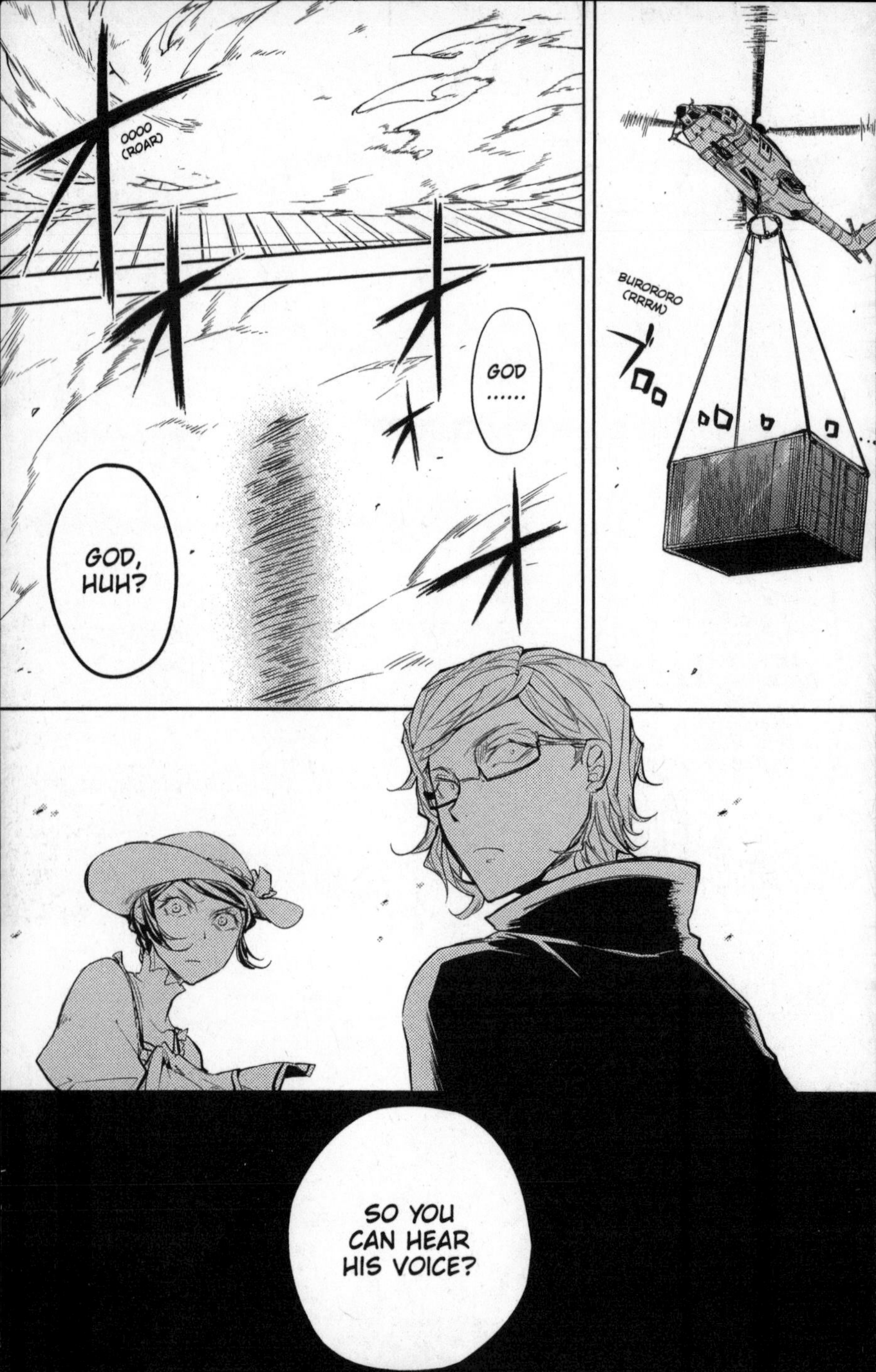
BURORORO (RRRM)
OOOO (ROAR)
GOD ......
GOD, HUH?
SO YOU CAN HEAR HIS VOICE?

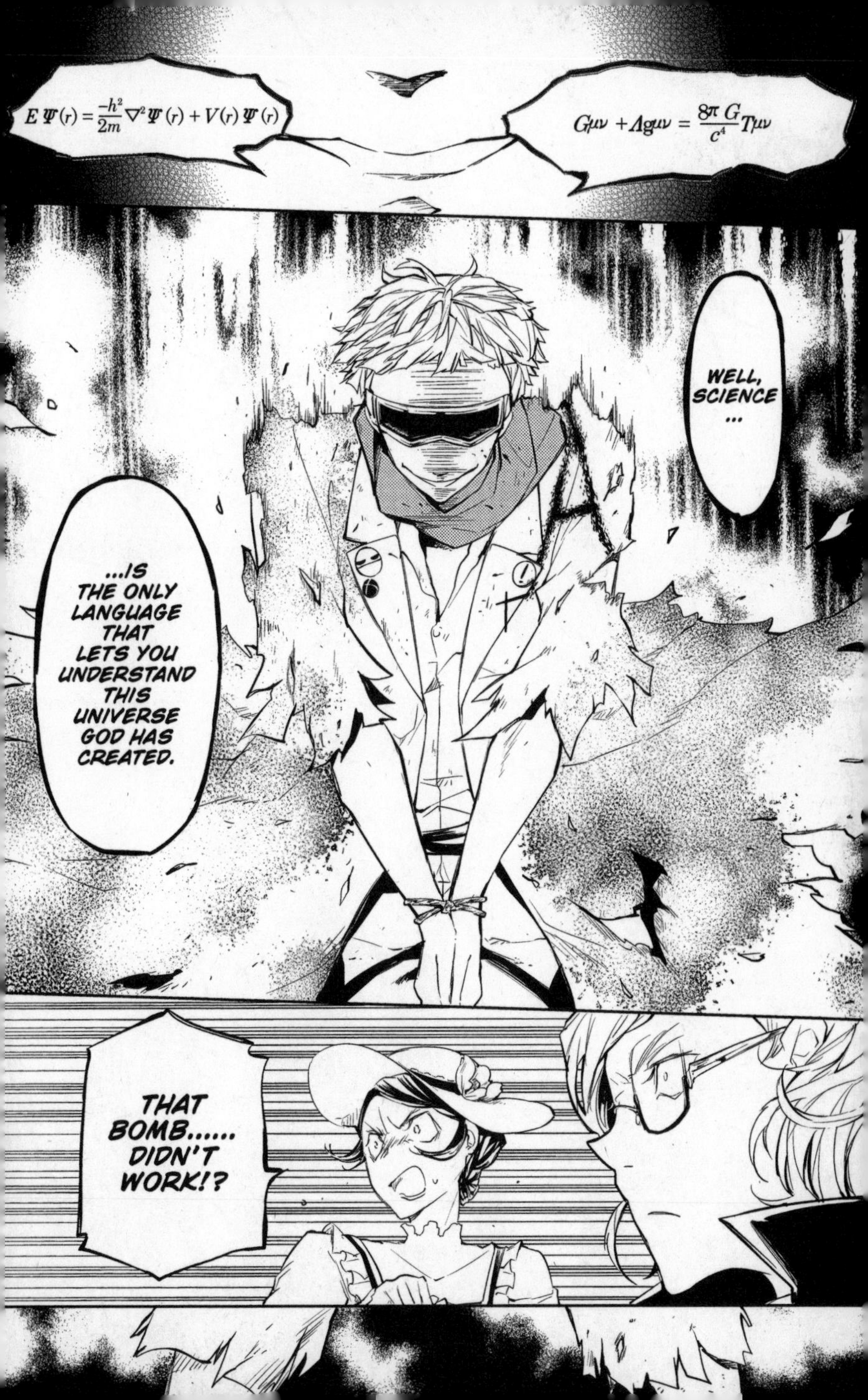
$G_{\mu\nu} + \Lambda g_{\mu\nu} = \frac{8\pi G}{c^4} T_{\mu\nu}$
$E\Psi(r) = \frac{-h^2}{2m}\nabla^2\Psi(r) + V(r)\Psi(r)$
WELL, SCIENCE ...
...IS THE ONLY LANGUAGE THAT LETS YOU UNDERSTAND THIS UNIVERSE GOD HAS CREATED.
THAT BOMB...... DIDN'T WORK!?

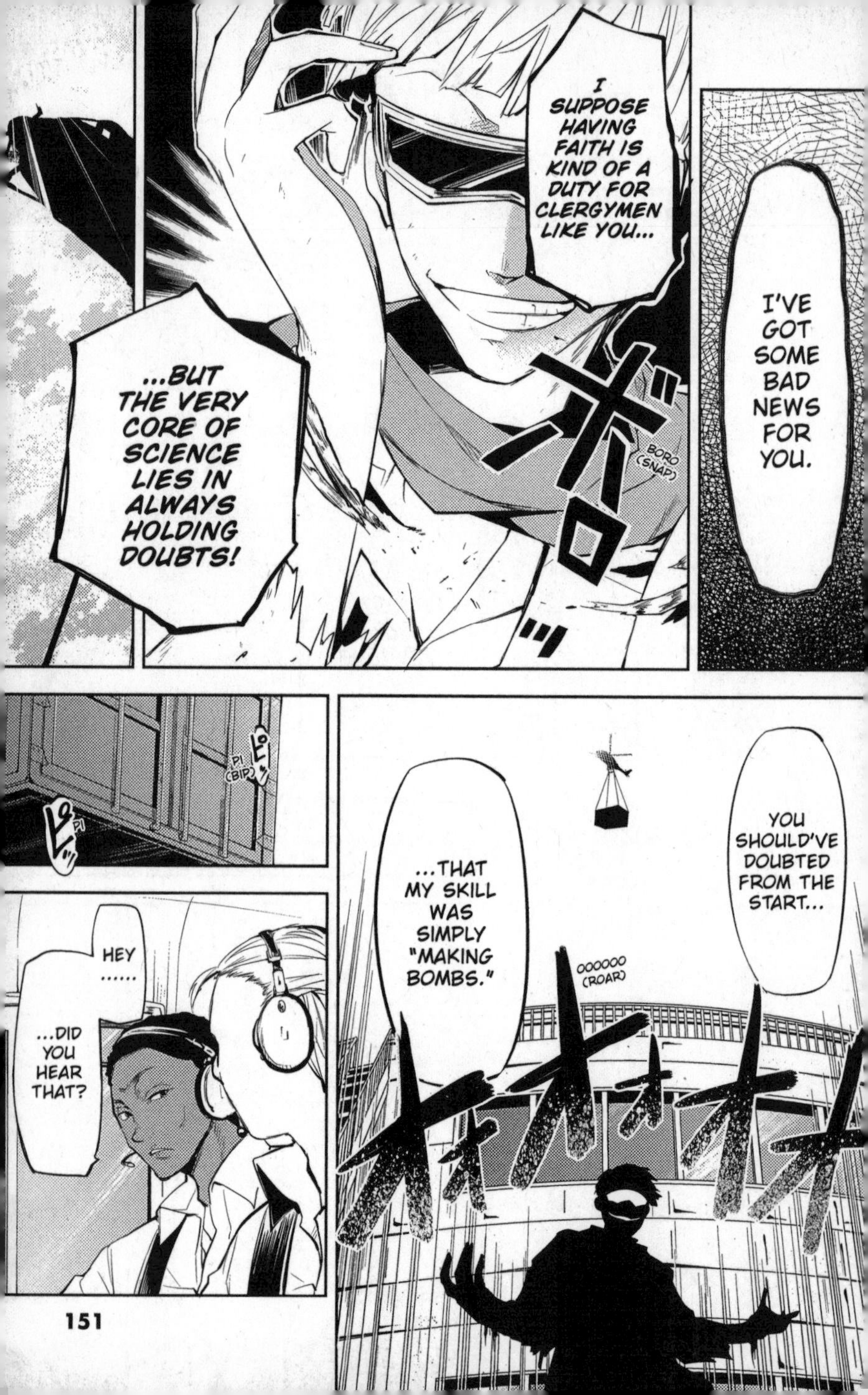
I'VE GOT SOME BAD NEWS FOR YOU.
I SUPPOSE HAVING FAITH IS KIND OF A DUTY FOR CLERGYMEN LIKE YOU...
BORO (SNAP)
...BUT THE VERY CORE OF SCIENCE LIES IN ALWAYS HOLDING DOUBTS!
YOU SHOULD'VE DOUBTED FROM THE START...
...THAT MY SKILL WAS SIMPLY "MAKING BOMBS."
OOOOOO (ROAR)
PI (BIP)
PI
HEY ......
...DID YOU HEAR THAT?

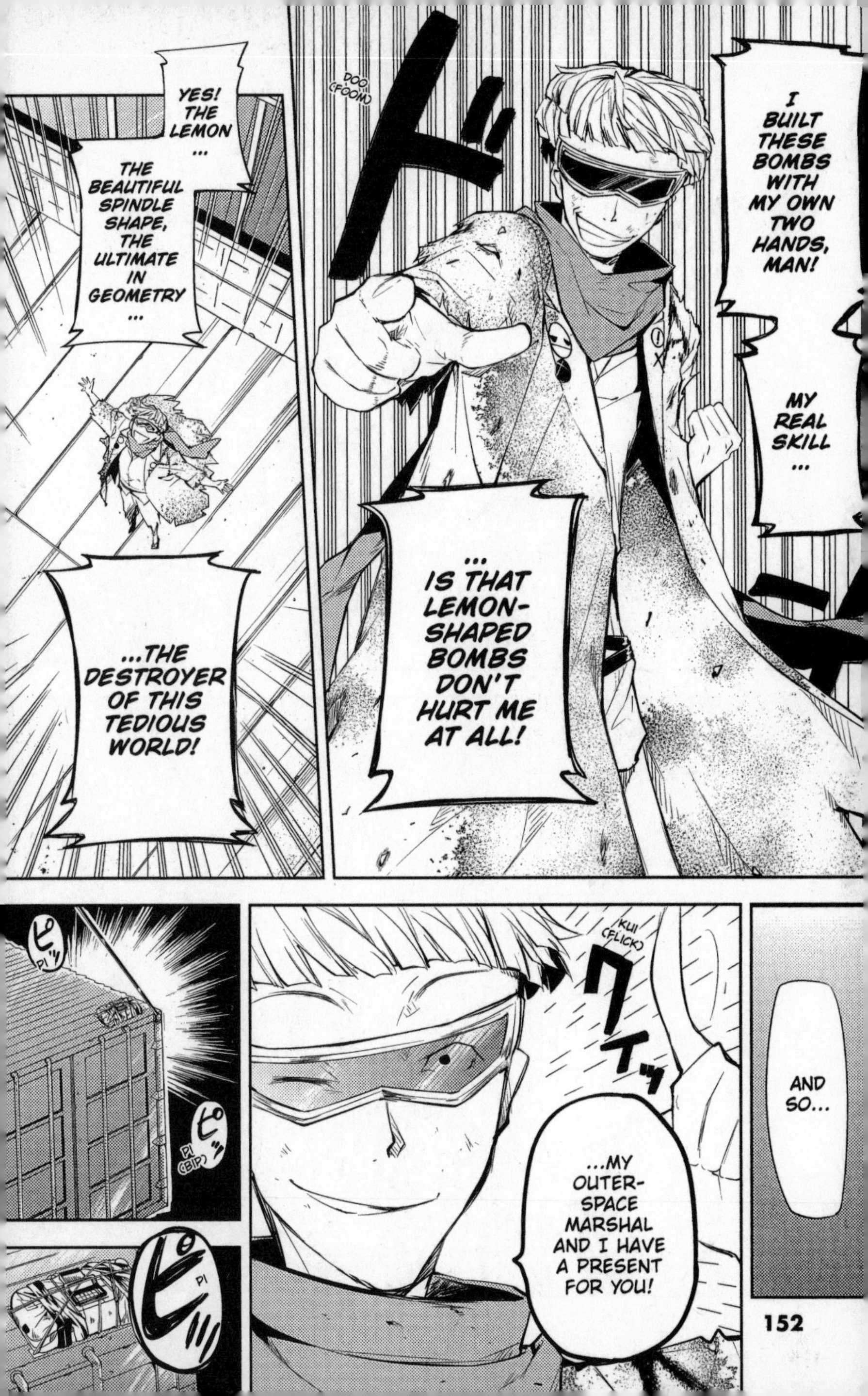
DOO (FOOM)
I BUILT THESE BOMBS WITH MY OWN TWO HANDS, MAN!
MY REAL SKILL ...
... IS THAT LEMON-SHAPED BOMBS DON'T HURT ME AT ALL!
YES! THE LEMON ...
THE BEAUTIFUL SPINDLE SHAPE, THE ULTIMATE IN GEOMETRY ...
...THE DESTROYER OF THIS TEDIOUS WORLD!
AND SO...
KUI (FLICK)
...MY OUTER-SPACE MARSHAL AND I HAVE A PRESENT FOR YOU!
PI
PI (BIP)
PI

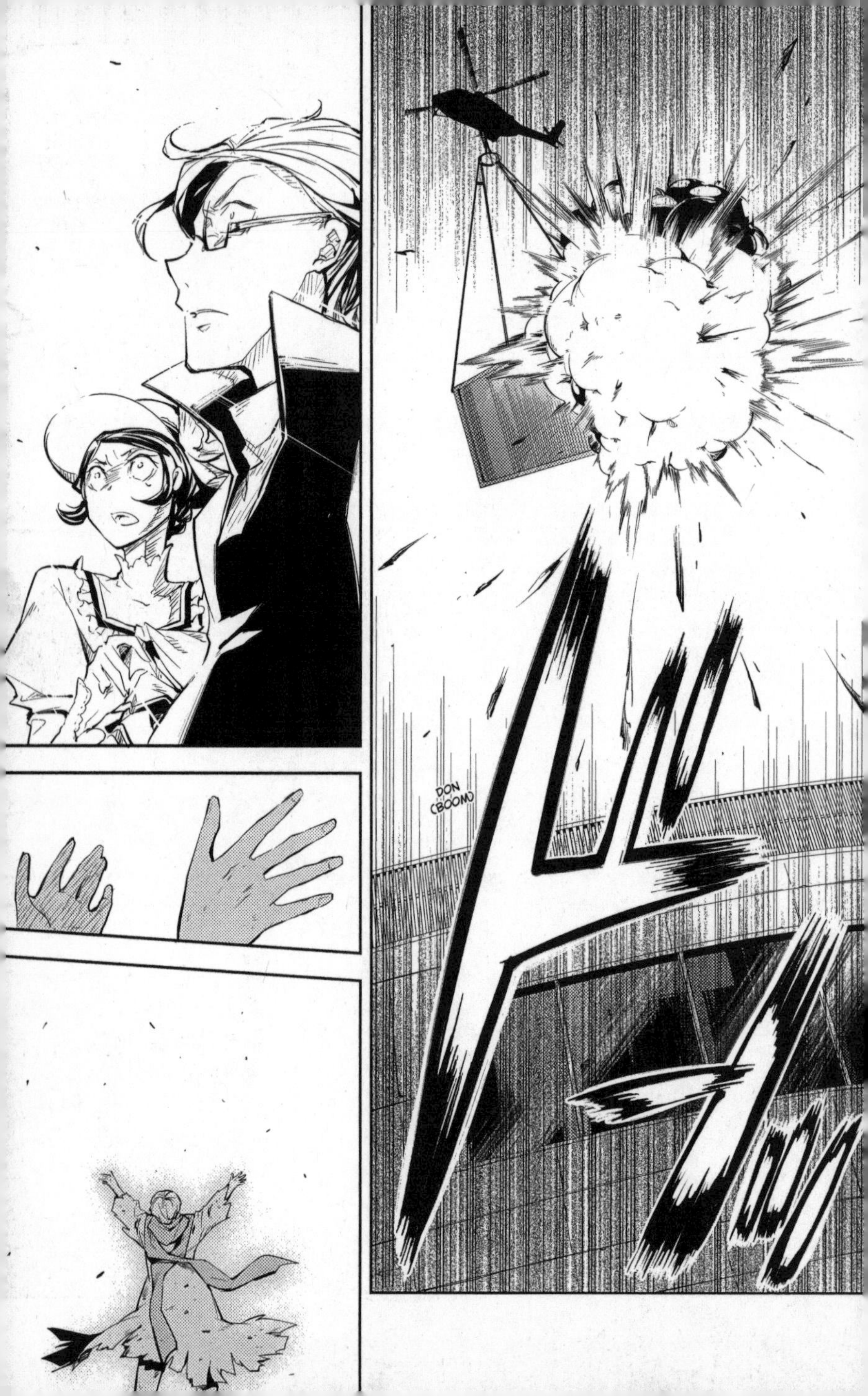
DON
(BOOM)

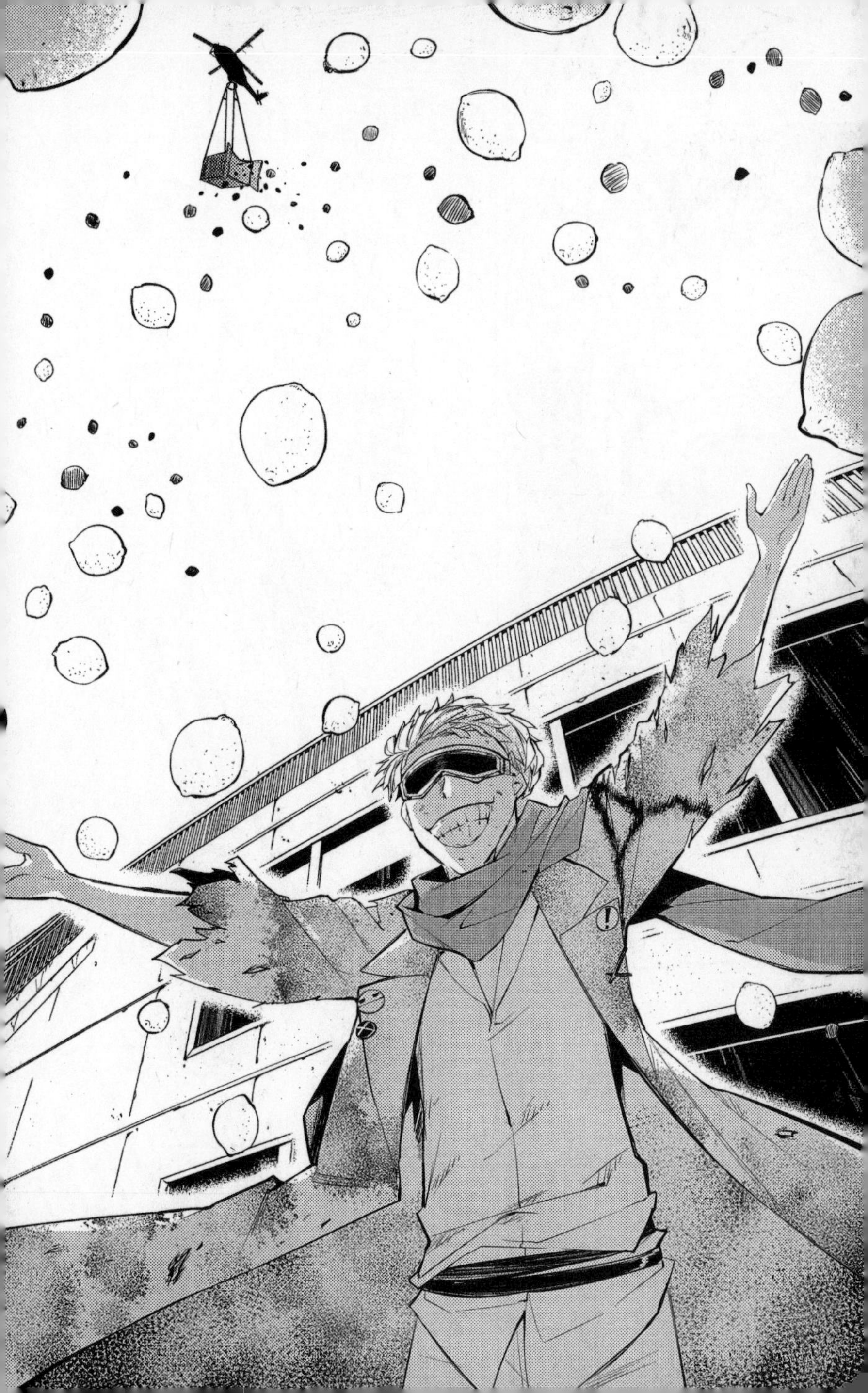

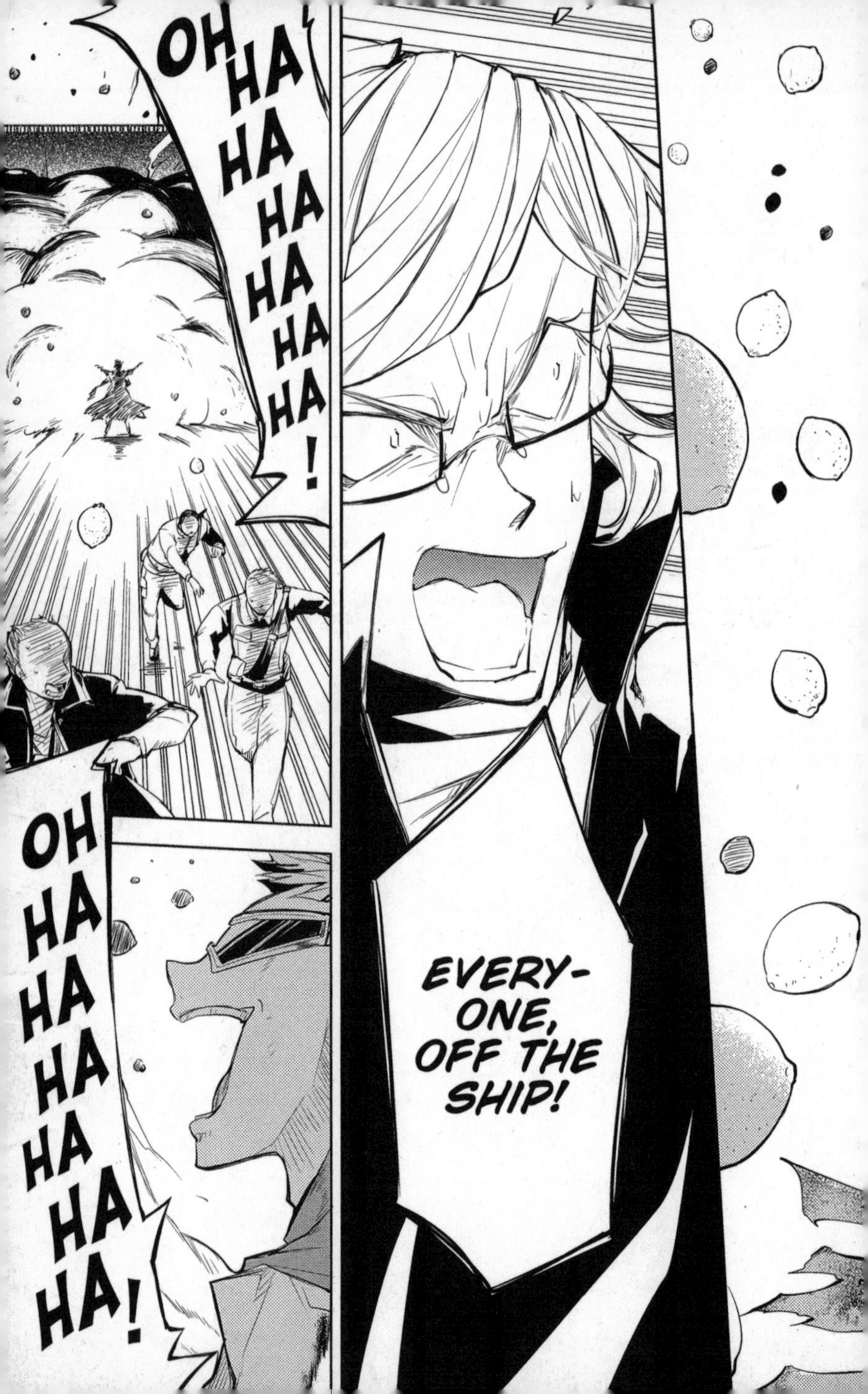
EVERYONE, OFF THE SHIP!
OH HA HA HA HA HA HA!
OH HA HA HA HA HA HA!

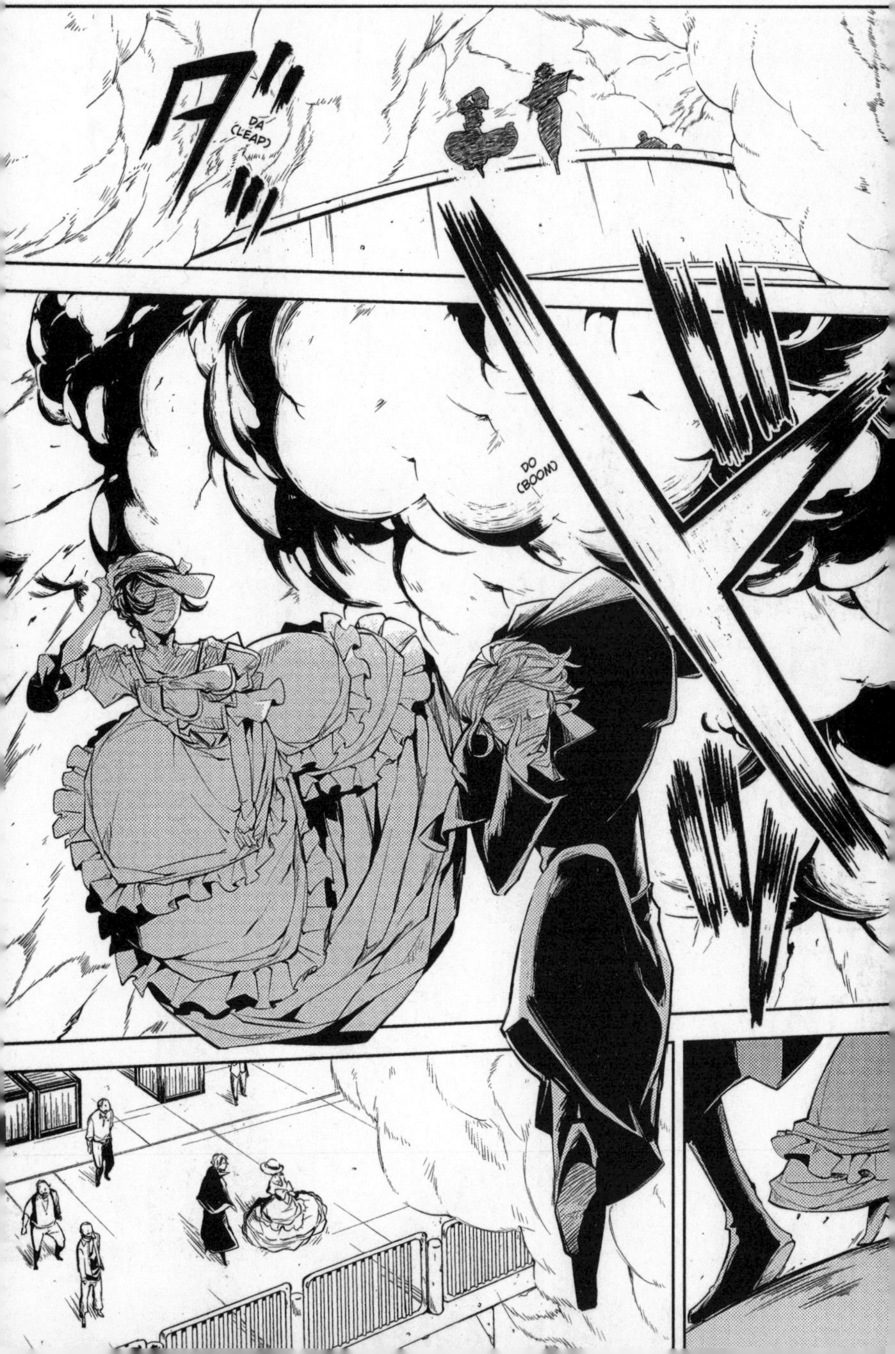
DA (LEAP)
DO (BOOM)

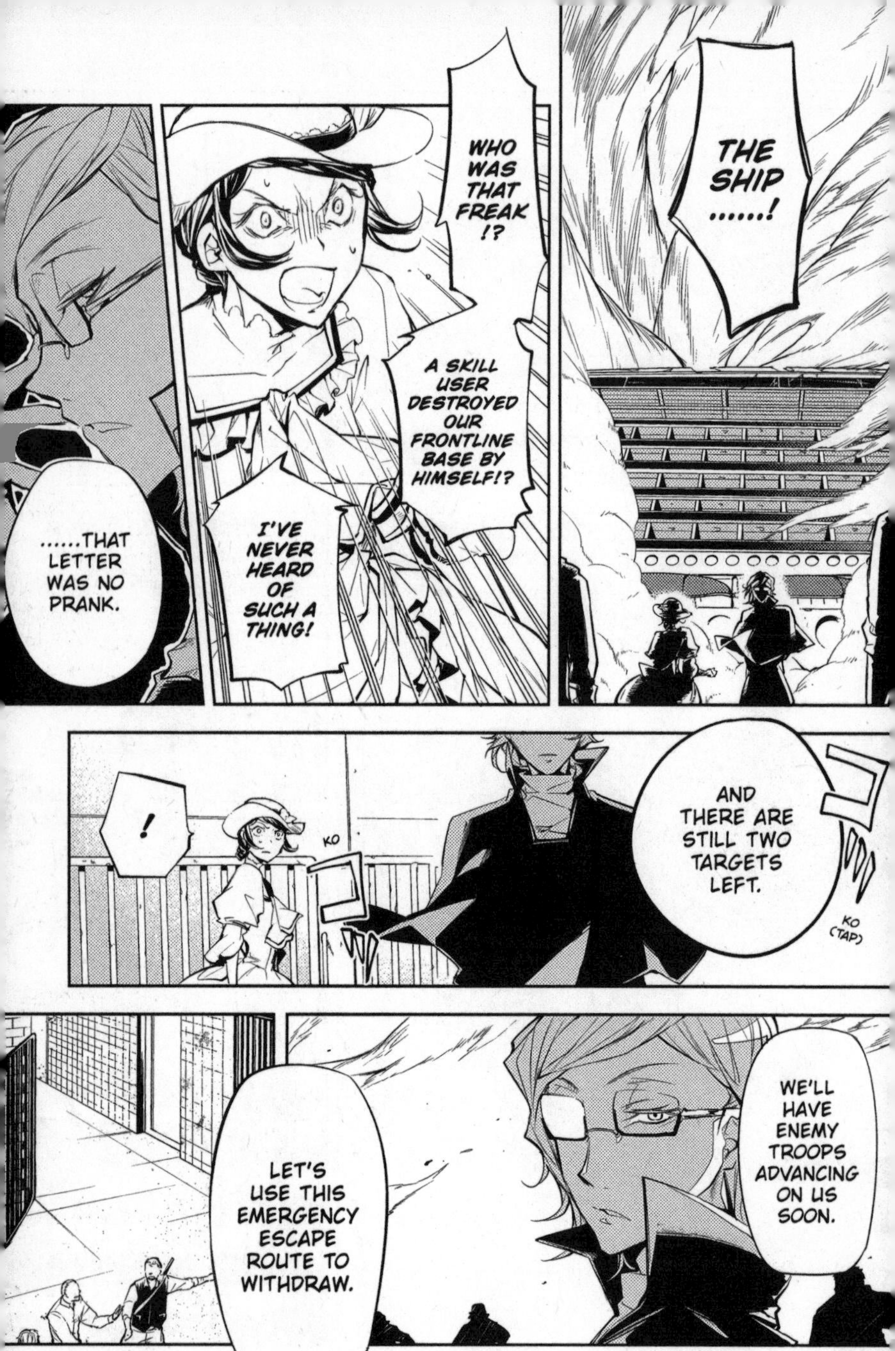
THE SHIP......!
WHO WAS THAT FREAK!?
A SKILL USER DESTROYED OUR FRONTLINE BASE BY HIMSELF!?
I'VE NEVER HEARD OF SUCH A THING!
......THAT LETTER WAS NO PRANK.
AND THERE ARE STILL TWO TARGETS LEFT.
KO (TAP)
KO
!
WE'LL HAVE ENEMY TROOPS ADVANCING ON US SOON.
LET'S USE THIS EMERGENCY ESCAPE ROUTE TO WITHDRAW.

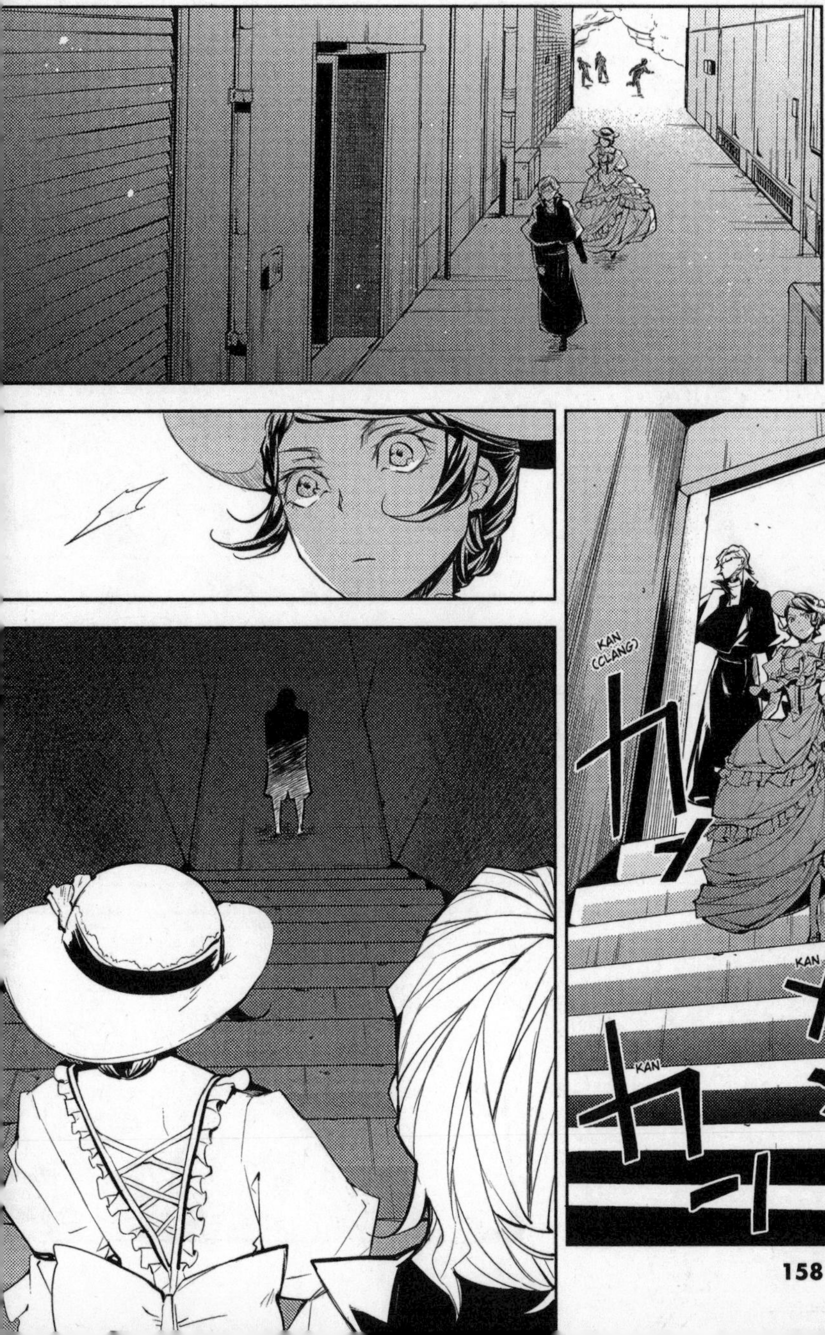
KAN (CLANG)
KAN
KAN

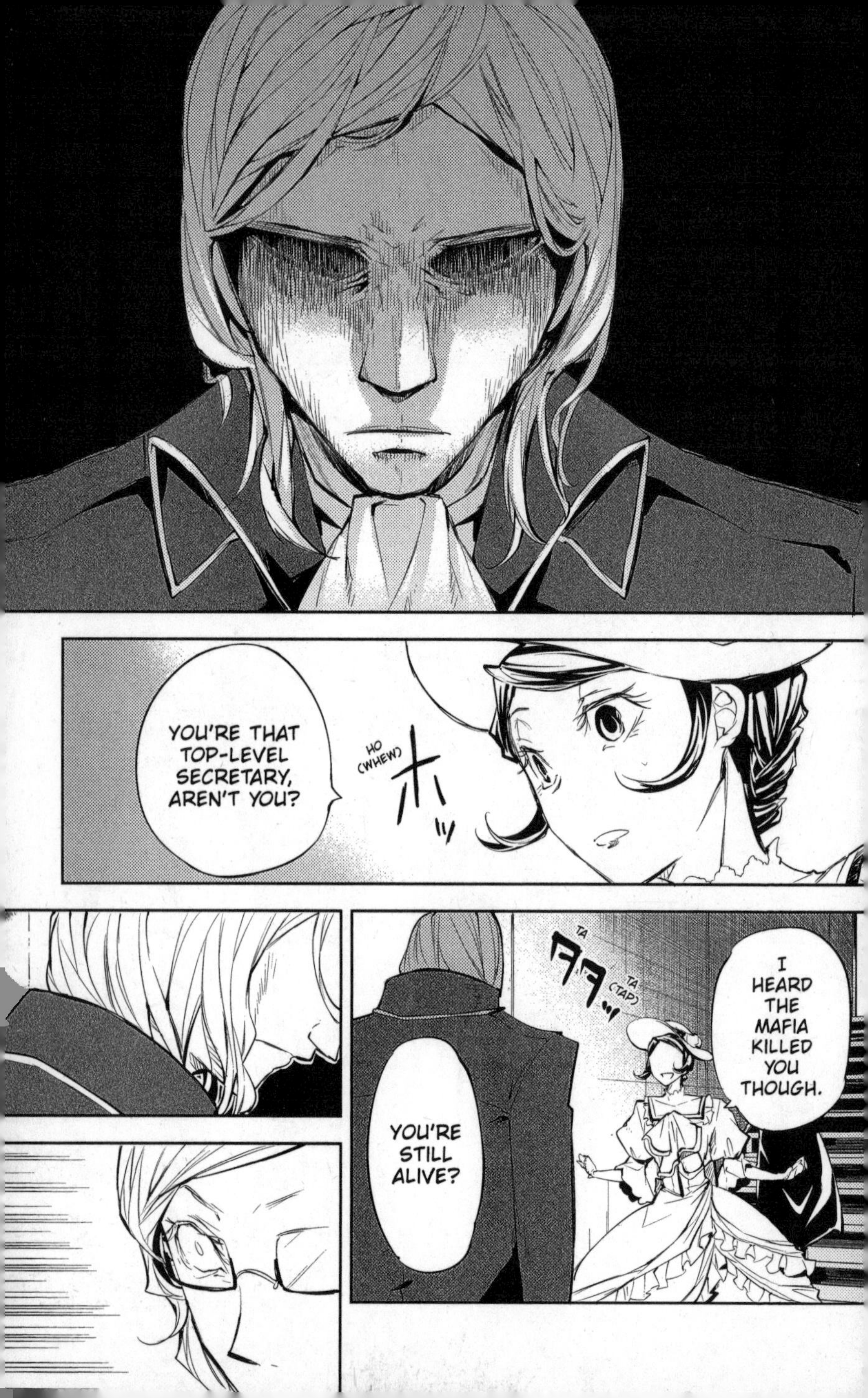
HO (WHEW)
YOU'RE THAT TOP-LEVEL SECRETARY, AREN'T YOU?
TA TA (TAP)
I HEARD THE MAFIA KILLED YOU THOUGH.
YOU'RE STILL ALIVE?

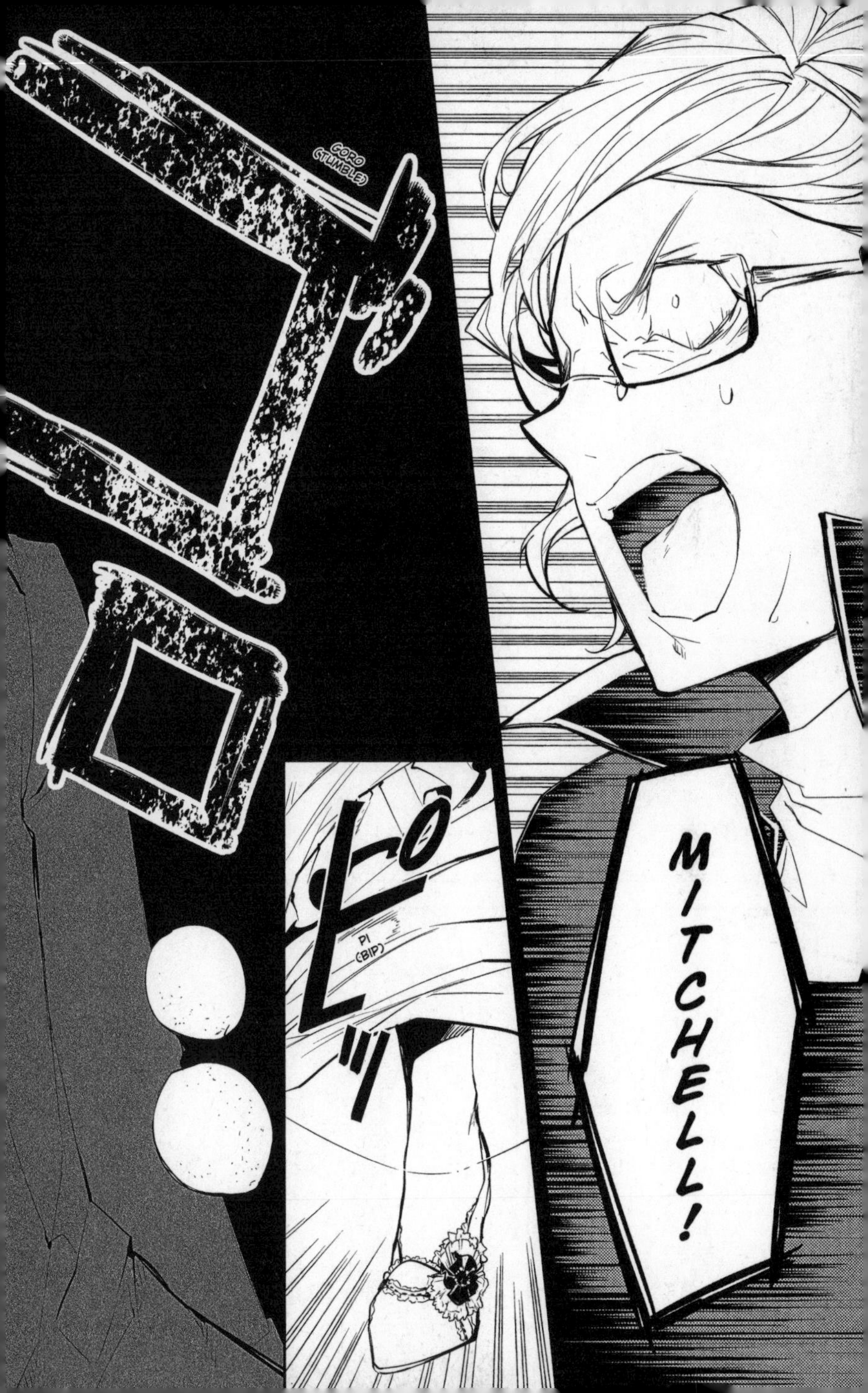
MITCHELL!
GORO (TUMBLE)
PI (BIP)

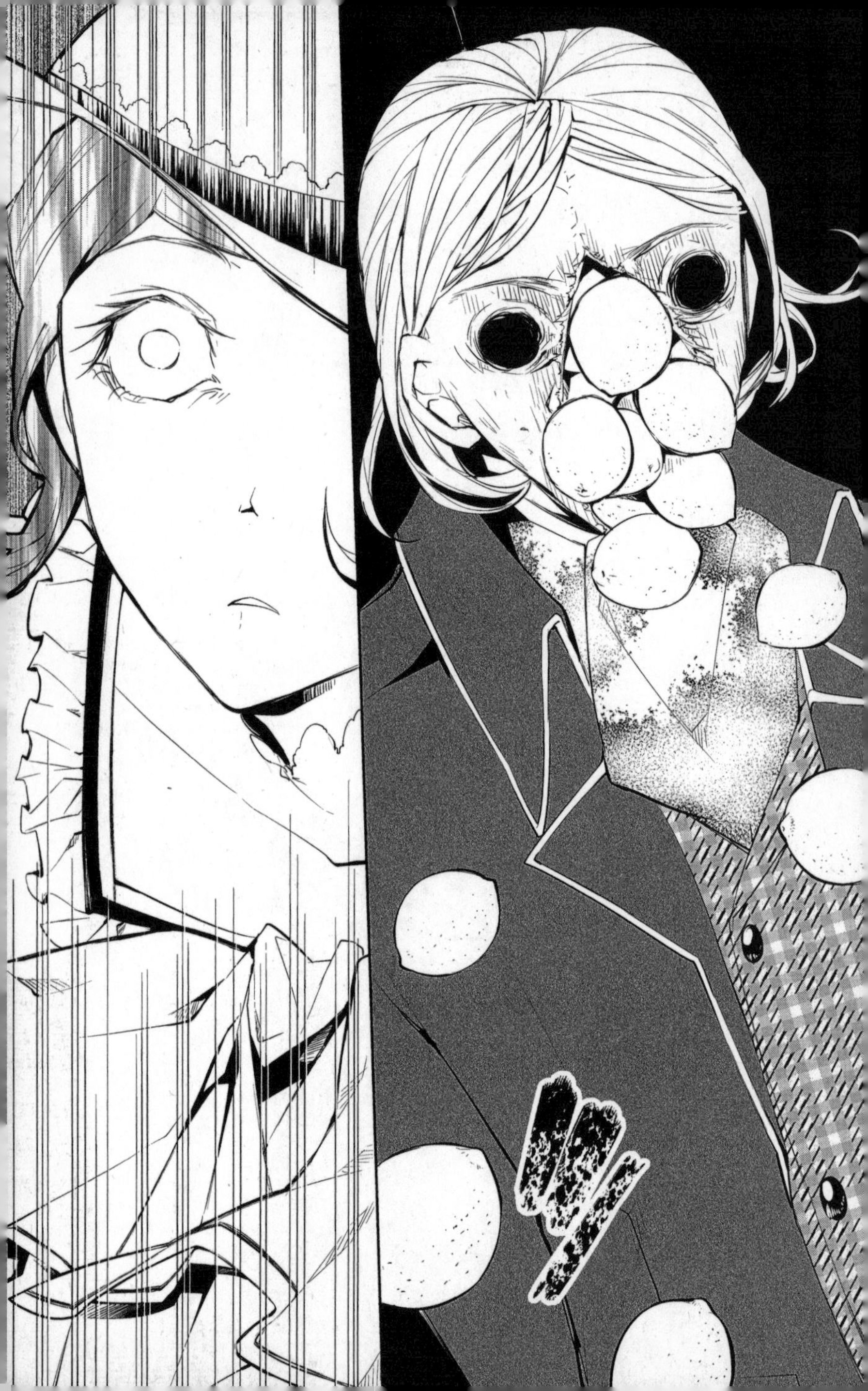

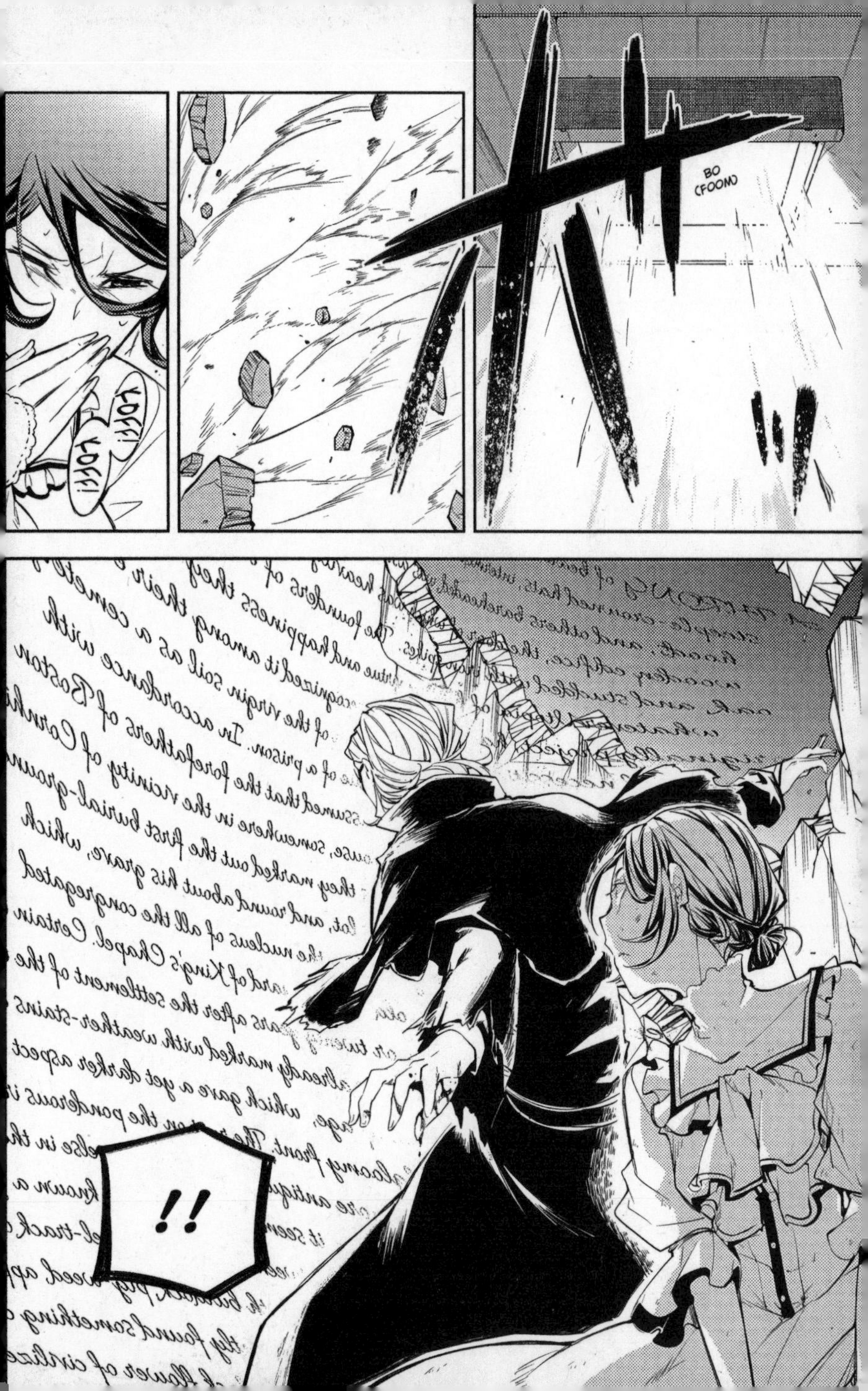
BO (FOOM)
!!
KOFF!
KOFF!
!!

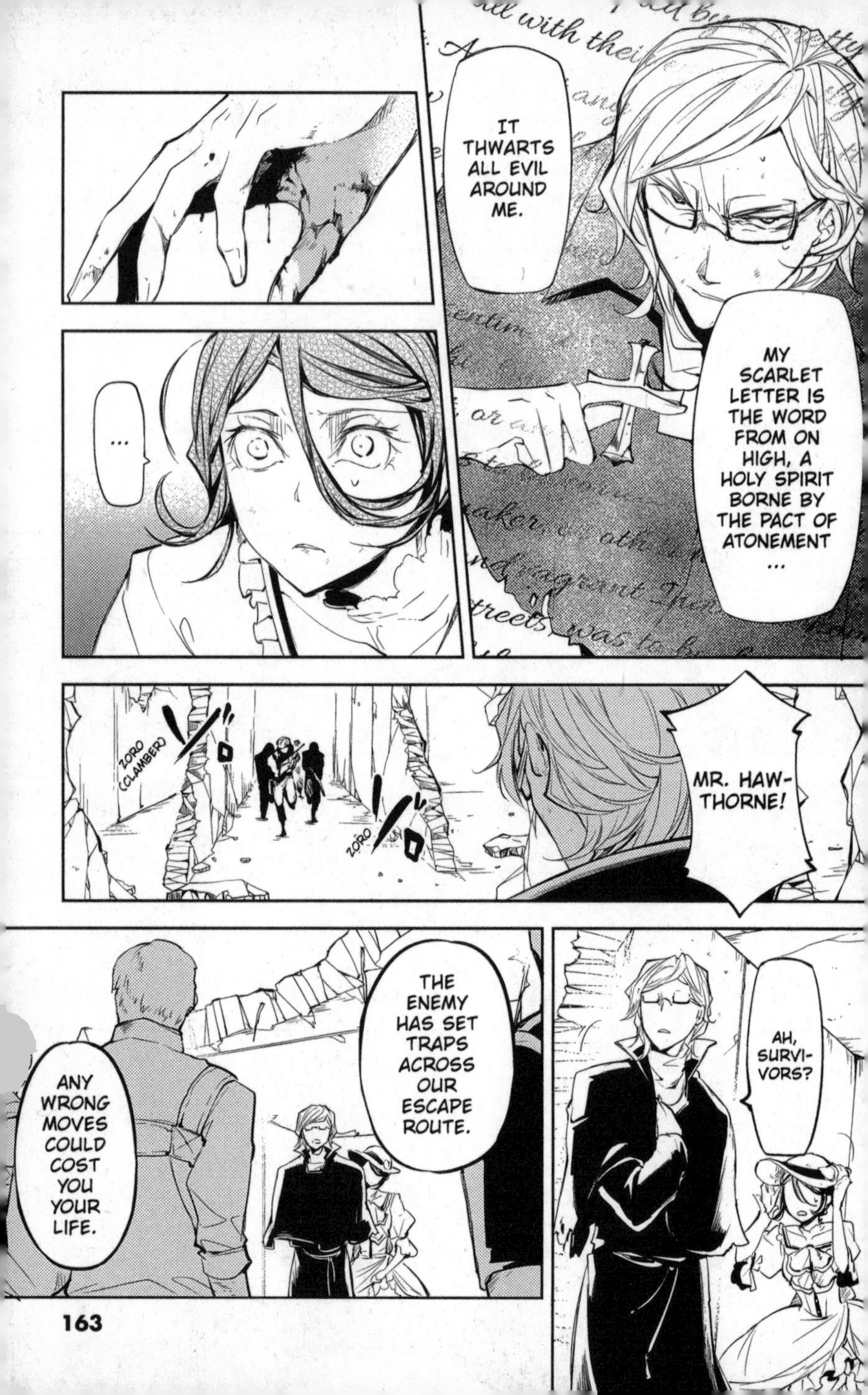
IT THWARTS ALL EVIL AROUND ME.
MY SCARLET LETTER IS THE WORD FROM ON HIGH, A HOLY SPIRIT BORNE BY THE PACT OF ATONEMENT ...
...
MR. HAW-THORNE!
ZORO (CLAMBER)
ZORO
AH, SURVI-VORS?
THE ENEMY HAS SET TRAPS ACROSS OUR ESCAPE ROUTE.
ANY WRONG MOVES COULD COST YOU YOUR LIFE.

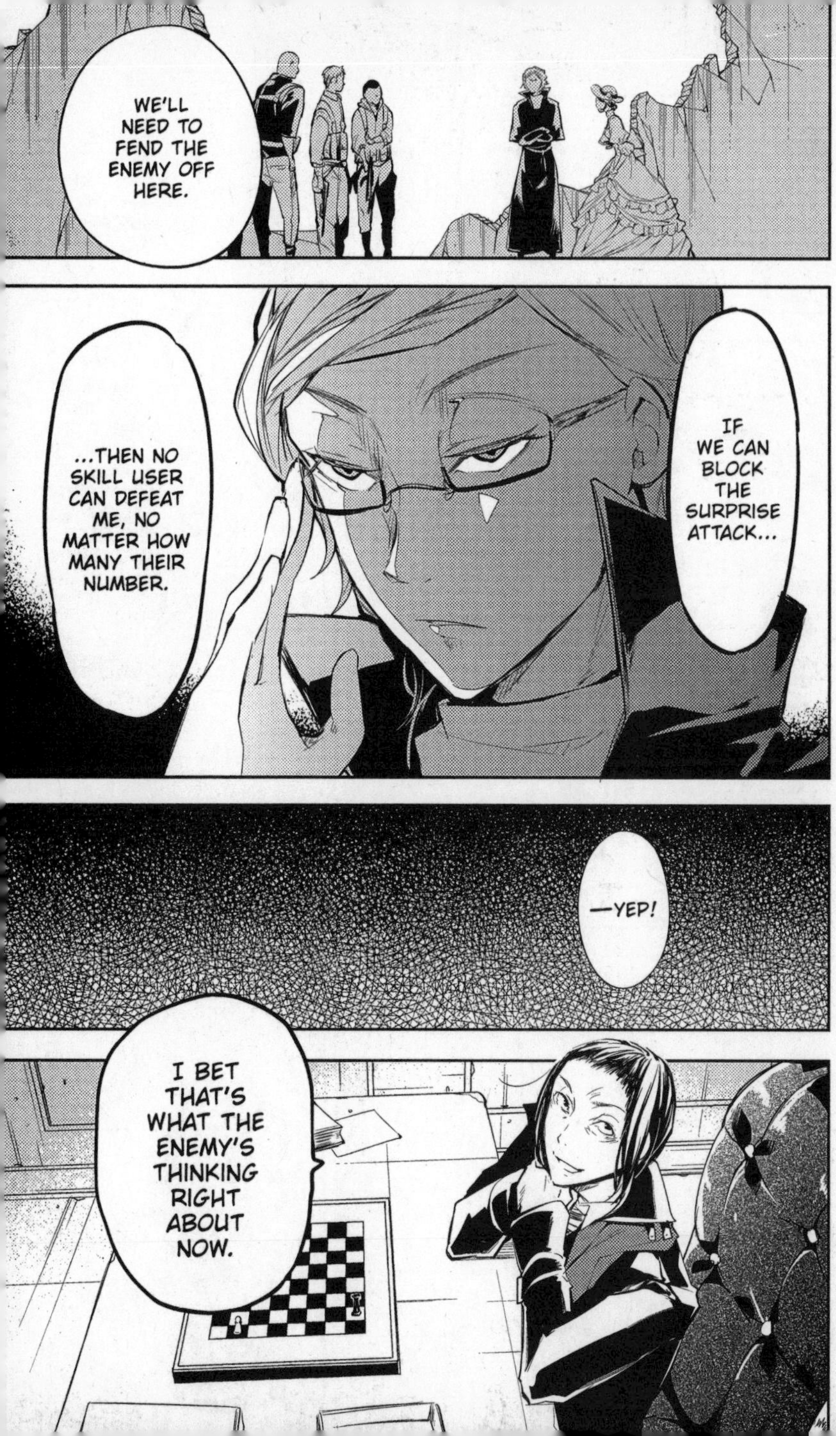
WE'LL NEED TO FEND THE ENEMY OFF HERE.
IF WE CAN BLOCK THE SURPRISE ATTACK...
...THEN NO SKILL USER CAN DEFEAT ME, NO MATTER HOW MANY THEIR NUMBER.
—YEP!
I BET THAT'S WHAT THE ENEMY'S THINKING RIGHT ABOUT NOW.

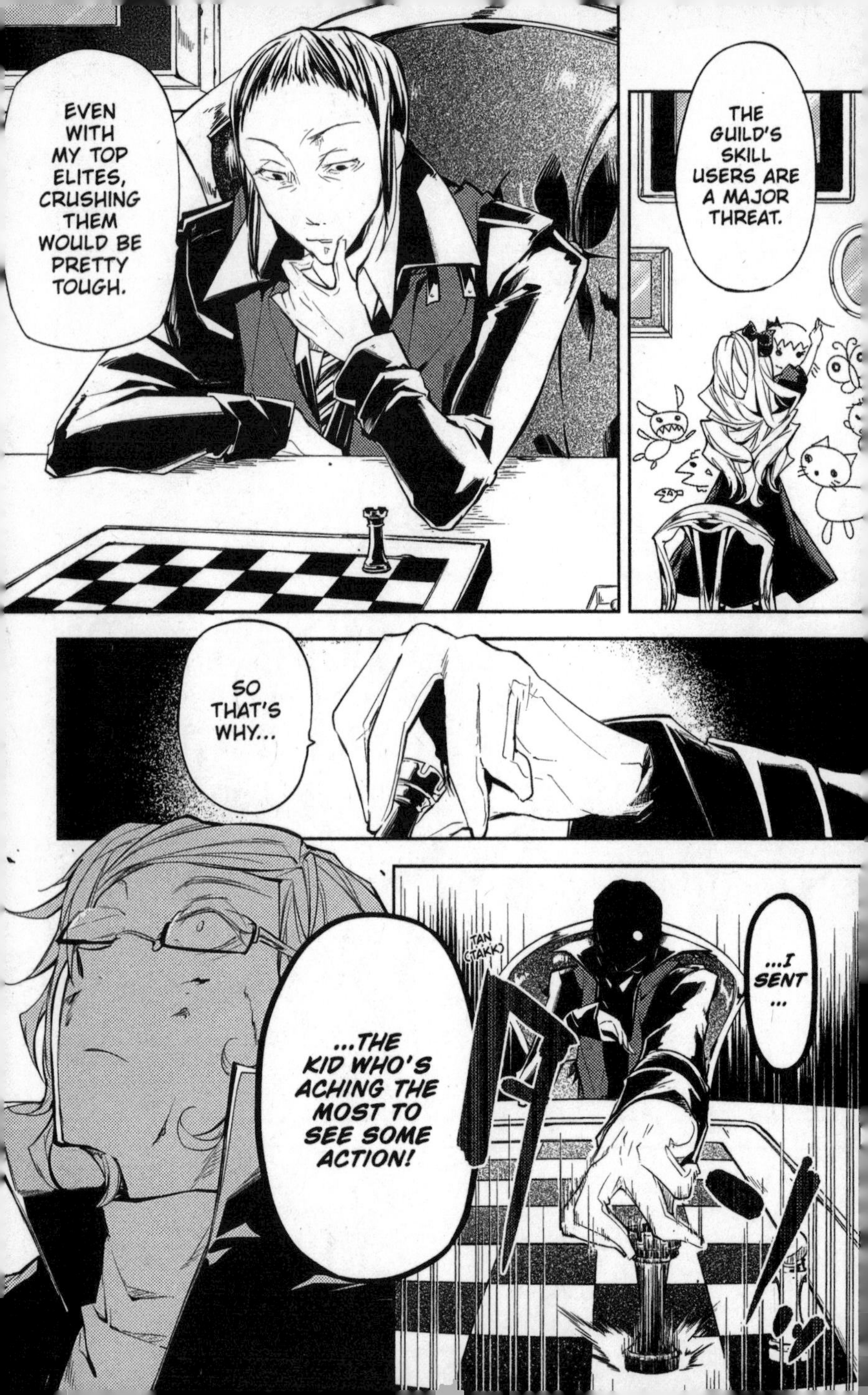
THE GUILD'S SKILL USERS ARE A MAJOR THREAT.
EVEN WITH MY TOP ELITES, CRUSHING THEM WOULD BE PRETTY TOUGH.
SO THAT'S WHY...
...I SENT ...
TAN (TAKK)
...THE KID WHO'S ACHING THE MOST TO SEE SOME ACTION!

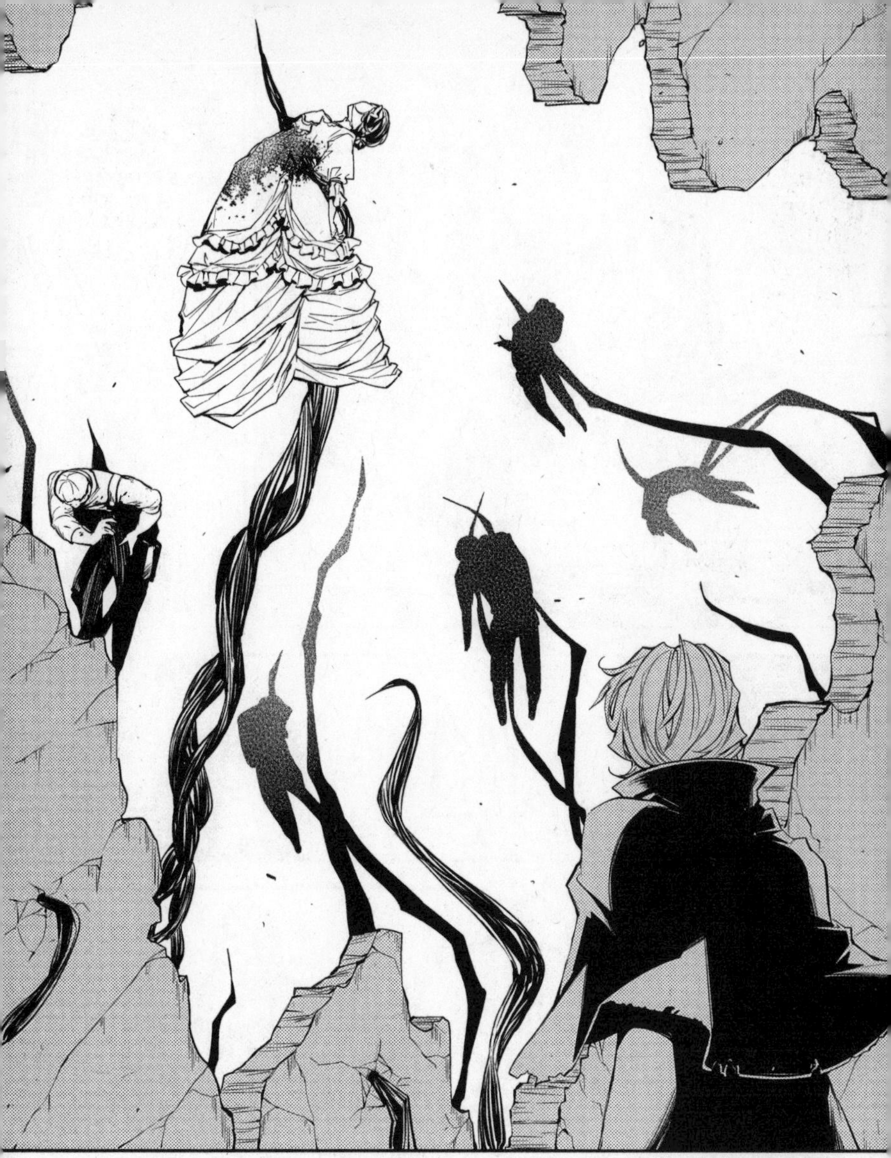

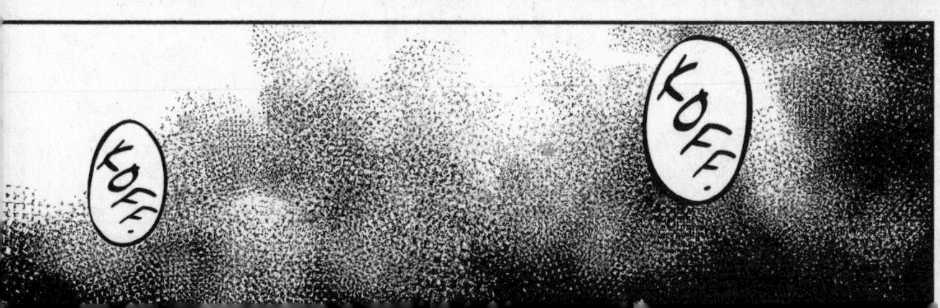
KOFF.
KOFF.

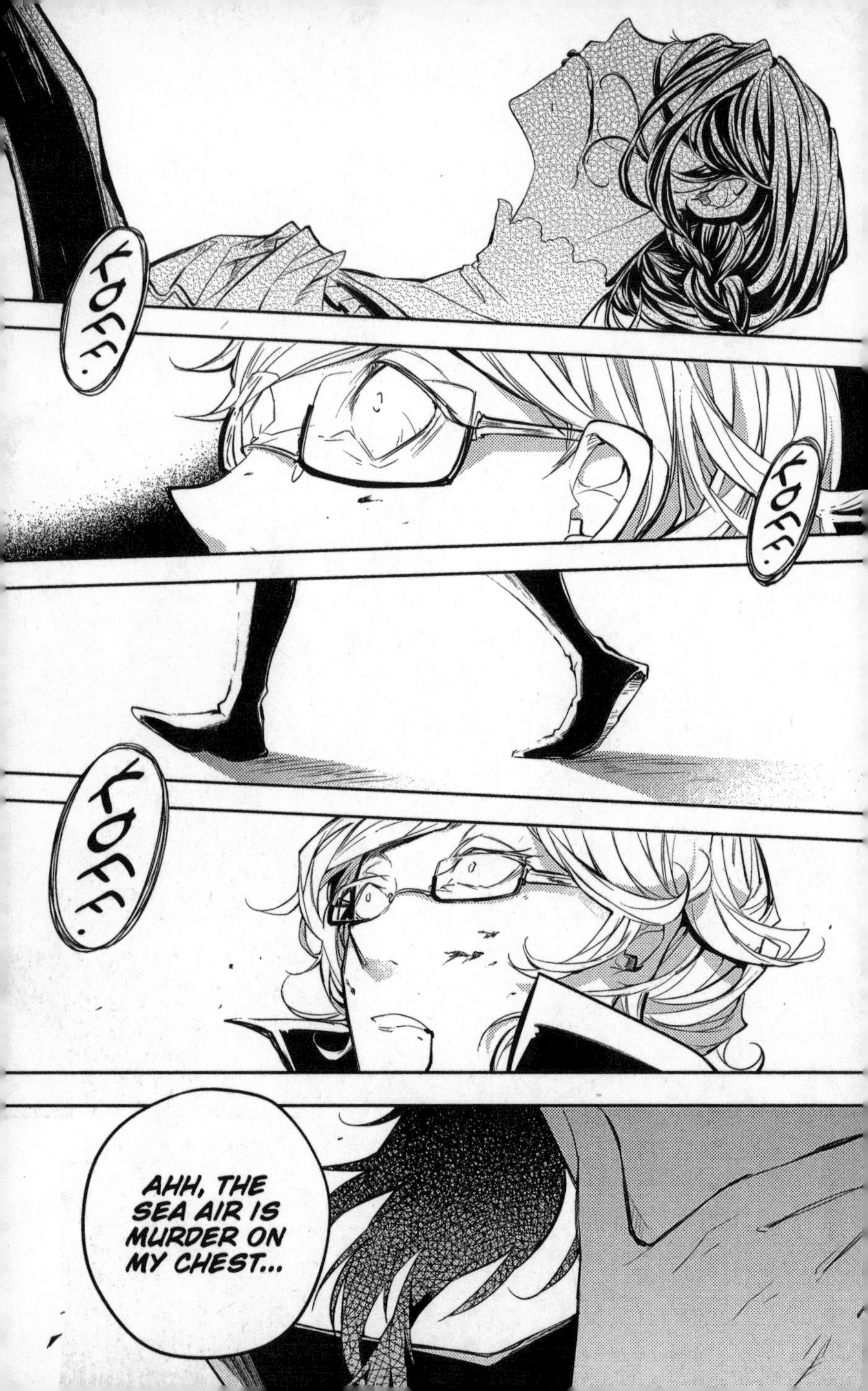
KOFF.
KOFF.
KOFF.
AHH, THE SEA AIR IS MURDER ON MY CHEST...

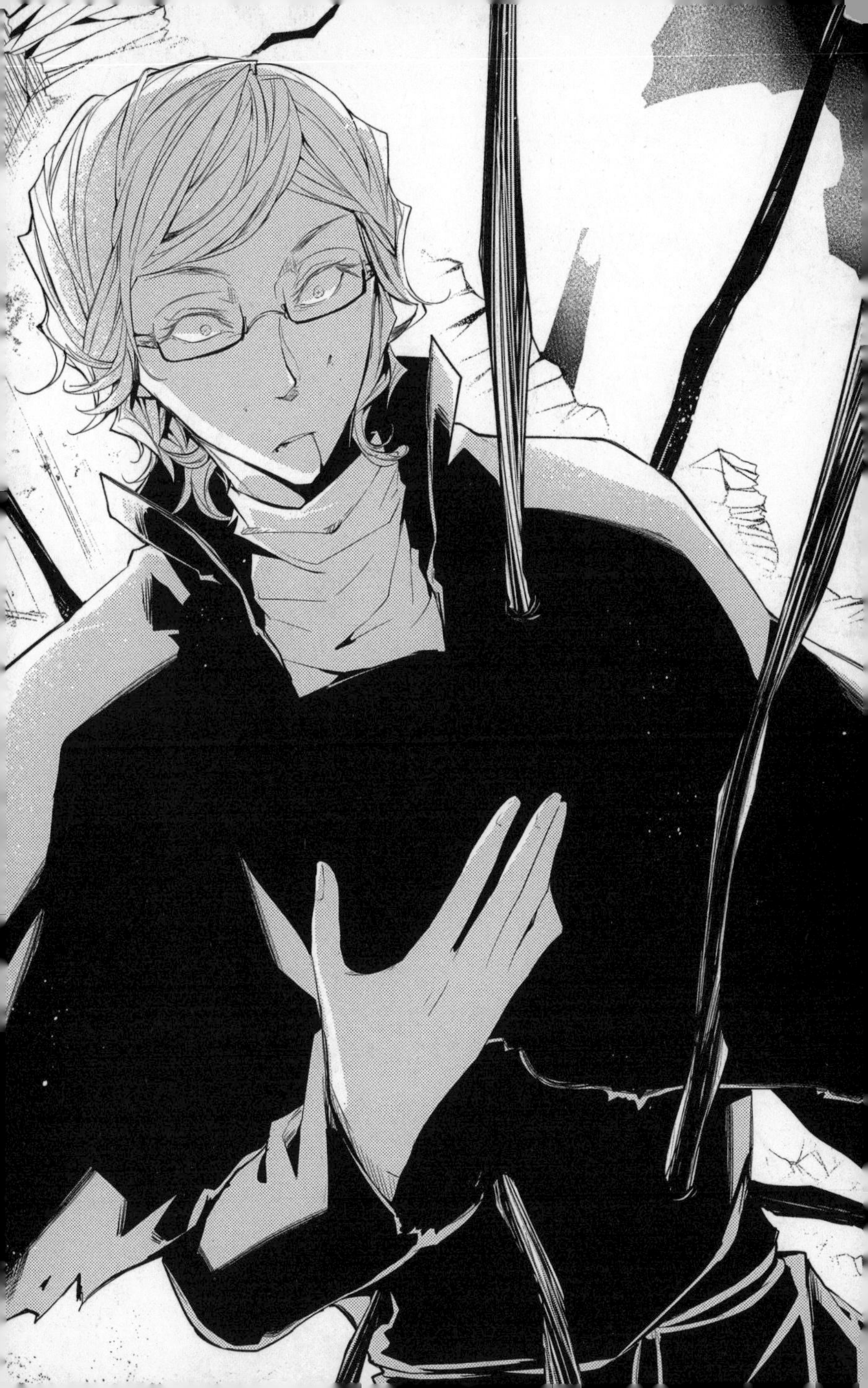

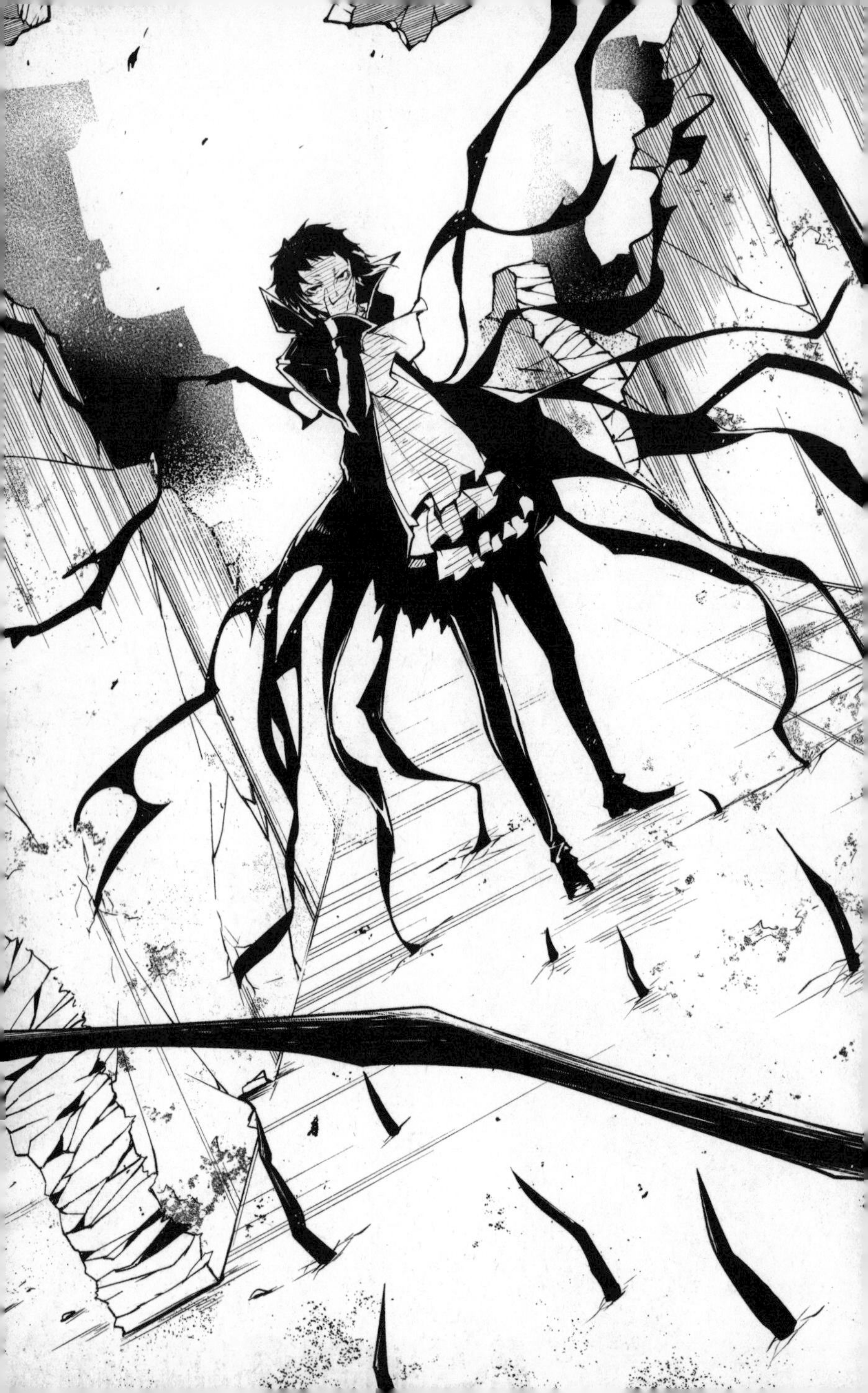

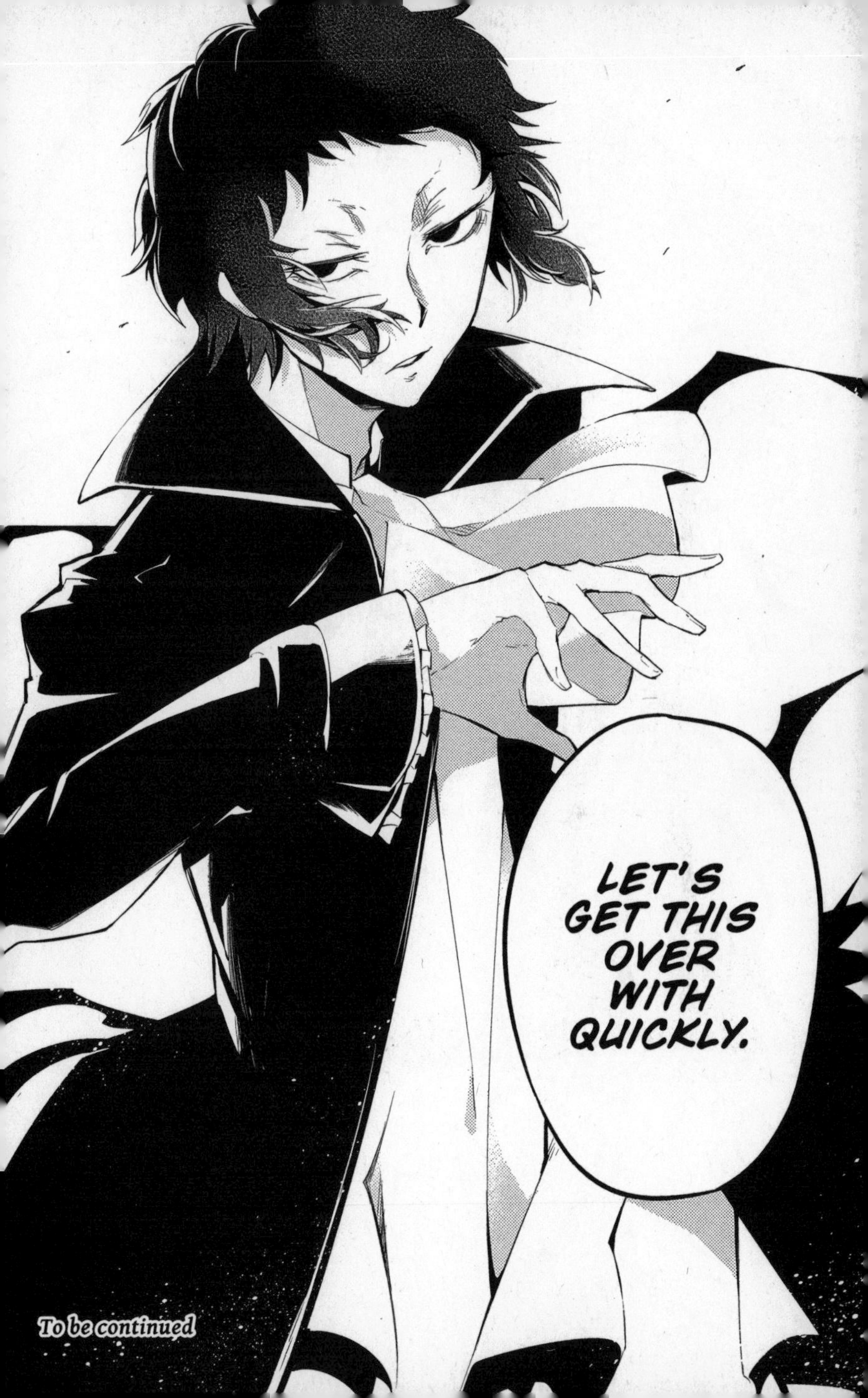
LET'S GET THIS OVER WITH QUICKLY.
To be continued

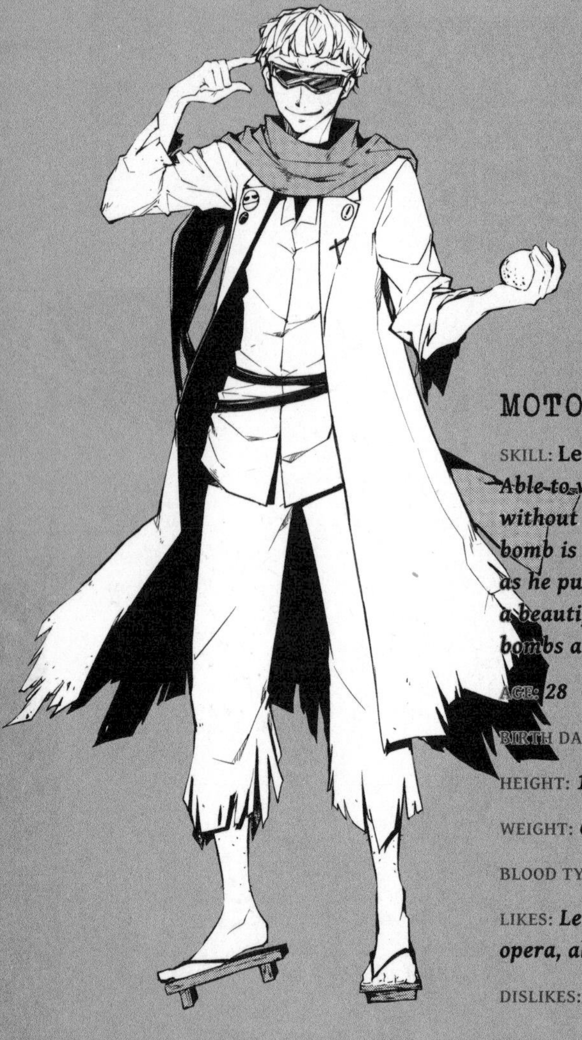

MOTOJIROU KAJII

SKILL: **Lemonade**
Able to withstand bomb blasts without injury, as long as the bomb is lemon-shaped—because, as he puts it, the lemon is such a beautiful spindle shape. His bombs are all handmade.

AGE: ***28***

BIRTH DATE: ***February 17***

HEIGHT: ***180cm***

WEIGHT: ***63kg***

BLOOD TYPE: ***B***

LIKES: ***Lemons, bombs, science, opera, alcohol***

DISLIKES: ***Main streets, jazz***

BUNGO
STRAY DOGS

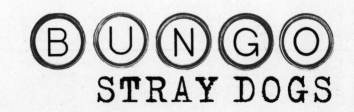

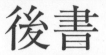

DAZAI: So, how about we kick off the first postscript in a while?

CHUUYA: Agh! Let me go, Dazai! Why do I have to sit here and engage in this worthless chatter with you!?

DAZAI: Easy there. I'm not exactly enjoying this either. But this is work, all right, Chuuya? I'm just picturing you as a giant Tosa mastiff in my mind to make this easier. Here, Chuuya, shake!

CHUUYA: Shut up! What do you even mean, "This is work"? Didn't you tell me once you'd rather starve to death than perform an honest day's work?

DAZAI: Oh, brother. I'm a believer in the laborer's faith, you know? Work hard, and you too can find salvation in the afterlife!

CHUUYA: Who's this so-called "job" for, anyway?

DAZAI: The editor.

CHUUYA: Oh. Well, can't do much about that, then...

DAZAI: Our topic today: "Exploring the great figures of literature"! You'll know our first subject pretty well—author of works like *Tsugaru*, *The Setting Sun*, *Run, Melos!* and *No Longer Human*, still enjoying a large and loyal fan base nearly seventy years after his death...I'm talking about none other than Osamu Dazai!

CHUUYA: Kind of playing favorites, aren't you?

DAZAI: Osamu Dazai tends to be thought of as a pessimist, someone who constantly probed at the nature of mankind with works like *No Longer Human*. However, he actually wrote quite a number of novels primarily meant to entertain readers—such as *Otogizoushi*, his collection of tales that parody popular Japanese mythology. And here's an interesting anecdote you might not know about him...

CHUUYA: Yeah?

DAZAI: In the book *One Hundred Views of Mount Fuji*, Dazai made up a story about how, while on a mountain-climbing trip with his friend and patron Masuji Ibuse, the two of them sat down to rest... and then Ibuse passed gas.

CHUUYA: That'd make anyone angry, wouldn't it?

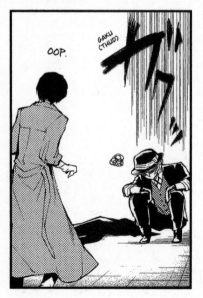

OOP.

GAKU (THUD)

DAZAI: Later, Dazai was out of money during a wild night of partying at an inn in Izu. His friend, the novelist and poet Kazuo Dan-sensei, came to check on him—and then Dazai made him stay at the inn and fled, promising he would be back with money. He never returned, though—he left old Dan-sensei in the lurch and kept partying back in Tokyo.

CHUUYA: We're talking about the same person who wrote something like *Run, Melos!*?

DAZAI: One time, he wanted to win the Akutagawa literary prize so badly that he prostrated himself before one of the judges, Yasunari Kawabata-sensei, and claimed he'd do anything ordered of him.

CHUUYA: He's...even more of a character than you, wasn't he?

DAZAI: ...Yeah...

CHUUYA: Oh, does that make you depressed? (* It makes the writer depressed, too.)

"Whenever one performs a good deed, one must always apologize while doing so, for there is nothing that hurts other people more than doing good."
—Osamu Dazai, "Handsome Devils and Cigarettes"

To be continued

GREETINGS

Due to my generally tongue-tied disposition, I've maintained my silence ever since the first volume. That makes this afterword the first real one I've ever written, I suppose. This is Harukawa, the artist. Thank you very much for purchasing Volume 5 of *Bungo Stray Dogs*.

I'm not entirely sure there are many interesting things an artist can say on a page like this, but since I've been given the opportunity, I think I'd like to talk about "eyes" for a moment.

This is something I do on my own prerogative—not something we discuss and formally decide upon—but when doing the art, the more dangerous a character is, the more I draw their eyes in a deadened kind of way, expanding out the black in them. Heavily black eyes have a way of projecting how "stained" a person's psyche is; that's my intention there. I think a lot of Mafia members have large black eyes, and for people who've been given a chance by the story to still "go back," their eyes are drawn relatively brighter. His goggles make it hard to tell, but actually, Kajii-san's eyes have no light in them whatsoever. (Looking over his design files, his eyes are completely dead...)

Kyouka-chan is something of an exception to this. Her eyes aren't deadened, but back in Volume 2 or so, I made an effort not to add highlights to them. I think you'll notice they've become brighter as the volumes go on. There's also someone—I won't say who—whose eyes get "tainted" a bit once their true nature comes to the surface. It could be a fun exercise for the reader to go back and check out those eyes, using them as a guide to the characters' mental states. Maybe.

Either way, I hope we'll get to see each other again in Volume 6.

春河35 SANGO HARUKAWA

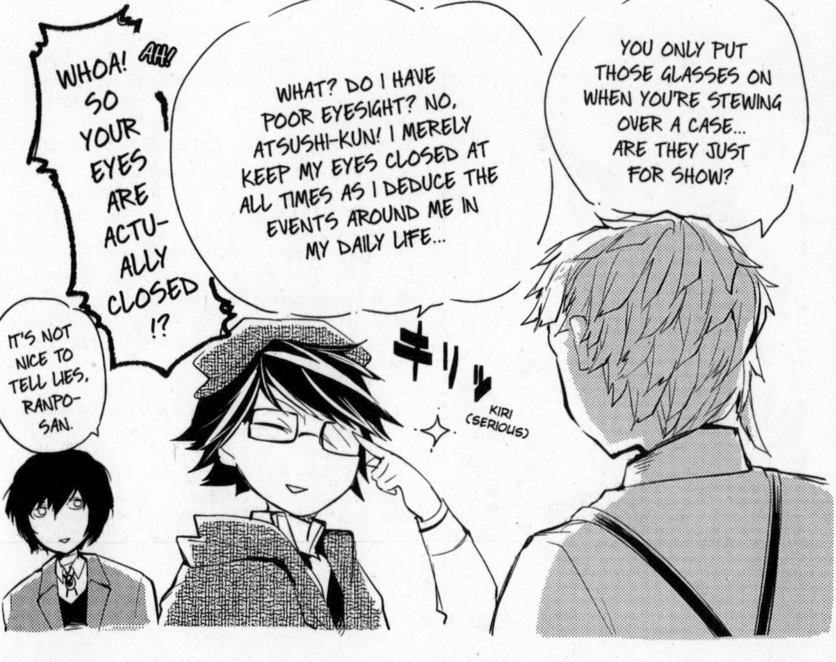
YOU ONLY PUT THOSE GLASSES ON WHEN YOU'RE STEWING OVER A CASE... ARE THEY JUST FOR SHOW?
WHAT? DO I HAVE POOR EYESIGHT? NO, ATSUSHI-KUN! I MERELY KEEP MY EYES CLOSED AT ALL TIMES AS I DEDUCE THE EVENTS AROUND ME IN MY DAILY LIFE...
キリッ
KIRI (SERIOUS)
WHOA! AH! SO YOUR EYES ARE ACTU-ALLY CLOSED !?
IT'S NOT NICE TO TELL LIES, RANPO-SAN.

Translation Notes

Page 5
***Hayashi* rice** is a Western-style Japanese dish consisting of diced-beef stew served over rice.

Page 37
Golden tempura, or *kinpura*, is a Japanese method of battering and deep-frying that uses more egg yolks than regular tempura does.

Page 92
Ane-san literally means "elder sister," but its usage is associated with how members of the Mafia speak in Japan—hence Dazai using it to address Kouyou.

Page 176
Jem, **Walter**, **Di**, **Nan**, **Shirley**, **Rilla**, and **Joyce** are the names of Anne Shirley's children in the *Anne of Green Gables* series by Lucy Maud Montgomery. Joyce dies in infancy—a bad sign for the man she's pointing at.

Page 177
Lady Cordelia Fitzgerald is a pretend identity Anne Shirley invents for herself in *Anne of Green Gables*. It's indicative of her hyperactive imagination at work—a quality reflected in the *Bungo Stray Dogs* character.

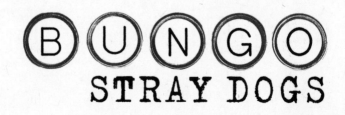

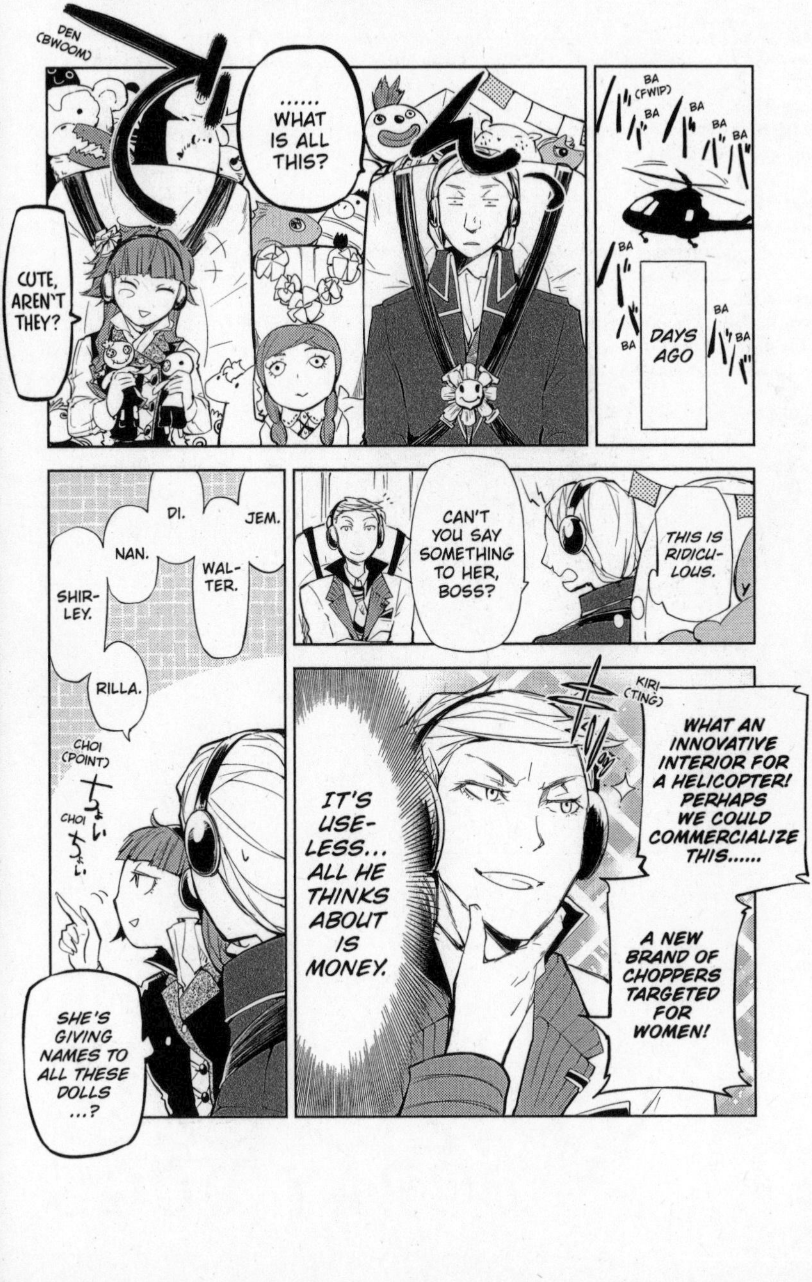
BA (FWIP) BA BA BA BA
BA BA BA BA
DAYS AGO
...... WHAT IS ALL THIS?
DEN (BWOOM)
CUTE, AREN'T THEY?
THIS IS RIDICULOUS.
CAN'T YOU SAY SOMETHING TO HER, BOSS?
KIRI (TING)
WHAT AN INNOVATIVE INTERIOR FOR A HELICOPTER! PERHAPS WE COULD COMMERCIALIZE THIS......
A NEW BRAND OF CHOPPERS TARGETED FOR WOMEN!
IT'S USELESS... ALL HE THINKS ABOUT IS MONEY.
JEM.
DI.
WALTER.
NAN.
SHIRLEY.
RILLA.
CHOI (POINT)
CHOI
SHE'S GIVING NAMES TO ALL THESE DOLLS ...?

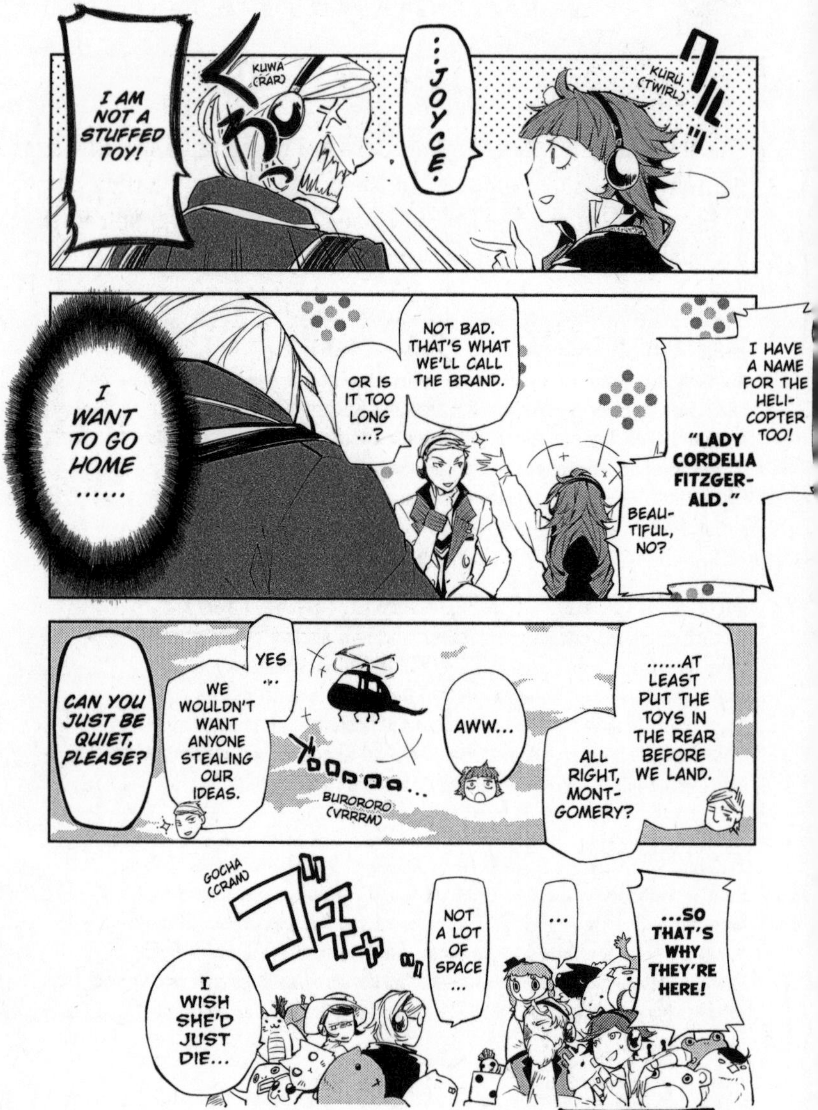
KURU (TWIRL)
...JOYCE.
KUWA (RAR)
I AM NOT A STUFFED TOY!
I HAVE A NAME FOR THE HELI-COPTER TOO! "LADY CORDELIA FITZGER-ALD."
BEAU-TIFUL, NO?
NOT BAD. THAT'S WHAT WE'LL CALL THE BRAND.
OR IS IT TOO LONG ...?
I WANT TO GO HOME ......
......AT LEAST PUT THE TOYS IN THE REAR BEFORE WE LAND.
ALL RIGHT, MONT-GOMERY?
AWW...
BURORORO (VRRRM)
YES ...
WE WOULDN'T WANT ANYONE STEALING OUR IDEAS.
CAN YOU JUST BE QUIET, PLEASE?
...SO THAT'S WHY THEY'RE HERE!
...
NOT A LOT OF SPACE ...
GOCHA (CRAM)
I WISH SHE'D JUST DIE...

※ CHAPTER 18, PRE-DROP

BUNGO STRAY DOGS

AUTHOR GUIDE (PART 2)

The characters of *Bungo Stray Dogs* are based on major literary figures from Japan and around the world! Here's a handy guide to help you learn about some of the writers who inspired the weird and wonderful cast of this series!

RANPO EDOGAWA (1894-1965)

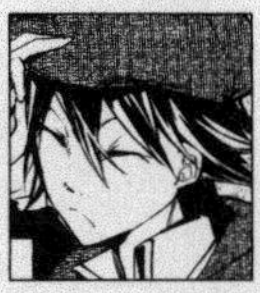

Arguably the greatest figure in Japanese mystery fiction. Many of Edogawa's characters—such as the detective Kogorou Akechi, the Boys' Detective Club, and the Fiend with Twenty Faces—remain popular. His mysteries often lean more toward the occult, owing to his fondness for Edgar Allan Poe—in fact, his pen name is a play on the famous American author ("Edgar Allan Poe" → "Edoga Waran Po").

JUNICHIROU TANIZAKI (1886-1965)

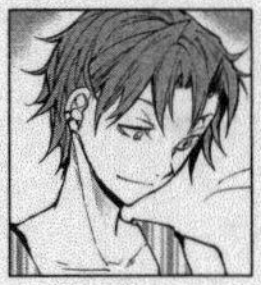

Writing mainly on obsession, passion, and how society changed over time, Tanizaki won the Asahi Prize in 1949 for his accomplishments. The skill *Light Snow* comes from a novel of the same name (translated into English as *The Makioka Sisters*) about the decline of an upper-middle class family leading up to World War II. *Naomi*, another novel, is about a man's obsession to groom a girl named Naomi into a Westernized woman.

KENJI MIYAZAWA (1896-1933)

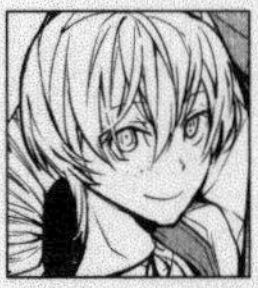

Born in Iwate, Miyazawa reflected through his writings a desire for harmony with nature and the universe, as well as a rejection of his family's wealth and status. The poem "Undefeated by the Rain" was likely written on the author's deathbed. The *Bungo Stray Dogs* character refers to his hometown as "Ihatovo"—the author's name for an alternate, idealized Iwate.

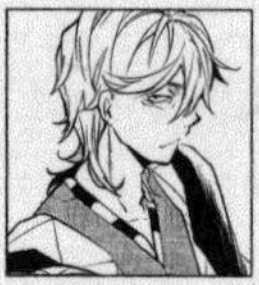

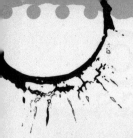

YUKICHI FUKUZAWA (1835-1901)

A liberal ideologist, prolific writer, critic, philosopher, educator, and more, Fukuzawa is seen as one of the fathers of modern Japan. The skill *All Men Are Equal* refers to *An Encouragement of Learning*, a seventeen-volume series on how equal opportunities for education are vital to society. Fukuzawa's face appears on the Japanese 10,000-yen bill.

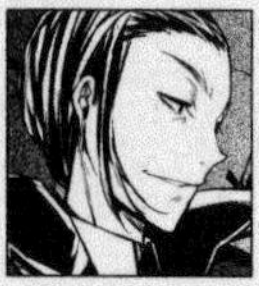

OUGAI MORI (1862-1922)

Originally enlisting in the Japanese military in order to study medicine, Ougai (real name Rintarou Mori) eventually rose to the rank of Surgeon General of the Army, the highest possible for a medical officer. Fluent in multiple languages, Ougai based his writings on his personal experiences. *Vita Sexualis* is an erotic novel that follows the main character's sexual experiences throughout his life.

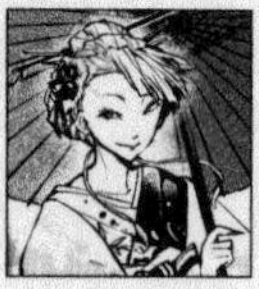

KOUYOU OZAKI (1868-1903)

A male writer, Ozaki was regularly published in the *Yomiuri Shimbun*, Japan's largest newspaper, and formed Japan's first literary society, "Kenyuusha." Among his many writing pupils was Kyouka Izumi. His novel, *The Golden Demon*, concerns the loss of humanity, social responsibility, and love in the face of modernization and money.

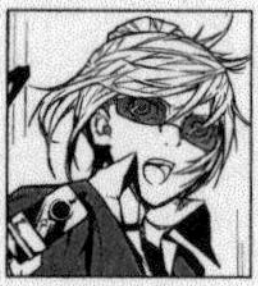

ICHIYOU HIGUCHI (1872-1896)

Best known for her short stories, Higuchi desired to create great literature (and not simply popular sellers). This led to a short yet tumultuous life, gaining fame and passing from tuberculosis by the age of twenty-four. Her writings aim for realistic depictions of the world and people, eschewing neat endings and feel-good fantasy.

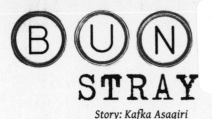

STRAY

Story: *Kafka Asagiri*   Art: *Sango Harukawa*

Translation: Kevin Gifford   †   Lettering: Bianca Pistillo

BUNGO STRAY DOGS Volume 5
©Kafka ASAGIRI 2014
©Sango HARUKAWA 2014
First published in Japan in 2014 by KADOKAWA CORPORATION, Tokyo.
English translation rights arranged with KADOKAWA CORPORATION, Tokyo through TUTTLE-MORI AGENCY, INC., Tokyo.

English translation © 2017 by Yen Press, LLC

Yen Press
1290 Avenue of the Americas
New York, NY 10104

Visit us at yenpress.com
facebook.com/yenpress
twitter.com/yenpress
yenpress.tumblr.com
instagram.com/yenpress

First Yen Press Edition: December 2017

Yen Press is an imprint of Yen Press, LLC.
The Yen Press name and logo are trademarks of Yen Press, LLC.

The publisher is not responsible for websites (or their content) that are not owned by the publisher.

Library of Congress Control Number: 2016956681

ISBNs: 978-0-316-46817-6 (paperback)
       978-0-316-46833-6 (ebook)

10 9 8 7 6 5 4 3 2 1

BVG

Printed in the United States of America